China in the World

A History Since 1644

Edited by the curriculum specialists at
Primary Source, Inc.

Foreword by Dr. Ezra Vogel
Introductory essay by Dr. William Kirby

Cheng & Tsui Company
Boston

Genevieve   Fahrner

16 15 14 13 12 11 10 09 08   1 2 3 4 5 6 7 8 9 10

Published by
Cheng & Tsui Company, Inc.
25 West Street
Boston, MA 02111-1213 USA
Fax (617) 426-3669
www.cheng-tsui.com
"Bringing Asia to the World"™

ISBN 978-0-88727-621-7

Cover design: Gia Giasullo, Studio eg
Interior design: Linda M. Robertson
Cover art: Shanghai skyline © iStockphoto/Robert Churchill. Used by permission. Presidential Palace, Nanjing, Gate of Heavenly Peace, Beijing, © Liz Nelson. Students © Primary Source. Used by permission.
Title page globe image © iStockphoto/Jan Rysavy. Used by permission.
Indexer: Kevin Millham, Windrose Writing Services.

Acknowledgments and copyrights can be found at the back of the book on pages 369–370, which constitute an extension of the copyright page.

Library of Congress Control Number: 2008927793

Printed in Canada

Table of Contents

UNIT III: Struggles to Create a Unified China (1911–1949)

UNIT IV: The People's Republic of China (1949–2000)

UNIT V: Contemporary China

Primary Source dedicates
China in the World: A History Since 1644
to the **Freeman Foundation**
which has so generously supported our work in
strengthening teaching about China.

Acknowledgments

Primary Source is deeply indebted to the scholars who freely shared their expertise, helped us shape the book, so patiently answered our many questions, and later reviewed the content of *China in the World*. We apologize for any errors that remain; they are the sole responsibility of the author.

Dr. Kenneth Hammond, New Mexico State University

Dr. Stephen R. Platt, University of Massachusetts, Amherst

Dr. Caroline Reeves, Emmanuel College

Dr. John Watt, Fairbank Center, Harvard University

Dr. Zheng Shiping, Bentley College

In addition, a number of scholars and educators provided valuable advice:

Dr. Dorothy V. Borei, Guilford College (retired)

Robert Daly, co-director of Nanjing-Hopkins Center, Nanjing, China

Dr. Christine Gilmartin, Northeastern University

Hong Zheng, principal, Dandelion School, Beijing, China

Dr. Anne Watt, co-founder, Primary Source

Dr. Ye Weili, University of Massachusetts, Boston

Dr. Zhu Fang, Fudan University, Shanghai, China

We thank the teacher-authors who contributed chapters to the book. They spent countless hours tracking down the most engaging primary sources, researching and writing the introductory essays, and developing tried and true activities. Without them, there would be no book.

Cara Abraham, Brookfield High School, CT

Michael Abraham, New Milford High School, CT

Ryan Bradeen, Director of Maine Programs, Primary Source

Philip Gambone, Boston University Academy and Harvard Extension School

David Green, doctoral candidate, Boston College;
    Acton-Boxborough Regional High School, MA

Shirley Moore Huettig, formerly of Concord Academy, MA

Jamie Moore, Newton Public Schools, MA

Todd Whitten, Beaver Country Day School, MA

Nan Ye, Bangor High School, ME

Rachel Zucker, doctoral candidate, Boston University; Burlington High School, MA

A number of additional educators offered guidance and materials. We thank you.

Marilyn Day, Marblehead Public Schools, MA

Rachel Eio, Brookline High School

Margaret Harvey, Winchester Public Schools, MA

Seth Kirby, Social Studies Chairperson, Boston College High School

Nicholas Krippendorf, Academy of the Pacific Rim, Boston

Richard Meegan, former Chair of Social Studies Department, Masconomet Regional High School, MA

Caroline Platt, (retired) Carlisle Public Schools, MA

David Walsh, Masconomet Regional High School, MA

For their photographs, we thank:

Michael Abraham, Ryan Bradeen, Christiane Corcelle-Lippeveld, Renee Covalucci, Abby Detweiler, Sarah Dorer, Eugene Dorgan, Margaret Harvey, Wanli Hu, Elizabeth Lewis, Kongli Liu, Liz Nelson, Julie Newport, and Anne Watt.

Primary Source Staff

Several staff members were key to the creation of *China in the World*. Ryan Bradeen, Peter Gilmartin, Wanli Hu, and Kongli Liu shared their knowledge on all things Chinese. Renee Covalucci contributed artistic expertise by creating slide shows and maps.

Liz Nelson, Editor

Ann Black, Administrative Coordinator

Ryan Bradeen, Director of Maine Programs

Renee Covalucci, Program Associate

Dr. Deborah Cunningham, Senior Program Director

Renata DeLellis, Program Associate

Abby Detweiler, Director of Program Operations

Kathleen M. Ennis, Executive Director

Peter Gilmartin, Associate Program Director, China/World Studies

Dr. Wanli Hu, Associate Program Director, China

Jennifer Hanson, Librarian

Eve Lehmann, Permissions Editor

Kongli Liu, Program Associate, China

Mark Lyons, Financial Administrator

Julie Newport, Marketing and Communications Director

Interns:

Catherine Hughes

Diana Lin, Graduate School of Education, Harvard University

Louisa Mardirossian, Belmont High School, MA

Dana Montalto, Wellesley College

Anya O. Priester, Cornell University

Foreword

There is tremendous dynamism in China, and it is unlikely that anything will stop the continued rise of China. Perhaps nothing is more important in maintaining peace between the largest power in the world today, the United States, and the greatest rising power, China, than better understanding between the people of the two nations.

The world is also becoming a smaller place. Over 20 percent of the world's population is Chinese, and Chinese people will play a larger role in affairs around the world in every arena—politics, business, art, music, sports—and in dealing with issues like managing the environment, aiding the poor people of the world, coping with disease, responding to terrorism.

People around the world may use the same cell phones and the same computers, but the people behind those cell phones and computers have a very different culture, a very different history, a very different way of thinking. It is important for American students to be prepared for a world in which they will be interacting with Chinese people.

Primary Source in the past four years has done a wonderful job of developing materials for use in the schools. It combines very close work with specialists in the field, who can bring to bear the most advanced research, with teachers, who know what works in the classroom.

China in the World: A History Since 1644 combines these two streams, the knowledge from specialists and the curriculum-building that comes from classroom teachers. It is a timely contribution to helping prepare Americans for the world they will face in the twenty-first century. It is well-rounded, covering many different topics from geography, to history, to society. We should all be thankful to the dedicated teachers who have put together these materials.
Jump in.

Ezra F. Vogel
Henry Ford II Professor Emeritus, Harvard University

Lessons of China's Modern International History

By William C. Kirby, Geisinger Professor of History and Director, Fairbank Center for Chinese Studies, Harvard University

It is a pleasure to introduce this extraordinary volume, *China in the World*. Its very title makes an important point: China cannot be studied in isolation. China has been shaped by the wider world and the world by China.

Until recently, scholarship on China (and indeed *in* China) emphasized China's insularity vis-à-vis other cultures. There are to be sure, both symbols and monuments of Chinese defensiveness, such as the Great Wall, built mostly as an anti-Mongol defense perimeter during the Ming era (1368–1644). But for the large majority of the imperial era, China-based empires crossed (often loosely defined) borders routinely, and for good reason: to engage in trade; to adjudicate diplomatic disputes; and to fight wars—that most common of human "international relations."

Particularly in the twentieth century, foreign relations became, quite simply, all penetrating, all permeating, all prevailing—*durchdringend*, as the Germans say—ultimately forcing their way into every part of Chinese society. In the realm of high diplomacy, Chinese statecraft delineated and protected the borders of the new nation-state to which all Chinese (and not a few non-Chinese) were now said to belong. China's modern economic development was founded in turn on an unprecedented opening to international economic influences. The early decades of the last century witnessed the first "golden age" of Chinese capitalism (we are now in the second) as well as the birth of modern state capitalism, neither of which could have existed without foreign partners. Patterns of dress and consumption would be influenced by international models, from the Sun Yat-sen (or "Mao") jacket, a military tunic adopted from Japan, to the nationwide addiction to nicotine, aided by the British-American Tobacco Company. Most striking of all in the twentieth century was the self-conscious attempt to overhaul Chinese culture, particularly political culture, according to international categories. Every government sought legitimacy in the context of one or another internationally authenticated "ism," from constitutionalism to communism.

What lessons might we draw from China's modern international history? Let us start a bit more than a century ago, in the mad summer of 1900.

On June 21, 1900, the Great Qing Empire declared war on eight countries, including the United States. The Qing—the Manchu dynasty that had ruled China since 1644—besieged the legations of the foreign powers in Beijing. During the "Fifty-five Days in Peking," as Hollywood would later film it, a small band of foreigners held out against great odds before an international expeditionary force could rescue it. This 20,000-man force then subdued an empire of 450 million subjects, making quick work of the Qing armies and the "Boxer" irregulars who joined them. The Western forces sacked and plundered Beijing, occupied its ancient palaces, and extracted an enormous indemnity. The humiliation of the Qing was complete. Eleven years later it collapsed, ending an imperial tradition of more than 2,000 years.

How the world changes. Little more than a century earlier, at the time of the American Revolution, the Qing dynasty presided over the strongest, richest, and most sophisticated civilization on the planet. It was supremely self-confident. It ruled China, and dominated East Asia, by a combination of power and cultural prestige. Through the famous examination system, it recruited the most learned men in the realm to government service. It did not want or need contact with the West. By 1895, however, China had been invaded, defeated and degraded by first the Western nations and then Japan. Such was the sudden, overwhelming power of the industrial revolution and the aggressive militarism of the imperialist age. The Boxer Uprising was a final, futile act of resistance by a government, and indeed an entire system of governance, that would be blown away. Today, more than a century after the Boxer Uprising, China is again formidable. It is an industrial power, a military power, and a growing economic power. It has become a great power because of, not despite, its relations with the rest of the world. Yet its power is at once shaped and constrained by its modern history.

China is an ancient civilization, but it is really a very young country. "China" as a political entity did not exist until 1912, when the Republic of China—Asia's first republic—was proclaimed as the successor to Manchu rule. The questions posed at that time are the dominant ones for Chinese history in this century. What would be China's physical domain? How would China interact with the outside world? What kind of government would replace that of the old empire? Let us discuss these questions, briefly.

China's Borders

The government that succeeded the empire in 1912 inherited not what one might call "historical China" but the vast Qing Empire, a multinational and multicultural expanse that included Manchuria, Mongolia, Eastern Turkestan, and Tibet, among other areas. No *Chinese* empire had ever been so big for so long as the Qing realm of the Manchus. The amazing fact of the twentieth century is that this space had not only been redefined, as "Chinese" and as the sacred soil of China, but also defended diplomatically to such a degree that the borders of the People's Republic of China today are essentially those of the Qing, minus only Outer Mongolia. The Qing fell but the empire remained.

These borders have enjoyed international diplomatic recognition since 1912, because the great powers of the day believed—rightly—that a divided China would be a source of international instability. But it was the job of Chinese governments to defend these borders, often from a position of great weakness, relying on a diplomacy that was hard-pressed, often creative and always obstinate.

For example, Chiang Kai-shek's Nationalist government, which ruled the Chinese mainland from 1927 to 1949, held on to at least nominal title to areas that the Manchus had governed but where the new Republic had little power: in Tibet, for example, where the Nationalists, like the Communists after them, would aim to undermine a stubbornly autonomous Dalai Lama by playing up the authority of a (China-friendly) Panchen Lama; or in the Muslim region of Xinjiang (Eastern Turkestan), in the far northwest, where Chinese rule was finally reasserted in the mid-1940s after a period of Soviet occupation. In each instance China used forms of what we would call the non-recognition doctrine: refusing to recognize anyone else's sovereignty until matters could be settled in China's favor. The non-recognition of unpleasant realities was carried to an art form in the case of Manchuria, which Japan occupied in 1931. It speaks volumes about the power of modern Chinese nationalism that China would mobilize for war—as it did in the 1930s—in defense of the *Manchu* homeland into which Chinese settlement had been legally permitted only since 1907. And it convinced the rest of the world not to legitimize Japan's conquest. If the case of Outer Mongolia turned out differently, this was because the Mongolians enjoyed powerful foreign support. In any event, this was the one part of the old Qing Empire where people actually got to vote whether they would be part of the Chinese nation. Mongolians ratified their independence in the Stalinesque plebiscite of October 1945. With the Russians counting, the vote was 487,000 to *nothing*.

This agenda of national unification is still very much alive. After the Nationalists lost the mainland to the Communists in 1949, and retreated to Taiwan, official maps in Taipei still showed Outer Mongolia as part of the Republic of China. The return of Hong Kong to China was something on which both Nationalists and Communists could agree.

Curiously enough, for most of the first half of the twentieth century, Taiwan was not *terra irredenta*, like Manchuria, but quite literally off China's map. Taiwan was not part of the old Manchu empire when it collapsed, because it had been ceded to Japan as the victor in the Sino-Japanese War of 1894–95. No Republican government challenged Japan's right to Taiwan until 1943, when Japan's defeat in World War II seemed likely. Taiwan first became part of the Republic of China in 1945. When the Nationalists made it their last bastion in 1949, and when the Americans intervened to protect them in 1950, Taiwan's "liberation" become, for the first time, a national cause on the Chinese mainland.

Now it is the last remaining cause of China's "reunification." It promises to be the most difficult cause. Taiwan's inhabitants, although culturally Chinese, were Japanese subjects from 1895 to 1945, and were largely removed from the growth of Chinese nationalism on the mainland. Many of them resented, and some resisted, Nationalist Chinese control after 1945. Taiwan's first reunification with the mainland did not go well. Taiwan's Democratic Progressive Party had its origins in Taiwanese resistance to Chinese mainlander domination. Now even the old Nationalist party, which for decades aimed to make (anticommunist) Chinese patriots out of the people of Taiwan, has itself become largely "Taiwanized." Gradually but surely, a separate, Taiwanese political identity is evolving on this island, even as its economic and cultural relations with the mainland deepen, and even as it retains the historic name of the Republic of China.

Meanwhile, on the other side of the Strait, the tenacity, obduracy, and overall *success* of China's twentieth-century diplomacy, which made the most distant regions of the Manchu realm part of "China," helps to explain the People's Republic's unyielding determination to "recover" Taiwan, even though the People's Republic of China (PRC) has never governed it for a single moment.

China's Internationalization

The demarcation of China's borders took place in a century of onrushing, inescapable internationalization at home. There is a great misperception that China "opened its doors" only in the last thirty years. This is not true. Rather, the years of isolationism (ca. 1960–72) are the great exception to the rule of China's international engagement in modern times.

Engagement was essential, for example, if China was to rid itself of the humiliations of the imperialist era. At the beginning of the twentieth century, foreigners in China enjoyed extraordinary privileges, extracted at gunpoint and by treaty. Through tough, relentless negotiations, by the mid-1940s China had regained full control of its "inner borders," that is, over the territorial concessions, monopolies, and special legal rights once held by foreigners.

China's commercial and industrial development in the twentieth century is unthinkable without internationalization, for it was founded on an unprecedented opening to international economic influences. The 1910s and 1920s witnessed the creation of a distinctly Chinese class of entrepreneurs, combining inherited and imported business cultures in a powerful way. Although the Communist revolution would force Chinese capitalism into temporary exile on China's periphery, its return to China after 1978, in the form of investments from Chinese in Hong Kong, Taiwan, and Southeast Asia, would be the driving force in the great boom of the 1980s and 1990s. The growth of modern state capitalism from the 1930s onwards was similarly dependent on foreign investment. In the late twentieth century, as Chinese state industries rusted and decayed, foreign capital was found to reinvent them through "corporatization."

Chinese higher education has similarly been shaped by the world at large. Beijing University, China's most venerable, is little more than a century old, and resides on the campus of the old Yenching University, which began as a missionary college. American, European, and Soviet models of higher education have each had their impact on the training of modern Chinese intellectuals. And waves of Chinese students have studied abroad: in Japan in the 1900s; in America in the 1910s and 1920s; in Germany in the 1930s; in the Soviet Union and Eastern Europe in the 1950s; and again, on a massive scale, in the United States in the 1980s and beyond. Only in the last case can one speak of a "brain drain" from China; and to judge from the case of Taiwan, which sent thousands of students to the United States beginning in the 1950s, it will prove a temporary phenomenon.

Political partnership with foreign powers was vital to China's very survival in the middle decades of the twentieth century. In the 1930s and 1940s, China entered into alignments with three of the world's most powerful countries—Germany, the Soviet Union, and the United States—in order to defend itself against the fourth, Japan. From 1942 to 1960 China sought security through formal alliances with two "superpowers," first with the United States, and then, after the Communist revolution, with the Soviet Union, in part to defend China *from* the United States.

Although from an American perspective China was "isolated" in the 1950s, China was never so deeply incorporated into an international system as it was in the hottest years of the Cold War. The Sino-Soviet alliance was the most fully articulated military alliance in China's history. It was an intense cultural and educational alliance, confirmed by the thousands of Chinese who studied in the USSR and the thousands of Russians who taught in China. It was an economic alliance of greater depth and complexity than any of modern China's foreign economic relationships. And it was an alliance based on an initially shared vision as to how a country should be governed.

Governing China

It is ironic but inevitable that modern China, in seeking to be master of its own fate, has so consistently looked abroad for its models of government. No government believed that China's twentieth-century crises could be solved by a return to the Qing state. There were certainly no clear precedents in Chinese political history for the task of integrating a new set of social groups—among them a bourgeoisie, a proletariat, an intelligentsia, and a permanent, professional military—into the altogether new structure of a nation-state. Therefore the last century was one of continual experimentation with political forms, not one of which was indigenous in origin: the parliamentary republic of 1912–13; the military dictatorship of 1913–16; the attempt at constitutional monarchy in 1916; the "Confucian fascism" of Chiang Kai-shek; and the several forms of communism under Mao Zedong and his successors.

Since the 1920s this experimentation has taken place within the framework of one enduring institution, the Leninist Party-State, of which there have been two incarnations—Nationalist and Communist. The Party-State is a *one*-party state. Sun Yat-sen, the father of the Nationalist state, defined the mission of the ruling Guomindang (Nationalist Party) as that of tutoring the Chinese people for democracy. "Tutelage" was to last six years. For Chinese under Nationalist rule on the mainland and on Taiwan, it lasted sixty. And when the Nationalists were ousted from the mainland in 1949, they were replaced by the other Chinese Party-State, of the Communists, in an intensification of Party-State rule that has survived until the present day.

The Party's purpose was not only to lead the government, but also to remake the Chinese people, to forge a citizenry for the new nation-state. Chiang Kai-shek's New Life Movement of the mid-1930s aimed to discipline an undisciplined populace, to give it a sense of obligation to the nation. Mao Zedong would take this transformative effort in a much different direction in his "Great Proletarian Cultural Revolution" of the 1960s.

The Party-State was a developmental state. It aimed to mobilize and industrialize China from the top down. Sun Yat-sen's famous work, *The International Development of China* (1921) was the first attempt to plot out the integrated economic development of a reunified China. It remains the most audacious and—still today, many Three-, Four-, Five-, and Ten-Year Plans later—the most memorable of national development programs. Sun's faith that international capital could be mobilized to construct Chinese socialism would be shared widely by Nationalist and Communist leaders. Sun's more concrete plans also left their mark. His two-paragraph proposal to "improve the upper Yangzi" with an enormous dam spawned seventy-five years of effort and debate before work on the great Three Gorges Dam finally began in the mid-1990s.

The Party-State was also a military state. Both the Nationalists and the Communists fought their way to power in the first half of the twentieth century, when China had more men under arms than any other part of the world. Western militarism (in its Soviet, German, and American national forms) was undoubtedly the single most successful cultural export from the West to China. Militarily defeated on the mainland, the Nationalists governed Taiwan on the formal basis of martial law until 1987. It was under Communist rule, however, that militarization would be taken furthest. Whereas the Nationalist military took oaths to defend the nation, the People's Liberation Army swore to uphold the rule of the Chinese Communist Party. This they did in the Tiananmen Incident of 1989. Through the 1990s, a significant part of the state sector of the economy (no one knows for sure how much) was owned and operated directly by the military. The People's Liberation Army, Incorporated, had become a state within the Party-State.

The Party-State had a Leader. The formal titles given first to Sun Yat-sen, Chiang Kai-shek, or Mao Zedong hardly captured the spirit and scope of their domination over their followers. Until very recently, both the Nationalist and Communist Party-States were led by a series of leadership cliques that are understood better as conspiratorial brotherhoods rather than as political factions. In short, for much of the twentieth century China was ruled by a very small group of men (one to two dozen) under one Leader. Whether as a continuation of monarchical political culture or as an example of Soviet and fascist influence, the Chinese Party-State demanded a single head, a *yuan-shou*—as the term *Führer* used to be translated into Chinese. Whether the Party-State can survive political competition (as in Taiwan) or collective leadership (in the PRC) remains to be seen.

Lessons

The emphasis on personal leadership reveals the greatest weakness of the Party-State: its inability to work together with civilian elites to erect an enduring, self-replicating system of government. Civilians could serve the Party-State, but could not govern separately from it. Like the Nationalist Party-State that preceded it (and the Manchu conquerors that preceded it) the People's Republic began as a military conquest regime. But as the old political wisdom goes: one conquers from horseback, but one cannot rule from horseback. Unlike the Manchus, who ruled China for 267 years, and unlike every other successful ruling house in Chinese history, by the early part of the twenty-first century the Chinese Communist Party had yet to show that its power could be transferred to, or even shared with, civilian political and legal institutions with enduring legitimacy. The Nationalists on Taiwan, by contrast, learned to cohabit with the sober-minded, authoritarian technocrats who guided Taiwan's economic miracle. But even these elites never exercised political power independent of the Party-State and never fundamentally challenged it. Even after the end of Party "tutelage" on Taiwan in 1987, certain habits of the Party-State died hard: in the late 1990s, after a decade of democratic reforms, the Guomindang's Central Executive Committee still met every Wednesday to set the agenda for the government Cabinet meetings on Thursday.

Pressures for Taiwan's eventual democratization would come from other quarters, above all from the Taiwanese majority who had long chafed under Nationalist Chinese rule. Is this a portent for other regions? Will ethnic challenges lead the process of political change in China itself? It is too early to say. But the evolution of a democratic, autonomous Taiwan in the past decade allows us to recast the question of China's "reunification." From the perspective of history, we may ask not how soon will Taiwan become enfolded in the arms of the motherland, but how long can China hold on to non-Chinese areas that were captured as part of the old empire, like Tibet, or Xinjiang? In the short run, the Chinese state is surely strong enough to retain these regions. But from a longer, historical perspective, we must remember that no Chinese empire, ever, has been so big, for so long, as the empire of the Great Qing and its Chinese successors. If the People's Republic is ultimately to get smaller, like all Chinese dynasties that preceded it, or simply "looser"—the Qing's great genius was to rule these territories with a "loose rein"—how it does so, and if it can do so peaceably, will be of enormous importance both to China and to the wider world.

Ultimately the key to China's future lies in the great, unresolved question of the last century: what kind of political system will, in the long run, take the place of the old empire? Chinese governments have been much more successful in defending territory and sovereignty than they have been in erecting stable political systems. Save for the 1990s, every decade in the twentieth century witnessed a major political upheaval. If twentieth-century history is any guide, when political change comes in China, it will be closely related to international political and intellectual currents.

For the present, as the immediate successor in our century to the old imperial system, the Chinese Party-State has shown that it can do many things better. It can organize. It can industrialize. It can militarize. And it can terrorize. But unlike that system that disappeared in 1912, it has not yet shown that it can *civilize*. One may use that term in two senses: first, to re-establish a lasting system of *civil* service, and indeed to institutionalize civilian rule, using the great talent of the Chinese people; and, second, to stand for something enduring in human values, for a civilization that goes beyond political control, material development and martial strength. This was the great strength of the old empire, for all its limitations. This was how its influence radiated throughout East Asia. Perhaps this will be the quest of political structures still unformed, once the Party-State has finally had its day.

Introduction

In his book *Arts of China*, Michael Sullivan writes, "The Chinese painter deliberately avoids a complete statement because he knows that we can never know everything. . . . All he can do is to liberate the imagination and set it wandering. . . . His landscape is not a final statement, but a starting point. Not an end, but the opening of a door." That is precisely how we view our book *China in the World: A History Since 1644*. Our goal is to introduce the reader to events that occurred in China and people who lived through them. In addition, in the final section, we take a look at contemporary China. Our book is a starting point for understanding the complex, vibrant, and sometimes violent recent history of a people with the longest continuous civilization in the world.

"In 1600, the empire of China was the largest and most sophisticated of all the unified realms on earth," writes Jonathan Spence in his seminal work *The Search for Modern China* (7). By 1800, the Chinese empire was not only still the most sophisticated state on earth, but had more than doubled in size. Why then, at the dawn of the twenty-first century, are we talking about China *becoming* one of the global superpowers? What happened in the intervening centuries?

Who Are We?

Primary Source is a non-profit educational resource center offering high-quality professional development and curriculum resources to K–12 teachers and school communities. Founded in 1988 by two committed and experienced educators, Anna Roelofs, M.Ed., and Anne Watt, Ed.D., the organization's mission is to promote social studies and humanities education by connecting educators to people and cultures throughout the world.

Primary Source is guided by a commitment to change the way students learn history and understand culture so that their knowledge base is broader, their thinking more flexible and given to inquiry, and their attitudes about peoples of the world more open and inclusive. By equipping teachers with the skills, knowledge, and resources to facilitate this type of learning, Primary Source prepares students for the challenges and complexities of our diverse nation and world. Our main content areas are East Asia, U.S. history with a special focus on African American studies, Africa, the Middle East, and Latin America. Although we feel a particular responsibility to social studies teachers, our programs are interdisciplinary, and teachers of all subjects will benefit from a broader understanding of peoples and cultures.

Our professional development opportunities include summer institutes, seminars, workshops and conferences. All programs are built around participation by scholars and lead teachers. By fostering a climate of intellectual exchange between university scholars and teachers, we acknowledge the pivotal role teachers play in the creation of a more sophisticated and aware American public.

Primary Source also develops publications for use by teachers. In the spring of 2004, Heinemann Publishing, Inc. released *Making Freedom: African Americans in U.S. History*, a series of five curriculum sourcebooks on African American history from the fifteenth century through the Civil Rights Movement.

Each book contains primary sources, including diaries, slave narratives, maps, official government documents, autobiographies, cartoons, broadsides, and photographs. We used the same model for *The Enduring Legacy of Ancient China*, published by Cheng & Tsui in 2006, and again in this volume, *China in the World: A History Since 1644*.

Using Primary Sources

Primary Source, the organization, takes its name from the term used by historians to distinguish original, un-interpreted material from secondary or third-hand accounts. Thus a photograph, a memoir, or a letter is a primary source, while an essay interpreting the photograph or memoir is usually, though not always, a secondary source. A textbook, still further removed, is a tertiary source.

China in the World utilizes a range of primary sources, some of which have never previously appeared in print. We include letters from American traders in Guangzhou (formerly Canton), writings of missionaries, treaties, imperial writings, woodcuts, propaganda posters, poetry, short stories, photographs, and more. All Chinese text has been translated, of course, making it, arguably, no longer a primary source. We have selected translations by eminent scholars to ensure the most accurate reading possible.

While it is imperative to read secondary sources in order to understand context and background, access to "the real stuff" (albeit some in translation) raises students' interest and curiosity and offers opportunities for them to make discoveries on their own. When textbooks are used as the only source of information, it is much more difficult for students to take ownership, both of their own learning and of a particular body of knowledge. It can be difficult to remember other people's generalizations or conclusions. Original source material provides students with rich opportunities for inquiry, and the chance to move from concrete to abstract thinking and back again.

How to Use This Book

The Organization of *China in the World*

The first two chapters in the book introduce information helpful to understanding all the chapters that follow. Chapter 1 looks at China's geography and its diverse population of today, and provides a sense of how the vast majority of China's people—the peasants—lived in much of the twentieth century and before. Chapter 2 steps back into the sixteenth century, the last century of Ming dynasty China, to showcase the cities and capture the lives of the elite who contributed to making the empire "the most sophisticated on earth."

The remaining chapters are arranged chronologically and clustered in units. Each unit begins with an overview and most also include a timeline that lists the events in China in the context of related events in regional and world history.

Each chapter contains:

- The Organizing Idea
- Key Questions
- An Introductory Essay
- Key Terms
- Primary Sources
- Activities Related to the Primary Sources
- Suggested Resources
- A Closer Look

Together, the **context essay** at the beginning of the book, the **unit overviews**, and the **introductory essays** to individual chapters provide background information necessary for understanding the primary sources and engaging in the activities. The book is designed so that chapters can be taught independent of each other. Teachers can select the topics that fit best into the time frame they have available. However, *we strongly recommend that a unit overview be read before an isolated chapter is selected*.

Because the essays and chapters were written by a group of scholars and teachers, they offer a variety of writing and instructional approaches. While the format of each chapter is the same, we have respected the authors' voices and have not edited them to a uniform length or style.

Key terms are included, and the words are defined in the **glossary**. (The glossary is in the book and on the CD-ROM.)

Each chapter includes a variety of **activities** designed to engage student interest. Excerpts of the **primary sources** appear in the book; in most cases, longer versions are included on the CD-ROM. *It is important to understand that in order to complete any of the activities, one must read the full text of the document.* Suggested activities include study and analysis of primary sources, mapping, research and writing, debating, and creative responses.

We would not expect teachers to use every activity in every chapter. Rather, just as they select the chapters, they should choose activities that dovetail best into their instructional plan and meet the instructional needs and learning styles of their students. We have set out a buffet—we do not intend for all of it to be consumed by each teacher.

A list of **Suggested Resources** is provided in each chapter. While every effort has been made to ensure that reputable websites are current and stable, material on the Internet does change. Teachers may wish to check websites before giving students assignments. Students should also be cautioned to carefully evaluate information found online, always considering who the author is, who sponsors the site, and what biases might be present.

Wherever applicable, chapters include the special feature **A Closer Look**. This feature gives the reader a more in-depth look at men and women who played key roles in events explored in the chapter.

 The CD-ROM

Most documents have been abridged in the book, and in some cases, where many photographs are available, not all appear in the book. However, **primary source materials**, including color images, appear in full on the accompanying CD-ROM, where they can be read on individual computers, printed out, or projected on a screen. In addition, the CD-ROM includes supplementary essays, an annotated bibliography, and teacher resources. The CD-ROM is compatible with both Windows and Macintosh computers.

A Note on the Text

In 1859, Sir Thomas Francis Wade, professor of Chinese at Cambridge University, created a system for the romanization of Chinese characters. His successor Herbert Giles revised it in 1892, establishing the Wade-Giles system, which served as the primary English-language method of writing Chinese in the roman alphabet until the middle of the twentieth century. In 1953, the People's Republic of China devised its own system of romanization, called *pinyin*. Most older translations use the Wade-Giles spelling of Chinese words, while recent publications have increasingly adopted *pinyin* as the standard. We use *pinyin* throughout *China in the World*, with just a few exceptions. The names of Chiang Kai-shek and Sun Yat-sen appear in their older romanized forms because those spellings are most familiar to the majority of readers.

In the introductory essays, the first time that key words or phrases appear, we have also included the word written in simplified Chinese characters.

All monetary figures cited in the book are given according to the currency of the time; they have not been converted into present-day terms.

Finally, many of the English primary source documents written in the eighteenth and nineteenth centuries include spelling, capitalization, and syntax typical for the period. We have left those unchanged. In a few letters, we did add periods where sentences end and capital letters where new ones begin for clarity.

China in the World

Primary Sources

DOCUMENT 1.1: Slide show "The Rural Landscape of China," 2000–2007

DOCUMENT 1.2: Excerpts from *Peasant Life in China* by Fei Xiaotong, 1938

DOCUMENT 1.3: Excerpts from *The Good Earth* by Pearl S. Buck, 1931

DOCUMENT 1.4: Excerpts from memoir by Li Xiuwen (1890–1992), describing life in the village where she grew up, early 20th century

DOCUMENT 1.5: Excerpts from "The Village With No Name," in *Daughter of Heaven* by Leslie Li, 2005

DOCUMENT 1.6: Slide show "Among the Peoples of China," 2006

DOCUMENT 1.7: Excerpts related to minority peoples from "The Common Program of the Chinese People's Political Consultative Conference," September 29, 1949

Supplementary Materials

ITEM 1.A: Outline map of the world

ITEM 1.B: Outline map of China

ITEM 1.C: Map of China's provinces, autonomous regions, and municipalities

ITEM 1.D: "Han Diversity and Unity," an essay

ITEM 1.E: China's national minorities and major areas of distribution

CHAPTER 1

China's Geography and Political Divisions

By Liz Nelson and Primary Source staff

Chapter Contents

Provinces, Autonomous Regions, and Municipalities

Ethnic Minorities

Landform

Rivers

Climate

Peasant Life

Organizing Idea

The People's Republic of China is a nation with a highly diverse landscape, climate, and people, all of which both enrich the country and pose challenges.

Key Questions

What are China's most important topographical features?

How are China's topography and climate related to population density?

Which regions of China are likely to be the most difficult to cultivate? Why?

Which borders would you guess have been the most troublesome for China's government in the past 250 years? Which are likely to be the cause of the most concern for China's government today? Why?

When and why were the autonomous regions established? In what ways are the regions "autonomous"?

When and why were the "municipalities" established?

Are the relationships between each of China's minority peoples and the central government the same? If not, how and why are the relationships different?

What were the characteristics of peasant life in China before the founding of the People's Republic of China in 1949? How has peasant life changed since that time?

Key Terms

jia   monsoon

loess

Essay

China (中国) is a country of enormous diversity. Over 60 percent of its land is more than a mile above sea level and includes some of the highest mountains in the world. Most of the uplands, however, are hills and plateaus. The country's climate ranges from tropical in the South to sub-arctic in the far North. The population is predominantly Han (汉) Chinese[1], but China also includes fifty-five distinct minority nationalities, whose languages and cultures differ significantly from those of the Han.

As for any other country, China's location, landforms, rivers, and climate play a crucial role in its history and culture. Since ancient times, Chinese men and women have been changing their environment through great cooperative human effort. They have built terraces on hills, drained marshes, created huge new waterways by building canals, and contained rivers by building massive dikes. Even level areas, such as plains and banks of rivers, have been modified by human action. Twenty-first–century projects, such as the Three Gorges Dam (三峡大坝) and the diversion of water from the South to the North, though they may be controversial, are in keeping with this tradition spanning millennia.

Administrative Units

Today more than 1.3 billion people live in China—roughly one out of five people on our earth. The present-day People's Republic of China (中华人民共和国) encompasses essentially the same land area that was controlled by the Qing (清) dynasty after 1750.[2] The country is divided into twenty-three provinces, four "Municipalities,"[3] five Autonomous

Regions,[4] and two Special Administrative Regions.[5] Chinese people identify strongly with their native provinces, several of which are larger than Germany, the biggest country in Europe.

Ethnic Minorities

Before World War II, the Chinese (Guomindang) government recognized four ethnic groups other than the Han Chinese: Manchus, Mongolians, Tibetans, and Chinese Muslims. After the People's Republic of China (PRC) was founded in 1949, the government began an inventory and identification of the many other minority peoples (*shaoshu minzu* 少数民族). According to the Common Program of 1949 and the subsequent 1954 constitution, the rights of all Chinese citizens are guaranteed, including those of ethnic minorities. In regions where a substantial proportion of the population includes minority nationalities, the PRC has established autonomous counties and provinces with the stated goal of ensuring the minority peoples' autonomy.[6] Different laws and

---

[1] More than 90 percent; however, given the size of China's population, the minority nationalities together comprise approximately 106 million people.

[2] Over the course of the first century of their rule, Qing dynasty (1644–1911) emperors greatly increased the size of China (see Chapter 3).

[3] Beijing, Shanghai, Tianjin, and Chongqing. The "municipalities" stand alone like provinces.

[4] Guangxi Zhuang, Xizang (Tibet), Xinjiang Uyghur, Ningxia Hui, and Nei Mongol. See Resources on the CD for additional information about Tibet and Xinjiang.

[5] Hong Kong and Macao (see Chapter 17).

[6] Ma Yin, ed., *China's Minority Nationalities* (Beijing: Foreign Languages Press, 1994) 25.

regulations apply to people designated as members of a minority. For example, they are permitted to have more than one child, and affirmative action programs help them enter universities. However, the "autonomous" regions are not independent in any political sense, and groups of activists the central government sees as potentially troublesome (such as those among the Uyghurs or Tibetans) are repressed, sometimes brutally.

While China is essentially the same size as the United States, only about 15 percent of its land is suitable for growing crops. (Approximately 40 percent of U. S. land could be cultivated.) As a result, 90 percent of China's population is concentrated in the eastern third of the country, where thriving cities and arable land lie.

The Rivers

Two major rivers are China's most prominent geographic features. From their sources in the western highlands, the Huang He and Chang Jiang flow for thousands of kilometers across the land to empty into the Pacific Ocean. The northernmost river is the Huang He (黄河) or Yellow River. The 5,464-kilometer-long[7] river gets its name from the amount of yellow earth—*loess* (黄土)—in the water. Loess is the fine, yellow wind-blown soil found in northern China, which blows in from the Gobi Desert and provides a wonderful base for agriculture. Vast quantities of loess are eroded by rainfall, carried into streams, and then into the Huang He as a dense sediment. In the lower reaches of the Huang He, the deposits of the eroded sediment constantly raise the riverbed's level. In some areas, because of natural and manmade banks along the river, the river itself actually flows above the level of the fields. When the river breaks through its banks, floods devastate the surrounding countryside and ruin the crops and livelihood of many farmers who live along it. As a result, the Huang He has earned the name "China's sorrow." However, the water and loess it carries have also made agriculture possible for millennia. In recent decades, the flow of the river has decreased substantially in the lower reaches of the Huang He, so that instead of a flood there is now only the trickle of a stream (see Chapter 20). Indeed, it is in the rich soil of the river's bottom that farmers now till their fields.

Another major river system is called the Chang Jiang (长江), also known in the West as the Yangzi River. It is the longest river in China and one of the five longest rivers in the world. It flows 6,380 kilometers[8] down through central China to the coast at Shanghai. Fed by snowmelt and heavy rain, this river and its tributaries (more than 3,000) provide the major transportation system for all of central China. Approximately 40 percent of China's grain production and 70 percent of its rice production occur in the river's huge basin. For these reasons, many of China's important cities have developed here.

Climate

China has great climatic differences resulting from the size of the country, the variety of its natural features, and the monsoon-like wind system that controls precipitation. Although China does not experience the prominent monsoons of South Asia, there is a monsoon-like seasonal reversal of winds in East Asia. This is especially true in winter, when winds blow out from central Asia, carrying cold, dry air toward the sea in North China, extending even into some areas of southern China. To some degree, this is like the arrival of the bitterly cold and dry Arctic air masses that sometimes affect the winter weather of the northern United States. In China, this occurs throughout every winter. From late spring to early fall, on the other hand, moist and hot air blows inland from the southeast seacoast and leads to substantial rainfall when the air rises over the hills and mountains.

[7] 3,395 miles

[8] 3,965 miles

Because of these monsoon-like seasonal reversals of winds, more rain falls in summer than in winter throughout China. Most parts of the country receive more than 80 percent of their rainfall from May to October. Moreover, far more rain falls on Southeast China than on North China, making it possible for farmers in the southeast to have two or even three harvests in a year. In the North, rainfall occurs mostly in the summer months, but it is unpredictable and varies from year to year, often creating problems of either drought or flooding.

Temperatures in China vary greatly from region to region. Northern and western China have cold and long winters like those in the north central United States. In South China winters are usually mild. Summer temperatures average about 26–32° Celsius[9] throughout much of China, but in southeastern China summers are also extremely humid.

Land formation and climate in China determine which crops are grown in different regions. This has, in turn, dictated people's diet. The staple foods in the North are noodles and dumplings made of wheat and other hardy grains such as millet and sorghum; even steamed bread is commonly eaten. In southeastern and eastern China, on the other hand, people generally eat rice, which can be made into noodles and dumplings in addition to being steamed. Poultry and pork are preferred meats because raising these animals requires little land, unlike the grazing of cattle. China's environment has influenced every aspect of its history and culture, from the location of major cities to innovative farming practices to the food people eat.

NOTE: For information about China's environmental challenges, see Chapter 20.

Primary Sources

DOCUMENT 1.1: Photographs from the slide show "The Rural Landscape of China," 2000–2007

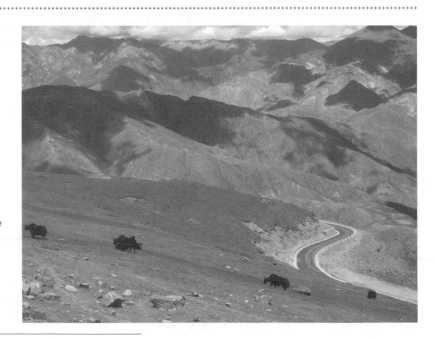

Yaks grazing; en route between Lhasa and Yamdrok-tso Lake, Xizang Autonomous Region (Tibet), 2005

(Photo by Abby Detweiler)

---

[9] 80–90 degrees Fahrenheit

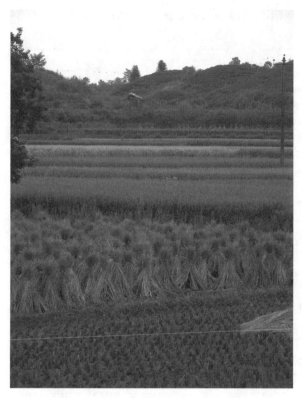

Harvested rice in the foreground, rice paddies in the center, and tea bushes in the background, Huangcun, Anhui Province, 2007

(Photo by Ryan Bradeen)

 The slide show "The Rural Landscape of China" is on the CD-ROM.

DOCUMENT 1.2: Excerpts from *Peasant Life in China* by Fei Xiaotong, 1938

The main purpose of marriage, in the village, is to secure the continuity of descent.... Beliefs connected with the relation of living descendants to the spirits of their ancestors are not clearly and systematically formulated among the people. The general view is that the spirits live in a world very similar to ours, but that economically they are partially dependent on the contributions of their descendents, which are made by periodically burning paper money, paper clothes, and paper articles. Therefore it is essential to have someone to look after one's well-being in the after-world....

The desire to have children is backed up by a two-fold motive; it ensures, in the first place, the continuity of the line of descent; and, in the second place, it is a concrete expression of filial piety by the future father towards his ancestors....[10]

SOURCE: Fei Xiaotong, *Peasant Life in China: A Field Study of Country Life in the Yangzi Valley* (New York: Oxford University Press, 1946), 30–31.

 The full text of Document 1.2 is on the CD-ROM.

---

[10] Traditionally men, not women, conduct the ancestor worship rites.

DOCUMENT 1.3: Excerpts from *The Good Earth* by Pearl S. Buck, 1931

[W]hen he had gone in the morning, [his wife] took the bamboo rake and a length of rope and with these she roamed the countryside, reaping here a bit of grass and there a twig or a handful of leaves, returning at noon with enough to cook the dinner. It pleased the man that they need buy no more fuel.

In the afternoon, she took a hoe and a basket and with these upon her shoulder she went to the main road leading into the city where mules and donkeys and horses carried burdens to and fro, and there she picked the droppings from the animals and carried it home and piled the manure in the dooryard for fertilizer for the fields....

And she took their ragged clothes and with thread she herself spun on a bamboo spindle from a wad of cotton, she mended and contrived to cover the rents in their winter clothes.... Day after day she did one thing after another, until the three rooms seemed clean and almost prosperous....

SOURCE: Pearl S. Buck, *The Good Earth* (New York: Washington Square Press, 1994 edition), 27–28.

 The full text of **Document 1.3** is on the CD-ROM.

DOCUMENT 1.4: Excerpts from memoir by Li Xiuwen (1890–1992), describing life in the village where she grew up, early 20th century

Usually farmers ate rice cooked with sweet potatoes or white potatoes with one dish of home-grown vegetables three times a day. Meat, mixed with vegetables, appeared at the table only on the New Year. People thought of eating melon or vegetables as producing cold in the body, so they ate hot peppers to counteract it. Therefore each family had a hot pepper stone grinding bowl in the house. Some nights, the farmers, after their hard day's work, went out to the river to catch fish, shrimp, and frogs. They would eat the frogs, and dry the fish, to save for meals in later days. In the busy farming season, farmers usually ate a little better. At dinner, they added a dish of fried soybeans, cooked dried fish, vegetables, and they might even drink some rice wine. Only the male workers drank rice wine, not female workers. Usually the men and women ate separately. The men's table had better food than the women's table.

SOURCE: Li Xiuwen, unpublished memoir.

DOCUMENT 1.5: Excerpts from "The Village With No Name," in *Daughter of Heaven* by Leslie Li, 2005

The village was enclosed, strangled really, by a high stone wall, which blocked out not only the sun's debilitating heat but also its life-giving light. Within this tight embrace, each lane—flanked by the outer stone walls of the two-story houses them-selves—was narrow and labyrinthine, its flagstones smeared with animal dung. Lanes led, torturously, to different family compounds, all in a sad state of disrepair and disuse. I peered inside the various gates at the wooden houses and open courtyards. Clucking hens wandered in and out of the rooms. A dirty, half-naked child played with a plastic rice bowl and a knotted piece of rope. A woman appeared in one doorway and stared at me with undisguised suspicion, then disappeared inside. A man in a stained tunic, smoking a pipe, studied me with grave indifference and held his ground…. There was no electricity, no plumbing here, not even an open sewer to flush away waste…. I was appalled by the poverty, the squalid living conditions….

SOURCE: Li, Leslie, *Daughter of Heaven: A Memoir With Earthly Recipes* (New York: Arcade, 2005), 222–225.

 The full text of **Document 1.5** is on the CD-ROM.

DOCUMENT 1.6: Photograph from the slide show "Among the People of China," 2006

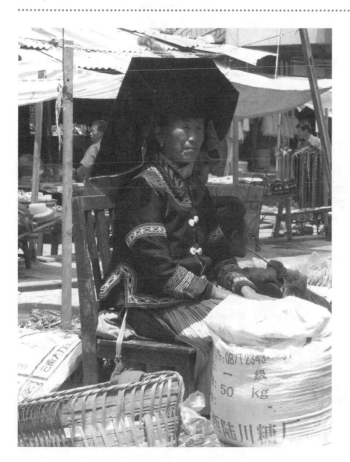

A Yi woman wearing a traditional headdress *(Photo by Michael Abraham)*

 The slide show "Among the Peoples of China" is on the CD-ROM.

DOCUMENT 1.7: **Excerpts related to minority peoples from "The Common Program of the Chinese People's Political Consultative Conference," September 29, 1949**

Article 50. All nationalities within the boundaries of the People's Republic of China are equal. They shall establish unity and mutual aid among themselves, and shall oppose imperialism and their own public enemies, so that the People's Republic of China will become a big fraternal and co-operative family composed of all its nationalities. Greater Nationalism and chauvinism shall be opposed. Acts involving discrimination, oppression and splitting of the unity of the various nationalities shall be prohibited.

Article 51. Regional autonomy shall be exercised in areas where national minorities are concentrated and various kinds of autonomy organizations of the different nationalities shall be set up according to the size of the respective populations and regions. In places where different nationalities live together and in the autonomous areas of the national minorities, the different nationalities shall each have an appropriate number of representatives in the local organs of political power....

SOURCE: The Important Documents of the First Plenary Session of the Chinese People's Political Consultative Conference (Beijing: Foreign Languages Press, 1949).

 The full text of **Document 1.7** is on the CD-ROM.

Activities

ACTIVITY 1: **What do you know?**

Part 1:

Before reading the essay, work in small groups to assess what you know.

1. List the names of the countries you think border China.
2. On individual copies of a blank world map (Item 1.A on the CD), draw in China. Compare maps and vote on which one the group thinks is (closest to) accurate.
3. How does China compare in size to Europe, Russia, Australia, Canada, Mexico, Brazil, and the United States?
4. How large is China's population? How does it compare to the populations of these other countries?
5. What kind of climate does China have?

Part 2:

Look at the slide show showing photographs taken since 2000 in the rural areas of various Chinese provinces (1.1). Please note that you are not seeing photographs of China's cities. For a look at urban China, see the slide show in Chapter 18.

1. What is most striking about the photographs?
2. What surprises you?
3. What can you conclude about China's landscape based on these photographs?
4. What can you conclude about farming practices?
5. Why might Chinese farmers terrace hillsides?
6. What crops do you see growing?

Read the introductory essay; using what you've learned from the slides, atlases, and online resources listed at the end of the lesson, find the correct answers to the first set of questions. Compare the accurate answers to your earlier guesses. What had you been relying on as sources for your first set of answers? If your initial answers were very different from the facts, what can you conclude from the ways in which you thought about China's location, population, and topography?

ACTIVITY 2: Creating Big Maps

Part 1:

Project an outline map of China (Item 2.B) onto a large piece of paper. Follow the instructions for making a Big Map in Resources on the CD, and create several copies. Working in small groups, using atlases and Internet resources, create a map showing one of the following topics. Establish map keys and a color code. The goal is for members of each group to become experts on their topic.

1. Topography with basic land formations—rivers, river basins, mountain ranges, lowlands, plateaus, deserts
2. Population density
3. Climate, including rainfall
4. Agricultural regions and crops
5. Autonomous regions
6. Major cities and municipalities
7. Bordering countries and the provinces or autonomous regions that lie on those borders

Part 2:

After the map is finished, as a group, create six questions related to your map for classmates to answer. Place all the maps, with the questions attached, around the room. Examine all the maps and answer the related questions.

Part 3:

Each group should briefly present its map and explain what group members discovered. The group should then elicit answers to the questions and clarify any misconceptions.

Part 4:

View the slide show again. Either on a Big Map or on individual copies of a map that shows China's provinces (Item 1.C), match the slides to the region and add the information you've learned. Alternatively, create a tour on Google Earth, inserting the photos provided on the appropriate provinces.

ACTIVITY 3: Peasant life

To better understand China and the appeal of the Chinese Communist Party, it is helpful to examine how peasants lived prior to Liberation in 1949. In addition, a look at the life of China's rural citizens today helps put future challenges in perspective. Begin with a discussion of the definitions of "farmer" versus "peasant." In Chinese, the word used is *nongmin*, which literally translated means "agriculture people."

Part 1:

Before coming to class, read excerpts from *Peasant Life in China* by one of China's renowned social scientists, Fei Xiaotong (1.2). Take notes on the topics addressed: the village site, the *jia*, population control, parents and children, and rural education.

Part 2:

In class, divide Documents 1.3–1.5 among small groups, so that each group is reading one account. Discuss the details in your group and add to your notes on peasant life. Reconvene in new groups that include individuals who have read different documents. Report on your reading to the new group and, as you hear new information, add to your notes.

Part 3:

Discuss as a class:

1. What is most striking about these descriptions of rural China?
2. Note one feature that is similar to something you have seen or read about.
3. Which aspects of peasant life appear to be distinctly Chinese?
4. Which aspects of peasant life appear to lend themselves to reform efforts, and which ones do you suspect would be difficult to change?

Creative extension:

Write a travel essay, a short story, or an illustrated children's book incorporating as many details of rural life in China as you can. Alternatively, working with a partner, create an electronic presentation, using for example PowerPoint® or Photo Story 3®, to depict rural life in China.

ACTIVITY 4: **Peasant life in film**

View any one of the films or documentaries that are either set in rural China in the past thirty years or specifically examine village life. Compare what you learned from the readings to the visual depictions. What has changed? What hasn't? What challenges remain and how might they best be addressed?

NOTE: For further information about rural education, see Chapter 19.

ACTIVITY 5: **Researching China's diverse peoples**

Part 1:

Begin by reading the essay about Han Chinese (Item 1.D), who make up more than 90 percent of China's population. Discuss as a class:

1. What unifies the Han Chinese?
2. What is the origin of the name "Han" Chinese? How far back does it date?
3. What are the differences among Han Chinese people? Give several specific examples.

Part 2:

Together, China's ethnic minorities add up to more than 100 million people, ranging from the Zhuang, who number more than 16 million, to the De'ang, who number around 18,000. Look at the slide show of a number of minority peoples in China (1.6). Discuss what you find most striking. (For example, consider the people's appearances, surroundings, relations with the camera, and so on.)

Read the excerpts from the Common Program (1.7). What rights did this document guarantee?

Look at the list of minority groups, as the Chinese government identifies them (Item 1.E). Working with a partner, choose one minority people you wish to learn about. (The larger groups have an asterisk.) Conduct research using the suggested online sources and create a presentation to share with the class (posters with captions, a PowerPoint® or Photo Story 3® slide show). Your presentation should include a map of China showing where the people live, ethnic identity (do they identify with a larger group?), economic life, customs, language, religion(s), dress, food, housing, etc., as well as challenges they may face.

ACTIVITY 6: Concluding discussion on ethnic minorities

After everyone has shared information about an ethnic group with the class, discuss:

1. How does the Chinese government define a minority nationality?
2. What is the purpose of this process?
3. How does it benefit a people?
4. How might it be detrimental?
5. Do other countries create similar categories? Which ones? For what purposes?
6. What is striking about *where* China's ethnic minorities live? What is the relationship between the regions where minority nationalities live and government policies toward them? (The class may want to create a Big Map showing the locations of all the minority nationalities they researched.)
7. Based on your research, what are the biggest challenges Chinese minority nationalities face in the twenty-first century?
8. How do these challenges compare to those faced by minorities in other countries? Consider, for example, the Sioux nation in the United States, Maori people in New Zealand, Muslims in a western European country, Asian Australians or any other minority people.

Suggested Resources

Books

Atlas of China: An Expansive Portrait of China Today with More Than 400 Maps and Illustrations. Washington, DC: National Geographic, 2008. *Fabulous maps, ranging from contemporary ones related to trade or tourism to historic ones; maps of key cities as well. Packed with information!*

Bailey, Alison et al., eds. *China: People Place Culture History.* New York: DK Publishing, 2007. *Stunning photographs and succinct information.*

Buck, Pearl S. *The Good Earth.* New York: Washington Square Press, 1931. *Written by an American woman raised in China by missionary parents, it gives a fine sense of traditional life in rural China before World War II. Pearl Buck won the Pulitzer Prize for this novel.*

Websites

Maps of provinces

http://www.ers.usda.gov/Data/China/Images/chinaProvinces.gif

http://earth.google.com/ Google Earth is available for free download.

https://www.cia.gov/cia/publications/factbook/print/ch.html The CIA World Fact Book provides excellent statistics on China today, including information about the geography.

http://afe.easia.columbia.edu The *Asia for Educators* site from Columbia University includes extensive information, many maps, and activities on China's geography.

http://www.askasia.org/teachers/essays/essay.php?no=10&era=&grade=&geo The site includes a long introductory essay, "Understanding the Geography of China," and multiple maps.

http://www.pbs.org/kqed/chinainside/soundmap/index.html PBS's "China from the Inside" site includes a soundscapes map of China, plus activities.

http://worldatlas.com/geoquiz/thelist.htm The site includes land, sea, and population statistics

http://plasma.nationalgeographic.com/mapmachine/ The site has an interactive map.

http://www.china.org.cn/english/features/43588.htm *Illuminating China's Provinces, Municipalities, and Autonomous Regions* provides information on geography, population, ethnicity, and more for all of China's regions.

http://depts.washington.edu/chinaciv/geo/geo.htm *A Visual Sourcebook of Chinese Civilization*, a site by Patricia Buckley Ebrey, shows China's geography with maps.

Autonomous Regions

http://www.paulnoll.com/China/Provinces/autonomous-regions.html Includes a map and short description.

http://depts.washington.edu/chinaciv/geo/maps/autonomous.htm Maps of the autonomous regions at the *Visual Sourcebook of Chinese Civilization* site.

http://www.usconstitution.net/china.html#Section6 The Chinese Constitution of 1982 with amendments; Articles 111–122 and 134 address the rights of autonomous areas.

Minority Peoples

http://countrystudies.us/china/36.htm This Library of Congress site provides online versions of materials written as part of the Country Studies/Area Handbook Series sponsored by the U.S. Department of the Army between 1986 and 1998. This particular essay, written in 1987, provides a good overview.

http://english.people.com.cn/data/minorities/ethnic_minorities.html China's major newspaper the *People's Daily* online offers detailed information.

http://www.lib.utexas.edu/maps/china.html The Perry-Castañeda Library Map Collection at the University of Texas at Austin offers easy-to-use online ethnolinguistic maps of some 40 different ethnic groups in China, as well as many other relevant maps.

http://depts.washington.edu/chinaciv/geo/people.htm#mapmino *Visual Sourcebook of Chinese Civilization* provides information about China's people, especially the minority populations.

http://www.c-c-c.org/chineseculture/minority/minority.html The Chinese Culture Center of San Francisco provides historical and demographic information about minority groups in China.

http://www.china.org.cn/e-groups/shaoshu/index.htm Photographs and very basic information from the Chinese government's official website.

http://www.travelchinaguide.com/intro/nationality/56list.htm Text and photos.

http://www.iisg.nl/~landsberger/xsmz.html From a professor of Sinology at Leiden University in the Netherlands, explanatory text and dozens of Mao-era propaganda posters featuring minority peoples.

Films

All Under Heaven (58 mins;1986) *Part of the* One Village in China *series, this documentary directed and produced by Carma Hinton and Richard Gordon captures the various ways in which the Communist Party of China has tackled the challenge of land reform and gives insight into rural traditions.*

Not One Less (106 mins; 1999) *In Chinese (Mandarin) with subtitles. The film tells the true story of Wei Minzhi, a fourteen-year-old girl who is ordered to a remote impoverished village in Hebei province to work as the substitute teacher for a month. Clueless when it comes to teaching, she is, however, extraordinarily determined to keep the class intact. Lead roles are played by the individuals themselves.*

The Road Home (89 mins; 2000) *In Chinese (Mandarin) with subtitles. This gently paced yet passionate love story is the work of acclaimed director Zhang Yimou. The film gives insight into life in rural China.*

Small Happiness (58 mins; 1984), produced and directed by Carma Hinton and Richard Gordon. *Another film in the three-part documentary series* One Village in China, *examining life in Long Bow, a rural community 400 miles southwest of Beijing; this segment looks at the lives of women.*

To Taste a Hundred Herbs (58 mins; 1986), produced and directed by Carma Hinton and Richard Gordon. *The third of the three-part documentary series* One Village in China, *this segment looks at the role of traditions and traditional Chinese medicine, and the lives of Chinese Catholics in the village.*

Primary Sources

DOCUMENTS 2.1, 2.2, AND 2.4: Excerpts from *The Journals of Matthew Ricci, 1583–1610* (not available on the CD-ROM)

DOCUMENT 2.3: Annual calendar of festival-related activities, 1635

DOCUMENT 2.5: "A Visit to High Beam Bridge" by Yuan Hongdao (1568–1610)

DOCUMENT 2.6: "Inscribed on the Doors of My Bookshelves," a poem by Yang Xunji (1456–1544)

DOCUMENT 2.7: Excerpt from *The Craft of Gardens* by Ji Cheng, 1630s

DOCUMENT 2.8: Slide show "A Nearby Journey Into Nature" on traditional Chinese gardens

DOCUMENT 2.9: Excerpts from the "Biography of Gentleman Wang," by Wang Daokun (1525–1593) (not available on the CD-ROM)

DOCUMENT 2.10: Poems written by women during the Ming dynasty (1368–1644)

DOCUMENT 2.11: Excerpts describing severe hardship in the lives of peasants during the latter part of the Ming dynasty

Supplementary Materials

ITEM 2.A: Additional information related to *The Journals of Matthew Ricci*

CHAPTER 2

An Introduction to Sixteenth-Century China

By Philip Gambone

Chapter Contents

Scholar-Officials

Literati

Merchants

Educated Women

Peasants

Organizing Idea

China's hierarchal society included at the top the scholar-officials. They, together with a thriving merchant class, created a vibrant urban culture in sixteenth-century China. Although in many ways a time of cultural and social continuation, the sixteenth century also ushered in an era of profound political and economic transformation that made China highly vulnerable to Western encroachment in the nineteenth century.

Key Questions

What was the traditional social hierarchy in China?

What characterized the lives of scholar-officials?

What was life like for educated Chinese women in the sixteenth century?

What was life like in the cities?

What challenges did peasants face?

Key Terms

Confucius	literati
connoisseur	magistrate
dynasty	Ming dynasty (1368–1644)
eunuch	scholar-official
Jesuit	*simin*
li	*tael*

Essay

For centuries, a child born in China grew up in a rigid social hierarchy. The so-called "four categories of the people" (*simin* 四民) reflected ancient Confucian beliefs and allowed for few opportunities to change one's social class. The traditional Confucian hierarchy placed scholar-officials at the top of society, followed by the peasants, then by artisans, then, at the bottom, merchants. Yet in the increasingly wealthy China of the sixteenth century, merchants flourished, and their actual role in society far outstripped their place in the traditional social hierarchy.

Civil Service Examinations

Over the course of its long history, Chinese leaders had administered the country in various ways. Ming (明) dynasty emperors, who ruled the country from 1368 to 1644, divided the country into fifteen major provinces, which were run by a hierarchy of government officials from provincial governors to local magistrates. In order to be assigned to a government position, a man had to pass the second in a series of increasingly difficult civil service exams: *shengyuan* (生员), *juren* (举人), and *jinshi* (进士).[1] The exams were based on memorization of four Chinese classics as a way to assess a man's grounding in Confucian tradition and his moral worth, rather than his administrative skills.[2]

The intent was to have only men who were educated and invested in Confucian ethics serving the people in government positions. However, Chinese official records, literature, and folktales are full of examples of corrupt, disengaged, or immoral officials, which suggests the system was far from perfect.

[1] A form of these exams had been in place for approximately 1,500 years.

[2] The four texts upon which the exams were based during the Ming dynasty were the *Analects of Confucius, Mencius, Doctrine of the Mean,* and the *Great Learning.*

Scholar-Officials

Passing the first of the three exams gave a man social standing as one of the educated members of the community. Passing the provincial *juren* exam would make him eligible for a government position, which would enable him to increase the family income. A comfortable income allowed a family to educate its sons, who would then be able to pass the civil service exams and ensure the family's prosperity. (While there were sons from poor families who managed to pass the civil service exams, this rarely happened because there was no free public education.) Scholar-officials generally earned their wealth from landownership, but they usually lived in larger towns and thus managed their properties as absentee landlords.

A scholar-official was expected to know history, classical literature, and art. As the ethical and cultural elite, scholar-officials not only ran the government bureaucracy and performed important ceremonial functions but also set the standard for moral behavior and artistic taste. Many were intellectuals who cultivated friendships with like-minded scholar-officials with whom they would enjoy conversation, poetry contests, and outings into the countryside. Aesthetic gardens graced their traditional courtyard homes (*siheyuan* 四合院). Connoisseurship—of painting, calligraphy, tea, porcelain, lacquerwork, even spider fighting!—was among their highest pleasures.

The Literati

As highly educated individuals, the literati were also among China's elite. Also educated in the classics, they were men who perhaps had failed one or more of the civil service exams and did not serve in the government, but rather dedicated their lives to scholarship and one or all of the "four accomplishments" (四艺)—calligraphy, poetry, painting, and music. A member of the literati was not necessarily wealthy, but those who were enriched their lives in the same ways as scholar-officials.

Women

The traditional Confucian view of women held that they were to be subservient to men. At the same time, during the Ming dynasty, women (at least those in the elite echelon of society) enjoyed greater literacy and freedom of expression than in earlier periods. An unprecedented number of female poets wrote during the Ming dynasty.

Commerce

Despite the traditional Confucian scorn for merchants, who were seen as profiting unfairly from the hard labor of the peasants, the fifteenth and sixteenth centuries in China were a time of enormously successful commercial activity. Small market towns thrived across the country, and regions became known for their agricultural and mercantile specialties. For example, cotton and silk came from the Yangzi River Delta, while in coastal Fujian Province, farmers grew tobacco and sugar cane. Jingdezhen in Jiangxi Province became famous for its porcelain.

Early European Presence

European traders and missionaries began to visit China and Southeast Asia in increasing numbers at this time, bringing with them new ideas, religious movements, and inventions. The Ming government slightly relaxed the previously imposed maritime trade restrictions, and in 1577, the Portuguese established a trading post at Macao (澳门). The Spanish, Dutch, and English ships that soon followed brought new products—potatoes, peppers, sweet potatoes, maize, and peanuts. Silk and porcelain were the principal commodities exported from China. Largely as a result of the Spanish discoveries of silver in South and Central America, huge quantities of silver poured into China in payment for the exports. This created new wealth and a corresponding desire for luxuries. As the Ming dynasty wore on, the well-to-do classes tended to cultivate their private lives at the expense of public service. Indeed, the elite enjoyed a higher standard of living than perhaps any of their contemporaries in the rest of the world.

This period set the stage for early modern China. On one hand, it represented economic expansion and the renewed development of the great artistic and cultural tradition of ancient China. On the other hand, rapid population growth, foreigners' interest in China, and economic disparity would lead to social turmoil in the eighteenth and nineteenth centuries.

Primary Sources

DOCUMENT 2.1: Excerpts from *The Journals of Matthew Ricci, 1583–1610* in which he describes Nanjing, ca. 1600

By the Ming dynasty, China had already been an urbanized culture for almost a thousand years. Cities like Nanjing, Xi'an, and Beijing were crowded, lively, and cosmopolitan centers of activity. As far back as Marco Polo's visit in the thirteenth century, Westerners had commented on the marvels and sophistication of city life in China. The Chinese, too, recognized their capital (with a population of approximately one million people) as a splendid one. Several guidebooks were published during the Ming. And like us today, city dwellers during the Ming complained of the congestion, the dirt, and the noise that were part of urban life.

Matteo (Matthew) Ricci, the author of this excerpt, was an Italian Jesuit missionary to China from 1582 until his death in Beijing in 1610. He targeted the literati class for Christian education, a "top-down" approach to conversion. Ricci became fluent in Chinese and wrote and translated several works into his adopted language.

In the judgment of the Chinese this city [Nanjing] surpasses all other cities in the world in beauty and in grandeur, and in this respect there are probably very few others superior or equal to it. It is literally filled with palaces and temples and towers and bridges, and these are scarcely surpassed by similar structures in Europe.... The climate is mild and the soil is fertile. There is a gaiety of spirit among the people, who are well mannered and nicely spoken, and the dense population is made up of all classes; of hoi-polloi, of the lettered aristocracy and the Magistrates [high-level scholar-officials]. These latter are equal in number and in dignity to those of Beijing, but due to the fact that the king does not reside here, the local Magistrates are not rated as equal with those of the Capital City. Yet in the whole kingdom of China and in all bordering countries, Nanjing is rated as the first city.

It is surrounded by three circles of walls. The first and innermost of these, and also the most decorative, contains the palace of the king. The palace, in turn, is surrounded by a triple wall of arches, and of circling moats, filled with circulating water.... The second wall, encircling the inner one, which contains the king's palace, encloses the greater and the more important part of the city. It has twelve gates, which are covered with iron plates and fortified by cannon from within.... The third and exterior wall is not continuous. At places that were judged to be danger spots, they scientifically added to natural fortifications. It is difficult to determine the full length of the circuit of this particular wall. The natives here tell a story of two men who started from opposite sides of the city, riding on horses toward each other, and it took a whole day before they came together.

This city was once the capital of the entire realm and the ancient abode of kings through many centuries, and though the king changed his residence to Beijing, in the north [in the early fifteenth century]... Nanjing lost none of its splendor or its reputation.

Source: Louis J. Gallagher, *China in the Sixteenth Century: The Journals of Matthew Ricci, 1583–1610* (New York: Random House, 1953), 268–270.

DOCUMENT 2.2: Excerpts from *The Journals of Matthew Ricci, 1583–1610* in which he describes Beijing, ca. 1601

[Beijing] is closed in on the south by two high, thick walls, wide enough for twelve horses to run along the tops of them without interference. These walls are built mostly of brick. At the foundations they are sustained by stones of tremendous dimensions, and the interiors are filled with prepared earth. They are not higher than city walls seen in Europe. On the north, the city is protected by a single wall. At night, all these walls are guarded by a host of soldiers, as numerous as if a war were raging. During the day, the city gates are guarded by the palace eunuchs, or at least they are supposed to be guarded, but these eunuchs are too busy taking tolls, something that is never done in other cities. The royal palace[3] is built into the southern wall, like an entrance to the city, and it extends clear to the northern wall, the entire length of the city and right through the middle of it. The rest of the town is spread on either side of the palace....

Very few of the streets in Beijing are paved with brick or stone, and it is difficult to say which season of the year is more objectionable for walking. The mud in the winter and the dust in the summer are equally obnoxious and fatiguing. As it seldom rains in this province, the surface earth dissolves into a coating of dust, which even a slight wind raises, blowing it into the houses, where it covers and soils nearly everything. In order to overcome this dust nuisance, they have introduced a custom which is probably unknown anywhere else. During the dust season here, nobody of any class would think of going out, either on foot or in conveyance, without wearing a long veil, falling in front from the hat, and thus sheltering the face. The material of the veil is fine enough to see through but no dust can penetrate it....

We have already noted that there is an abundance of everything in Beijing, most of which is brought into the city, but despite this fact, living in Beijing is difficult, save for such as are wealthy and do not have to retrench. Firewood is always lacking here, but this shortage is made up for by a bituminous substance, which for want of a better name, we shall call asphalt or mineral pitch.[4] It is a sort of fossil tar, dug out of the earth... The Chinese use it for cooking and also for heating their houses during the extreme cold of winter... The abundance of this material makes up nicely for the lack of firewood. The beds here are built up with bricks with a hollow space underneath, through which pipes from a fireplace are passed, creating a heat chamber beneath the bed. One does not have to keep the heat on during the night because the chamber stays hot for a long time. This kind of bed is in common use through all the northern provinces. The northern Chinese are more warlike and courageous than those from the south but less alert mentally. Such is the balance of human nature, that some are superior in one respect and some in another.

SOURCE: Louis J. Gallagher, *China in the Sixteenth Century: The Journals of Matthew Ricci, 1583–1610* (New York: Random House, 1953), 309–311.

---

[3] The Forbidden City; see Chapter 3.

[4] Coal was used in China long before it was known in the West.

DOCUMENT 2.3: Annual calendar of festival-related activities, 1635

Date	Activity
Lichun	Prefect and elites "welcome spring" in the eastern suburbs.
1/1–15[5]	Lunar New Year. Families celebrate the new year at home and call on relatives and friends over the next weeks. Visit certain temples.
1/8–18	Lantern market. Buy, display, and view lanterns on city streets.
1/15	Lantern festival. Everyone can stroll the streets and stay out all night.
1/25	Cook and eat a huge meal of special cakes, called "filling up the granaries."
2/2	Clear out insects and eat special foods associated with the "dragon raising his head."
Qingming	Commemorate deceased ancestors by visiting family graveyards.
3/28	Birthday of the god of the Eastern Peak, celebrated in his temple.
4/8	Birthday of Shakyamuni, celebrated in Buddhist monasteries
4/18	Birthday of Bixia Yuanjun, celebrated in various temples
5/5	Visit scenic spots. Take prophylactic measures to "avoid poisons" thought to be in the air.
5/13	Birthday of Guan Yu, celebrated at his temples
6/6	Air books and clothing, at homes and in temples.

SOURCE: *Dijing jingwu lue* ("Description of the Scenery of the Imperial Capital"), 1635. Quoted in Susan Naquin, *Peking: Temples and City Life, 1400–1900* (Berkeley: University of California Press, 2000), 275.

 The full text of **Document 2.3** is available on the CD-ROM.

DOCUMENT 2.4: Excerpts from *The Journals of Matthew Ricci, 1583–1610* in which he describes the literati

The sect of the Literati is proper to China and is most ancient in the kingdom. They rule the country, have an extensive literature, and are far more celebrated than the others…. Confucius is their Prince of Philosophers, and according to them, it was he who discovered the art of philosophy. They do not believe in idol worship. In fact they have no idols. They do, however, believe in one deity who preserves and governs all things on earth. Other spirits they admit, but these are of less restricted domination and receive only minor honors. The real Literati teach nothing relative to the time, the manner, or the author of the creation of the world….

The ancients scarcely seem to doubt about the immortality of the soul because, for a long time after death, they make frequent reference to the departed as dwelling in heaven. They say nothing, however, about punishment for the wicked in hell. The more recent Literati teach that the soul ceases to exist when the body does, or a

---

[5] The 1/1–15 does *not* correspond to the Western New Year, January 1, but rather to the months of the traditional Chinese lunar calendar. The Chinese New Year falls on the eve of the second new moon following the winter solstice.

short time after it…. [T]his school teaches that only the souls of the just survive. They say that the soul of a man is strengthened by virtue and solidified to endure, and since this is not true of the wicked, their souls vanish, like thin smoke, immediately after leaving the body….

Although the Literati, as they are called, do recognize one supreme deity, they erect no temples in his honor. No special places are assigned for his worship…. Neither are there any public or private prayers or hymns to be said or sung in honor of a supreme deity. The duty of sacrifice and the rites of worship for this supreme being belong to the imperial majesty alone. This is so true that if anyone else should offer such a sacrifice in usurpation of this right, he would be punished as an intruder upon the duty of the emperor and as a public enemy….

The most common ceremony practiced by all the Literati, from the emperor down to the very lowest of them, is that of the annual funeral rites…. As they them-selves say, they consider this ceremony as an honor bestowed upon their departed ancestors… They do not really believe that the dead actually need the victuals which are placed upon their graves, but they say that they observe the custom of placing them there because it seems to be the best way of testifying their love for their dear departed…. [I]t was [also] hoped that children, and unlearned adults as well, might learn how to respect and to support their parents who were living, when they saw that parents departed were so highly honored by those who were educated and prominent….

The Temple of Confucius is really the cathedral of…the Literati. The law demands that a temple be built to the Prince of Chinese Philosophers in every city…. In the most conspicuous place in the temple there will be a statue of Confucius, or if not a statue, a plaque with his name carved in large letters of gold….

The ultimate purpose and the general intention of…the Literati is public peace and order in the kingdom. They likewise look toward the economic security of the family and the virtuous training of the individual….Their writings explain at length the second precept of charity: "Do not do unto others what you would not wish others to do unto you." It really is remarkable how highly they esteem the respect and obedience of children toward parents, the fidelity of servants to a master, and devotion of the young to their elders.

Source: Louis J. Gallagher, *China in the Sixteenth Century: The Journals of Matthew Ricci, 1583–1610* (New York: Random House, 1953), 94–97.

DOCUMENT 2.5: "A Visit to High Beam Bridge" by Yuan Hongdao (1568–1610)

....

[The bridge] has the best view in the capital area. The embankment lies in the middle of water. Weeping willows extend for more than three miles. The river flows rapidly. The water is so clear that even the fins and scales of the fish at the bottom of the river can be seen. Buddhist temples dot the scene like pieces on a chessboard. Crimson towers and pearly pagodas beam among green trees. The Western Hills seem to be right within one's reach, enchanting tourists with their colors from morn-ing till night. In the height of spring, gentlemen and ladies from the city gather there, and the crowd is thick as clouds. No government official would ever refrain from making a trip there unless he were extremely busy.

On the first day of the third month, I had an outing with Wang Changfu and the Buddhist monk Jizi. A fresh green was sprouting at the tip of the willow branches. The hills shone from behind a thin mist. The river water rose up almost to the level of the embankment, and musicians were playing on their strings and pipes along both banks. Squatting on the root of an old tree, we drank some tea in place of wine, and, to accompany our drink, we looked at the patterns of ripples and the shade of trees and watched, like a stage performance, the birds in the air, the fish in the water, and the people who walked back and forth.

SOURCE: Yang Ye, ed. and trans., *Vignettes from the Late Ming: A Hsiao-p'in Anthology* (Seattle: University of Washington Press, 1999), 50–51.

 The full text of Document 2.5 is available on the CD-ROM.

DOCUMENT 2.6: "Inscribed on the Doors of My Bookshelves," a poem by Yang Xunji (1456–1544)

> When angry, I read and become happy;
> When sick, I read and am cured.
> Piled helter-skelter in front of me
> Books have become my life.
> The people of the past who wrote these tomes,
> If not sages, were certainly men of great wisdom.
> Even without opening their pages,
> Joy comes to me just fondling them.

SOURCE: Yang Hsün-chi, "Inscribed on the Doors of My Bookshelves," trans. John Timothy Wixted, *The Columbia Anthology of Traditional Chinese Literature*, ed. Victor H. Mair (New York: Columbia University Press, 1994), 273.

 The full text of Document 2.6 is available on the CD-ROM.

DOCUMENT 2.7: Excerpt from *The Craft of Gardens* by Ji Cheng, 1630s

Generally, in the construction of gardens, whether in the countryside or on the outskirts of a city, a secluded location is the best. In clearing woodland one should select and prune the tangled undergrowth; where a fine piece of natural scenery occurs one should make the most of it. Where there is a mountain torrent one may cultivate orchids and angelica together. Paths should be lined with the "three auspicious things"[6] whose property it is to symbolize eternity. The surrounding wall should be concealed under creepers, and rooftops should emerge here and there above the tops

[6] Pine, bamboo, and flowering plum; or rocks, bamboo, and flowering plum.

of the trees. If you climb a tower on a hill-top to gaze into the distance, nothing but beauty will meet your eye; if you seek a secluded spot among the banks of bamboo, intoxication will flood your heart. The pillars of your verandah should be tall and widely spaced; your windows and doors should give an unimpeded view.

Source: Ji Cheng, *The Craft of Gardens*, trans. Alison Hardie (New Haven: Yale University Press, 1988), 43.

 The full text of **Document 2.7** is available on the CD-ROM.

DOCUMENT 2.9: Excerpts from the *Biography of Gentleman Wang* by Wang Daokun (1525–1593)

This biography written by a Ming scholar-official, Wang Daokun, gives us a portrait of a successful merchant during the late Ming dynasty. Wang is a common Chinese surname. The author and the subject of the biography are not related.

Even at his great age [of ninety] Mr. Wang is a man of the highest integrity; therefore I now extol his deeds in order to show my respect for virtuous old men.... Mr. Wang lives in Shanghai. Even as a teenager, he was famous for his skill in making money. Being open and confident, he has attracted the respect of many capable and prosperous people who compete to attach themselves to him. At first, Mr. Wang's capital was no greater than the average person's. Later, as he grew more prosperous every day, the number of his associates also steadily increased. To accommodate his apprentices, Mr. Wang built buildings with doors on four sides. Whenever customers came, they could be taken care of from all four directions; thus, no one ever had to wait long.

Mr. Wang set up the following guidelines for his associates: do not let anyone who lives in another county control the banking; when lending money, never harass law-abiding people unnecessarily or give them less than they need; charge low interest on loans; do not aim at high profit and do not ask for daily interest. These principles led customers to throng to him, even ones from neighboring towns and provinces. Within a short time, Mr. Wang accumulated great wealth; in fact, of all the rich people in that area he became the richest.

Mr. Wang liked to help people and to give assistance to the poor. If anyone among his kinsmen could not afford a funeral for his parents, Mr. Wang would always buy some land and build a tomb for him. As soon as he heard someone could not make ends meet, he would buy land to rent to him. Whenever he was out traveling and met some unburied spirit, he would bid his servants bury it and present some offering.

The biography goes on to describe how Mr. Wang gave advice on how to distribute grain during a drought. He gave money to repair a bridge and an ancestral temple.

Later, when Mr. Zhu set up dikes, a dispute occurred which involved thousands of people. The official tried to straighten out the merits of the case, but still it could not be resolved. Therefore the official asked Mr. Wang to take a hand in the matter. He successfully mediated the dispute merely by sending out a long letter. Later he was singled out to promote good community relations in Linhe and resolved all the quarrels there. Thus everybody praised him, saying, "Mr. Wang is capable of mediating disputes. He has the manner of a gentleman of national stature, and even the gentlemen of antiquity were not his equals."

SOURCE: Patricia Buckley Ebrey, ed., *Chinese Civilization and Society: A Sourcebook* (New York: Free Press, first edition 1981), 159–160.

DOCUMENT 2.10: Poems written by women during the Ming dynasty (1368–1644)

"Hardships of the Road," by Lu Qingzi

With orchid and musk tapestried quilts perfumed;
Behind silk screens breezes of spring still cold.
When I bound up my hair and became your bride
We were always together like a bundle tied:
You were my heart's beloved.

We were lacquer and glue; who could come between?
We were metal and stone, enduring to the end.
Then a mere word, by chance caused the ruin of all my hopes;
Your angry glance was the first sign of ill will.

The lady's beauty gradually faded away;
The shining mirror took leave of the soaring phoenix.
I mounted the carriage, went out the gate and left.
The knot of our bond for a thousand miles unraveled.

When I was young, I enjoyed your loving favor;
Who could know then my road would be hard to travel?
Thought it hasn't been long they speak of someone new;
Your generous love for me is truly already spent!

SOURCE: Kang-I Sun Chang and Haun Saussy, eds., *Women Writers of Traditional China: An Anthology of Poetry and Criticism,* (Stanford, CA: Stanford University Press, 1999), 256.

 Additional poems are available on the CD-ROM.

DOCUMENT 2.11: Excerpts describing severe hardship in the lives of peasants during the latter part of the Ming dynasty

Excerpt A: "Letter to a Friend" by Wang Wenlu, 1545

The drought in Haiyan county began in 1538 when a tidal wave crossed the sea wall in the south, inundating the fields with saltwater, and then flowed north and attacked the crops. What with the blazing autumn sun and no sources of fresh water to irrigate, the rice put forth ears that did not turn to seed, or produced seed that then rotted. Growing plants shrank and turned to weeds, the fields yellowed: as far as you looked it was a scene of desolation. The officials did not report this to the throne. The stricken were excused from paying taxes, yet the prosperous were so pressed that they also became impoverished. Paddy rice did not come on the market and the price of rice went even higher. People fed themselves first on chaff and bean pods, then on tree bark and weeds. In 1539 and 1544 we suffered virulent epidemics. Both in the country villages and in the towns, nine out of ten houses stood empty. In any village, half the girls and boys were sold off. Now it is spring, and as we wait for the end of the summer growing season, the corpses of the starved lie everywhere—beside the monasteries, below the fords, within the suburban gates, in the middle of the roads—and everywhere the sound of wailing pierces our ears.

Source: Qtd. in Timothy Brook, *The Confusions of Pleasure: Commerce and Culture in Ming China* (Berkeley: University of California Press, 1998), 105–106.

 The full text of **Document 2.11** is available on the CD-ROM.

Activities

ACTIVITY 1: **Life in the cities**
....

Documents 2.1–2.3 provide glimpses into the daily life of urban citizens in the early 1600s. After reading them, select one or more of the following activities.
  Discuss in class:

1. What is most striking about Matteo Ricci's accounts of Nanjing and Beijing?

2. How do his descriptions compare to your sense of how China's cities once looked?

3. How did China's cities of 1600 compare to a city elsewhere in the world during the same era?

4. Using the documents as evidence, pretend you are a European merchant or missionary. Write a letter home, describing life in the city that you are visiting. Alternatively, create a travel poster.

5. Ricci describes "a bituminous substance"—coal—that the residents of Beijing used as fuel. Research the history of coal. What did people in Europe and other parts of the world use for fuel at this time? When did Europeans discover coal? Did they discover it independently or was it introduced by the Chinese? You may also want to research various other Chinese discoveries and inventions.

6. Research several key festivals listed in the "Annual Calendar, 1635" (2.3)

7. What religions and beliefs are reflected in this calendar?

8. What values does this list of celebrations reflect?

Extended research:

Working with a partner or in a small group, compare these Chinese celebrations to ones celebrated elsewhere in the world in the seventeenth century (e.g., France, Mexico, England, Brazil, Puritan Massachusetts, Virginia, Japan, India, etc.). The class could make a chart comparing and contrasting festivals around the world.

NOTE: For more information about Chinese festivals, see Lesson 9 in *The Enduring Legacy of Ancient China* (Cheng & Tsui, 2006).

ACTIVITY 2: The lives of scholar-officials and literati

Part 1:

Documents 2.4–2.6 give a taste for what the lives of scholar-officials and the literati were like. After reading the selections, choose from among the following activities:

1. Is there evidence of bias in Ricci's account of the literati (2.4)? What is his understanding of their spiritual beliefs? Who is at the center of the beliefs? According to Matteo Ricci, what do members of this class value?

2. What differences do you see between an outing into the countryside on which you might go and the one described by Yuan Hongdao in "A Visit to High Beam Bridge" (2.5)?

3. Illustrate the setting in Yuan's description.

4. What differences between the scholar-officials and the merchant class does the poem "Inscribed on the Doors of My Bookshelves" (2.6) emphasize?

5. Describe the tone of the poem and how the poet views himself.

6. Adopting the persona of a scholar-official, write one or two diary entries describing daily life. Make sure you account for various roles: official, amateur artist, and connoisseur.

NOTE: For a deeper understanding of the values of scholar-officials and the literati, read the lessons on the Four Accomplishments—calligraphy, poetry, painting, and music—in *The Enduring Legacy of Ancient China* (Cheng & Tsui, 2006).

Part 2:

Read the excerpt from Ji Cheng's book (2.7) and look at the PowerPoint slide show of classical Chinese gardens (2.8). Discuss:

1. What is most striking about the description and the images of the gardens?

2. What appear to be consistent features?

3. Given the values of scholar-officials and the newly wealthy merchant class, do you think that the gardens of the scholar-officials served purposes that were similar to or different from those of the merchants?

Creative extensions:

- Draw or paint a Ming dynasty garden based on Ji's description and the photos. Alternatively, using these sources and additional information from books and websites, sketch a plan for a small Chinese garden.

- Other important crafts during the Ming dynasty included furniture making and the manufacture of blue-and-white porcelain. Work with a partner or in a small group to create a presentation on either of these.

Extended research:

- The "three auspicious things" Ji mentions (in 2.7) may be pine, bamboo and flowering plum (*Prunus mume*), also known as the "three friends in winter," or rock, bamboo and flowering plum. Find out why these would be considered the "three auspicious things."

- Why did garden design rise to become such an art in China? Do some research on Daoism and/or read some Chinese landscape poetry to further your understanding.

- Some cities outside of Asia have small Chinese (or Japanese) gardens, either within the city's park system or at a museum. If there is a Chinese or Japanese garden near you, visit it. What are the differences and similarities between Chinese and Japanese gardens? Compare these gardens to city parks and/or other gardens with which you are familiar.

ACTIVITY 3: The life of a merchant

Read the *Biography of Gentleman Wang* (2.9) and make a list of the qualities that helped make Mr. Wang a successful businessman. Are these the same qualities we would find in businesspeople today? Why or why not?

1. What prejudices against merchants come through in this short biography?

2. Review Mr. Wang's four guidelines. Why were they so effective in generating business? Would these guidelines work today? Why or why not?

3. Compare Mr. Wang's examples of philanthropy with the philanthropic activity of today's successful businesspeople like Bill Gates.

4. The author of this biography calls the man "virtuous." Would you agree? What do you think a scholar-official of the Ming dynasty would have to say about businessmen such as Mr. Wang?

ACTIVITY 4: The lives of women

After reading the selections of poetry (2.10), discuss:

1. What are the subjects of these poems?
2. What were these women's joys? What were their sorrows?
3. What values are reflected in the poems?
4. One poem is by a concubine; the others are not. How are they similar and different?
5. What is the picture of the lives of Ming dynasty women that comes through in these poems? What assumptions do the women make about their lives?

The preface to one anthology of Chinese women poets, written late in the Ming dynasty, says, "Men must travel to all the corners of the earth in order to know the world….But women never have to do that. They have country villages right on their pillows and mountain passes in their dreams, all because they are so pure…. Alas! How far in their skillfulness men fall behind women!"[7] Do you agree? What prejudices are embedded in this statement?

NOTE: To deepen understanding of the lives of educated women during the sixteenth century, read more of their poems in *Women Writers of Traditional China* (see Suggested Resources).

Creative extension:

Write a poem in the voice of a Ming dynasty woman. Or write a pair of poems: one in the voice of a Ming dynasty woman and the other in which a present-day individual responds to her words.

ACTIVITY 5: Life of the peasantry

Read Document 2.11, which includes four selections describing conditions for the vast majority of the people in the 1500s, the last century of the Ming dynasty. (Refer to Chapter 1 for additional primary sources describing rural life.) Then choose from among the following activities:

1. Using the documents as evidence, write a diary, letter, or story in the voice of a sixteenth-century peasant describing the conditions in his or her *li* (neighborhood).
2. In the persona of a sixteenth-century Chinese peasant, dictate a petition to a person in your village who is literate. The petition will be presented to the local official describing the dire conditions in your farming area. What should the official do to help?
3. In these accounts, we get various glimpses of government officials. (Liu in excerpt C is also an official.) Make a list of the qualities of a good government official, either today or in Ming dynasty times. (You might want to do research

---

[7] qtd. in Chang and Saussy, *Women Writers in Traditional China*, 9–10.

to find out how Confucius thought a good government official should behave.)

4. In these accounts, the starving peasants resort to dire, even gruesome, measures in order to survive—selling one's wife, selling one's children, cannibalism. What do these things tell us about the power of hunger? Where else have you heard of individuals having to make unbearable choices? You might want to research the peasant revolts that occurred toward the end of the Ming dynasty and report to the class.

5. Are there places in the world today where conditions exist similar to the ones described in these documents? Research a region in the world plagued by droughts, floods, or other conditions that hinder good farming.

6. Is the present situation exactly like that of these sixteenth-century peasants? If not, how is it different?

7. What is being done to help the people affected by catastrophic conditions?

8. Is one form of government better able to address the problems of farmers than another? Why?

EXTENDED RESEARCH:

To get a deeper understanding of various aspects of life in sixteenth-century China, explore any one of these topics:

- The life of Matteo Ricci, Jesuit living in China

- The bed "built up with bricks" (Document 2.2) is called a *kang* in Chinese. Research this and other aspects of courtyard homes (*siheyuan*).

- Research a topic such as calligraphy, the tea ceremony, or Ming dynasty poetry.

- Learn about the Confucian examination system through which all scholar-officials had to pass before they could serve in the government. The class might want to debate the merits and liabilities of such a system.

- Read *The Examination* by Malcolm Bosse (see Suggested Resources) and report on what you learn about Ming dynasty China from the book.

Suggested Resources

Books

Good general introductions to the Ming dynasty include

Chan, Albert. *The Glory and Fall of the Ming Dynasty*. Norman, OK: University of Oklahoma Press, 1982.

Clunas, Craig. *Fruitful Sites: Garden Culture in Ming Dynasty China*. Durham, NC: Duke University Press, 1996.

Grousset, René. "A National Restoration: The Ming Dynasty" in *The Rise and Splendor of the Chinese Empire*. Berkeley: University of California Press, 1953.

Roberts, J. A. G. "The Early Modern Period: The Ming and Early Qing" in *A Concise History of China*. Cambridge, MA: Harvard University Press, 1999.

Other specialized, but quite readable, studies on various topics in the Ming dynasty include

Brook, Timothy. *The Confusions of Pleasure: Commerce and Culture in Ming China*. Berkeley: University of California Press, 1998.

Knapp, Ronald, Jonathan Spence, and A. Chester Ong. *Chinese Houses: The Architectural Heritage of a Nation*. Rutland, VT: Tuttle Publishing, 2005.

Levathes, Louise. *When China Ruled the Seas: the Treasure Fleet of the Dragon Throne 1405–1433*. New York: Simon & Schuster, 1994.

Tsai, Shih-shan Henry. *The Eunuchs in the Ming Dynasty*. Albany: State University of New York Press, 1996.

Spence, Jonathan D. *The Memory Palace of Matteo Ricci*. New York: Penguin, 1985. *An excellent book on Ricci and the Jesuits in China.*

For women's poetry

Chang, Kang-i Sun, and Haun Saussy, eds. *Women Writers of Traditional China: An Anthology of Poetry and Criticism*. Stanford, CA: Stanford University Press, 1999.

See the bibliography on the CD-ROM for several excellent anthologies of Chinese literature, all of which contain selections from Ming prose and poetry.

Bosse, Malcolm. *The Examination*. New York: Farrar, Straus & Giroux, 1994.

 An excellent historical novel that captures many features of life in Ming China, including the civil service examination process.

Websites

http://www.chinavista.com/travel/13tomb/main. html This website, entitled *The Thirteen Tombs of the Ming Dynasty: World's Largest Concentration of Royal Tombs*, provides a visual tour of the imperial tombs including the gateways, the Sacred Way, the mausoleums, etc.

http://www.travelchinaguide.com/cityguides/ beijing/forbidden.htm One of many websites devoted to the Forbidden City built by the third Ming emperor, Zhu Di, between 1407 and 1420.

http://www.gotheborg.com This fully searchable site dedicated to antique Chinese and Japanese porcelain, is, according to the creators, "the largest information resource on Chinese and Japanese antique porcelain on the Internet."

http://archive.tpt.org/china/TGuide/china. pdf This Teacher's Guide, written to accompany *Fine Art from the Middle Kingdom to Minnesota*, a six-part series produced by Twin Cities Public Television, features, among other units, one on the creative life of the Chinese literati.

http://www.wsu.edu/~dee/WORLD.HTM An award-winning website, Washington State University's *World Civilizations: An Internet Classroom and Anthology* includes sections on Ming dynasty China, including copious links to other relevant sites.

http://hua.umf.maine.edu/China/ming. html Provides an extensive bibliography on Ming dynasty China. This site is a great place to consult for further serious reading.

http://www.hsofmich.org/~asia/bibs/bibebrey. html Compiled by Patricia Ebrey, a leading scholar of ancient China, this site provides a reading list on women in Chinese history. An excellent place to start research projects on women in the Ming dynasty.

http://www.portlandchinesegarden.org/

http://www.portlandchinesegarden.org/ awakening/orchids/info/C4/ Provides maps and plantings of a traditional Chinese garden in Portland, Oregon and its designers' collaboration with the city of Suzhou, China. An infusion of horticulture and philosophy.

http://www.seattlechinesegarden.org/index.php?p =Four+Elements&s=14 Information on the four traditional elements of a Chinese garden as well as the design, horticulture and symbolism of plants found in this traditional Chinese garden in Seattle, Washington.

http://www.metmuseum.org/TOAH/hd/cgrk/ hd_cgrk.htm The Metropolitan Museum of Art's Timeline of Art History website describes Chinese gardens and collector's rocks in their many varieties, with links to scholar-officials and items they used and made.

Film

The Emperor's Eye (58 mins; 1990) *This documentary captures the preeminence of the arts in Chinese culture.*

UNIT TWO

The Qing Dynasty
(1644–1911)

UNIT OVERVIEW

By Liz Nelson

After the last Ming emperor to rule from Beijing hanged himself in 1644, the Manchu people swept down from the northeast and gradually took control of China. They established the **Qing dynasty**, only the second non-Chinese dynasty ever to control all of China.[1] Over the course of the next century, Qing forces expanded and solidified China's borders, creating an immense continental power. Under the reigns of **three powerful emperors: Kangxi, Yongzheng, and Qianlong**, China enjoyed more than a century of peace during which culture and commerce could flourish. These three rulers and their successors incorporated Chinese values and aesthetics into Manchu court life, while at the same time keeping a firm grasp on military power. Chinese scholar-officials continued to be appointed to government positions, ensuring their support.

The Chinese had had experience interacting with peoples beyond their borders for centuries. For example, Chinese merchants were engaged in trade over the Silk Routes for extended periods of time, first during the Han dynasty (206 B.C.E.–220 C.E.) and again during the Tang dynasty (618 C.E.–907 C.E.). During the latter period, Xi'an,[2] the start of the trade route, was the most cosmopolitan city in the world. By the thirteenth century, the Chinese had developed the most reliable ocean-going vessels in the world, with watertight bulkheads and moveable rudders. This advanced technology allowed them, 200 years later, to launch an enormous fleet of 300 vessels on tributary missions in South and Southeast Asia, the Persian Gulf, and East Africa.

Each dynasty conducted its relations with non-Chinese-speaking peoples (regarded as "barbarians") with the understanding that China was the Middle Kingdom, just as its name *Zhongguo* suggests. (In much the same way, "Mediterranean" means "middle of the earth," with Rome at the center.) The emperor was the Son of Heaven and all foreign rulers owed him allegiance as heads of what the Chinese rulers considered **tributary states**.

In the late 1700s, the emperors of the Qing dynasty continued to focus on their immediate neighbors and had little knowledge of or interest in **European imperial powers**. When they

---

[1] The Mongols' Yuan dynasty, from 1279 to 1368, was the other.

[2] Formerly known as Chang'an

TIMELINE

Elsewhere in the world as the Manchus founded the Qing dynasty:

- The Ottoman Empire, founded in 1288 and ruled from present-day Istanbul, spanned southeastern Europe, the Middle East, and North Africa. At its height, it stretched from the Strait of Gibraltar to the Caspian Sea.

- Africa knew this as the period of Great African Kingdoms (e.g. Dahomey, Great Zimbabwe, and Axum).

- The Mughal Empire, in existence from the early 1500s, stretched across the Indian subcontinent.

- In Korea, the Joseon dynasty began rule in 1392.

- In Japan, during the Tokugawa or Edō period, the country was unified under a military government, beginning in 1600.

- In Vietnam, the Le dynasty had ruled since 1428.

1600

1602 Dutch East India Company established

1644: Qing dynasty established

1648: Taj Mahal completed in India

1650: Dutch East India Company brings tea to New Amsterdam (later New York City)

1652–1654: The English begin to drink tea

1661: The first of two 17th-century civil wars in Vietnam between Trinh in the North and Nguyen in the South (the second civil war begins in1672)

1662: Kangxi Emperor begins his reign (1662–1722)

1670: England's King Charles II expands powers of British East India Company

1683: Qing annex Taiwan

1689: Peter the Great becomes emperor of Russia

1689: Treaty of Nerchinsk signed with Russia

1697: Qing conquer western Mongolia

had to, they dealt with them as they had with other nations—as unequal parties. But with the Industrial Revolution underway in the West, China was up against a new kind of "barbarian," and China's lack of knowledge cost the Chinese dearly. Western imperial powers, followed by Japan later in the nineteenth century, were transforming themselves from agrarian into industrial nations with new kinds of weaponry and territorial ambitions. Their merchant fleets traded all over the world, and their citizens eagerly purchased the tea, silk, and porcelain from China that ships brought home. China, however, had no interest in Western products

and restricted Western traders to Guangzhou[3] in what was known as the **Canton System**. The Chinese government also demanded payment in silver, supplies of which were plummeting in the West. British and American merchants began to import opium into China, and after Qing officials banned its production, use, and importation, Western vessels smuggled the drug in via eager Chinese middlemen.

Tension between China and the West escalated until in 1839, the British government

---

[3] Formerly known as Canton

1700

1700s Age of Enlightenment in Europe

1700: As Mughal authority weakens, regional powers rise in India

1711: East India Company establishes trading post in Guangzhou

1720: Tibet becomes Qing protectorate

1723: Emperor Yongzheng begins his reign (1723–1736)

1729: Opium smoking prohibited in China

1736: The reign of Qianlong, China's longest-ruling emperor, begins (1736–1795)

1750 Population of China 177.5 million

of Europe 140 million

of the 13 North American colonies 1.3 million

1757: Battle of Plassey; victory gives East India Company control of Bengal, beginning expansion of British rule in India

1759: Qing annex Xinjiang

1770: Bengal Famine kills an estimated 10 million people, one third of the population in the affected area

1771: The Tay Son Revolt topples the Le dynasty in Vietnam

1773: British Parliament passes the Tea Act, sparking protests in Boston, Massachusetts

1775–1783: American War for Independence

1784: The vessel *Empress of China* opens trade between the United States and China

End of 18th century: Industrial Revolution begins in Great Britain

1789–1799: French Revolution

1793: The Macartney embassy meets with Emperor Qianlong

1793–1815: Napoleonic Wars; end with Napoleon's defeat at Waterloo

1796–1805/06: White Lotus uprisising

used its state-of-the-art weaponry and highly trained soldiers to conduct "gunboat diplomacy." China lost both what became known as **Opium Wars** and the Manchus were coerced into signing a series of **unequal treaties**, thus ushering in what the Chinese refer to as their "century of humiliation."

At the same time that Qing leaders were coping with pressure from the West, various factors contributed to **social unrest** in many areas of the country. The population of China had tripled from 143 million in 1741 to 430 million in 1850, but arable land had only increased by about 35%, exacerbating hardship for peasants. The ever-growing smuggling of opium had now reversed the trade balance: more silver was leaving China than entering. As a result, the price of silver rose sharply, and members of the working class, who were paid in copper coins, found it increasingly difficult to pay taxes in silver currency as the government required. In the 1840s and 1850s, millions also suffered from natural disasters: droughts and floods. The educated elite had trouble finding employment. Some who did have government positions had bought them rather than having passed the traditional examinations, and corruption was widespread. In addition, the

1800

1800: Dutch East India Company dissolved

1802: Nguyen dynasty founded in Vietnam

1807: British Atlantic slave trade ends

1810–1820: The majority of Latin American countries declare independence from Spain and Portugal

1811: Population of China 358.5 million

1812–1815: War of 1812 fought between United States and Great Britain

1813: Opium smoking banned in China

1819: The British establish Singapore as a colony

1826: Cholera pandemic begins in India and spreads from Russia to Central Europe to Scotland by 1832

1839–1842: Opium War fought between Britain and China ending with the Treaty of Nanjing, the first of the "unequal treaties"

1849: First Chinese immigrants arrive in Peru

1850: Emperor Xianfeng begins his rule

1848–1858: California Gold Rush; first Chinese immigrants begin to arrive in the United States

1851: Population of China 431.9 million

1850s: First Chinese immigrants arrive in Australia

1851–1854: Taiping Rebellion led by Hong Xiuquan

1851–1868: Nian Rebellion led by Zhang Luoxing

1853–1856: Crimean War between Britain, France, the Ottoman Empire, and Russia

1854: Convention of Kanagawa negotiated by Commodore Matthew Perry ends Japanese isolation policy

1858: Treaty of Tianjin

1858: British East India Company's rule ends, and direct British rule begins in India

1861–1865: United States Civil War

1862: Treaty of Saigon is the first unequal treaty between France and Vietnam

---

army was in dismal shape: poorly equipped and, like all other segments of society, riddled with opium addicts. Four major rebellions rocked the Qing dynasty mid-century, the most significant of which was the **Taiping Rebellion** (1851–1864).

The combination of internal strife and external pressure damaged the Qing dynasty beyond repair. While a number of prominent Chinese scholar-officials launched many thoughtful plans to reform China, their **self-strengthening efforts** were up against an entrenched bureaucracy and a dynasty desperate to hang onto power. Chinese students studied abroad, and foreign language schools and armories were established at home, but no multi-faceted program took hold. China lagged decades behind the West and Japan rather than forging centuries ahead as it had in the past.

Merchants from Britain, France, Portugal, the United States, and Russia set aside segments of China's port cities, such as Shanghai and Tianjin, as their own "concessions," where *their* legal systems applied instead of China's. Now they traded freely with inland China, too. Thousands of Protestant and Catholic **missionaries** proselytized and established schools and hospitals across the country. Much of their

1862: Six-year-old Tongzhi becomes emperor; Cixi acts as Empress Dowager; Tongzhi Restoration

1863: Cambodia becomes a protectorate of France

1868–1912: Meiji Period in Japan begins, launching the Meiji Restoration

1875: Tongzhi dies; three-year-old Guangxu appointed emperor; Empress Dowager Cixi continues to rule

1882: Chinese Exclusion Act passed in the United States

1887: French create the Indochinese Union (ICU), which includes Cochinchina (southern Vietnam) as a colony and Annam (central Vietnam), Tonkin (northern Vietnam), and Cambodia as protectorates; Laos added as a protectorate in 1893

1894–1895: Sino-Japanese War. Treaty of Shimonoseki cedes Taiwan to Japan and gives Japan control of Korea

1897–1910: Emperor Gojong proclaims the Republic of Korea

1898–1901: Boxer Uprising

1900

1900: Commonwealth of Australia established

1901: Australia passes the Immigration Restriction Act, also known as the "White Australia Policy"

1904–1905: Russo-Japanese War won by Japan; Treaty of Portsmouth ends hostilities

1905: Abolition of traditional Confucian examination system

1906: Great Earthquake of San Francisco

1908: Empress Dowager Cixi dies; Puyi becomes emperor

1910: Japanese colonial rule in Korea begins

1910: Slavery abolished in China

1911: Qing dynasty falls to revolutionary forces led by Sun Yat-sen

social work improved the lives of countless Chinese men, women, and children. But increasing hardships for the Chinese peasantry made foreigners an easy target for mistrust, and violence broke out a number of times, culminating in North China in the **Boxer Uprising** of 1900.

As increasing numbers of upper-class Chinese men and women studied abroad (especially in Japan), they became keenly aware of the disparities between industrialized nations and China. Expatriates, such as **Dr. Sun Yat-sen**, gathered supporters and funds, eager to end imperial rule and establish a republic in China. Several revolts failed, but eventually one that began by accident in Wuhan spread rapidly. The formal **abdication** by the child-emperor Puyi on February 12, 1912 marked the end of more than two millennia of dynastic rule in China.

Primary Sources

DOCUMENT 3.1: Excerpts from "Shi Lang's Memorial on the Capture of Taiwan" 1683

DOCUMENT 3.2: Excerpts from the Treaty of Nerchinsk signed by China and Russia in 1689

DOCUMENT 3.3: Excerpts from the *Analects of Confucius*

DOCUMENT 3.4: The Kangxi Emperor's "The Sacred Edicts," 1670

DOCUMENT 3.5: Excerpts from "Demonstrate Ceremony and Deference in Order to Improve Popular Customs," 1700s (not available on the CD-ROM)

DOCUMENT 3.6: "Fan Jin Passes the Juren Examination," an excerpt from *The Scholars* by Wu Jingzi, c. 1740

DOCUMENT 3.7: Excerpts from "Yuanchun Visits Her Parents on the Feast of Lanterns," *The Dream of Red Mansions* by Cao Xueqin, 1792

DOCUMENT 3.8: Excerpts from "A Worthless Son Receives a Fearful Flogging," *The Dream of Red Mansions* by Cao Xueqin, 1792

DOCUMENT 3.9: "Portrait of the Qianlong Emperor (r.1736–1796) as the Bodhisattva Manjusri"

DOCUMENTS 3.10a–n: Photographs of the Forbidden City, Beijing, 2006 & 2007

Supplementary Materials

ITEM 3.A: Map of China during the Ming dynasty (1368–1644)

ITEM 3.B: Map of China during the Qing dynasty (1644–1911)

CHAPTER 3

Three Manchu Emperors

By Jamie Moore

Chapter Contents

The Manchu Invasion

Qing Dynasty Expansion

Manchu and Chinese Cultures Integrate

Organizing Idea

The Manchu were an ethnically non-Chinese people who in the seventeenth and eighteenth centuries controlled the largest territory that China had ever possessed in one of the country's most prosperous periods. Qing rulers kept their own Manchu identity, while at the same time incorporating and preserving Chinese culture and values.

Key Questions

What were the effects of foreign, Manchu rule on China?

What were the challenges and benefits of territorial expansion for the Qing dynasty?

In what ways did Qing rulers preserve Chinese values? What did they emphasize? What did they control?

Key Terms

civil service examination system	Han Chinese
courtesan	Manchu
Confucianism	maxim
dynasty	Qing
edict	queue
eunuch	treaty

Essay

The Manchu Invasion

In the early 1600s, the Manchus (满族), who lived in the northeast in what are now Liaoning (辽宁), Heilongjiang (黑龙江), and Jilin (吉林) provinces, began to consolidate their forces north of the Great Wall. They took advantage of the declining Ming (明) dynasty (1368–1644) to begin their gradual conquest of China. In the twelfth century, their ancestors had ruled northern China as the Jin (晋) dynasty. The Manchus used this historical connection as a justification for the legitimacy of their rule.

Nurhaci (努尔哈赤) (1559–1626), the *khan* or ruler of the Manchus, organized his military forces into eight units known as "banners" that consisted of soldiers and their family members. This was an efficient way to keep track of people and plan strong military advances. As the *khan* conquered Chinese territory, he encouraged the Chinese to join him by giving them powerful leadership positions. After Nurhaci's death, his sons pushed for the complete defeat of the Ming, and in 1636, Huang Taiji (皇太极) (r.1626–1643) officially named the new dynasty "Qing" (清), meaning "pure" or "clear." After an uneasy first forty years, the dynasty's early history was one of relative stability, unity, and success. This can be attributed to the rule of three powerful Qing emperors: Kangxi (康熙), Yongzheng (雍正), and Qianlong (乾隆). They ruled the largest land empire of the time from 1662 to 1796, a period heralded by scholars as one of the most stable in China's history.

Territorial Expansion

Kangxi, the first of these three emperors, came to power in 1662, and under his leadership, the Qing dynasty quickly consolidated territory in southern and southwestern China that had previously been controlled by three warlords. In addition, the Qing also expanded and solidified borders. To suppress resistance by Ming dynasty loyalists who had retreated to Taiwan, they captured the island in 1683 and made it part of the Qing empire. (See Additional Resources on the CD for an overview of Taiwan's history.) The Qing then solidified the northeast border of China by signing the Treaty of Nerchinsk with Russia in 1689. A subsequent treaty outlining the border west of the 1689 treaty was signed in 1727 under the Yongzheng emperor.[1] The Manchus defeated the Eastern Mongols in the 1630s and the nomadic Zunghar tribes (western Mongols) in 1696. They also invaded Tibet (西藏) (an area almost twice the size of the state of Texas) in 1720, continuing a long legacy of Chinese involvement in and efforts to control the region. (See Additional Resources on the CD for an overview of Tibet's history.) In the 1750s, Manchus conquered the vast, primarily Muslim territory of Xinjiang (新疆). Over the course of a century, the Qing had significantly increased land holdings north, south, and west, which included people of many ethnicities. As the empire expanded, however, the Manchus also faced the task of coping with periodic rebellions, which were often led by secret societies such as the White Lotus (see A Closer Look at the end of the chapter).

Manchu and Chinese Cultures Integrate

Throughout their rule, the three emperors (Kangxi, Yongzheng, and Qianlong) balanced ways to maintain military and civil power with practices that integrated Confucian-trained Chinese intellectuals into the Manchu government. On the one hand, the Manchus established dominance by requiring Chinese men to wear a braided queue in the Manchu style. They prohibited Manchu women from binding their feet, which limited intermarriage between Manchu women and Chinese men since Chinese men believed bound feet to be a sign of refinement. The Qianlong emperor also persecuted Chinese writers suspected of harboring anti-Manchu sentiments. On the other

---

[1] The Treaty of Kiakhta

(Minneapolis Institute of Art)

hand, when the Qing established six ministries of government (Civil Affairs, Finance, Rituals, War, Justice, and Public Service), they had a Manchu and a Chinese leader for each ministry. They also kept the civil service examination system, which was based on knowledge of four key Confucian books and five ancient Chinese classics. They even added a special exam in 1679 for men of great talent, to draw more Chinese into their government.

The three emperors incorporated Chinese culture to make the Chinese more accepting of their rule. The Kangxi emperor not only studied and debated proper moral behavior and values found at the heart of the ancient classics, but wrote his "Sacred Edicts" in 1670, summarizing sixteen maxims that he considered to embody Confucius's most important moral values. In 1724, the Yongzheng emperor added his own comments to these edicts and mandated that they be publicly presented to the common people twice a month. The Qing court sponsored literary endeavors, such as the writing of encyclopedias. The Qianlong emperor sponsored a major compilation of famous literary and historical works known as the *Complete Library of the Four Treasuries*. He is also noted for having studied Tibetan Buddhism in order to model himself as a Buddhist savior kind to his non-Chinese subjects.

Emperors Kangxi, Yongzheng, and Qianlong expanded the empire and solidified key borders, which allowed China to prosper culturally and economically. The few Europeans who visited China were stunned by the sheer opulence and wealth of the Qing court. Until the nineteenth century, the high standard of living, material resources, and inventions of Manchu China were unrivaled in the rest of the world.

Primary Sources

DOCUMENT 3.1: Excerpts from "Shi Lang's Memorial on the Capture of Taiwan," 1683

Cannon shot and arrows fell like rain; smoke and flame covered the sky. It was impossible to see even a foot beyond the ships…. The fighting went on from the early morning until the late afternoon. Our sailors fought without regard for their own lives and used all of their energy to attack and kill the bandits. Eighteen of the bandits' big gunboats were set aflame and destroyed by our navy's incendiary buckets and grenades. Eight other heavy gunboats were sunk by cannon fire. Thirty-six large "birdboats," sixty-seven silk junks, and five refitted foreign ships were also burned and destroyed. Moreover, our navy used the wind to propel incendiary boats into other bandit ships; one "birdboat" and two silk junks were destroyed in this way. The rebellious bandits fought feverishly and when their forces were exhausted, [they] packed gunpowder in holds of their own ships and blew themselves up. In this way, they burned nine gunboats and thirteen "birdboats." Some bandits panicked and jumped into the sea and, in this way, we captured two "birdboats," eight silk junks, and twenty-five two-masted junks. What was to be burnt was burnt; those to be killed were killed….

SOURCE: Rpt. in Pei-Kai Cheng, Michael Lestz, and Jonathan Spence, eds., *The Search for Modern China: A Documentary Collection* (New York: W.W. Norton, 1999), 50–51.

 The full text of **Document 3.1** is available on the CD-ROM.

DOCUMENT 3.2: Excerpts from the Treaty of Nerchinsk signed by China and Russia in 1689

II

Likewise, the river called Argun which falls into the river Amur is thus decreed the frontier, so that all lands that make up the left side, going along that river to its very sources, are under the dominion of the Khin khan [Chinese ruler]; likewise, all lands contained on the right side are in the domain of the czarist majesty of the Russian state, and all buildings on the southern bank of that river Argun shall be moved to the other side of that same river.

III

The town of Albazin which was built by the czarist majesty will be destroyed to its foundations and those people living there with all military and other supplies shall be returned to the side of the czarist majesty, and none of their losses, however small the things, shall be left there.

IV

Fugitives, whether they were, up to this peace decree, from either the side of the czarist majesty or from the side of the Bugdykhan highness are [permitted] to be on either side without being exchanged, but those who after this decreed peace shall pass over, such fugitives shall be expelled without delay from either side and [turned over] immediately to the frontier voevodas.[2]

SOURCE: Rpt. in Pei-Kai Cheng, Michael Lestz, and Jonathan Spence, eds., *The Search for Modern China: A Documentary Collection* (New York: W.W. Norton, 1999), 53–54.

 The full text of **Document 3.2** is available on the CD-ROM.

DOCUMENT 3.3: Excerpts from the *Analects of Confucius*

Confucius is believed to have been born around 551 B.C.E., during the time of the Warring States and great political disorder in China. He became a scholar and traveled from province to province hoping to spread his ideas about good moral behavior and the proper way for rulers to treat their subjects. While he never had the impact he hoped for during his lifetime, Confucius's thoughts were recorded by his students in the Analects. *Since the Han dynasty (206 B.C.E.–220 C.E.), Confucius's ideas have shaped Chinese society and were used as the foundation for political and social life in dynastic China long after his death.*

---

[2] Local administrators with political and judicial powers

1.2 You Zi (a disciple of Confucius) said, "It is rare for a man whose character is such that he is good as a son and obedient as a young man to [go against] his superiors… Being good as a son and obedient as a young man is perhaps the root of a man's character."

1.6 The Master said: "At home, a young man must respect his parents; abroad, he must respect his elders. He should talk little, but with good faith; love all people, but associate with the virtuous. Having done this, if he still has energy to spare, let him study literature."

1.16 The Master said, "Don't worry if people don't recognize your merits; worry that you may not recognize theirs."

2.3 The Master said, "Guide them by edicts, keep them in line with punishments, and the common people will stay out of trouble but will have no sense of shame. Guide them by virtue, keep them in line with the rites, and they will, besides having a sense of shame, reform themselves."

2.7 Nowadays people think they are dutiful sons when they feed their parents. Yet they also feed their dogs and horses. Unless there is respect, where is the difference?

2.15 Confucius said, "To study without thinking is futile. To think without studying is dangerous."

SOURCES: D.C. Lau, trans., *Confucius: The Analects* (Hong Kong: The Chinese University Press, 2000). Simon Leys, trans., *The Analects of Confucius* (New York: W. W. Norton, 1997).

DOCUMENT 3.4: The Kangxi Emperor's "Sacred Edicts," 1670

1. Highly esteem filial piety and the proper relations among brothers in order to give due importance to social relations.
2. Give due weight to kinship in order to promote harmony and peace.
3. Maintain good relations within the neighborhood in order to prevent quarrels and lawsuits.
4. Give due importance to farming and the cultivation of mulberry trees in order to ensure sufficient clothing and food.
5. Be moderate and economical in order to avoid wasting away your livelihood.
6. Make the most of schools and academies in order to honor the ways of scholars.
7. Denounce strange beliefs in order to elevate the true doctrine.
8. Explain laws and regulations in order to warn the ignorant and obstinate.
9. Show propriety and courtesy to improve customs and manners.
10. Work hard in your professions in order to quiet your ambitions.
11. Instruct sons and younger brothers in order to prevent their committing any wrong.
12. Put a stop to false accusations in order to protect the good and honest.
13. Warn against giving shelter to deserters in order to avoid punishment with them.
14. Promptly and fully pay your taxes in order to avoid forced requisition.

15. Get together in groups of ten or a hundred in order to put an end to theft and robbery.
16. Free yourself from resentment and anger in order to show respect for your body and life.

Source: Paul Brians et al., ed., *Reading About the World,* Volume 2 (Fort Worth, TX: Harcourt Brace CustomBooks, 1999). http://www.wsu.edu/~wldciv/world_civ_reader/world_civ_reader_2/kang_hsi.html

DOCUMENT 3.5: Excerpts from "Demonstrate Ceremony and Deference in Order to Improve Popular Customs" by Wang Youpu, 1700s

In the seventeenth and eighteenth centuries, the Qing dynasty ordered that lectures be given to the common people twice a month to explain the "Sacred Edicts," first issued in 1670 by the emperor Kangxi. The lecturer's task was to appeal to and reach the common people by using examples and simpler language. This piece, an excerpt of such a speech, was given by Wang Youpu, a salt commissioner from the eighteenth century.

Popular customs vary greatly: in some places people are kindly, in others, reserved; in some places they are extravagant and pompous, in others frugal and simple. Because the customs of every place differed, the ancient sages created ceremonial practices in order to standardize conduct. The sage [Confucius] said that to secure the ease of superiors and bring order to the people, nothing is better than ceremony (*li*)....

[Y]ou soldiers and common people...all possess the basic elements of ceremonial behavior. For example, you know that there should be filial piety towards parents, honor and respect for superiors, harmony between husband and wife, affection among brothers, honesty among friends, and mutual responsibility among those of the same lineage. This proves that internally you already possess the basic elements of ceremony and deference....If you could really, in dealing with others, be extremely cooperative, in conducting yourselves be extremely obliging, in the family express the affection appropriate between parents and children, elder and younger brothers, in your villages maintain accord between the old and the young, the great and the small, then those habits of struggling over minor differences and getting into noisy disputes would be reformed and the tendency toward indulgent and degenerate conduct would be restrained....

It is just that people love to quarrel and will not give in to others.... Farmers are also in the habit of quarreling about their fields. I say that you have encroached on the dike a little; you say that I have ploughed a furrow too many. Perhaps some animal, an ox or a sheep, has trodden down the grain, and this gives rise to a quarrel. Or perhaps one person dams up the water till it overflows his own fields, not letting it pass by and irrigate those of his neighbor, and this leads to a struggle. Craftsmen are also quick to get into violent quarrels. You want to keep me down and I want to keep you down; I try to turn your employer against you and you try to turn mine away from me. We each care for our own prosperity only, with no regard to whether the other lives or dies....

Let all of you—scholars, farmers, artisans, merchants, and soldiers—take care in practicing ceremonial deference. If one place becomes good, then many places will become so and finally the entire realm will be in excellent harmony. Won't we then have a world in perfect concord?...

The ancients said it very well: "A person who always makes way for others on the road won't waste one hundred steps in his whole life. He who always gives in on questions of boundaries won't lose even a single section over the course of his life." Hence it can be seen that yielding and ceremony bring gain and never humiliation....

If you are able to get along with others, those who are rude will imitate you and learn to get along. If you are able to manage business fairly, those who are honest will learn to be fair by following you. When one person takes the lead all the rest will follow. When one family follows, then the whole village will do the same. From near to far, everywhere people will be good. At first it will take effort, but constant practice will make it easy. Men will become honest and popular customs pure and considerate. Only this could constitute full adoption of the meaning of the Yongzheng emperor's repeated instructions to you.

SOURCE: Rpt. in Patricia Buckley Ebrey, ed., trans., *Chinese Civilization: A Sourcebook* (New York: The Free Press, 1993), 297–300.

DOCUMENT 3.6: "Fan Jin Passes the Juren Examination," an excerpt from *The Scholars* by Wu Jingzi, c. 1740

"This is to announce that the master of your honourable mansion, Fan Jin, has passed the provincial examination in Guangdong, coming seventh in the list. May better news follow in rapid succession!"

Fan Jin feasted his eyes on the announcement, and, after reading it through once to himself, read it once more aloud. Clapping his hands, he laughed and exclaimed, "Ha! Good! I have passed." Then, stepping back, he fell down in a dead faint. His mother hastily poured some boiled water between his lips, whereupon he recovered consciousness and struggled to his feet. Clapping his hands again, he let out a peal of laughter and shouted, "Aha! I've passed! I've passed!" Laughing wildly he ran outside, giving the heralds and the neighbours the fright of their lives. Not far from the front door he slipped and fell into a pond. When he clambered out, his hair was dishevelled, his hands muddied and his whole body dripping with slime. But nobody could stop him. Still clapping his hands and laughing, he headed straight for the market.

They all looked at each other in consternation, and said, "The new honour has sent him off his head!"

His mother wailed, "Aren't we out of luck! Why should passing an examination do this to him? Now he's mad, goodness knows when he'll get better."

"He was all right this morning when he went out," said his wife. "What could have brought on this attack? What *shall* we do?"

SOURCE: Wu Jingzi, *Rulin waishi* [*The Scholars*], trans. Yang Xianyi and Gladys Yang. (Beijing: Foreign Languages Press, 1999).

 The full text of **Document 3.6** is available on the CD-ROM.

DOCUMENT 3.7: Excerpts from "Yuanchun Visits Her Parents on the Feast of Lanterns," *The Dream of Red Mansions* by Cao Xueqin, 1792

For a long time they waited in silence, Jia She and the young men of the family by the entrance of the west street, the Lady Dowager and the women in front of the main gate.

Then two eunuchs wearing scarlet uniforms rode slowly up to the entrance of the west street. Dismounting, they led their horses behind the screens, then stood to attention, their faces turned towards the west. After some time another pair appeared, then another, until there were ten pairs lined up and soft music could be heard in the distance.

And now a long procession approached: several pairs of eunuchs carrying dragon banners, others with phoenix fans, pheasant plumes and ceremonial insignia, as well as gold censers burning Imperial incense. Next came a curved-handled yellow umbrella on which were embroidered seven phoenixes, and under this a head-dress robe, girdle and slippers. After this came attendant eunuchs bearing a [Buddhist] rosary, embroidered handkerchiefs, a rinse-bowl, fly-whisks and the like.

Last of all, borne slowly forward by eight eunuchs, came a gold-topped palanquin[3] embroidered with phoenixes....

SOURCE: Hsueh-chin Tsao and Ngo Kao. *A Dream of Red Mansions*, trans. Yang Hsien-yi and Gladys Yang (Boston: Cheng & Tsui Company, 1996), 116.

 The full text of **Document 3.7** is available on the CD-ROM.

DOCUMENT 3.8: Excerpts from "A Worthless Son Receives a Fearful Flogging," *The Dream of Red Mansions* by Cao Xueqin, 1792

The sight of his father paralyzed Huan with fright. He pulled up short, hanging his head.

"What are you rushing about for?" demanded Jia Zheng.... As he shouted for the servants who accompanied Huan to school, the boy saw a chance to divert his father's anger.

"I wasn't running to begin with," he said. "Not until I passed the well where that maid drowned herself. Her head's swollen up like this, and her body's all bloated from soaking in the water. It was such a horrible sight that I ran away as fast as ever I could."

Jia Zheng was astounded. "What maid here had any reason to throw herself into a well?" he wondered. "Such a thing has never happened before in this house. Since the time of our ancestors we have always treated our subordinates well. Of late, though, I've neglected household affairs and those in charge must have abused their power, resulting in this calamitous suicide. If word of this gets out, it will disgrace our ancestors' good name."

He called for Jia Lian, Lai Da and Lai Xing. Some pages were going to fetch them when Huan stepped forward and caught hold of his father's gown, then fell on his knees.

---

[3] A covered litter, or elaborate arm chair, carried by poles on the shoulders of two or more men.

"Don't be angry, sir!" he begged. "No one knows about this except those in my lady's apartment. I heard my mother say...." He stopped and looked around, and Jia Zheng understood. At a glance from him the servants on both sides withdrew.

"My mother told me," Huan went on in a whisper, "that the other day Brother Baoyu grabbed hold of Jin Zhuan in my lady's room and tried to rape her. When she wouldn't let him, he beat her. That's why she drowned herself in a fit of passion." Before he had finished Jia Zheng was livid with fury.

"Fetch Baoyu! Quick!" he roared....

SOURCE: Hsueh-chin Tsao and Ngo Kao. *A Dream of Red Mansions*, trans. Yang Hsien-yi and Gladys Yang (Boston: Cheng & Tsui Company, 1996), 200–201.

 The full text of **Document 3.8** is available on the CD-ROM.

DOCUMENT 3.9: "Portrait of the Qianlong Emperor (r. 1736–1796) as the Bodhisattva Manjusri," by Jesuit missionary Giuseppe Castiglione

This painting shows Qianlong in the center of a *thangka*—a Tibetan religious painting of a divinity. Bodhisattvas are individuals who have achieved great moral and spiritual wisdom, and Manjusri is the Tibetan Bodhisattva of Wisdom. The inscription on the painting states that Manjusri is the ruler of the Buddhist faith. Qianlong embraced Buddhism, frequently studying it at his court. *(Courtesy of Freer Gallery of Art, Smithsonian Institution, Washington, D.C.)*

DOCUMENTS 3.10a–n Photographs of the Forbidden City, Beijing, 2006–2007

(Photos by Julie Newport)

 Additional photographs are on the CD-ROM.

Activities

ACTIVITY 1: An introduction to the Qing dynasty

Read the introductory essay and discuss:

1. Why were the Manchus able to gain power?
2. How did the status of the Manchus as foreigners affect their rule?
3. What about the three emperors stands out to you?
4. What characteristics would you assume early Qing leaders had (qualities, skills, abilities) that contributed to their success?
5. Compare the Manchu occupation of China to that of another military power occupying a country.

ACTIVITY 2: Examining the capture of Taiwan

Read "Shi Lang's Memorial on the Capture of Taiwan" (3.1) and discuss:

1. How was the battle described? Which side was superior and why?
2. What language or adjectives were used to describe enemy forces? Qing forces?
3. How were the enemies treated when they were captured? Based on the way the Qing treated the rebels, what messages were they sending?

ACTIVITY 3: Analyzing the treaty with Russia

Divide into six groups. Each group will read a part of the Treaty of Nerchinsk (3.2) and will prepare a presentation that paraphrases the agreed-upon point. Be sure to use a map if explaining geographical terms. After presenting:

1. Identify the boundaries on a map. What did Russia and Qing dynasty China gain and lose?
2. What do you notice about the stipulations of the treaty?
3. Why was the treaty so significant for the Manchus?
4. What does the treaty say about the Qing dynasty?

ACTIVITY 4: Mapping the Qing dynasty

Examine maps of China (Items 3.A, 3.B on the CD-ROM). Locate and compare the size of:

- the Manchu homeland
- China under the Ming dynasty
- China's borders under the Qing after a century of their rule
- China's borders today

When you have become familiar with the maps, begin to discuss:

1. What does this expansion tell you about the Qing? What would they have needed in order to do this?

2. What challenges does any empire face when adding so much territory? (e.g. consider treatment of minority groups, differences in culture, organization, communication, etc.)

Extended activity:

Look up maps showing the boundaries of earlier Chinese dynasties (for example, on the website *The Art of Asia* from the Minneapolis Institute of Arts: http://www.artsmia.org/art-of-asia/history/ming-dynasty-map.cfm) and discuss the implications of the changes in China's borders over the centuries.

ACTIVITY 5: Analyzing and writing about cultural values

Part 1:

In groups, read excerpts from the *Analects of Confucius* (3.3). Each group should put the analects in their own words, then decide what general category each belongs to (family, government, education, etc). Each group will establish its own categories, so there will be some variety.

Part 2:

Read and paraphrase the Kangxi emperor's sixteen "Sacred Edicts" (3.4). Again, each group should paraphrase and categorize the edicts, as they did with the *Analects*. Discuss:

1. What are the similarities/differences between Kangxi's edicts and the *Analects*?

2. What did the Qing emperor emphasize?

3. According to the Qing emperor, what qualities make a good subject? What behavior should be avoided?

4. How could these edicts have been used to solidify the emperor's power and create harmony in society?

5. What conclusions can be drawn from the similarities between the Kangxi edicts and Confucius's *Analects*?

Part 3:

Read the excerpts from Wang Youpu's speech to the common people (3.5). As a class, compare and contrast Wang Youpu's speech, the *Analects of Confucius*, and Kangxi's edicts.

1. Which qualities or attributes are most emphasized?
2. What are the key points?
3. How might Wang Youpu's speech appeal to the average person?

Writing Connections:

Choose from the following:

1. Write an essay addressing how leaders can consolidate and solidify their control over their subjects. Consider:
   a. How did the Qing emperors consolidate and solidify their control?
   b. How have other empires achieved these goals?
2. Write an essay addressing how cultural values are imposed or spread. Consider:
   a. What written materials in your culture are used to disseminate values and ideals?
   b. What do you believe are the most effective ways to promote civility and harmony among people?
3. Pick two maxims from the Kangxi emperor's "Sacred Edicts" (3.4) that still apply to our world today. In the style of Wang Youpu (3.5), write an example using everyday behavior that would convey the message to the general public.

ACTIVITY 6: Using literature to learn about society

Part 1:

Read the excerpt from *The Scholars*, "Fan Jin Passes the Juren Examination" (3.6). Discuss:

1. What elements of Chinese society are evident in the story?
2. What do you think is the basis of Wu Jingzi's criticism of the examination system? Why does he use satire to make his point?
3. Do you think that he is justified?
4. How would having an examination system such as this for all civil service jobs affect government?
5. Should people pass exams to serve in certain jobs? Which jobs? Is this fair for everyone?

Part 2:

Read the excerpts from *A Dream of Red Mansions*. (Document 3.7 details a visit to the wealthy Jia family by one of their daughters who was one of the emperor's courtesans. Document 3.8 gives insight into the hierarchy and relationships in the Jia family.)

For Document 3.7, discuss:

1. What did the family do in preparation for the courtesan's visit?
2. Who were the eunuchs? What was their role?
3. What was the role of the imperial courtesans in society?
4. What does this description show about China at that time?

For Document 3.8, first diagram the family hierarchy. Then discuss:

1. How do various members of the household react to Jin Zhuan's suicide? What is thought to have pushed the maid to suicide? What conclusions can be drawn from the reactions?
2. What has Baoyu done to enrage his father and how does the father respond?
3. Which behavior is considered the worst? Why?
4. Who ultimately speaks to Jia Zheng about the way he punished his son? What happens next?
5. What does it mean to be "filial"?
6. What questions do you have and where might you find answers?

Discuss as a class: How does literature help us learn about another culture and era? What are the advantages and disadvantages of relying on literature for insights?

Write a reaction piece describing your impressions of a wealthy family during the Qing dynasty.

ACTIVITY 7: Interpreting visual art

In the 1720s, the Qing rulers were drawn into Tibet and added the devoutly Buddhist region to the area under their control. (For more information about Tibet's history, read the essay in Additional Resources on the CD-ROM.) Examine the painting "Portrait of the Qianlong Emperor (r. 1736–1796) as the Bodhisattva Manjusri" (3.9).

1. Describe the painting. What do you notice?
2. What relationship is the painting suggesting exists between Manjusri—the Bodhisattva of Wisdom—and the Qianlong emperor?
3. What do you think Qianlong's objective was in commissioning this painting?
4. What can we learn about the Qing dynasty from this painting?
5. Can you think of other examples of government figures taking on a guise for a similar purpose?

For homework:

- Find an article about an ethnic minority or national group within China and its relationship with the Chinese government today (for example, the Uyghur or Tibetans).
- Find information about an ethnic group anywhere in the world who wants independence from what it feels is rule by a foreign power.

Summarize the information you find and share it with classmates.

ACTIVITY 8: Exploring the Forbidden City

Examine the photographs of the Forbidden City posted at different stations around the room (3.10a–n) and research online how the palace functioned for 500 years, until the early 1900s. Discuss as a class:

1. What is most striking?
2. How did the Forbidden City reflect the relationship among various elements of Chinese society?
3. What additional information does it give us about the Qing dynasty?
4. Compare the way the Forbidden City functioned to the government structure and operations in another country in the same time period (e.g. France, Great Britain, the North American colonies, or Japan during the period 1650–1750).

EXTENDED RESEARCH:

To further your understanding of Qing dynasty China, research any one of the following topics and present your findings in a paper, Powerpoint presentation, or visual display.

- The role of eunuchs in the imperial court
- Secret societies (such as White Lotus, Triad, etc.)
- The role of concubines
- *Dream of Red Mansions* theme parks in China today
- Present-day Chinese soap operas set during the Qing dynasty
- Tibetan Buddhism
- Taiwan

Suggested Resources

Books

Bosse, Malcolm. *The Examination*. New York: Farrar, Straus & Giroux, 1994.
This young-adult historical novel gives an excellent sense of the civil service examination system and secret societies.

Cao Xueqin. *The Story of the Stone*. Trans. David Hawkes. Vol. 1. London: Penguin Books, 1973.
A very readable translation of the famous novel also known as A Dream of Red Mansions.

Websites

http://www.learn.columbia.edu/nanxuntu/start.html *Recording the Grandeur of the Qing* is an excellent interactive website on various aspects of the Qing dynasty. From the Metropolitan Museum of Art and Columbia University.

http://www.wsu.edu/~dee/CHING/CHING.HTM This website from Washington State University has great background information on the Qing and some primary sources.

http://afe.easia.columbia.edu Columbia University's *Asia for Educators* website has great maps and information on each dynasty.

http://www.artsmia.org/art-of-asia/history/ming-dynasty-map.cfm This website from the Minneapolis Institute of Arts has maps visible on one screen, showing China's shifting boundaries across the millennia.

http://www.mnsu.edu/emuseum/prehistory/china/later_imperial_china/qing.html This website from Minnesota State University Mankato has good information on imperial China.

http://www.askasia.org This website from the Asia Society includes lesson plans, maps, and images.

http://www.c-c-c.org/chineseculture/minority/minority.html The Chinese Cultural Center of San Francisco, a non-profit organization, has information about ethnic groups in China.

http://www.museum.upenn.edu/Mongolia/section3a.shtml From the University of Pennsylvania Museum of Archeology and Anthropology, an exhibit on the government structure of the Manchu dynasty.

http://www-chaos.umd.edu/history/toc.html Good introductory information on imperial China from Leon Poon at the University of Maryland.

http://www.threeemperors.org.uk/index.php?pid=21 An online companion to the Royal Academy of Arts' exhibit *China: The Three Emperors, 1662–1795*.

Forbidden City

http://www.travelchinaguide.com/cityguides/beijing/forbidden.htm

http://www.chinavista.com/beijing/gugong/map.html Includes a palace map and virtual tour.

Film

The Emperor's Eye (58 mins; 1990) *The documentary captures the preeminence of the arts in Chinese culture as it weaves together the stories of the Qing emperor Qianlong, his remarkable collection of art, and its journey to the Palace Museum in Taipei, Taiwan.*

■ **A CLOSER LOOK**

The White Lotus Society Rises in Protest

Though the early Qing years were times of relative peace and stability, small rebellions did occur, many inspired by secret societies. The White Lotus Society first emerged in the late thirteenth century during another period when China was ruled by foreigners. The Society originated in Sichuan Province in central China and its members were millennialists: They believed that the end of the world was close at hand. The Society drew on a sort of folk Buddhism, Daoism, and a belief in the support of the "Eternal Venerable Mother" goddess. Smaller branches believing in the same principles appeared again and again in later centuries. They usually rose in objection to the ruling dynasty of the time, but especially objected to the foreign Manchu rule.

White Lotus rebels, under the leadership of Wang Lun, emerged in the eighteenth century with the goal of reestablishing the Ming dynasty, whom they saw as the legitimate rulers of China. Most White Lotus followers were poor peasants, workers, and demobilized soldiers— those disaffected by society. The White Lotus also appealed to women, as the society promoted social equality. While it is not clear whether there was a specific trigger to their rebellions, the movement suggests deep discontent in society.

Several factors may have led to the rise of the White Lotus Society: the poor management of emergency granaries (for use in time of famine); cruel and brutal treatment by Manchu soldiers; a growing population; high taxes; and government corruption. During the Qing dynasty, followers of the White Lotus often clashed with local officials and landlords and had to be subdued by the military. While these societies did not overthrow the Qing, they ultimately contributed to the dynasty's demise.

■ *Discuss: What secret and/or illegal organizations do you know of elsewhere in the world that destabilize a government? How do they operate?*

Primary Sources

DOCUMENT 4.1a & b: Stamps issued commemorating Jesuit missionary Ferdinand Verbiest

DOCUMENT 4.2: Excerpts from the letter King George III of England wrote to the Chinese emperor and sent with Lord Macartney, 1792

DOCUMENT 4.3: Two edicts from the emperor Qianlong in reply to Lord Macartney's mission to China, September 1793

DOCUMENT 4.4: Requests by English merchants and responses from a Chinese official, 1793

DOCUMENT 4.5: A description of various European countries and their people by Xie Qinggao, a Chinese sailor, between 1783 and 1797

DOCUMENT 4.6a & b: Excerpts from a letter by William Trotter of Philadelphia, trading in Guangzhou, 1797

DOCUMENT 4.7: Excerpts from a letter Edward King wrote from Guangzhou to his brother, October 31, 1835

DOCUMENT 4.8a & b: Examples of *chinoiserie* (ca. 1800 and ca. 1810)

DOCUMENT 4.9: Excerpts from a letter of instructions from the owners of the vessel *Mentor* to Captain John Suter, 1816

DOCUMENT 4.10: "A Voyage with Opium Smugglers" by William Hunter, between 1825 and 1844

Supplementary Materials

ITEM 4.A: Opium Trade statistics

ITEM 4.B: Information about the Willow pattern

ITEM 4.C: *Qianlong Meets Macartney: Collision of Two World Views*, a play by John Watt

CHAPTER 4

China's Foreign Relations (1644–1839)

By Shirley Moore Huettig

Chapter Contents

Bureaus for Foreign Affairs

Jesuit Missionaries

The Canton System

Chinoiserie

Opium Trade and Smuggling

Organizing Idea

Despite restrictions enforced by the Qing dynasty, an active exchange of goods and ideas continued to exist between China and the Western powers. However, in the mid-eighteenth century, Europeans, especially Great Britain, began pressuring the Qing government for broader access to Chinese markets.

Key Questions

What diplomatic and trade relationships did the Qing dynasty establish with foreign nations?

What roles did missionaries play in China in the seventeenth and eighteenth centuries?

Why did the Qing restrict trade with Westerners but allow relative freedom of trade with other Asian nations?

How and why did Western nations try to change diplomatic and trade relations with China? To what extent were they successful in the period 1638–1839?

Key Terms

astronomy	homage
cartography	kowtow
chinoiserie	memorial
decentralized	tributary

Essay

Until the late seventeenth century the Chinese world view was one of concentric circles in which China, known to Chinese then and now as *Zhongguo*, the "Middle Kingdom," was at the center and all people on the borders and beyond were considered subordinate or "barbarians" (蛮夷). International relations and trade were conducted using a tributary system in which foreign trade missions would pay homage to the Chinese emperor, bring him gifts, and conduct trade under tightly controlled conditions. The Qing (清), foreign invaders themselves from Manchuria (满洲),[1] recognized the need to interact carefully with people along their borders. They created a series of agencies to communicate with various groups of foreigners, reflecting their view of the nations involved.

Early Management Approaches

The Office of Border Affairs (*Lifan Yuan* 理番院) had been created in 1638 by Nurhaci, who had led the conquest of China, to address the growing challenges from peoples north and west of China, such as the Russians and Mongolians. Qing emperors saw these peoples as a threat because they sought territorial expansion into China, so their movement and trade within China was carefully controlled and monitored.

The Board of Rites (*Li Bu* 礼部) was responsible for non-Chinese people whose cultures were similar to the Chinese and who were not seen as a territorial threat, such as Koreans, Japanese, and Vietnamese. They were allowed much more lenient trade rights, though they were still limited to coastal cities and not permitted to travel inland. Early European traders were also included in this group because they did not at first fit into the other categories.

The Imperial Household (*Neiwufu* 内务府) was responsible for overseeing the activities of European missionaries, who were welcomed into the imperial court and served as advisors to the emperor in technology, astronomy, and determining the calendar. In fact, several Jesuit missionaries held the important position of director of the Bureau of Astronomy from the beginning of the Qing era to the late eighteenth century.[2] Jesuit missionaries had also spread thinly into northern and western China. Their roles, however, were strictly limited so as to keep them from encroaching too much into Chinese society. Eventually, Kangxi (康熙) (r. 1661–1722) expelled missionaries who refused to accept his position that Confucian rites did not conflict with Catholic faith.

In the late 1600s, China's international relations began to change significantly. European and American missionaries participated in trade agreements and Western nations pressured the emperor for new diplomatic relations and broader trading rights. In 1689, the Chinese signed the Treaty of Nerchinsk[3] with Russia (see Chapter 3, Document 3.2) and, significantly, retreated from their traditional tributary system for the first time, acknowledging Russia as a sovereign state and giving the Russians trading rights in Kiakhta. China continued to maintain tight control over who traded in China and where they were allowed to ply their trade.

The Canton System

By 1759, the British, who by then dominated the China trade among the European nations, formally petitioned the emperor for more lenient trade rights, access to higher officials in the Chinese government, and fewer taxes levied

---

[1] Now Northeast China

[2] Directors included Father Ferdinand Verbiest in the late seventeenth century, best known for his updated map of the world. In the late eighteenth century, Father Michel Benoist introduced Copernicus's heliocentric theory, in addition to many other scientific discoveries from Europe, to the emperor and his government.

[3] Jesuit missionaries helped with the negotiations.

on their trade. In response, the Qing government created an even more restrictive system to protect itself against European incursion: the Canton System (广东体制). European traders were only allowed to trade in Canton, a southeastern port city now known as Guangzhou. Furthermore, Chinese authorities restricted Westerners to one section of the city where the foreigners had their living and business quarters, called "factories." The Chinese permitted Westerners to live there only during the tea-trading season (after which time they had to return to Portuguese-controlled Macao) and insisted they conduct their business with Chinese intermediaries, the *Cohong* or *Hong* merchants (行商). In 1793, frustrated by the limitations, the British sent Lord Macartney on a mission to the emperor, again requesting changes in trade policies. Through an unfortunate series of misunderstandings and cultural conflicts, the mission failed and left the Chinese increasingly resistant to European pleas for greater freedom in China.

Active Trade

Despite the restrictions, trade flourished between China and the West. Europeans and merchants from the newly founded United States of America bought large quantities of tea, silk, and porcelain.[4] In addition, ideas and artifacts from China and Western cultures become known and appreciated by the other. *Chinoiserie*, a style of art and architecture reflecting a strong Chinese influence (though idealized and fanciful) became popular in Europe. Europeans had begun to imitate China's blue-and-white porcelain during the Ming era and later started to include Chinese-inspired design and images on furniture and small pagoda-styled garden buildings. In China, meanwhile, the Qianlong (乾隆) emperor hired Westerners to work collaboratively with Chinese architects to build his summer palace, the Yuanming Yuan (圆明园), in a mixed Italianate and Chinese style.

By the late eighteenth century, Great Britain's trade deficit with China had grown to alarming levels.[5] China required payment in silver, but silver was increasingly expensive, and British merchants began to import opium as the medium of exchange. Taking vast quantities of opium grown in their colony in India, the British shipped it to China, where growing numbers of addicts kept demand high. By the early 1800s, China was experiencing a trade deficit with Great Britain; the tables had turned. The emperor and court officials were appalled by the rate of addiction and wrote several edicts; first in 1800 the government banned importation and domestic production of opium, then in 1813 smoking it was banned as well. Tension between China and Great Britain over the smuggling of opium into the country grew until in 1839 it erupted into war.

---

[4] In 1784, the *Empress of China* sailed out of New York City bound for Guangzhou, opening the United States–China trade.

[5] By 1800, the East India Company, which operated all British trade to India and China, was buying more than 23 million pounds of tea a year, at a cost of £3.6 million (Spence, *The Search For Modern China*, 122.) When converted into the purchasing power of the dollar in 2006, this is equivalent to approximately $19 billion. (www.measuringworth.com).

Primary Sources

DOCUMENT 4.1a & b: Stamps issued commemorating Jesuit missionary Ferdinand Verbiest

DOCUMENT 4.2: Excerpts from the letter King George III of England wrote to the Chinese emperor and sent with Lord Macartney, 1792

We rely on your Imperial Majesty's wisdom and justice and general benevolence to mankind so conspicuous in your long and happy reign, that you will please to allow our Ambassador and Representative at your court to have the opportunity of contemplating the examples of your virtues and to obtain such information of your celebrated institutions, as will enable him to enlighten our people on his return; he, on our part, being directed to give as far as your Majesty shall please to desire it, a full and free communication of any art, science or observation either of use or curiosity which the industry, ingenuity and experience of Europeans may have enabled them to acquire; and also that you will be pleased to allow to any of our subjects frequenting the coasts of your dominions, and conducting themselves with propriety, a secure residence there, and a fair access to your markets, under such laws and regulations as your Majesty shall think right, and that their lives and properties shall be safe under your imperial protection....

SOURCE: *British Illustrations*, http://www.king-books.com/en/h02.asp

 The full text of **Document 4.2** is available on the CD-ROM.

DOCUMENT 4.3: Two edicts from the emperor Qianlong in reply to Lord Macartney's mission to China, September 1793

I have perused your memorial: the earnest terms in which it is couched reveal a respectful humility on your part, which is highly praiseworthy. In consideration of the fact that your Ambassador and his deputy have come a long way with your memorial and tribute, I have shown them high favour and have allowed them to be introduced into my presence. To manifest my indulgence, I have entertained them at a banquet and made them numerous gifts. I have also caused presents to be forwarded to the Naval Commander and six hundred of his officers and men, although they did not come to Peking, so that they too may share in my all-embracing kindness.

As to your entreaty to send one of your nationals to be accredited to my Celestial Court and to be in control of your country's trade with China, this request is contrary to all usage of my dynasty and cannot possibly be entertained....

Our dynasty's majestic virtue has penetrated unto every country under Heaven, and Kings of all nations have offered their costly tribute by land and sea. As your Ambassador can see for himself, we possess all things. I set no value on objects strange or ingenious, and have no use for your country's manufactures....

SOURCE: *British Illustrations*, http://www.king-books.com/en/h01.asp

 The full text of **Document 4.3** is available on the CD-ROM.

DOCUMENT 4.4: Requests by English merchants and responses from the Chinese official, 1793

Request II: When we [the English] pass through [the river] between Guangzhou and Macao, both toll tax and goods tax are to be collected. If this is required by the original regulation, we beg your Excellency to give us a list of what we should pay; if these taxes are not required by the original regulation, we beg your Excellency to abolish them.

Endorsement: The toll tax and the goods tax were originally illegal and were abolished in the eleventh month of the fifty-eighth year of [the emperor] Qianlong, by official proclamation. We have punished the soldiers and servants one by one who dared to demand this illegal levy.... Now we shall publish another official proclamation to renew the prohibition. If they still dare to demand money, we shall allow the barbarians[6] to present a petition of accusation in order to try them...."

SOURCE: Lo-shu Fu, *A Documentary Chronicle of Sino-Western Relations (1644–1820)* (Tucson: University of Arizona Press, 1966), 327–328.

 The full text of **Document 4.4** is available on the CD-ROM.

---

[6] Common word for "foreigner," anyone who was not literate in the Chinese language and literature.

DOCUMENT 4.5: A description of various European countries and their people by Xie Qinggao, a Chinese sailor, between 1783 and 1797

England is located southwest [*sic*] of France and could be reached by sailing north from St. Helena for about two months. It is a sparsely settled island, separated from the mainland, with a large number of rich families. The dwelling houses have more than one story. Maritime commerce is one of the chief occupations of the English, and wherever there is a region in which profits could be reaped by trading, these people strive for them, with the result that their commercial vessels are to be seen on the seven seas. Commercial traders are to be found all over the country. Male inhabitants from the ages of fifteen to sixty are conscripted into the service of the king as soldiers. Moreover, a large foreign mercenary army is also maintained. Consequently, although the country is small, it has such a large military force that foreign nations are afraid of it....

SOURCE: Jeannette Mirsky, ed., *The Great Chinese Travelers*, (New York: Pantheon, 1964), 266–71, rpt. in Mark A. Kishlansky, ed., *Sources of World History*, vol. 2 (New York: HarperCollins College Publishers, 1995), 126–128.

 The full text of **Document 4.5** is available on the CD-ROM.

DOCUMENT 4.6a & b: Excerpts from a letter by William Trotter of Philadelphia, trading in Guangzhou, 1796

The City of Canton [Guangzhou] is situated on the north side of the River Zhu [Pearl River]...about 80 miles from the Sea; it is surrounded by a thick wall about 20 feet in height, and according to information about 10 miles in circumference. There are several arched passages through the walls, by which the inhabitants of the Suberbs [*sic*] have communication with the City; to these passages are large iron gates, which are guarded during the day and shut every night. Of the interior part of the City, we can only judge from the suburbs, as the jealous laws of Chinese prohibit all Foreigners from entering. I was assured by a respectable Merchant they were much the same. The suberbs of Canton are very extensive and exceeding populous. The streets are irregular and very narrow, and so crowded with People that a stranger frequently finds great difficulty in passing them. The Houses are built of brick and wood and generally more than a story high, with a kind of balcony facing the street. The front part of the Houses and especially those near the European Factories are fitted up as shops, which [are] painted and gilded in a fancified manner. The Warehouses of some of the Silk Merchants are very large and well stocked with the valuable article they trade in.

SOURCE: William Trotter to William Sansom, 13 April 1796, William Trotter letter, Massachusetts Historical Society, Boston.

 The full text of **Document 4.6a** is on the CD-ROM. **Document 4.6b**, also on the CD, has longer excerpts from Trotter's letter.

DOCUMENT 4.7: Excerpts from a letter Edward King wrote from Guangzhou to his brother, October 31, 1835

I arrived in this city on Thursday evening the 29th … [I] intend taking on board a Cargo of Teas for home…

People live here in great style and have everything very comfortable. Servants in abundance one for every person. I have been much pleased with the appearance of the Chinese. They are extremely neat, that is the better class. Our passage up from Linten was quite interesting though. We were confined in a small fishing boat covered up to prevent our being seen. We saw I should think a million or more of people in Boats. All the way up the river from Whampoa there are villages of 50,000 and more. There are hundreds of kinds of boats. That is of different forms and sizes, from the sampan to the junk of 1,000 tons. Opposite the city, the river is completely covered with Boats, which are anchored in which are thousands of inhabitants.…

What I have seen of the shops has pleased me. The Chinese are a shrewd set. Silks are high, 20% more than last year.… The Chinese are a very industrious people. They are always busy about something. I today went with Mr. Coolidge to see some of the Hong Merchants. We called on Hougus, the senior Hong Merchant. He is quite old, about 80 years of age. He is the richest man in Canton, and one of the most intelligent. We also saw Toushing and Kingqua who are also Hong merchants. The Hong merchants are the only persons allowed by the Government to sell Teas to foreigners.

SOURCE: Edward King to George King, 31 October 1835, Edward King papers, Massachusetts Historical Society, Boston.

 The full text of **Document 4.7** is available on the CD-ROM.

DOCUMENT 4.8a & b: Examples of *chinoiserie*

Blue and white porcelain platter, ca. 1800

Blue and white porcelain lunch plate, ca. 1810

(Courtesy of Lovers of Blue and White.)

DOCUMENT 4.9: Excerpts from a letter of instructions from the owners of the vessel *Mentor* to Captain John Suter, 1816

Your Ship is equipped and provisioned for a three years' Voyage and you are furnished with a Cargo both for trade with the natives and Russian settlements in that quarter of the Globe. Although they prepared for two Seasons it would be highly beneficial if the Voyage could be accomplished in one, and we think it very possible that this may be the case. If when you arrive on the Coast you think there is a fair probability of your being able to collect, the first Season, both from the Russians and Natives, a quantity of Furs, equal to Three thousand Merchantable Sea Otter Skins, we recommend your finishing your Voyage [from there to Guangzhou, China] by all means the first year,...

The articles which compose your Russian assortment are probably better than have ever been carried there before, the Rum is not lower than third proof and the Brandy is all fourth, the Wine may want to be fined which can easily be done with a little Isinglass, Milk or Eggs. For the Natives you have the best assortment we have known to have been carried. The Muskets are unequalled by any ever shipped from this Country and will sell very readily. As more of the same kind will undoubtedly follow, we recommend your selling them as expeditiously as possibly without undervaluing them....

We leave you at full liberty to pursue any course which you may deem for our interest either by purchasing Furs, by killing them or employ the Ship in any other way, taking care however never to attempt any illicit trade against which your Ship is not insured, although She is against all the usual and ordinary perils of the Voyage. When you arrive at Canton [Guangzhou] you will find instructions from us for your future government. Should you not you will apply to Messrs Perkins & Company who will assist you in transacting your business then....

SOURCE: Bryant Sturgis to John Suter, 6 August 1816, John Suter papers, Massachusetts Historical Society, Boston.

 The full text of **Document 4.9** is available on the CD-ROM.

DOCUMENT 4.10: "A Voyage with Opium Smugglers" by William Hunter, between 1825 and 1844

Needless to say, the opium trade was prohibited by Imperial edicts as well by proclamations of the Guangzhou authorities. The Chinese who dealt in "foreign mud" [opium] were threatened even with capital punishment, but so perfect a system of bribery existed (with which foreigners had nothing whatever to do) that the business was carried on with ease and regularity....

The [official and his secretary] were then invited to the cabin to refresh, which being done, we proceeded to business. The Mandarin [Chinese official] opened by the direct questions, "How many chests have you on board? Are they all for Namao? Do you go further up the coast?"…Then came the question of [the bribe], and that was settled on the good old Chinese principle (that customs in such matters are the same everywhere). Everything being thus comfortably arranged, wine drunk, and [cigars] smoked, His Excellency said: "I announce my departure."…

SOURCE: W. C. Hunter, *The "Fan Kwae"* [7] *at Canton Before Treaty Days, 1825–1844* (London: Kegan Paul, Trench and Company, 1882), 64–70. Rpt. in Hyman Kublin, ed., *China: Selected Readings* (Boston: Houghton Mifflin, 1968), 117–120.

 The full text of **Document 4.10** is available on the CD-ROM.

Activities

ACTIVITY 1: Examining Jesuit contributions

Part 1:

Examine the two commemorative postage stamps (4.1a and 4.1b) and investigate some of the links for "Science and the Jesuits" in the Suggested Resources section to answer the following questions individually or in a class discussion.

1. Why would Chinese emperors have been so interested in astronomy and cartography? Why would they want to know more about Western advances in particular?

---

[7] *Fan Kwae* is another Chinese word for "barbarian," a foreigner, someone not literate in Chinese.

2. What roles did Jesuits play in the imperial government of China in the seventeenth and eighteenth centuries?

3. Why was Ferdinand Verbiest so important a figure at this time?

4. Choose one of the five instruments shown on the stamp from Macao and learn how it was used. Why would each instrument have been important to the emperor?

5. Why would Belgium and Macao create these commemorative stamps of Verbiest?

Extended activity: Examine Verbiest's map using the link in Suggested Resources.

1. Which parts of the map are most accurate?

2. Which are very different from modern maps?

3. Why do you think some parts of the map are accurate and others are not?

4. Consider again, based on this evidence, why the emperor would have wanted Western cartographic expertise.

ACTIVITY 2: Trade between Great Britain and China: A Jigsaw

Part 1:

Divide the class into three teams. Each team will become experts on one of the following documents: 4.2, 4.3, or 4.4. Each team member will read the document on his or her own. The team will then gather to discuss:

1. Who is the author? What tone (collegial, condescending, patronizing, subservient, etc.) does the author use? Is it consistent throughout the document?

2. Who is the recipient?

3. When was the document written?

4. What is the purpose of the document? What does the author want?

5. Does the author comment on the recipient or his country? What kinds of things does he write? Is he complimentary? Critical?

6. What promises, if any, does the author make to the recipient?

7. If you were the recipient of this document, how would you respond to its tone and content?

8. Individually, write a response as if you were the recipient writing back to the author of the document.

Part 2:

Reconvene in groups of three, with each member of the new group an expert on a different document. Share with each other pertinent details related to your document (date, author, tone, content, etc.) Then discuss:

1. To what extent are the authors of the documents in agreement? On which points do they disagree?

2. In your opinion, is one author more reasonable than the others? What evidence do you see of misunderstandings between cultures? How might these misunderstandings have been avoided or cleared up?

3. As a group, draft a letter addressing the authors of all the documents. Imagine you are a "disinterested third party" and make recommendations for resolving the points of conflict found among these documents.

Part 3:

Return to a whole class discussion and share the letters of resolution drafted in your small groups.

Creative extension:

To further explore the issues involved in the Macartney mission, perform *Qianlong Meets Macartney: Collision of Two World Views*, a play by John Watt. (See Suggested Resources on the CD-ROM for the link.)

ACTIVITY 3: Exploring foreigners' perceptions

Read documents 4.5, 4.6a, and 4.7. For each document, answer the following questions.

1. What is the nationality of the author? What foreign culture or nation is he describing?

2. What is the author doing in that part of the world?

3. What part of the culture does the author discuss the most? Do you think the answer to question 2 is related to your answer to this question? How?

4. How is the author's description different from what you expected?

5. Is the author's tone complimentary or derogatory? Or is it neutral—merely descriptive? Is there any evidence of cultural bias?

6. Compare the writing of these three authors, commenting on the presence or absence of cultural bias. What does this suggest to you about their cultures at the time of writing?

Writing extension:

Imagine you are a member of one of the cultures being described. Write a response to the author regarding his description of your culture.

ACTIVITY 4: *Chinoiserie*: discovering legends and images

Reread the section on *chinoiserie* in the introductory essay to this chapter, and read about the Spode Willow Pattern (Item 4.B on the CD). Examine the porcelain in the images (4.8a and 4.8b) and answer the following questions:

1. Who was Josiah Spode, and why do you think he produced blue and white porcelain dishes?
2. Why would Europeans have adapted, or made up, a legend to go with the Spode dish pattern?
3. Which of the pieces of porcelain (4.8a or 4.8b) uses the Spode Willow Pattern? (The other is called Forest Landscape, also by Spode.)
4. Why do you think the Willow Pattern was the most popular one? How do you think the legend played into that popularity?

Creative extensions:

Choose one:

- Draw your own interpretation of the legend of the Willow Pattern.
- Read the longer excerpts from William Trotter's letter (4.6b on the CD) and design your own porcelain pattern based on one of Trotter's descriptions. Remember, your pattern should be "idealized and fanciful" and show both Chinese and European influences. Look at links in Suggested Resources under "Asian Export Art / *Chinoiserie*" for additional ideas.

ACTIVITY 5: Mapping and analyzing early nineteenth-century trade between China and the United States

1. On an outline map of the world, trace the routes of the ships *Mentor* and *Rose* described in 4.9 and 4.10 as best you can from the landmarks provided in the text. Illustrate on each leg of the journeys those items being transferred to the next location.
2. How far from Guangzhou (Canton) was the Russian trade that the *Mentor* engaged in (4.9)?
3. Which leg of the journey was the longest for the *Mentor*?
4. How far from Guangzhou (Canton) did Hunter's vessel, the *Rose,* "wander" (4.10)?
5. Based on your knowledge of the China trade, what items do you think Captain Suter would have been instructed to purchase and take back to Boston?
6. What kind of advice and warnings did the ship owners (Bryant and Sturges) give Captain Suter regarding trade and getting the best deal?
7. Once at sea, how did ship captains communicate with ship owners 200 years ago?

8. Compare how trade was conducted in 1816 to what you know about international trade today.

9. Why might traders have resorted to trading opium instead of the items mentioned in Suter's letter?

10. Based on the statistics from Item 4.A (on the CD), evaluate the extent to which opium was a large part of trade in China by the time Suter's ship the *Mentor* arrived in 1816.

11. What, if anything, surprises you about the description of the illegal opium trade in William Hunter's account (4.10)?

EXTENDED RESEARCH:

Conduct research on any of the topics below and present your findings in a paper, a visual display, or an electronic slideshow, using, for example, PowerPoint® or Photo Story 3®.

- Tea use in Great Britain and/or the British North American colonies in the eighteenth century
- The tributary system (e.g. relations between China and Korea)
- Trade conducted on the traditional Chinese sailing vessels called "junks" by Westerners
- Hong merchants
- Hong merchant Pan Changyao, known as Conseequa to Westerners, an exceptionally wealthy man
- The Kangxi and Qianlong emperors
- Using the descriptions in William Trotter's letter (4.6b), compare any one aspect of life in 1797 Guangzhou (Canton) to another country in the same time period (e.g. a city in South America to Guangzhou; vessels in Europe to vessels in China; the lives of women in the United States to the lives of women in China; formal gardens in France to the merchant's garden outside Guangzhou).

Suggested Resources

Book

Kerr, Phyllis Forbes. *Letters from China: The Canton-Boston Correspondence of Robert Bennet Forbes, 1838–1840.* Mystic, CT: Mystic Seaport Museum, 1996.

Websites

Science/Jesuits

http://hua.umf.maine.edu/China/astronomy/index.html University of Maine site run by Marilyn Shea offers information on Chinese astronomy.

http://www.asia.si.edu/EncompassingtheGlobe/default.htm Arthur M. Sackler Gallery exhibit on Portuguese exploration and the explorers' contact with and influence on the Chinese. This site includes a great Google Earth animation with routes of exploration and explanations of interactions at each stop. See stops in Beijing and Macao in particular. (Google Earth animation requires downloading Google Earth, http://earth.google.com.)

http://www.newadvent.org/cathen/15346a.htm Biography of Verbiest in the *Catholic Encyclopedia*; includes a description of competition between Eastern and Western science.

http://u21museums.unimelb.edu.au/museumcollections/glasgow/hunterian/map.html An image of the Eastern Hemisphere of Verbiest's map, easily enlarged and zoomed for close examination and detail.

http://www2.library.tohoku.ac.jp/kano/mado/index-eng.html A high-resolution image of Matteo Ricci's world map; sections can be enlarged for close examination and detail.

China trade

http://www.primarysource.org/resources/default.php?sectionPage=China%20Source&id=Lesson%20Plans *Qianlong Meets Macartney: Collision of Two World Views,* a play by John Watt.

http://afe.easia.columbia.edu/china/modern/tch_mcem.htm#Two *Asia for Educators*: "Macartney and the Emperor"

http://www.nps.gov/sama/historyculture/trade.htm Salem, Massachusetts and the China Trade

http://afe.easia.columbia.edu/china/for_pol/ch_trade.htm "200 Years of U.S. Trade with China"

http://image.sl.nsw.gov.au/Ebind/c192/a1162/a1162031.html for transcripts of letters between a Mr. Drummond and a Mr. Bishop regarding the details of trade and the central role Conseequa played in the financing of trade.

Asian Export Art/Chinoiserie

http://www.pem.org/collections/asian_export.php The Peabody Essex Museum holds one of North America's premier collections of Asian export art, with many images available online.

http://www.mfa.org/index.asp (Search for 25.407 and look in "collections.") Image of plate with scene of two Europeans fishing, but scenery is of Chinese design.

http://www.vam.ac.uk/vastatic/microsites/british_galleries/bg_styles/Style04c/index.html Victoria and Albert Museum, London

Opium: From Use to Abuse

Opium is harvested from the unripe seedpods of the opium poppy. The seedpods release a milky latex that turns into a gummy substance when it comes in contact with air. Raw opium can be ground into powder, or sold as lumps, cakes, or bricks, and when treated further, morphine, codeine, and heroin can be made from it. Opium and all the drugs created from it are called opiates. People have known about the medicinal and sedative properties of opium for millennia. It has been widely used as a painkiller, but in addition to alleviating pain, opium gives users a feeling of calm, well-being, and drowsiness.

Turkish and Arab traders first brought opium to China in the late sixth or early seventh century. For some one thousand years the Chinese swallowed raw bitter-tasting opium, using it in limited quantities to reduce pain and stress. But in the 1720s, smoking a mix of opium and tobacco started to become popular. The Portuguese imported opium into China early in the eighteenth century, and the British became the leading suppliers by the early 1770s. The drug also made its way overland through Tibet and Burma into China's western provinces. By 1729, addiction had increased so dramatically that the Yongzheng emperor issued an edict prohibiting selling opium for anything but medicinal use. This had little effect. From 200 chests of opium in 1729, British imports increased to more than 4,000 chests in 1796 (see Item 4.A on the CD-ROM). Addiction grew so high that it began to affect both the Qing troops and scholar-officials responsible for local and provincial governing. Despite further imperial edicts that banned importation, domestic production, and later, smoking of opium, the problem only grew worse.

■ *Discuss: What responsibility does a supplier of a drug bear for increasing addiction? What else might the European merchants have used for trade?*

Primary Sources

DOCUMENT 5.1: Painting, "View of Guangzhou," ca. 1800

DOCUMENT 5.2: Painting, "Factory site, Guangzhou," 1865

DOCUMENT 5.3: Excerpts from Lin Zexu's letter to Queen Victoria, 1839

DOCUMENT 5.4: Excerpts from William Gladstone's speech to Britain's House of Commons, 1840

DOCUMENT 5.5: Excerpts from the Treaty of Nanjing, August 1842

DOCUMENT 5.6: Excerpts from the Treaty of Wangxia, July 3, 1844

DOCUMENT 5.7: Excerpts from "The Land System of the Heavenly Kingdom," 1853

DOCUMENT 5.8: Excerpts from *The Wealth of Nations* by Adam Smith, 1766 [only on CD]

Supplementary Materials

ITEM 5.A: "Hong Xiuquan and the Taiping Rebellion," an essay

ITEM 5.Ba–c: Photographs from the Presidential Palace, Nanjing, commemorating the Taiping Rebellion, 2006

ITEM 5.C: Replica of a robe worn by Hong Xiuquan, Nanjing, 2006

CHAPTER 5

Nineteenth-Century Strife

By Liz Nelson

Chapter Contents

The Opium Wars
Unequal Treaties
The Taiping Rebellion

Organizing Idea

Great Britain and its allies fought two wars in part to protect their lucrative opium trade, but more broadly to coerce China into becoming part of the Western trade and diplomatic system. These wars and the subsequent "unequal treaties" were watershed events in Chinese history. Together with the rebellions that broke out in various provinces, they put immense political and economic pressure on the Qing dynasty.

Key Questions

Why did hostilities break out between China and Western nations in the 1840s and again in the late 1850s?

What were the short-term and long-term results of the treaties signed between Western nations and China?

Why do many historians—Chinese and Western—consider the Opium Wars as the beginning of modern Chinese history?

What appear to have been the root causes of the rebellions that broke out across China during this time period?

Key Terms

barbarian

"factory"

gunboat diplomacy

Manchu

tariff

treaty

Essay

At Jinghai Temple (静海寺), the large room in which the Nanjing Treaty (《南京条约》) of 1842 was negotiated was opened to the public in 1997. But there is no information, either in Chinese or in English, about what led up to this "treaty" between Great Britain and China, nor what it forced the Qing dynasty emperor to concede. In answer to the question "Why?" the guide shrugged her shoulders and said, "Everybody knows about it." When pressed further, she acknowledged, "We are ashamed of what happened here."

Westerners Smuggle Opium

British exports of opium to China from its colony India multiplied sevenfold in the second half of the eighteenth century, to 4,570 chests—each holding 130 to 160 pounds of opium.[1] Despite the imperial decrees banning Chinese production, importation, and use of opium, British exports rose further to 40,000 chests in 1838,[2] and the British were also selling the drug to merchants from other nations, such as the United States, to export to China. Not only were merchants and corrupt officials reaping huge profits, but so was the British treasury in the form of taxes from the trade. (For further information on the opium trade, see Chapter 4.)

Britain's Gunboat Diplomacy

In 1838, the emperor appointed Lin Zexu (林则徐) (see A Closer Look) to cut opium importation off at its source: Guangzhou (广州).[3] Lin imposed increasingly severe penalties on

---

[1] Jonathan D. Spence, *The Search for Modern China* (New York: W. W. Norton, 1999), 129–130.

[2] Spence, *The Search for Modern China*, 151.

[3] formerly known as Canton

users and traffickers and destroyed 20,183 chests of confiscated opium: cargo he insisted the foreigners surrender. In response, British merchants, who had lost the most in the confrontation, pressured their government for a military response. The debate in Great Britain was extensive and the vote in the House of Commons close, but the advocates for a military response prevailed 271 to 262. Parliament never officially declared war; rather, the nation with the most formidable navy in the world sent a fleet to exact "satisfaction and reparation."

The first Opium War (鸦片战争) (1839–1842) was fought in fits and starts and consisted primarily of the British blockading harbors and seizing several key Chinese cities. When British forces threatened Nanjing (南京), the Qing government capitulated and agreed to the terms of the Nanjing Treaty. Britain's steam-powered Royal Navy and state-of-the-art weapons forced China to open five ports to trade, to pay $21 million in reparation, and to cede to Britain the island of Hong Kong (香港) "in perpetuity." The emperor refused, however, to legalize opium, writing: "nothing will induce me to derive revenue from the vice and misery of my people." Sadly, the emperor's stand had no effect on the quantities of the drug smuggled into China.

In 1843, the Treaty of the Bogue (《虎门条约》) extended further rights to the British, including the critical most-favored-nation clause: whatever additional rights China gave to other nations would immediately apply to the British, too. The United States signed their first treaty with China, the Treaty of Wangxia (《望厦条约》), in July 1844; the French signed the Treaty of Whampoa (《黄埔条约》) with the Qing government the following October.

Social Unrest

While their first direct confrontation with powerful Western nations resulted in a shocking loss of face for the Qing government, internal rebellions in the mid-nineteenth century had a far more devastating effect on the people, as well as on Qing power. Violence and famines, which were in part a result of the chaos, left tens of millions dead or homeless by the time order was restored.

The Taiping Rebellion (太平天国运动) (1851–1864) was the most significant of four major rebellions at this time. It began in Guangxi Province (广西) under the leadership of Hong Xiuquan (洪秀全). Hong (1813–1864) initially attracted followers primarily from among the Hakka (客家) minority people and others outside the mainstream of Chinese society. Anti-Confucian and practicing a mutated kind of Christianity, the movement was committed to destroying the Manchu Qing dynasty. In December 1850, Qing forces tried but failed to quash the movement, which was growing rapidly. Soon thereafter, Hong appointed himself Heavenly King of the *Taiping Tianguo* (太平天国, Heavenly Kingdom of Great Peace).

In the fall of 1851, the Taiping began to conquer one city after another, massacring all people of Manchu descent as they marched north. In March 1853, they took Nanjing, established a theocracy, and ruled for eleven years. Their rebellion affected sixteen of China's eighteen provinces but never succeeded in toppling the Qing dynasty. Ultimately, the Taiping failed for a variety of reasons, including a collapse of their leadership. (See Item 5.A on the CD for a detailed account of the Taiping Rebellion.) But the Qing court would also have to wage costly battles against three more rebellions before social unrest was quelled.

The Second Opium War (1856–1860)

While Qing dynasty officials were embroiled in suppressing the Taiping and other rebellions, the British, French, and Russians (with Americans in tow) pushed the Qing for further concessions. The British, for example, wanted to live wherever they wished in Guangzhou, rather than be restricted to the area designated for foreigners. They insisted on having an ambassador at the imperial court in Beijing, who could argue on behalf of the merchants. Qing officials absolutely refused to allow foreigners into their capital, seeing it as an admission to equal status.

The second war, like the first, concentrated for the most part on port cities and around access to key waterways. Chinese and Manchu soldiers fought valiantly, but once again, their antiquated weapons were no match for Western technology. After two years of sporadic conflict, and with the British and French navies threatening to sail up to Beijing, the Qing government signed the Tianjin Treaty (《天津条约》) in 1858. Although the Western powers did not get everything they wanted in the treaty, they were mindful of the concurrent Taiping threat. "If you humiliate the Emperor beyond measure [by entering the capital], if you seriously impair his influence over his own subjects…[you] throw the country into confusion and imperil the most lucrative trade you have in the world," warned Lord Elgin, Britain's senior official in China. But as hostilities continued, the British and French eventually took the capital. First, though, they plundered the imperial Summer Palace, just outside Beijing's city walls. Then, to revenge the death of several British prisoners of war, on October 18, 1860 Lord Elgin ordered the palace buildings burnt to the ground. A week later, Chinese officials signed the Convention of Peking (《北京条约》),[4] in which the emperor apologized for the execution of the British captives, agreed to pay 8 million *taels*[5] of silver in reparation, opened Tianjin to trade, and permitted a British ambassador to maintain year-round residency in the capital. The French signed a similar agreement the following day.

While the Europeans and Americans had been coercing the Chinese into granting them more favorable commercial rights, the Russians had been pressing for territorial gains north of the Amur River and east of the Ussuri River. Taking advantage of China's weakness, they

---

[4] Former name for Beijing

[5] A *tael* is approximately an ounce of silver, or approximately 37 grams.

too were part of the agreements reached at the Convention of Peking, which gave Russia more than 300,000 square miles of formerly Chinese territory. As a result of the most-favored-nation clause, Russia also benefited from anything the British and French had gained. The Chinese continue to refer to the hundred years that followed as their "century of humiliation."

Primary Sources

DOCUMENT 5.1: Painting, "View of Guangzhou," ca. 1800

DOCUMENT 5.2: Painting, "Factory site, Guangzhou," 1865

(Images courtesy of the Peabody Essex Museum, Salem, MA)

DOCUMENT 5.3: Excerpts from Lin Zexu's letter to Queen Victoria, 1839

We find your country [Great Britain] is sixty or seventy thousand *li* from China. Yet there are barbarian ships that strive to come here for trade for the purpose of making a great profit. The wealth of China is used to profit the barbarians. That is to say, the great profit made by barbarians is all taken from the rightful share of China. By what right do they then in return use the poisonous drug to injure the Chinese people? Even though the barbarians may not necessarily intend to do us harm, yet in coveting profit to an extreme, they have no regard for injuring others. Let us ask, where is your conscience? I have heard that the smoking of opium is very strictly forbidden by your country; that is because the harm caused by opium is clearly understood. Since it is not permitted to do harm to your own country, then even less should you let it be passed on to the harm of other countries—how much less to China! Of all that China exports to foreign countries, there is not a single thing that is not beneficial to people: they are of benefit when eaten, or of benefit when used, or of benefit when resold: all are beneficial.

SOURCE: Ssu-yü Teng and John Fairbank, *China's Response to the West: A Documentary Survey, 1839–1923* (Cambridge, MA: Harvard University Press, 1954), rpt. in Mark A. Kishlansky, ed., *Sources of World History*, vol. 2 (New York: HarperCollins CollegePublishers, 1995), 266–269. http://cyber.law.harvard.edu/ChinaDragon/lin_xexu.html

 The full text of **Document 5.3** is available on the CD-ROM.

DOCUMENT 5.4: Excerpts from William Gladstone's speech to Britain's House of Commons, 1840

[The Chinese government] gave you notice to abandon your contraband trade. When they found you would not do so, they had the right to drive you from their coasts on account of your obstinacy in persisting with this infamous and atrocious traffic [in opium]… justice, in my opinion, is with them; and whilst they, the Pagans, the semi-civilized barbarians have it on their side, we, the enlightened and civilized Christians, are pursuing objects at variance both with justice and with religion… a war more unjust in its origin, a war calculated in its progress to cover this country with a permanent disgrace, I do not know and have not read of. Now, under the auspices of the noble Lord [Macaulay], that flag is become a pirate flag, to protect an infamous traffic.

SOURCE: qtd. in W. Travis Hanes III and Frank Sanello, *The Opium Wars: The Addiction of One Empire and the Corruption of Another* (Naperville, IL: Sourcebooks, Inc., 2002), 78–79.

 The full text of **Document 5.4** is available on the CD-ROM.

DOCUMENT 5.5: Excerpts from the Treaty of Nanjing, August 1842

II.

His Majesty the Emperor of China agrees, that British subjects, with their families and establishments, shall be allowed to reside, for the purposes of carrying on their mercantile pursuits, without molestation or restraint, at the cities and towns of Guangzhou, Xiamen, Fuzhou, Ningbo, and Shanghai...

III.

It being obviously necessary and desirable that British subjects should have some port whereat they may [maintain] and refit their ships when required, and keep stores for that purpose, His Majesty the Emperor of China cedes to Her Majesty the Queen of Great Britain, &c., the Island of Hong-Kong, to be possessed in perpetuity by Her Britannic Majesty, her heirs and successors, and to be governed by such laws and regulations as Her Majesty the Queen of Great Britain, &c., shall see fit to direct.

IV.

The Emperor of China agrees to pay the sum of 6,000,000 of dollars, as the value of the opium which was delivered up at Guangzhou in the month of March, 1839, as a ransom for the lives of Her Britannic Majesty's Superintendent and subjects, who had been imprisoned and threatened with death by the Chinese High Officers....

 The full text of **Document 5.5** is available on the CD-ROM.

DOCUMENT 5.6: Excerpts from the Treaty of Wangxia, July 3, 1844

ARTICLE XVII.

Citizens of the United States residing or sojourning at any of the ports open to foreign commerce, shall enjoy all proper accommodation in obtaining houses and places of business, or in hiring sites from the inhabitants on which to construct houses and places of business, and also hospitals, churches and cemeteries. The local authorities of the two Governments shall select in concert the sites for the foregoing objects, having due regard to the feelings of the people in the location thereof... any desecration of said cemeteries by subjects of China shall be severely punished according to law....

ARTICLE XXI.

Subjects of China who may be guilty of any criminal act towards citizens of the United States, shall be arrested and punished by the Chinese authorities according to the laws of China: and citizens of the United States, who may commit any crime in China, shall be subject to be tried and punished only by the Consul, or other public functionary of the United States, thereto authorized according to the laws of the

United States. And in order to the prevention of all controversy and disaffection, justice shall be equitably and impartially administered on both sides.

Source: Jules Davids, ed. *American Diplomatic and Public Papers: The United States and China* (Wilmington, DE: Scholarly Resources, Inc., 1973), 122–124.

 The full text of **Document 5.6** is available on the CD-ROM.

DOCUMENT 5.7: Excerpts from "The Land System of the Heavenly Kingdom," 1853

Throughout the [Taiping] empire the mulberry tree is to be planted close to every wall, so that all women may engage in rearing silkworms, spinning the silk, and making garments. Throughout the empire every family should keep five hens and two sows, which must not be allowed to miss their proper season. At the time of harvest, every sergeant shall direct the corporals to see to it that of the twenty-five families under his charge each individual has a sufficient supply of food, and aside from the new grain each may receive, the remainder must be deposited in the public granary. Of wheat, pulse, hemp, flax, cloth, silk, fowls, dogs, etc., and money, the same is true; for the whole empire is the universal family of our Heavenly Father, the Supreme Lord and Great God....

For every twenty-five families there must be established one public granary, and one church where the sergeant must reside. Whenever there are marriages, or births, or funerals, all may go to the public granary; but a limit must be observed, and [money] not be used beyond what is necessary. Thus, every family that celebrates a marriage or a birth will be given one thousand cash and a hundred catties of grain....

Source: Franz H. Michael, *The Taiping Rebellion: History and Documents*, vol. 2, Documents and Comments (Seattle: University of Washington Press, 1971), 313–315, 319–320.

 The full text of **Document 5.7** is available on the CD-ROM.

Activities

ACTIVITY 1: Examining visual sources

Before reading any of the materials for this lesson, examine the two paintings of Guangzhou (5.1 and 5.2).

1. What does each painting show?
2. Which countries had a presence in Guangzhou (Canton) in 1800? Which had a presence in 1865? How can you tell? Had anything changed in the way in which these countries were present?
3. Compare the two paintings, listing all the differences and similarities.

4. What might be the reasons behind the differences? Discuss the significance (or lack thereof) of each change.

5. What surprises you about the paintings?

Now read the unit overview and the introductory essay to the chapter. Re-examine the paintings. What do they reflect?

ACTIVITY 2: Evaluating the controversy over the opium trade

After reading Commissioner Lin's letter intended for Britain's Queen Victoria (5.3), consider:

1. What do you learn about trade between China and Western nations from this document?

2. What is the overall tone of the letter?

3. How does the letter reflect Chinese perceptions of themselves and China's traditional values?

4. On what arguments did Lin Zexu base his appeal?

5. In what other situations have people used similar arguments? What were the results?

6. How do Commissioner Lin's efforts to eradicate opium use in China compare to efforts to eliminate drug abuse around the world today?

Now compare Lin's arguments with those that William Gladstone, a member of the British Parliament, gave in his speech (5.4).

1. From Gladstone's speech what can be concluded about the members of Parliament and their knowledge of the ethical issues involved in the opium trade?

2. What factors likely led Parliament to vote in favor of a military response?

Creative extension:

Create an anti-opium-importation poster, either from the point of view of members of Britain's Parliament who opposed the trade or from the point of view of someone on Commissioner Lin's staff.

ACTIVITY 3: Comparing Unequal Treaties

Define the word "treaty" as a class. What would you expect to read in a treaty between two countries? Then, half the class should read the Treaty of Nanjing between China and Great Britain (5.5) while the rest reads the Treaty of Wangxia between China and the United States (5.6).

1. List the key components of each treaty in your own words.

2. Why did these and several subsequent treaties between Western nations and China earn the term "unequal treaties"?

3. Working with a partner who read the other treaty, analyze the similarities and differences between the two treaties. How does the content of each treaty reflect the motives that drove Britain and the United States?

4. Now compare either treaty with the Treaty of Nerchinsk between Russia and China in 1689 (Chapter 3, Document 3.2). What conclusions can be drawn from the differences among the treaties? How had the position of Qing dynasty China changed?

To role play, divide into six groups (members of the negotiating team who represented China, Great Britain, and the United States in the treaty negotiations, scholar-officials in the Qing court, members of Parliament, and U.S. Senators). Each negotiating team must report back to its government on the terms of its respective treaties and convince the government that the treaty should be ratified. Government representatives should be prepared to ask questions to ensure that the treaty is in their country's interest before they take a vote.

ACTIVITY 4: Reflecting in writing

Choose one of the following options:

1. W. Travis Hanes, in his book *Opium Wars,* describes this period of Chinese history as "a cultural confrontation—a confrontation between two great world civilizations, one new and one ancient, each believing itself to be the pinnacle of civilization on the planet" (p. 12). Refer to Chapter 4 for additional information, and then write an essay in response to this statement.

2. Write an editorial for a newspaper from the perspective of a scholar-official in the Qing court, William Gladstone, Commissioner Lin, or an American or British ship owner who has been involved in the opium trade, giving your view of the war and subsequent treaties.

3. Write an essay suggesting how China should respond to these encounters with the West in order to protect its interests.

ACTIVITY 5: Concluding discussion

Discuss as a class:

1. Why does China consider the wars and signing of the treaties as the beginning of its "century of humiliation"?

2. How might you expect these events in the nineteenth century to affect China's foreign policy today?

ACTIVITY 6: Analyzing the Taiping Rebellion

∙∙∙

Read a summary of the Taiping Rebellion (Item 5.A). Then, working with a partner, examine "The Land System of the Heavenly Kingdom" (5.7).

1. List the principles upon which the government was established.
2. Summarize the organizational structure.
3. Why might this type of government have appealed to so many people?
4. How does the Heavenly Kingdom compare to other forms of government or utopian communities?

ACTIVITY 7: The Taiping in Nanjing

∙∙∙

Working in small groups, examine the photographs taken in the wing dedicated to the Taiping Rebellion at the Presidential Palace in Nanjing (Item 5.Ba–c) and of the replica of Hong's robe (Item 5.C).

1. What can you conclude from the appearance of the two rooms?
2. What, if anything, surprised you about the rooms? Why?
3. List words to describe the statue of Hong Xiuquan.
4. Does the king's robe surprise you in light of the principles of the Heavenly Kingdom? Why or why not? What is the significance of the color?

EXTENDED RESEARCH:

∙∙∙

To explore this period of Chinese history further, research:

- The Nian Rebellion (1851–1868)
- Muslim revolts in Yunnan (1855–1873) and in Shaanxi and Gansu provinces (1862–1873)
- The economist Adam Smith's writing on China (see 5.8 on the CD-ROM) in *The Wealth of Nations*, 1766
- The treaties of Tianjin between China and the United States (June 18, 1858), and China and Great Britain (June 26, 1858); the full text of each can be accessed online at http://web.jjay.cuny.edu/jobrien/reference/ob27.html and http://web.jjay.cuny.edu/jobrien/reference/ob28.html
- The Taiping Rebellion by reading Katherine Paterson's novel *Rebels of the Heavenly Kingdom* (see Suggested Resources)

■ **A CLOSER LOOK**

Lin Zexu: The Commissioner Takes Charge

In 1838, the emperor appointed Lin Zexu (1785–1850) to enforce the ban on opium by cutting it off at the source: Guangzhou (Canton). Commissioner Lin was an exemplary official by all accounts. He held a *jinshi* degree, having passed the most difficult of the civil service exams. A literary scholar, reformer, and skilled diplomat, he was incorruptible. Lin took a multifaceted approach to the opium problem: favoring rehabilitation for addicts, appealing to Britain's Queen Victoria on moral grounds, and destroying drug-related paraphernalia. By the spring of 1839, he had arrested 1,600 Guangzhou residents and confiscated 42,000 opium pipes. By mid-summer, he had seized 14,000 drug-filled chests. After a battle of wills, he forced Western merchants to surrender the opium on their vessels: 20,000 chests (worth about $12 million), which the commissioner destroyed. In future, he declared, if any vessel were found to have opium on board, he would order the entire crew executed. In Britain, economics peppered with national pride trumped moral arguments and the British with their allies fought two wars in part to protect the lucrative opium trade. Commissioner Lin's best efforts were no match for Britain's gunboat diplomacy. By 1879, opium imports to China had risen to an astronomical 105,000 chests.

■ *Discuss: How else might Commissioner Lin have approached the task of ridding Guangzhou and hence inland China of opium? Were his efforts inevitably doomed to fail? Why or why not?*

Dr. Peter Parker: Beyond Evangelical Work

Peter Parker (1804–1888) was the first Protestant medical missionary to China. He was born in Framingham, Massachusetts, the son of devout farmers. After graduating from Yale College in 1831, he studied medicine and theology. In 1834, he earned his M.D., was ordained as a Presbyterian minister, and sailed for Guangzhou. There he opened an opthalmic hospital. Throughout his years in China, he specialized in diseases of the eye, but also performed other surgeries, especially ones involving removal of tumors. Dr. Parker introduced Western anesthesia (sulphuric ether) to China. Medicine and preaching were of equal importance to him. He offered free treatment at the hospital to rich and poor alike and held regular religious services there. His goal, he said was to "open China for the gospel with the lancet." During the first Opium War, Dr. Parker left China, did extensive fundraising back in the States, then returned to China in 1842. Two years later, he took on a diplomatic role: he was of invaluable assistance to U.S. envoy Caleb Cushing in his efforts to negotiate the first treaty between the U.S. and China. From 1855 to 1857, Dr. Parker served as the American Commissioner and Minister to China.

■ *Discuss Peter Parker's work in China. Compare it to the work of earlier missionaries (see Chapter 4). How was Dr. Parker's presence similar to and different from that of other Westerners in Guangzhou? Do present-day missionaries combine their evangelical work with social services, too? Where? How?*

Suggested Resources

Books

Hanes, W. Travis III and Frank Sanello. *The Opium Wars: The Addiction of One Empire and the Corruption of Another.* Naperville, IL: Sourcebooks, Inc., 2002.
A very readable history of the events.
Paterson, Katherine. *Rebels of the Heavenly Kingdom.* New York: Puffin Books, 1983.
Paterson grew up in China as the daughter of missionaries and was a missionary herself for a brief time. Her young-adult historical novel, the result of careful research and first-hand knowledge of China, gives a poignant look at how two teenagers experienced the Taiping Rebellion. An excellent read.

Spence, Jonathan D. *God's Chinese Son: The Taiping Heavenly Kingdom of Hong Xiuquan.* New York: W. W. Norton, 1996.
A careful analysis of Hong Xiuquan, who led the Taiping, by a master historian.

Websites

http://www.exeas.org/resources/opium-trade. html The Opium Trade lesson is one of many online lessons at Columbia University's *Expanding East Asian Studies* website.

http://digital.library.mcgill.ca/westchina/trade. htm McGill University Library's *Trade and Gunboat Diplomacy* website includes a brief overview with several interesting primary sources.

CHAPTER 6

Exploring Solutions (1861–1894)

By Shirley Moore Huettig

Chapter Contents:

The Self-Strengthening Movement

Missionaries in China

The Chinese Diaspora

Organizing Idea:

The period 1861–1894 witnessed the Chinese turning to ideas that included both accommodation and resistance in order to strengthen themselves in their dealings with foreign powers. In addition to their increased contact with foreign governments and traders, the Chinese witnessed a flood of missionaries into their country, as well as an exodus of Chinese individuals to other parts of the world.

Key Questions:

How did the Chinese both accommodate and resist foreigners?

What initiatives did the Chinese launch as part of the Self-Strengthening Movement?

What was the relationship between missionaries and the Chinese?

What factors contributed to the large number of Chinese people choosing to emigrate in the late nineteenth century?

What were some common experiences of Chinese people working and living overseas?

Key Terms

accommodation

coolies

conservative

diaspora

immigrant

incursion

indenture

missionary

progressive

proselytize

restoration

Essay

In the second half of the nineteenth century, the Qing (清) dynasty faced growing incursion by foreign nations and dissatisfaction from within China. Conservative and progressive voices within China argued over the country's relationship with the outside world; some called for restoring a more isolationist stance, while others advocated learning from the foreigners in order to resist them. For some Chinese, one of the most visible examples of Western incursion was the presence of missionaries, especially from Britain and the United States, whose numbers in China grew significantly after 1860. Finally, in response to conditions at home, thousands of Chinese chose to leave in search of a better life in areas as far flung as Australia, the West Indies, and the United States.

Restoration and Self-Strengthening

Although the Qing dynasty was greatly weakened after the treaty settlements of 1860, it was able to continue in power. Many Chinese intellectuals saw the dynasty's survival despite the crisis as a sign for "restoration" (*zhongxing* 中兴). But others were less optimistic and called for "self-strengthening" (*ziqiang* 自强). They urged changes in policy, suggesting that the Chinese engage and learn from foreigners so as to resist further incursions. Most of the arguments between those who supported restoration and those who called for self-strengthening revolved around education, the traditional foundation of Chinese government. Among those who promoted self-strengthening was the provincial leader Zeng Guofan (曾国藩),[1] who recorded in his diary:

If we wish to find a method of self-strengthening, we should begin by considering the reform of government service and the securing of men of ability as urgent tasks, and then regard learning to make explosive shells and steamships and other instruments as the work of first importance. If only we could possess all their [Westerners'] superior techniques, then we would have the means to return their favors when they are obedient, and we would also have the means to avenge our grievances when they are disloyal.[2]

Unfortunately, despite the efforts of a number of visionary and talented individuals, China made little headway compared to the achievements in the West and Japan. "They never dreamed of remaking China into a modern state," writes historian Immanuel Hsü in *The Rise of Modern China*. "In fact, they strove to strengthen the existing order rather than to replace it. They had absolutely no conception of economic development, industrial revolution, and modern transformation." The movement did, however, mark "the beginning of industrialization… in China."[3]

Empress Cixi (慈禧), who served as regent for a series of young boy-emperors, was positioned between the "restoration" and "self-strengthening" efforts as she tried to maintain imperial power. At first, she tried to balance calls for traditional versus Western education and policy. Later, however, she realized it was only through the restoration of the traditional Confucian system of government that she would retain her power over the young emperors and, therefore, the government.[4]

---

[1] Zeng Guofan was a Confucian statesman/general/scholar, who brought an end to the Taiping Rebellion by defeating the Taiping in Nanjing (see Chapter 5).

[2] http://www.lcsc.edu/modernchina/Zenggf3.html

[3] Immanuel C.Y. Hsü, *The Rise of Modern China* (New York: Oxford University Press, fourth edition, 1990), 288, 290.

[4] Joanna Waley-Cohen, *Sextants of Beijing: Currents in Chinese History* (New York: W. W. Norton, 1999), 168.

Foreign Relations

In 1861 the Qing government created the *Zongli Yamen* (总理衙门, Office for the Management of the Business of All Foreign Countries).[5] It was headed by Prince Gong (恭亲王), the emperor's uncle, who had gained important experience in dealing with foreigners in his role negotiating the 1860 peace settlement with the British, French, and Russians (see Chapter 5). He had come to appreciate that the West had good ideas to offer in the realm of manufacturing as well as international law and treaties. As a result, several schools to train translators and interpreters were set up on the eastern seaboard. The first, the *Tongwen Guan* (同文馆), had a curriculum that included foreign languages, taught mostly by missionaries who were restricted from proselytizing at any time, as well as Western science, technology and mathematics, also taught by foreigners, and classical Chinese studies.

Despite the best efforts of the *Zongli Yamen*, foreign nations continued their encroachment on what the Chinese had long considered tributary lands. In 1879, Japan occupied the Liuqi Islands and was quickly followed by Russia in the Yili Valley in 1881, France in Vietnam in 1885 and Laos in 1893, and Britain expanding its empire into Burma in 1886.[6] Within China's borders, foreigners continued to extract more favorable trade arrangements and greater access to interior sections of the country.

Missionaries

After 1861, Europeans and Americans also made their presence felt in China with a significant increase in missionary activity, both Protestant and Catholic. Especially active during the period 1861–1885, missionaries built orphanages and schools, where they offered Western curricula including English language, science and technology, medicine, and law, as well as religious studies. Catholic missions emphasized religious conversion, while Protestants maintained a more secular curriculum. In dramatic contrast to Chinese tradition, missionaries opened schools for girls. Despite these seemingly useful contributions, the presence of Western missionaries was fraught with tension, which periodically erupted in violence.

Emigration

As the Atlantic slave trade slowed and countries abolished slavery, a huge international demand for labor arose.[7] Despite Confucian ethics, which emphasized that an adult son should remain at home in order to take care of aging parents, and a Qing edict (1672) that prohibited Chinese individuals from emigrating, an estimated three million impoverished Chinese, especially from rural areas, left in the late nineteenth century in search of a better life overseas.[8] They boarded ships in southern China only to find crowded, unhealthy passage to work on plantations, in mines, and on railroads in the Caribbean, Southeast Asia, Latin America, South America, Australia, and the United States. Once there, the immigrants found the work to be little better than slave labor. Belying its image as a land of equal opportunity, the United States greeted Chinese immigrants with discrimination, derision, and physical harm. Immigrants in many other lands fared similarly. Forced to watch out for themselves, Chinese immigrants settled together in neighborhoods, creating "Chinatowns" in large cities such as Havana, Cuba; Georgetown, Guyana; Liverpool, England; and San Francisco, U.S.A.

---

[5] Prior to this, China's foreign relations were divided among three bureaus. (See Chapter 4.)

[6] In Japan, the Liuqi Islands are called the Ryukyu Islands.

[7] For example, Peru abolished slavery in 1854, the United States in 1865, and Cuba in 1886.

[8] Wei Djao, *Being Chinese: Voices from the Diaspora* (Tucson: University of Arizona Press, 2003), 26. This figure covers the period between 1840 and 1911.

Primary Sources

DOCUMENT 6.1: Letter from Zeng Guofan and Li Hongzhang to *Zongli Yamen* (the Foreign Relations Bureau) on sending young men abroad to study, March 1871

[After a delegation sent by the empress dowager Cixi] had traveled in various countries… they saw the essential aspects of conditions overseas, and they found that cartography, mathematics, astronomy, navigation, shipbuilding, and manufacturing are all closely related to military defense. It is the practice of foreign nations that those who have studied abroad and have learned some superior techniques are immediately invited upon their return by academic institutions to teach the various subjects and to develop their fields. Military administration and shipping are considered as important as the learning that deals with the mind and body, and nature and destiny of man. Now that the eyes of the people have been opened, if China wishes to adopt Western ideas and excel in Western methods, we should immediately select intelligent young men and send them to study in foreign countries….

SOURCE: Rpt. in William Theodore de Bary and Richard Lufrano, *Sources of Chinese Tradition*, vol. 2 (New York: Columbia University Press, 2000), 241.

 The full text of **Document 6.1** is available on the CD-ROM.

DOCUMENT 6.2: Excerpts from the autobiography of Yung Wing, *My Life in China and America*, describing his efforts to modernize China, 1909

The proposition was for the government to send picked Chinese youths abroad to be thoroughly educated for the public service…. As to the character and selection of the students: the whole number to be sent abroad for education was one hundred and twenty; they were to be divided into four installments of thirty members each, one installment to be sent each year for four successive years at about the same time. The candidates to be selected were not to be younger than twelve or older than fifteen years of age. They were to show respectable parentage or responsible and respectable guardians. They were required to pass a medical examination, and an examination in their Chinese studies according to regulation—reading and writing in Chinese—also to pass an English examination if a candidate had been in an English school….

SOURCE: Wing Yung, *My Life in China and America* (New York: Henry Holt and Company, 1909), 173, 183–184.

 The full text of **Document 6.2** is available on the CD-ROM.

DOCUMENT 6.3: Excerpt from letter by Zhu Yixin in response to the Self-Strengthening Movement, late 1800s

The barbarians do not recognize the moral obligations between ruler and minister, parent and child, elder brother and younger brother, husband and wife. There is your change in principles. Do you mean that the classics of our sages and the teachings of our philosophers are too dull and banal to follow, and that we must change them so as to have something new? Only if we first have principles can we then have institutions. Barbarian institutions are based on barbarian principles. Different principles make for different customs, and different customs give rise to different institutions. Now, instead of getting at the root of it all, you talk blithely of changing institutions. If the institutions are to be changed, are not the principles going to be changed along with them?

SOURCE: William Theodore de Bary and Richard Lufrano, *Sources of Chinese Tradition*, vol. 2 (New York: Columbia University Press, 2000), 277.

 The full text of **Document 6.3** is available on the CD-ROM.

DOCUMENT 6.4: Excerpts from the writings of British evangelical Protestant missionary J. Hudson Taylor regarding the foundation and functioning of the China Inland Mission in 1865

A journey taken in the spring of 1855 with the Rev. J. S. Burdon of the Church Missionary Society (later the Bishop of Victoria, Hong Kong) was attended with some serious dangers.... We went to Tongzhou [in Jiangsu Province], and of our painful experiences there the following journal will tell....

A respectable man came up, and earnestly warned us against proceeding, saying that if we did we should find to our sorrow what the Tongzhou militia were like.... After this my wheelbarrow man would proceed no farther, and I had to seek another, who was fortunately not difficult to find.... Long before we reached the gate, a tall powerful man, made tenfold fiercer by partial intoxication, let us know that all the militia were not so peaceably inclined, by seizing Mr. Burdon by the shoulders.... At once we were surrounded by a dozen or more brutal men, who hurried us on to the city at a fearful pace.... We demanded to be taken before the chief magistrate, but were told that they knew where to take us, and what to do with such persons as we were, with the most insulting epithets.... He all but knocked me down again and again, seized me by the hair, took hold of my collar so as to almost choke me, and grasped my arms and shoulders, making them black and blue....

As we were walking along Mr. Burdon tried to give away a few books that he was carrying, not knowing whether we might have another opportunity of doing so; but the fearful rage of the soldier, and the way he insisted on manacles being brought, which fortunately were not at hand, convinced us that in our present position we could do no good in attempting book distribution....

SOURCE: J. Hudson Taylor, *The Autobiography of a Man Who Brought the Gospel to China* (Minneapolis: Bethany House, 1986), 64, 66, 68–69.

 The full text of **Document 6.4** is available on the CD-ROM.

DOCUMENT 6.5: Excerpts from letters from China by Presbyterian missionary Kate Mills to her father in Windsor, Connecticut, 1883, 1886, and 1888

November 12, 1883

My Dear Papa,

Many of the natives are sorry-looking creatures. Those who have plenty of clothes fare poorly enough, but those who have none look as if they would freeze. You know they have no fires in their houses except when they cook their meals, and on a sunny day they may [be] seen in the streets sunning themselves. Their houses are nothing more than sheds. The wind can come in anywhere it will. Consequently they leave their doors open thinking, I suppose, that it is warmer outdoors than in, and they are usually right. But the worst of it is that they do not comprehend the difference when they get into a house that is tight and where there is a fire, or else they think our fire will warm all outdoors. I do not know which. They first leave the kitchen door open thus making that room cold and then all the doors as far as they go....

June 29, 1886

You asked about the situation of Hangzhou.... The number of inhabitants are variously estimated from 5 to 800,000. Probably the number you saw (700,000) was about right, although I think it would be largely guess work for probably no such thing as a census was ever taken. The most you can say is that they are packed in like sardines. One room as large as Laurie's bedroom would be considered immense for a whole family, so they take in the pigs to help fill it up. They all seem perfectly at home together.

I do not see how they live with hot weather. Even the cleanest of them has an odor as bad as any dirty Irishman. Our teacher manages to keep himself quite respectable, but this morning one came in that I have usually thought very neat, but I did want to use the campher [*sic*] bottle....

May 23, 1888

One of the queer things of this country is that everything in the line of eatables will be under lock and key. Thus anything needed for cooking must be dealt out in the necessary quantities every day. It is a nuisance but is done all around us. It is said that if that is not done, things have a very mysterious way of disappearing no one knows where. For it is universally acknowledged that all Chinese will cheat and steal some, even the Christians. Even the best of them will do it, and taking certain things is not considered stealing by them....

SOURCE: Kate Mills Papers, M-3281.1, M-3288. William L. Clements Library, University of Michigan. Ann Arbor, Michigan.

 The full text of **Document 6.5** is available on the CD-ROM.

DOCUMENT 6.6 Letters from Southern Baptist missionary Lottie Moon, published in the *Foreign Mission Journal*, October 1888 and June 1898

June 30, 1898

Tongzhou, China

Dear Dr. Willingham,

I have visited during this Quarter [three months] twenty different towns & villages. At many of them, I remained several days. At others, I have made but brief visits, going out after dinner & returning about sun-set. I have had much to encourage me in the work. The people are very friendly & more ready to listen to the gospel than I have ever known them to be. In two places, there are, apparently, some genuine inquirers. I have been pressingly invited to go to a new village to visit a family said to be very favorably disposed to Christianity & I have promised to go. It is a source of sorrow that I cannot meet the numerous calls. I have simply to decide what cases & places most urgently demand attention & to neglect many others to which I would gladly go, were I free to do so. We need at least three more single women here. Miss Hartwell is doing noble work in the school, but, thus far, this year has been unable to leave the city. There are about thirty towns & villages connected with the Tongzhou station, that ought to have visits of several days duration, at least twice a year. With our present force, this is simply impossible.

We are rejoiced at the good news from the Convention. To have that awful debt rolled off, what a blessing.

With best wishes & earnest prayers for a blessing upon your labors,

Yrs. sincerely,

L. Moon.

SOURCE: Lottie Moon to Robert J. Willingham, 30 June 1898. *Lottie Moon Letters*, ed. International Mission Board (Southern Baptist Convention), accession no. 192. https://solomon.imb.org/public/ws/lmcorr/www/lmcorr/SimpleSearch

 Additional letters from Lottie Moon are available on the CD-ROM.

DOCUMENT 6.7: Excerpts from a report by the commissioner of three northern ports describing the Tianjin Massacre, June 1870

I find that in the Tianjin region, since summer began the weather has been hotter and drier than usual, and the popular mood is unsettled. Among the populace, rumors have been rife. There are those who say that [the foreigners] use medicine to kidnap youths and children. There are those who say that there are cases of the corpses and bones of youths and children being exposed in the public cemetery. There are those who say that the exposed corpses are all those abandoned by the church. Also, there are those who say that the Catholics gouge out eyes and cut out hearts. Rumors spread in great confusion, but without any firm basis....

People from everywhere were summoned by gong. The church was burnt down, and also the Renci Hall outside the Eastern Gate was destroyed by fire. In other places "preaching halls" were pulled down. Missionaries and those practicing the faith, both Chinese and foreign, were injured and killed. Your servant rushed to supervise with the local civil and military officials and also sent troops to put down [the disturbance]. Alas, the masses were [too] numerous, with the force of a mob, and in a short while the killing, wounding, burning, and destroying were already *faits accomplis....*

SOURCE: Gengyin Chonghou, untitled memorial, 23 June 1870, trans. Howard R. Spendelow. http://www9.georgetown.edu/faculty/spendelh/china/TJ700623.htm

 The full text of **Document 6.7** is available on the CD-ROM.

DOCUMENT 6.8: Excerpts from the "Autobiography of Mr. Kwan Hong Kee," describing his early years in Australia, January 1938

In 1885, Kwan Hong Kee borrowed $100 from his brother to pay for his passage from Hong Kong to Australia. He worked as a cook on board the vessel. After arriving in Sydney, he borrowed more money to send a letter home, letting his family know he had arrived safely, and to buy European clothes. His first job was in Newcastle as a cook in a Chinese store. He was provided with room and board but received no pay.

Each day after cooking breakfast, I worked as a hawker selling goods until 4 o'clock in the afternoon, when it was time to cook the evening meal. I did this for a period of three months, after which through another friend I got work in Sydney at "Sarm Choy" store. This store imported and sold Chinese goods. My wages were fifteen shillings a week. After two years I was promoted to salesman and received one pound a week. [Four years later] my work included selling, back store work, receiving and delivering goods, in fact all general work. I tried my best, my boss was pleased with my work over the six years. I then returned to China again and married....

SOURCE: Kwan Hong Kee, "Autobiography of Mr. Kwan Hong Kee," Hong Kong, January 1938. *Golden Threads,* Australian Museums & Galleries Online, Nov. 2003. http://amol.org.au/goldenthreads/stories

 The full text of **Document 6.8** is available on the CD-ROM.

DOCUMENT 6.9: Excerpts from a contract of indenture for Chinese emigrants sailing to Guyana, 1873

1. I agree to work in British Guyana as I may be directed by the Government Immigration Agent or for any person to whom he may transfer this Contract....

3. I agree to do any kind of work that I may be lawfully directed to do, whether in town or country, in fields, in factories, in private houses &c....

8. Wherever I may work or in whatever family I may be employed, I must obey the lawful regulations there in force; on the other hand should I at any time feel aggrieved at the conduct of my master towards me, all reasonable facility shall be afforded me, for laying my complaint before the proper officers of the Colony....

12. Every day, food will be issued as follows; 8 oz. salt meat and 2½ lbs. of other articles, all of which shall be good and wholesome....

14. Each year there will be given me one suit of clothes and one blanket....

19. I the said coolie now agree that my wages shall be four dollars a month and I declare my willingness, before my departure, to go to British Guyana, it is therefore understood that hereafter if I hear or ascertain that the labourers in British Guyana receive more wages than myself, I must still be satisfied with the wages and other compensating advantages secured to me by this Contract....

SOURCE: Trev Sue-A-Quan, *Cane Reapers: Chinese Indentured Immigrants in Guyana* (Vancouver, BC: Riftswood Publishing, 1999), 323–327.

 The full text of **Document 6.9** is available on the CD-ROM.

DOCUMENT 6.10a & b: Excerpt from "Our Misery and Despair" by Denis Kearney of the California Workingmen's Party and a letter in response by Kwang Chang Ling, published in the *San Francisco Argonaut*, 1878

From Kwang Chang Ling's response:

■ You are continually objecting to [the] morality [of the Chinese]. Your travelers say he is depraved; your missioners call him ungodly; your commissioners call him unclean... Yet your housewives permit him to wait upon them at table; they admit him to their bedchambers; they confide to him their garments and jewels; and even trust their lives to him by awarding him supreme control over their kitchens and the preparation of their food. There is a glaring contradiction here....

■ The slender fare of rice and the other economical habits of the peasant class [of China], which are so objectionable to your lower orders and the demagogues who trumpet their clamors, are not the result of choice to Chinamen; they follow poverty. The hard-working, patient servants that you have about you today love good fare as well as other men, but they are engaged in a work far higher than the gratification of self-indulgence; they are working to liberate their parents in China [from poverty].... When this emancipation is complete, you will find the Chinamen [sic] as prone as any human creature to fill his belly and cover his back with good things.

SOURCE: Kwang Chang Ling, letter in San Francisco *Argonaut*, 1878. *Becoming American: The Chinese Experience*, PBS. http://www.pbs.org/becomingamerican/ce_witness2.html

 The full text of **Document 6.10** is available on the CD-ROM.

DOCUMENT 6.11: Cartoon in Australia's *Queensland Figaro*, April 1888

APRIL 28, 1888.   THE QUEENSLAND FIGARO.   729

M'ILWRAITH TO THE RESCUE.

Should I return to power I will at once take action both separately and jointly with the other Colonies to secure the total and *immediate* exclusion of Chinese from Australia.—*Sir Thomas M'Ilwraith's Manifesto.*

DOCUMENT 6.13a–d: Photographs of Chinatowns around the world today

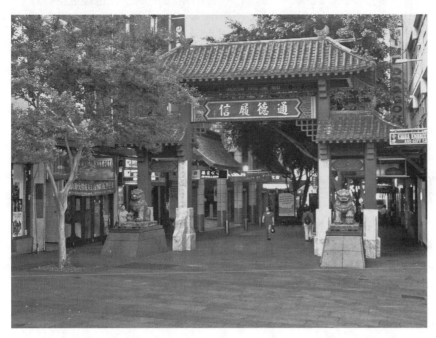

Chinatown in Sydney, Australia *(Photo by Liz Nelson)*

 Additional photographs are available on the CD-ROM.

Activities

ACTIVITY 1: Exploring solutions: reading, discussing, and writing

Part 1: Text on text discussion

Seated in a circle in groups of three, read and respond to each document (6.1, 6.2 or 6.3; see Item 6.A for directions).

1. How does this person feel about China's relationship with foreign countries?
2. What does he think should be done in response? What specific solutions does he recommend? Does he advocate "restoration" or "self-strengthening"?
3. Are you convinced by his argument? Why or why not?

Part 2: Inside/Outside class discussion

Create two groups, making sure that each group has a mix of "experts" on each of the three documents 6.1, 6.2, and 6.3.

One group sits in a tight circle in the middle of the room with its members facing each other. The other group sits in a larger circle around the first group. The inner group begins a discussion of the questions students addressed in part 1. When they are done, the groups switch. The new inside group can add to the first group's discussion as well as address the original questions. When they are done, the groups switch again. The first group returns to the middle to finish the discussion of the questions.

Writing extension:

Write a letter to the emperor from the point of view of one of the authors of these documents, with recommendations regarding China's relationship with foreigners and steps to take to keep China strong or make it stronger. Do you advocate "restoration" or "self-strengthening"? Be sure to support your argument with specifics from the document. Alternatively, write a formal persuasive essay.

ACTIVITY 2: The missionary presence: reading, discussing, and writing

Part 1: Text on text discussion

After reading documents 6.4–6.7, work in small groups to answer the following questions:

1. What was the role of missionaries in China?
2. How well did the missionaries integrate with the Chinese population?
3. How did the missionaries treat the Chinese? How did the Chinese treat the missionaries?
4. How were the authors of these documents similar to and different from each other?

Regroup with your classmates and discuss opinions about missionaries in China.

Writing extension:

Write a letter either as a church elder or a Chinese peasant or official to one of the denominations sending the missionaries, with recommendations regarding their presence in China. Would you allow missionaries to stay? What restrictions, if any, would you place on their activities (traveling, proselytizing, or conducting business)? Be sure to support your argument with specifics from the documents.

ACTIVITY 3: The Chinese diaspora: reading and discussing

Part 1:

Working in small groups, examine documents 6.8–6.11 and discuss:

1. Why did Chinese people leave China? Where did they go?

2. What challenges and opportunities did Chinese immigrants face in their new homes?

3. What factors contributed to the discrimination Chinese immigrants experienced?

Part 2:

Conduct an Inside/Outside group discussion (see Activity 1, Part 2) on the issue of Chinese immigration.

ACTIVITY 4: Analyzing data from shipping records

Refer to the instructions in Item 6.B to prepare for working with the shipping records (6.12 on the CD-ROM). Answer the following questions:

1. Which ship made the most voyages to Guyana? How was the name of the ship ironic?

2. What was the height of the immigration from China to Guyana? How did you define the "height" of the trade? Based on your knowledge of Chinese history (see Chapter 5), how can you explain the increase in emigration?

3. From which Chinese port did most ships sail? What was the second most common port of departure?

4. Which was the longest voyage? Which was the shortest? What was the average length of a voyage from China to Guyana?

5. At what time of year did most voyages take place? In which months did these voyages generally not sail? Why do you suppose this was?

6. What was the highest number of people transported on one ship? The lowest number? Notice the difference between the numbers in column L and those in column R. How might you account for the differences? What was the largest number of people "lost" on one voyage? How might you account for the change in the number who embarked and those who disembarked on the *Montmorency* in 1861?

7. Who accounted for the most emigrants: men, women or children? Why do you suppose this was true?

Propose other questions and experiment with other sorting methods to further examine the data for information about emigration from China to Guyana.

ACTIVITY 5: Self-evaluation

Write a one-page summary of your participation in the group work. How much did you contribute? Did you dominate the conversation? How well did you listen to others? How did you show that you were listening well? What might you have done differently to be a better participant in the discussion?

Creative extensions:

For documents 6.8–6.12, create a corresponding written or visual response. For example:

1. What recommendations would you make to *Zongli Yamen* (the Foreign Relations Bureau; see Introductory Essay) about China's role in the lives of Chinese emigrants?

2. Write an editorial to a newspaper in a country to which Chinese people moved. Address the topic of assimilation or treatment of the Chinese immigrants. Be sure to support your argument with specifics from the documents.

3. Design a cartoon from the Chinese perspective that summarizes the experience of the Chinese immigrant: conditions, reception, family life, etc.

4. Create a sculpture or write a poem in response to any one of the documents.

5. Write a letter as though you are a Chinese immigrant to your family back in China. Who are you—gender, age, occupation, location? What is your life like? Would you recommend that your family come join you? Why or why not? For additional resources, visit http://www.rootsweb.com/~guycigtr/ or http://memory.loc.gov/learn/features/immig/chinese3.html.

6. Design a pamphlet to attract Chinese coolies to come to Guyana to live and work.

7. Write a report from a Chinese investigating committee to the *Zongli Yamen* (the Foreign Relations Bureau) on the conditions in Guyana, Peru, or San Francisco.

ACTIVITY 6: Carousel brainstorming

In brainstorming, members of a group all respond by calling out words that they associate with the image. The recorder should write down all of the ideas; there is no censoring in brainstorming. Don't criticize or question anyone's idea. As a class, brainstorm about Chinatown:

1. What is a Chinatown?

2. What do you expect to see? What don't you expect to see?

3. Where do you think Chinatowns are located?

Working in small groups, examine one of the photographs 6.13a–d. One member of each group should record the group's ideas. On a single sheet of paper, record at the top the names of the students in the group and the location of the Chinatown.

1. Brainstorm for five minutes together, with the recorder writing down all the responses. Consider: What do you see? What don't you see that you might have expected? What surprises you about the image?

2. When the time is up, put the paper on which the group's ideas were recorded in the middle so all can see. Write several summary statements about the image, using the responses from the whole group.

3. Reconvene as a class and share one summary statement from your own work. (Statements can be read out loud or written on the board for others to record.)

4. Discuss the many ideas elicited by the pictures. To what extent did the images of Chinatowns match the ideas from the initial brainstorming?

NOTE: This activity can also be done using the topic of the reactions of native populations to Chinese immigration, referring to Document 6.11 and the additional cartoons listed in Suggested Resources.

EXTENDED RESEARCH:

Choose one of the topics below and create a final product (a paper, an electronic presentation using a program such as PowerPoint or Photo Story 3, or a creative response) to share the information with classmates.

1. Choose another country that has faced or currently faces the need to modernize, and show how the country did it (e.g. Japan, Russia, or a developing country today).

2. To what extent has China "caught up to" or surpassed the West in manufacturing, weapons, or other technologies? What is China's role in the global economy now?

3. Where else did missionaries go in the nineteenth century? How successful were their efforts in other places?

4. Where do missionaries go today? How do they work?

5. Explore immigration issues such as:

   a. What are a host country's responsibilities toward immigrants?

   b. What responsibilities does the country of origin have for the people who left?

   c. Compare the response of United States citizens to the Chinese to their response to other immigrant groups.

   d. Compare the response of the United States to Chinese immigrants to the response of another country to Chinese immigration, such as Australia, Cuba, Peru, Great Britain, etc.

   e. Choose one country and explore the emigration or immigration issues that country faces today.

6. Search the Internet for Chinatowns all over the world. Using a world map or Google Earth, mark all the cities where Chinese immigrants created communities in the past that are still present today.

Suggested Resources

Books

McCunn, Ruthanne Lum. *God of Luck*. New York: Soho Press, 2007.
A wrenching story of a young Chinese man kidnapped in southern China, shipped to Peru, and coerced to work there. The novel is based on extensive research by the author. See Additional Resources on the CD-ROM for a teaching guide for both of McCunn's books.

McCunn, Ruthanne Lum. *Thousand Pieces of Gold*. Boston: Beacon Press, 1981.
Set first in rural China, the book tells the true story of Lalu, sold into slavery to a saloon owner in a gold-mining town of the American West. Poignant and powerful.

Sue-A-Quan, Trev. *Cane Reapers: Chinese Indentured Immigrants in Guyana*. Vancouver, BC: Riftswood Publishing, 1999.
The book reveals the experiences of the author's own ancestors among the many Chinese who were "hired" to work in the Caribbean and northern South America. The book is difficult to obtain and not indexed, but it contains an interesting account of the Chinese Diaspora beyond the United States.
Consider also Cane Ripples, *a sequel to* Cane Reapers *that describes the experiences of the Chinese in Guyana, presented in the form of short stories about individuals and families in their working and recreational lives. You can contact the author and order either of these books at: http://www.rootsweb. com/~guycigtr/Book.htm*

Yep, Lawrence. *Dragonwings*. New York: Harper & Row, 1975.
A Newbery Honor Book, Dragonwings *is a beautifully written story of a child who leaves his mother and (paternal) grandmother in China to join his father in San Francisco. Told from the perspective of the young boy, the book captures the experience of Chinese immigrants and the traditions they brought with them to an often hostile new setting.*

Websites

Restoration/Self-Strengthening

http://en.wikipedia.org/wiki/Self-strengthening_movement For a detailed introduction.

http://web.pdx.edu/~lorz/texts.htm The *Yung Wing Project* includes his autobiography and many additional related papers, including letters written to their U.S. host families by Chinese students who had studied in Hartford and returned to China.

Empress Cixi

http://www.chinapage.com/biography/cixi.html

http://departments.kings.edu/womens_history/ tzuhsi.html Thomas J. Gilroy at King's College (Pennsylvania) provides a biography of Cixi.

Li Hongzhang

http://www.hfly.gov.cn/Eng/OldTown3.html See this site for a photograph of Li.

http://www.hfly.gov.cn/Eng/OldTown4. html Information about the Shrine Hall of Li.

Missionaries

http://ime.imb.org/LottieMoon/letters.asp This site provides a collection of her letters and additional information about Moon.

Chinese Diaspora

http://memory.loc.gov/learn/features/timeline/ riseind/chinimms/chinimms.html A Library of Congress *American Memory* site: *Chinese Immigration to the United States, 1851–1900*.

http://memory.loc.gov/ammem/award99/ cubhtml/cicSubjects1.html#bottom Information from the Library of Congress on Chinese immigrants in California: text, cartoons, and photographs.

http://www.cetel.org/index.html The Center for Educational Telecommunications' *Ancestors in the Americas* site has a three-part series on Chinese Americans.

http://www.latinamericanstudies.org/chinese-immigrants-1.htm Illustrations of Chinese immigrants in the United States.

http://www.rootsweb.com/~guycigtr/ Trev Sue-A-Quan's website *Chinese in Guyana: Their Roots*.

http://www.guyana.org/history.html A brief introduction to the history of Guyana.

http://archive.amol.org.au/goldenthreads/ stories/ A website from Australian Museums and Galleries Online focusing on Chinese contributions in New South Wales, Australia.

http://www.teachingheritage.nsw.edu.au/ d_reshaping/images_meta1.html A brief summary of Chinese immigration to Australia.

http://www.abc.net.au/federation/fedstory/ep2/ ep2_culture.htm *The Chinese and the New Gold Mountain* [Australia]. An exploration of early Chinese immigration from the Australian Broadcasting Corporation.

http://immigration.museum.vic.gov.au/Origins/ history.aspx?id=9 *Immigrant Communities in Victoria, Australia*; includes overview and photo gallery.

http://www.mccunn.com Ruthanne Lum McCunn's site provides additional information on her books.

Film

http://www.cctv.com/video/documenta- ry/2006/08/documentary_128_20060816_2. shtml Boy Students, *from the Chinese broadcaster CCTV, is about the boys at the China Education Mission in Hartford, Connecticut.*

■ **A CLOSER LOOK**

Li Hongzhang: Reformer and Diplomat

Li Hongzhang (1823–1901) was a central figure in China's Self-Strengthening Movement and foreign policy in the late nineteenth century. He was born in Anhui Province near the capital city of Hefei, and at the young age of twenty-four, passed the highest level civil service examination, the *jinshi*. Li gained notice and promotions for his military and administrative abilities leading forces against the Taiping, Nian, and Tianjin rebellions (see Chapter 5). He worked tirelessly to quell aggression against the Qing dynasty, as well as against foreigners. His military successes were due to a well-paid and loyal army, but also to foreign-made arms and patrol boats, which he used after witnessing their effectiveness. By the early 1870s, Li had been promoted to the grand council of the empire and was appointed the superintendent of trade, a position that put him in regular contact with the international community. In this role, Li effectively led Chinese foreign policy.

With his experience using Western technology in battle and negotiating treaties with foreign countries, Li Hongzhang became an early and staunch supporter of strengthening the empire. He ardently supported the use, and later the construction, of Western artillery, as well as efforts to bring Western education to China, including the China Education Mission begun by Yung Wing.

Li Hongzhang continued to play an important role in Chinese foreign relations, traveling to the United States to advocate for more lenient immigration laws following the Chinese Exclusion Act in 1882. Li died only months after signing the treaty ending the Boxer Uprising and negotiating the withdrawal of foreign troops from Beijing in 1901 (see Chapter 7, Document 7.2).

■ *Discuss why the Qing government depended on Li's military and diplomatic skills so often. What appear to have been his strengths?*

■ **A CLOSER LOOK**

Empress Cixi: The Power Behind the Throne

Cixi was born in 1835 to a low-ranking Manchu government official. She moved to Beijing during her childhood and was offered to the Xianfeng emperor as a concubine when she was fifteen years old. Chosen from a group of sixty young girls, Cixi entered the Forbidden City as a low-ranking concubine with little power, but when she gave birth to the only male offspring of the Xianfeng emperor in 1856, Cixi quickly moved up the ranks among the most favored women, second only to the emperor's mother.

When the Xianfeng emperor died, his heir apparent was only five years old, which left the leadership of the country in turmoil. Cixi, an intelligent, realistic, and energetic woman, knew well how the court operated. Through a series of plots, alliances, and executions Cixi positioned herself as the de facto ruler of China as empress dowager for her son, the Tongzhi emperor, and later her nephew, the Guangxu emperor. She was the power behind the throne for forty-seven years, from 1861 to her death in 1908.

During most of her reign, the empress made conservative decisions, fighting to maintain the traditional Confucian system of government that she had manipulated to put her in power and keep her there, and resisting the incursion of foreign manufacturers and ideas into China. But at times Cixi made non-traditional choices, such as the handing over of military leadership against the Taiping to Han Chinese generals rather than to Manchu generals traditionally favored by the Manchu Qing dynasty.

Among Empress Cixi's most questionable decisions was her use of the budget intended for the Imperial Navy to renovate the Summer Palace, including having a marble boat built, which never floated. Harshly criticized, Cixi continued to make decisions that would maintain both her power in the government and the splendor she associated with her station.

In the end, the Empress Cixi is generally blamed for contributing to the fall of the Qing dynasty and the imperial system in China because of her self-serving motives and poor decisions. She died three years before the Republican Revolution of 1911.

■ *Read more about Empress Cixi and then discuss: In what ways did she benefit China? What decisions did she make that give credence to historians' generally negative portrayal of her?*

CHAPTER 7

The End of Imperial Rule

By Jamie Moore

Chapter Contents

The Rise of Japan
The "Hundred Days Reform"
The Boxer Uprising
Qing Reforms
The Revolution of 1911

Organizing Idea

China's humiliating defeat by Japan in 1895 precipitated reforms and violence. Ultimately, a combination of internal and external pressures such as land shortages, famine, and high population; foreign encroachment on Chinese territory; and an increasing sense of nationalism brought an end to two thousand years of dynastic rule, paving the way for a new period in Chinese history.

Key Questions

What factors led to the Boxer Uprising? What effects did the uprising have?

What were the goals of the revolutionaries? How did they become more radical over time?

What role did foreign pressure (Western and Japanese) play in the demise of the Qing dynasty?

What factors led to the fall of dynastic China?

How did Sun Yat-sen symbolize a new direction for China? How is he portrayed in China today?

Key Terms

abdication	Manchu
Boxer Uprising	Manchuria
censorate	mausoleum
feudal Japan	Meiji Restoration
imperial power	reparation
industrialized	tributary relationship

Essay

By the end of the nineteenth century, the Qing (清) dynasty was crumbling. In addition to growing territorial pressures from European powers, China had to contend with an increasingly strong Japan, which had imperialistic dreams of its own.

The Rise of Japan

While both Japan and China had come under political and economic pressure from the West in the middle of the nineteenth century, the two countries had responded differently. In 1868, Japan had begun a tremendous transformation known as the Meiji ("Enlightened Rule") Restoration. From 1868 to 1912, Japan built a powerful militarized and industrialized nation that not only resisted Western pressure but competed with the West in empire-building.

In the latter part of the nineteenth century, Japan began to encroach on countries that had a long-standing tributary relationship with China. First, in 1879, Japan annexed the Liuqi Islands.[1] Fifteen years later a rebellion broke out in Korea, and China intervened, sending reinforcements in support of Korea's Joseon dynasty. The Japanese sank one of the ships carrying Chinese soldiers to Korea, and war broke out between China and Japan. The Sino-Japanese War was a disaster for China, quickly demonstrating Japan's new military strength. Now Japan concluded its own "unequal treaty" with China. (See Chapter 5 for the initial series of unequal treaties.) In the 1895 Treaty of Shimonoseki (《马关条约》), China was forced to give up Taiwan to the Japanese and to open four more cities to Japanese trade, including Chongqing (重庆) far up the Yangzi River (长江). China also agreed to recognize "the independence of Korea." (In reality, however, Korea became a Japanese colony.) The Chinese had to allow the Japanese to build factories in their Chinese ports and to pay the Japanese reparations of 200 million *taels* (两) of silver.[2] China's defeat at the hands of the country that had once looked up to them as the source of civilization was profoundly humiliating to China's educated populace.

In 1905, Japan further demonstrated its strength to the rest of the world by winning a war against Russia. For the first time, the "yellow man" had beaten the white man, and fear of the "yellow peril" began to spread in the West. Distrust and racism targeting the Chinese in the United States had begun in the middle of the century and led to the Chinese Exclusion Act of 1882, which limited the number of Chinese eligible to immigrate. In Australia, the Immigration Restriction Act of 1901 achieved similar ends. Japan's climb to power only increased the West's anxiety over the rise of Asian power and further exacerbated discrimination against individuals of Chinese heritage. Yet at the same time, the strength of an Asian nation was inspiring to progressive Chinese.

The "Hundred Days Reforms"

By the end of the nineteenth century, China was a country of sharp contrasts. Evidence of modernization and industry could be found along the coast, where contact with the outside world was the strongest, but not inland. The Qing bureaucracy and the vast majority of Chinese were still firmly rooted in tradition and age-old practices. When Western powers increased their claims in China, this only heightened fears among the Chinese. Some, though, recognized that change needed to occur in China if the country were to survive and keep its independence. Among them was the relatively young emperor Guangxu (光绪). In late 1898, he issued a number of edicts, which

---

[1] In Japan, the Liuqi Islands are known as the Ryukyu Islands.

[2] A *tael* is approximately one ounce of silver, or about 37 grams.

became known as the Hundred Days Reforms (百日维新). He insisted on changes in education and economic development. He ordered the rebuilding of the navy and training of militias, and he mandated that the bureaucracy be made more efficient. His aunt, the empress dowager Cixi, promptly quashed his efforts. She placed the emperor under "house arrest" (in the Forbidden City) and executed many of his key advisors.

The Boxer Uprising

Meanwhile, outside of Beijing (北京), calls for change took a different form. In the late 1800s and early 1900s many secret societies had formed in China, continuing a long historical tradition of rural anti-government protest (see A Closer Look at the end of Chapter 3). During this period, however, the secret societies also opposed the increasing presence of Western missionaries. The Boxers United in Righteousness (义和拳) emerged in Shandong Province in 1898. As did past secret societies, they practiced martial arts (giving them the name "Boxers"), used magic to ward off evil, and took oaths. Some believed they had special powers that could even protect them from bullets. The group appealed mostly to landless young peasants, as well as boatmen, former soldiers, and vagrants whose lives had been devastated by famine or poverty. Young women also joined the Boxers, including a group called the Shining Red Lanterns (红灯照). The Boxers blamed the problems of society on foreigners and Chinese Christian converts. Initially, they destroyed their property. Then in June of 1900, violence escalated when Boxers killed foreigners and Chinese Christians in Tianjin (天津), Beijing, and other cities. The empress dowager Cixi at first wavered in her support of the Boxers, then publicly backed them. Alarmed, foreign nations (including Japan, Russia, Great Britain and the United States) raised a force of 20,000 soldiers and began in August of 1900 to subdue the uprising that was holding many of their citizens under siege. The foreign powers insisted that China execute Boxer supporters and pay staggering reparations: 450 million *taels* of silver.[3] Among other concessions, China was to cancel civil service exams for five years in cities where foreigners had died.

Qing Reforms

Finally, following humiliation after humiliation, Qing rulers of the early 1900s seemed ready for reform. In 1905, they sent delegates to five Western countries to study their governments, and they ended the centuries-old examination system. In 1908, the empress dowager Cixi stated that a full constitutional government would be incorporated in China within nine years. The Qing also worked to modernize schools and restructure and centralize the army. Unfortunately for the Qing, many forward-thinking Chinese considered this too little, too late.

Revolution of 1911

The Boxer Uprising, foreign encroachment throughout China, and other problems such as high taxes (issued to pay for new reforms and reparations) and catastrophic flooding led people to call for the end of Manchu rule.[4] Fear of being carved up by the West and anger at the government's ineffectiveness spurred a growing sense of nationalism. Chinese students who had studied abroad and experienced Western and Japanese industrialized, modern societies led the drive to overthrow the Qing dynasty.

The most famous of the revolutionaries was Dr. Sun Yat-sen (孙逸仙) (1866–1925), who came to be the leader of the Revolutionary Alliance (同盟会) in the early 1900s. The goal of Sun Yat-sen and his followers was to expel the Manchus, restore China to the Chinese, and establish a republic. They met in secret, raised funds from expatriates, and, most importantly, gained support in the army and among provincial leaders. (See A Closer Look at the end of the chapter for further information on Sun Yat-sen.)

In November 1908, the empress dowager Cixi died. A day earlier, in a suspicious coincidence, so had the (imprisoned) Guangxu emperor. Puyi (溥仪)—a toddler—was named emperor and Manchu regents as his "advisors." In October of 1911, an accidental bomb explosion sparked the revolution. Within weeks, many of the provinces joined the uprising. The Qing called on Yuan Shikai (袁世凯)—leader of a powerful North China army and a general in the Qing military—to put down the rebellion. He, however, worked both sides, negotiating the best position for himself. On December 25, 1911, Sun Yat-sen, who had been gathering support for the revolution overseas, returned to China to be named provisional president of the Republic. In February 1912 the Qing court abdicated, and two thousand years of dynastic rule ended. A new age for China began.

---

[3] This represented more than twice the government's total annual revenue.

[4] The Manchus, a foreign people from what are now Liaoning, Heilongjiang, and Jilin provinces, had invaded Ming dynasty China in the early 1600s and in 1644 established the Qing dynasty. See Chapter 3.

Primary Sources

DOCUMENT 7.1: **Painting of Treaty of Shimonoseki negotiations**

Japanese and Chinese officials negotiate the treaty at Shimonoseki in 1895 to end the Sino-Japanese War.

DOCUMENT 7.2: **Excerpts from "Li Hongzhang Negotiates with Japan, 1895"**

H.E[5]. LI. And if I sign this gruesome Treaty I am certain to bring down another avalanche of curses on my head. Think of it!... The Chinese in [Taiwan] are unwilling to remove and are equally unwilling to sell their property. If hereafter Proclamations are issued requiring them to do so and they revolt, the Chinese Government cannot be held responsible.

H.E. ITO. My Government will assume all future responsibility.

H.E. LI. I have received a telegram from the Governor of [Taiwan] stating that the [Taiwanese] have revolted and swear that they will not be subject to Japan.

H.E. ITO. Let them revolt. We can manage that.

H.E. LI. This is not said to alarm you. I am telling you the truth out of good-will.

H.E. ITO. I have heard of it.

H.E. LI. If the [Taiwanese] kill the officials and band together to resist, you must not blame me.

H.E. ITO. Let China transfer the sovereignty to us and the whole responsibility will be assumed by the Japanese Government... Our intention is to send troops and officials to take [Taiwan] over within a few weeks after the Treaty has been ratified.

---

[5] H.E. stands for His Excellency.

H.E. LI. Someone can be appointed to consult with the Governor of [Taiwan] about all matters pertaining to the transfer.

H.E. ITO. As soon as ratifications have been exchanged the Chinese officials should proclaim the transfer to the [Taiwanese] and we will send troops and officers to take charge...

H.E. LI. One month is rushing the matter. The Zongli Yamen[6] and myself are too far removed from [Taiwan] to know the actual situation there. It would be much better for China to delegate the Governor of [Taiwan] to arrange with the Japanese Governor on the spot what the conditions of transfer shall be. Then, the Treaty having been exchanged we shall be on friendly terms and arrangements can readily be made.

H.E. ITO. One month is sufficient.

SOURCE: Rpt. in Pei-kai Cheng, Michael Lestz, and Jonathan Spence, eds., *The Search for Modern China: A Documentary Collection* (New York: W.W. Norton , 1999), 173–174.

 The full text of **Document 7.2** is available on the CD-ROM.

DOCUMENT 7.3: Excerpts describing Emperor Guangxu and his 1898 reforms

The *Peking[7] Gazette* continued to come daily, bringing with it the following twenty-seven decrees in a little more than twice that many days. I will give an epitome of the decrees so that the reader at a glance may see what the emperor undertook to do. Summarized, they are as follows:

1. The establishment of a university at Beijing.
2. The sending of imperial clansmen to foreign countries to study the forms and conditions of European and American government.
3. The encouragement of the arts, sciences and modern agriculture.
4. The emperor expressed himself as willing to hear the objections of the conservatives to progress and reform.
5. Abolished the literary essay as a prominent part of the governmental [civil service] examinations...
12. Special rewards were offered to inventors and authors.
13. The officials were ordered to encourage trade and assist merchants.
14. School boards were ordered established in every city in the empire.
15. Bureaus of Mines and Railroads were established.
16. Journalists were encouraged to write on all political subjects.
17. Naval academies and training-ships were ordered.

SOURCE: Isaac Taylor Headland, *Court Life in China: The Capital, its Officials and People* (New York: Fleming H. Revell, 1909). 137–139.

 The full text of **Document 7.3** is available on the CD-ROM.

---

[6] Chinese bureau that managed foreign affairs; see Chapter 6.

[7] Former name for Beijing

DOCUMENT 7.4: Excerpts describing the activities of the "Boxers" during the uprising, by Fei Qihao, 1900

As we traveled, the young soldier who had taken my horse away walked close behind my cart, never taking his eyes off me. I thought that he was angry because I had objected to giving him the horse, so I gave little attention to it. Then I noticed something strange in his way of looking at me, as if there was something he wished to say to me. After we had gone on a little farther with the soldier walking behind the cart, still keeping his eyes on me, he heaved a great sigh, and said: "Alas for you—so very young!"

The soldier walking at the side looked sternly at the speaker and said something to him, which I could not hear, but I heard the reply: "This is our own countryman, and not a foreigner." When I saw the expression on their faces and heard these words, suddenly it flashed across me that they had some deep meaning, and I asked the young soldier what was up.

"I don't know," he replied.

"If anything is going to happen," I said, "please tell me."

He hung his head and said nothing, but followed still close to the cart, and after a while said to me plainly: "You ought to escape at once, for only a short distance ahead we are to kill the foreigners."

SOURCE: Fei Ch'i-hao, *Two Heroes of Cathay*, ed. Luella Miner (New York: Fleming H. Revell, 1903) 63–128.

 The full text of **Document 7.4** is available on the CD-ROM.

DOCUMENT 7.5: Excerpts from a letter written by missionary Nellie N. Russel to relatives in Chicago, describing the Boxer Uprising, 1900

That afternoon about 4 o'clock the first attack on us here was made, and the bullets fell like rain for a few moments. Just before we came here, very early one morning, Mr. Ament went in around the back way to our place and the sight made him sick. The houses, two churches, printing office, school buildings, all were in ruins. Most of the brick walls had been carried away, and not enough wood was left in the place to make a toothpick he said.... We heard from the Chinese officials of the taking of the forts at Tianjin, but we did not believe it, for it did not seem possible such a thing would be done with the ministers shut in the enemy's country—and that a heathen one—with no possible way out. The day after we came in here the custom-houses were fired and the Austrian legation was abandoned. The Boxers, flourishing knives, approached the legation, and the machine guns were turned on them, killing and wounding sixty. This only drove them away for the time. They started fires all about us. The next few days we had to fight fire. We ladies formed in line and passed back the pails and other receptacles for water. Such an olio of articles for fighting fire and for one's life—pitchers, large and small, wash bowls of all sizes, pails, tin cans, flower pots, etc. The Chinese seemed determined to burn us out, and it was not till all about us was either burnt by them, or by us as a protection, that they gave up that time.

SOURCE: Qtd. in J. Martin Miller, *China, the Yellow Peril: At War With the World* (Chicago: Monarch Book Co., 1900) 423–424.

 The full text of **Document 7.5** is available on the CD-ROM.

DOCUMENT 7.6: Interviews with individuals recalling the Shining Red Lanterns movement

3. [The town of] Fenglou had the Shining Red Lantern. All the Shining Red Lanterns were women who dressed up completely in red. They waved red fans and carried red lanterns and they could get wind or rain or ride the clouds and call in the mist. Two women facing each other would wave their fans and while waving them would ascend into the sky. That was the kind of thing they did…I used to go to watch the hustle and bustle…

—*Interview with Zhang Yuqi, age 82, Ma Village, Sanlitun Commune, Renping County, January 1966.*

5. Girls who joined the Boxers were called "Shining Red Lanterns." They dressed all in red. In one hand they had a little red lantern and in the other a little red fan. They carried a basket in the crook of their arm. When bullets were shot at them they waved their fans and the bullets were caught in the basket. You couldn't hit them! Some were also possessed by spirits and would say that they were Ma Guiying or Hu Jinchan [famous women warriors who were often portrayed in popular dramas in North China].

—*Interview with Zhu Yunze, age 82, Zhu village, Yeguantun Commune, Renping County, December 1965.*

SOURCE: Pei-kai Cheng, Michael Lestz, and Jonathan Spence, eds., *The Search for Modern China: A Documentary Collection* (New York: W.W. Norton, 1999) 185–186.

 The full text of **Document 7.6** is available on the CD-ROM.

DOCUMENT 7.7a: Excerpts from the preface to *China the Yellow Peril: At War With the World* by J. Martin Miller, 1900

Never before has one nation of the world stood against allied civilization as China has stood against Europe and America in the unique contest [the Boxer Uprising]—military, diplomatic and commercial—which is here related…

In a prolonged journey through the Chinese Empire in 1899, the author gathered the historical and descriptive matter which comprise the chapters devoted to those phases of the subject, as well as many of the photographs, which appear as illustrations…. Careful study has been made of the works of the best authors, English, German, French, and American, with assurance that the best book is the one that seeks the best sources for its complete information. The resulting work is here presented with the hope and belief that it will prove of service to its readers.

SOURCE: J. Martin Miller, *China, the Yellow Peril: At War With the World* (Monarch Book Co., 1900). 9–10.

 The full text of **Document 7.7** is available on the CD-ROM.

DOCUMENT 7.8: Excerpts from "The Yellow Peril," an essay by Jack London, 1904

The menace to the Western world lies, not in the little brown man, but in the four hundred millions of yellow men should the little brown man undertake their management. The Chinese is not dead to new ideas; he is an efficient worker; makes a good soldier, and is wealthy in the essential materials of a machine change. Under a capable management he will go far. The Japanese is prepared and fit to undertake this management. Not only has he proved himself an apt imitator of Western material progress, a sturdy worker, and a capable organizer, but he is far more fit to manage the Chinese than we are. The baffling enigma of the Chinese character is no baffling enigma to him. He understands as we could never school ourselves nor hope to understand. Their mental processes are largely the same. He thinks with the same thought-symbols as does the Chinese, and he thinks in the same peculiar grooves. He goes on where we are balked by the obstacles of incomprehension. He takes the turning, which we cannot perceive, twists around the obstacle, and, presto! is out of sight in the ramifications of the Chinese mind where we cannot follow.

SOURCE: Jack London, "The Yellow Peril" (1904). Rpt. in *Major Problems in Asian American History*, Lon Kurashige and Alice Yang Murray, eds. (Boston: Houghton Mifflin Co., 2003) 182.

 The full text of **Document 7.8** is available on the CD-ROM.

DOCUMENT 7.9: Excerpts from Sun Yat-sen's Reform Proposal, 1893

I have always felt that the real reason for Europe's wealth and power lies less in the superiority of its military might than in the fact that in Europe every man can fully develop his talent, land resources are totally utilized, each object functions to its maximum capacity, and every item of merchandize [*sic*] circulates freely...these four items are the most basic if our nation is to become wealthy, strong, and well governed. For our nation to ignore these four items while concerning itself exclusively with ships and guns is to seek the insignificant at the expense of the basic...

It has been thirty years since we began to imitate the West. We have language schools, as well as military and naval academies, to train specialists in Western affairs. We have mining and textile enterprises to open up financial resources. We have steamship and railroad companies to facilitate transportation. Yet we still lag behind Europe in overall achievement. Why? The reason is that we have not, really, embarked upon the completion of the four tasks, as described above, on a nationwide basis.

When we do, given China's human and natural resources, we should be able to overtake Europe in twenty years.

SOURCE: Pei-kai Cheng, Michael Lestz, and Jonathan Spence, eds., *The Search for Modern China: A Documentary Collection* (New York: W.W. Norton, 1999) 169–171.

DOCUMENT 7.10: Excerpts from a revolutionary proclamation published by the *Zhonghua Tongmeng Hui* (Chinese Alliance Association), 1907

A PUBLIC DECLARATION

Since the beginning of China as a nation, we Chinese have governed our own country despite occasional interruptions. When China was occasionally occupied by a foreign race, our ancestors could always in the end drive these foreigners out, restore the fatherland, and preserve China for future generations of Chinese. Today when we raise the righteous standard of revolt in order to expel an alien race that has been occupying China, we are doing no more than our ancestors have done or expected us to do. Justice is so much on our side that all Chinese, once familiarizing themselves with our stand, will have no doubt about the righteousness of our cause....

We...strive not only to expel the ruling aliens and thus restore China to the Chinese but also to change basically the political and economic structure of our country. While we cannot describe in detail this new political and economic structure since so much is involved, the basic principal behind it is liberty, equality, and fraternity. The revolutions of yesterday were revolutions by and for the heroes; our revolution, on the other hand, is a revolution by and for the people....

At this juncture we wish to express candidly and fully how to make our revolution today and how to govern our country tomorrow.

1. *Expulsion of the Manchus from China.* The Manchus of today were known as the Eastern Barbarians *Dong Hu* during bygone years. Toward the end of the Ming dynasty they repeatedly invaded our border areas and caused great difficulties. Then, taking advantage of the chaotic situation in China, they marched southward and forcibly occupied our country. They compelled all Chinese to become their slaves, and those who did not wish to subjugate themselves were slaughtered, numbering millions. In fact, we Chinese have not had a country for the past two hundred and sixty years. Now that the day has finally arrived when the brutal and evil rule by the Manchus must come to an end, we do not expect much resistance when our righteous army begins to move. We shall quickly overthrow the Manchu government so as to restore the sovereignty of China to the Chinese....

2. *Restoration of China to the Chinese.* China belongs to the Chinese who have the right to govern themselves. After the Manchus are expelled from China, we will have a national government of our own....

3. *Establishment of a Republic.* Since one of the principles of our revolution is equality, we intend to establish a republic when we succeed in overthrowing the Manchu regime. In a republic all citizens will have the right to participate in the government, the president of the republic will be elected by the people, and the parliament will have deputies elected by and responsible to their respective constituents.

A constitution of the Chinese Republic will then be formulated, to be observed by all Chinese. Anyone who entertains the thought of becoming an emperor will be crushed without mercy.

4. *Equalization of landownership.* The social and economic structure of China must be so reconstructed that the fruits of labor will be shared by all Chinese on an equal basis....

To attain the four goals as outlined above, we propose a procedure of three stages. The first stage is that of a military rule.... [D]uring the first stage, the Military Government, in cooperation with the people, will eradicate all the abuses of the past; with the arrival of the second stage the Military Government will hand over local administration to the people while reserving for itself the right of jurisdiction over all matters that concern the nation as a whole; during the third or final stage the Military Government will cease to exist and all governmental power will be invested in organs as prescribed in a national constitution. This orderly procedure is necessary because our people need time to acquaint themselves with the idea of liberty and equality. Liberty and equality are the basis on which the Republic of China rests....

The brilliant achievements of China have been known throughout the world, and only recently has she suffered numerous difficulties. We shall overcome these difficulties and march forward....

SOURCE: Pei-kai Cheng, Michael Lestz, and Jonathan Spence, eds., *The Search for Modern China: A Documentary Collection* (New York: W.W. Norton, 1999) 202–205.

DOCUMENT 7.11: Excerpts from "The Revolutionary Army" by Zou Rong, 1903

I offer to my most revered and beloved 400 million countrymen of the great Han people to prepare them for the path they are to follow:

- China is the China of the Chinese. Countrymen, you must all recognize the China of the Chinese of the Han race.
- Not to allow any alien race to lay their hands on the least rights of our China...
- To set up a central government, which will act as a general body to run affairs.
- In each area and province a deputy to a general assembly is to be elected by vote in public elections. From these deputies, one is to be elected by vote to serve as provisional president to represent the whole country A vice-president is also to be elected, and all *zhou* [prefectures] and *xian* [counties] are to elect a number of deputies.
- The whole population, whether male or female, are citizens.
- All men have the duty to serve as citizen-soldiers.
- Everybody has the duty of bearing the burden of taxation.

SOURCE: John Lust, trans., *The Revolutionary Army: A Chinese Nationalist Tract of 1903* (Paris: Mouton, 1968).

 The full text of **Document 7.11** is available on the CD-ROM.

DOCUMENT 7.12: Photograph of Sun Yat-sen's mausoleum, Nanjing, 2006

The mausoleum was built just outside Nanjing by the Guomindang government in 1926 to honor Sun Yat-sen. Nanjing, at that time, was the capital of China. The stairway is 323 meters long and 70 meters wide. One of the signs in English reads: "The map of the whole mausoleum looks like an alarm bell, which symbolizes the neverending struggling spirit of Dr. Sun Yat-sen and his devotion of himself to the cause of waking up the masses and saving the Chinese nation and state." The site continues to be visited by tens of thousands of people every year. This photograph was taken on a weekday in May.
(Photo by Liz Nelson)

DOCUMENT 7.13: Sign describing Sun Yat-sen, 2006

(Photo by Liz Nelson)

DOCUMENT 7.14: Excerpts from Emperor Puyi's abdication, 1912

The Whole Country is tending towards a republican form of government. It is the Will of Heaven, and it is certain that we could not reject the people's desire for the sake of one family's honor and glory.

We and His Majesty the Emperor hand over the sovereignty to the people. We decide the form of government to be a constitutional republic.

In this time of transition, in order to unite the South and the North, We appoint Yuan Shikai to organize a provisional government, consulting the people's army regarding the union of the five peoples, Manchus, Chinese, Mongolians, Mohammedans [Muslims], and Tibetans with their territories. These peoples jointly constitute the one great Republic of China.

We and His Majesty the Emperor will retire to a peaceful life and will enjoy the respectful treatment of the nation.

This was signed by the emperor, by Yuan Shikai as prime minister, and also by the other ministers.

SOURCE: Eva March Tappan, ed., *China, Japan, and the Islands of the Pacific*, The World's Story: A History of the World in Story, Song, and Art, vol. 1 (Boston: Houghton Mifflin, 1914) 261.

Activities:

ACTIVITY 1: Overview of the Manchu decline

Review events from earlier in the nineteenth century (see Chapters 4–6), and read the introductory essay. Discuss:

1. What was going wrong for the Manchus?
2. How was the population changing, and what effect might this have had? (See Suggested Resources for additional information on China's demographics.)
3. What role did modernity play in the demise of the dynasty?
4. What were the effects of foreign encroachment? How did the Manchu government respond? What might they have done differently?

ACTIVITY 2: Examining the results of the Sino-Japanese War, 1895

Look at the painting of the negotiations (7.1) and write down everything you notice.

1. Who is depicted in the painting?
2. What differences in posture and dress can you see?
3. From looking at this painting, what can you infer about each side and the negotiations?

Read the transcript of negotiations between the Chinese delegate Li Hongzhang and the Japanese delegate Ito Hirobumi at Shimonoseki (7.2).

1. What tone does each delegate take with the other?
2. What is each side trying to convey?
3. Who has the upper hand, and why?

Discuss the final treaty and its cost to China.

1. How do you think the Chinese intelligentsia felt?
2. How were the Chinese perceived by the rest of the world?
3. How does the tone of the negotiations compare to the painting?

ACTIVITY 3: Analyzing the effects of imperialism in China

View the map "Imperialism in the Nineteenth Century" (Item 7.A). Remember that in the eighteenth century, China had strongly resisted foreign influence. Examine all the places where Western powers had influence in and around China.

Discuss:

1. How did Western powers gain influence in China?
2. What areas did they control and why?
3. What does this tell us about the Qing dynasty in the nineteenth century?
4. How does this compare to the Qing dynasty of the eighteenth century? (See Chapter 4.)
5. Compare the Qing territorial expansion of the seventeenth century with the growing foreign influence of the nineteenth century. (See Chapter 3 and Item 3.B.) What conclusions can you draw?
6. If this map of the late nineteenth century were shown to a Chinese citizen of the time, how might he or she feel? (Remember that many educated Chinese people were aware of what had happened to India and countries in Africa at the hands of imperialists.)

ACTIVITY 4: Analyzing and promoting Emperor Guangxu's reforms

Examine the emperor's proposals for change (7.3). In small groups, discuss:

1. What subjects did the emperor's reforms include?
2. What problems did these proposed reforms appear to address?
3. Based on the proposed reforms, what did Emperor Guangxu see as the role of government?
4. Would it be possible to do all that he proposed? What would it have taken to accomplish his goals? What countries have undertaken and succeeded at such wide-ranging reforms?
5. Which, if any, government departments or ministries in your country address these subjects?

Creative extension:

Design a poster promoting Emperor Guangxu's reforms.

ACTIVITY 5: Exploring the Boxer Uprising

Work in a small group on one of the documents related to the Boxer Uprising (7.4–7.6). After reading it carefully, discuss in your group:

1. Who created or wrote the text, and for what purpose?
2. How does this affect the content of the document?
3. Extract at least six key pieces of information from the document.
4. How does this document further inform us about the Boxer Uprising?
5. Was religion the issue? If so, in what way? If not, what was at the heart of the violence?

Form groups of three in which each member has read a different document. Share with each other the information you extracted from your primary source. As a class, compare the Boxer Uprising to other episodes of significant social unrest about which you have learned.

1. How was the Boxer Uprising similar to and different from other social unrest?

2. How was the way the uprising was put down similar to or different from the ways that other episodes of social unrest ended in other parts of the world?

3. What conclusions can you draw from the comparisons?

4. How might the Boxer Uprising be used by the government to promote nationalism?

5. How does the Boxer Uprising compare to anti-religious violence that erupted in China later in the twentieth century?

ACTIVITY 5: The rise of the "Yellow Peril"

Read the preface to J. Martin Miller's book *China the Yellow Peril: At War With the World* and examine several photographs he included in his book (7.7a–d on the CD-ROM). Discuss:

1. What ideas are included in the choice of words in the title? What does the title lead you to expect?

2. What does Miller say was his purpose in writing this book?

3. How did he go about writing it? Was it a reasonable way to approach the writing of a country's history? Why or why not?

4. What responses do the photos evoke now? What responses do you think they were likely to evoke in 1900? Why do you think Miller chose to include them?

5. How might a book such as this affect people's opinions and views of China, Asia, and/or Chinese Americans?

Read and discuss the excerpts from Jack London's essay "The Yellow Peril" (7.8).

1. What is the significance of the title?

2. What is most striking about this essay?

3. How does London describe the Chinese? The Japanese? The West? Make a three-column list on the board with examples of each.

4. What does London see as the connection between the Chinese and Japanese?

5. Why does London not fear the "Brown Peril"?

6. When did the "Yellow Peril" become a concern for Westerners? Why?

7. Writing in 1904, what did London see as the future? Were his predictions accurate? In what way?

After reading both excerpts, what do you think was the source of Western fears?

ACTIVITY 6: A Debate: Toward Revolution

Divide into three groups, so that each group looks at one of the three revolutionary documents (7.9–7.11) either as homework or in class. Examine the document from a number of perspectives:

1. Who is the author? To whom is he writing? Does this piece of writing follow any specific event in China's history?
2. What overall goals does the author propose?
3. What method or methods does he suggest to achieve the goals?
4. What is the tone of the piece of writing?
5. How does the proposal for change compare to the reforms proposed by Emperor Guangxu in 1898 (7.3)? Why didn't the author(s) of the work consider reforms such as these instead?

Use books or online sources to learn more about each revolutionary. Prepare notes and brief quotes or examples from the document so that you can successfully present your author's ideas and goals in a debate.

ACTIVITY 7: Examining the legacy of Sun Yat-sen

Read about Sun Yat-sen in the introductory essay and A Closer Look at the end of the chapter. Examine the photographs of his mausoleum (7.12) and the sign describing Sun Yat-sen (7.13). Discuss:

1. Why would the Guomindang government have decided to build this for Sun Yat-sen? Compare the layout to other important historic sites in China, such as the Temple of Heaven in Beijing and the Monument to Martyrs in Nanjing.
2. Why do you think he was so widely admired over other revolutionaries?
3. When you read the sign, pay attention to the language used. What did the Chinese government want people to think about Sun Yat-sen?
4. What can you conclude from the fact that both the Guomindang government and the Chinese Communist Party claim Sun Yat-sen as the father of the nation? (See Chapter 9 for more information.)

ACTIVITY 8: Manchu abdication

The Qing dynasty ended in 1911. Read the Manchu abdication edict as a class (7.14). Discuss:

1. What do you notice about the edict?
2. What language is used? What is the tone?
3. What was the role of Yuan Shikai in the revolution?
4. What role is the emperor hoping for in the future? Do you think that this will happen? Why or why not?

Watch part of the film *The Last Emperor* up to the Japanese invasion. What do you learn about life within the confines of the Forbidden City? How does the life of the Qing leaders compare with that of leaders in other countries around the world in the same time period?

ACTIVITY 9: Reflection: The end of the imperial era

As a class, brainstorm based on classwork and readings: Why did the Qing dynasty fall? List the possible reasons where everyone can see them. When finished, pick one or two reasons that the majority agree were the most significant. Discuss why these reasons were so important.

In groups or individually, research revolutions in other countries in the world (e.g. the United States, France, or countries in Africa, South America, or Central America). Each group will have a different country. Address:

1. What happened in your country?

2. What factors caused the people to revolt? Was there a final straw, or was it a culmination of events?

3. How does this revolution compare to the 1911 revolution in China?

Each group will present its findings, and this can lead to a discussion about revolution in general and the forces that guide it.

Suggested Resources

Book

Aisin-Gioro, Pu Yi. *From Emperor to Citizen.* Beijing: Foreign Languages Press, 1989. *The autobiography of the last Qing emperor, who came to the throne as a toddler.*

Websites

http://afe.easia.columbia.edu Columbia University's *Asia for Educators* site has great maps and information on each dynasty.

http://afe.easia.columbia.edu/china/geog/population.htm *Asia for Educators* also has an introduction to population growth and challenges.

http://ocw.mit.edu/ans7870/21f/21f.027j/yellow_promise_yellow_peril/yp_core_04.html A great site constructed by John W. Dower of MIT; focuses on Western perceptions of Japan but has excellent images and information on the Yellow Peril in general.

Boxer Uprising

http://www.fordham.edu/halsall/eastasia/eastasiasbook.html The *East Asian History Sourcebook* site from Paul Halsall at Fordham University includes additional first-hand accounts.

http://www.travelchinaguide.com/intro/history/qing.htm This Chinese site provides concise information on the rise and decline of the Qing, written from the government-approved perspective.

http://www.wsu.edu/~dee/MODCHINA/MODCHINA.HTM Richard Hooker's *Modern China* site from Washington State University provides information on reforms, revolution, and Sun Yat-sen.

Film

The Last Emperor (162 mins; 1987) *The film poignantly captures the anachronism of a child-emperor coming to power in China in the early twentieth century and the subsequent political turmoil. Directed by Bernardo Bertolucci.*

■ **A CLOSER LOOK**

Dr. Sun Yat-sen: Father of the Nation

Sun Yat-sen was born in 1866 to a poor rural family near Guangzhou (formerly Canton). He received his early education in a local village school, but the rest of his schooling took place at assorted educational institutions associated with missionary efforts in Hawaii (where his elder brother had a business), Hong Kong, and Guangzhou. He completed medical school in Hong Kong in 1892. As he experienced more of the industrialized West, he became increasingly involved with revolutionaries, including members of secret societies. Influenced by Western ideas and a nationalistic desire to improve China, he formed an organization called the Revive China Society (*Xingzhonghui*), which eventually had branches in a number of countries. In 1894, he wrote to a high-ranking Qing official explaining his ideas for how China needed to reform and modernize (see 7.9). His ideas were ignored and in 1895, he helped plan an uprising in Guangzhou. The plot was exposed, and Sun Yat-sen fled to Hong Kong and then Japan. Living in exile, he cut his queue and began to wear Western clothes. In 1896, he was briefly arrested in London by Qing authorities but was able to effect a dramatic rescue, which made him internationally famous. For years Sun Yat-sen traveled in Europe, the United States, and Japan, speaking, writing, and raising funds.

By 1905, he had refined his ideas and developed the Three Principles of the People (*Sanmin Zhuyi*): nationalism, democracy, and social welfare. He also organized the Revolutionary Alliance (*Tongmenghui*), whose goal was to overthrow the Qing dynasty and establish a Chinese republic. Sun Yat-sen's message and desire for revolution appealed to many who had studied abroad, as well as women and the poor, who felt marginalized.

Between 1906 and 1911, the Alliance planned several uprisings, all of which failed.

Sun Yat-sen was not in China at the time of the revolution of October 1911, but returned in December to accept the title of Provisional President of the Chinese Republic. Though his tenure as leader was brief, Sun Yat-sen worked until his death trying to promote a unified Republican nation in the face of constant opposition from warlords (see Chapter 9). He died of cancer in early 1925 while he was in Beijing to negotiate with warlord leaders. Despite his many setbacks, the vast majority of Chinese regard Sun Yat-sen as the father of the nation (*Sun Guofu*).

■ *Read more about Dr. Sun's ideas in his essay "Fundamentals of National Reconstruction," available online at http://acc6.its. brooklyn.cuny.edu/ ~phalsall/texts/sunyat.html. Discuss: How was Sun Yat-sen similar to and different from revolutionary leaders in other countries?*

■ **A CLOSER LOOK**

Qiu Jin: Revolutionary Heroine

Today Qiu Jin is considered a heroine for her fight as a revolutionary against Manchu rule in China. She was born in 1875 to a relatively well-to-do family and was one of the few girls in China to receive an education. In 1904, unhappy in the marriage her parents had arranged, Qiu Jin left her husband and two children to study in Japan. Like others who studied abroad, she was struck by Western ideas and modernization. She attended a vocational school, but her passion lay with revolutionary politics and feminist issues. Qiu Jin wrote on both topics, pushing for an overthrow of the Qing as well as for greater equality between men and women, and an end to practices such as foot-binding, female infanticide, and arranged marriages. In 1906, she returned to China, where she taught at a school in Zhejiang Province and founded the *Chinese Women's Journal*. Contemporaries considered Qiu Jin's occasional preference for men's clothing and participation in military drills shocking. She continued her efforts to bring political change to China by working to unite different revolutionary groups to better ensure success. But in 1907, Qing officials captured and executed her for participating in revolutionary activities. After the fall of the dynasty, Qiu Jin became an inspiration for girls all over China. A nationalist and revolutionary, she had the courage to take a stand against the government and a society that oppressed women.

■ *Compare Qiu Jin to female role models in other countries.*

UNIT THREE

Struggles to Create a Unified China

(1911–1949)

UNIT OVERVIEW

By Ryan Bradeen and Liz Nelson

The fledgling Republic of China built from the ashes of the Qing dynasty was soon itself in tatters, with the country split between bickering **warlords** constantly battling for power. While the armies fought, young men and women from all walks of life tried to find solutions to the deep-seated problems that threatened to destroy the country. From this dangerous and unsettled period, the leaders of New China would emerge. The carving of China into independent territories during the Republican period echoed the fragmentation that had followed the end of many previous dynasties[1]. One of the most notable aspects of Chinese history is that during these chaotic periods, peasants and intellectuals alike believed that a politically unified China should be the goal.

In China's earlier periods of disunity, vicious warfare and turmoil created desperate times for the general populace. The rural population suffered from the destruction of crops, the marching of armies back and forth across their lands, the loss of young men pressed into military service, endless taxes, and the disruption of economic activity. Cities were the targets of conquests, and as a result urban residents were often caught in the middle of pitched battles, their homes and business confiscated or destroyed, their families separated. The turmoil of the Republican era was no different; modern weaponry made the conflicts only more deadly and devastating.

Throughout China's history, the downfall of powerful empires and fragmentation of the country into contending regions also had surprising and positive side effects: great outpourings of intellectual activity. In the confusion of periods of disunity, no single philosophy, religion, or ideology was held up by the central government as the official belief system to which the populace should adhere. Therefore, philosophers, scientists, and writers were much

---

[1] At the end of the Tang dynasty (907 C.E.) China was embroiled in fifty-three years of warfare for supremacy. At the end of the Han dynasty (220 C.E.), the empire was divided for more than 300 years. The 254 years that followed the end of the Zhou dynasty are referred to as the "Warring States" period.

TIMELINE (1911–1949)

1910–1945 Japanese colonial rule in Korea

1911–1912 Republican Revolution and the founding of the Republic of China

1912: Guomindang (the National People's Party) formed

1913: United States extends full diplomatic recognition to the Republic of China

1913: 13th Dalai Lama returns to Tibet and assumes temporal and spiritual leadership

1914: World War I breaks out after the assassination of Archduke Franz Ferdinand

1915: Japan issues the Twenty-One Demands

1916–1928: Warlord Period

1917: Russian Revolution

1918–early 1920s: Red Scare in the United States

1918: Armistice between Allies and Germany signed on November 11

1919: Paris Peace Conference concludes with the signing of the Treaty of Versailles

1919: May Fourth Movement begins

1920: League of Nations founded in Paris

1920: Nazi Party formed in Germany

1921: Chinese Communist Party formally organized at First Congress in Shanghai

1922: Soviet Union established

1926: Communists and Guomindang work together in First United Front: Northern Expedition against warlords

1927: Guomindang turn on Communists in Shanghai

1929: World economic crisis follows "Black Friday"; stock exchange collapse in New York

1929: Joseph Stalin, general secretary of the Communist Party of the Soviet Union since 1922, becomes de facto dictator

1930: Indochina Communist Party founded

1931: Mukden (Shenyang) Incident

1932: Franklin Delano Roosevelt sworn in as 32nd president of the United States

1933: Japan withdraws from the League of Nations

1933: Adolf Hitler appointed chancellor of Germany

1934: Puyi becomes emperor of Manchukuo under Japanese auspices

---

freer to explore new intellectual territory.[2] During the first half of the twentieth century, a similar **intellectual vitality** characterized China.

---

[2] During the Warring States period (475–221 B.C.E.), for example, intellectual activity is described with the moniker "One Hundred Schools of Thought," referring to the many philosophers of religion, government, war, and diplomacy who established schools, traveled broadly, and freely debated during this period of chaos. Confucius and several of his most important disciples, the early Daoists, Sun Zi (author of *The Art of War*), and the founders of Legalist thinking all grew out of this vibrant intellectual environment.

Out of the political and military upheaval created by the warlords and the intellectual turmoil resulting from the **May Fourth Movement**, two leaders emerged who would lead China on a path to resurgence: **Mao Zedong** and **Chiang Kai-shek**. Each man would come to the fore of opposing political factions, the **Chinese Communist Party** (CCP) and the **Guomindang**, with competing beliefs about how to unify the nation and heal the deep political and social wounds. Mao was primarily concerned with conditions in rural China, where the vast majority of the population lived. His proposals called for sweeping change—revolution—to overturn the long-standing rural

1934: Soviet Union joins the League of Nations

1934–1935: Long March

1936: Zhang Xueliang and his supporters kidnap Chiang Kai-shek in Xi'an, Second United Front formed

1937: Japan occupies eastern China; Nanjing Massacre

1939: World War II begins: Nazi Germany invades Poland, and France and Britain declare war on Germany

1941: Japan attacks Pearl Harbor; the United States declares war on Japan, Germany, and Italy

1941–1945: Japan occupies Vietnam

1943: Cairo Conference; Chiang Kai-shek and Madame Chiang Kai-shek meet with President Roosevelt and British Prime Minister Winston Churchill

1945: "V-E Day" ends war in Europe

1945: United States drops two atomic bombs on Japan; Japan surrenders August 14

1945–1952: Japan occupied by Allied Powers, chiefly the United States

1945: World Bank founded

1945: Korea liberated from Japanese control but soon divided into zones of occupation by the United States and Soviet Union

1945: Taiwan, under Japanese control since 1895, is returned to China

1945: Ho Chi Minh declares the founding of the Democratic Republic of Vietnam

1946–1954: First Indochina War between France and the Viet Minh

1946: Marshall Mission to China

1946–1949: Civil war in China

1947: New constitution in Japan creates a parliamentary state

1947: India and Pakistan gain independence from Great Britain

1947: Taiwan becomes a separate province of China

1948: Mahatma Gandhi assassinated

1949: India adopts a constitution

1949: On October 1 Mao Zedong declares the founding of the People's Republic of China

1949: Chiang Kai-shek and Guomindang forces flee to Taiwan

social structures and empower the peasants. Chiang, on the other hand, proposed to lead citizens into a reinvigorated Chinese lifestyle rooted in ancient traditions. At times, these two leaders would collaborate, forming "united fronts" against the common enemies. But more often they saw each other as deadly archrivals to be destroyed for the sake of the nation.

By the early 1930s, the power of the warlords had diminished as the Guomindang and the Communists grew into increasingly potent military and political organizations controlling more and more of China's land mass. But the two parties had to contend with a menacing **Japanese Army** that threatened the entire nation with colonialization. One could picture the situation as a boxing match with three contenders in the ring at the same time, each trying to knock out the other two. In 1934, Chiang and his Guomindang forces, determined to eliminate the Communists, drove the CCP out of southeastern China on the legendary **Long March**; the Communists regrouped at Yan'an in Shaanxi Province.[3]

As the Japanese continued to encroach, two of Chiang's generals kidnapped him to try to

---

[3] North central China, in a region north of the city of Xi'an.

force him into creating a **United Front** against Japan. The **Xi'an Incident**, as it became known, ended with a fragile alliance among the Chinese warring factions. China's armed forces, however, were no match for Japan's imperial army. By the end of 1937, the Japanese occupied key cities and the most fertile regions in eastern China. Chiang's Guomindang government retreated into the country's interior, to Chongqing. The Communists continued to rebuild their strength in Yan'an. The horrors of the **Nanjing Massacre** were followed by years of brutal occupation by the Japanese, which included **biological warfare**.

After World War II ended, any semblance of cooperation between the Communists and the Guomindang disappeared. Representatives of the United States tried to broker a collaborative new government, and when that failed to materialize, they supported Chiang Kai-shek's efforts to take control of China. The CCP, on the other hand, had help from the Soviet Union. The **civil war** that had plagued the country in the 1930s broke out again in 1946. The Guomindang government was unable to stem spiraling inflation, nor could it effectively counter the compelling communist ideology that spread throughout China. As the CCP's People's Liberation Army (PLA) mounted one successful military campaign after another, the Guomindang government retreated to the island of Taiwan. On October 1, 1949, Mao Zedong proclaimed the founding of the **People's Republic of China**.

Primary Sources

DOCUMENT 8.1: "Medicine," a short story by Lu Xun, first published in *Xin Qingnian* (*New Youth* magazine), May 1919

DOCUMENT 8.2: Excerpts from Act 2 of *Teahouse,* a play by Lao She, 1957

DOCUMENT 8.3: Table of Contents from *Xin Qingnian* (*New Youth* magazine), Vol. 6 No. 5, May 1919

DOCUMENT 8.4: Excerpts from "Why I Write Poems in the Vernacular" by Hu Shi, in *Xin Qingnian* (*New Youth* magazine), May 1919

DOCUMENT 8.5: Excerpts from "My View on Marxism" by Li Dazhao, in *Xin Qingnian* (*New Youth* magazine), May 1919

DOCUMENT 8.6: Slide show "Duolun Road" on the New Culture Movement in the 1920s and 30s in Shanghai

DOCUMENT 8.7: Excerpts from a memoir by Li Xiuwen (1890–1992), describing the political turmoil of the 1920s

DOCUMENT 8.8: Clips from Northeast Historic Film, 1934 (on CD-ROM)

CLIP 1: "Americans living in Shanghai"

CLIP 2: "The Paper Chase"

CLIP 3: "An American Family Tours the Countryside"

Supplementary Materials

ITEM 8.A: Map of areas controlled by warlords, 1925

CHAPTER 8

Early Republican Period (1912–1928)

By Ryan Bradeen and Nan Ye

Chapter Contents

The Rise and Fall of the Republic
The Reign of the Warlords
Intellectual Vitality
The May Fourth Movement

Organizing Idea

Like the end of many previous dynasties, the fall of the Qing was followed by a period of division when competing warlords battled for power. But the disunity also heralded intellectual exploration that led to the development of ideas and the emergence of leaders who would found a New China.

Key Questions

What were the characteristics of the Early Republican Period?

Why did warlords come to power and how did they preserve their power?

Why did the political disunity of the Early Republican Period lead to intellectual vitality?

What were the characteristics and legacy of the May Fourth Movement?

Key Terms

Guomindang
ideology
Treaty of Versailles
vernacular
warlords

Essay

The overthrow of the Qing (清) dynasty ushered in a shockingly brief period of hope for rejuvenating China and tackling the dire issues that confronted the nation. After working for years to bring about the downfall of the Manchu government, Sun Yat-sen (孫逸仙) was elected president of the Republic of China (中华民国) on January 1, 1912. He held the post for six weeks.

The troops who had mutinied against the Manchus were no match for the imperial armies stationed around the capital. Without the support of the Qing military—especially its most senior general, Yuan Shikai (袁世凱)—the Republic would be short-lived. On the very day of his election, Sun Yat-sen sent a telegram to Yuan Shikai, stating "[The presidency] is actually waiting for you, and my offer will eventually be made clear to the world."[1] Yuan accepted the offer, forced the abdication of the last Manchu emperor, and on February 13, 1912 became president of the Republic of China.

The new government immediately planned national elections for December 1912. Sun Yat-sen's Guomindang Party (国民党, the National People's Party) won a majority of seats.[2] It soon became apparent, however, that Yuan Shikai had no intention of following the new Republican laws. The newly elected Guomindang party leader, Song Jiaoren, was assassinated by figures associated with Yuan Shikai. By October 1913, Yuan had outlawed the Guomindang and forced its members out of the legislature. Hunted by Yuan's troopers, Sun Yat-sen slipped out of the country, leaving Yuan as virtual dictator of the Republic of China.

While Yuan Shikai had eliminated the Guomindang—his most pressing threat—he had also undermined his own support among the military, many of whom genuinely believed that the Republic was China's best chance to modernize the nation. The final straw was Yuan's December 1915 attempt to install himself as the new emperor of China. Massive protests sprang up all over the country. Even Yuan's old officers rebelled, declaring themselves and their provinces independent. Coincidentally, within six months, Yuan was dead of kidney failure. The Republic of China survived, but only in name. For the next decade, the Republican government carried on at the whim of whichever military leader was strong enough to control the capital, but the central government did not have complete control over the country. The basic functions of law, order, and public works were left to the provinces.

The Reign of the Warlords

The men who assumed control of the provinces most often were provincial army commanders. These generals-turned-warlords were a varied bunch. The most prominent were professional soldiers who had been trained in China's New Army, established in 1895 under the command of Yuan Shikai. Many were committed to the ideal of a unified China, especially one in which they themselves would play a starring role. Some warlords, like Yan Xishan in Shanxi Province, were quite progressive, establishing schools and promoting social reforms. Others were little more than overgrown thugs who had consolidated a base of power through crime and intimidation.[3]

The handful of major warlords who dominated the 1910s and 1920s commanded sizeable regions, populations, and deposits of resources. For example, the smallest of the major warlord regions, Yan Xishan's Shanxi Province, was approximately the same geographic size as modern Greece or Louisiana and had huge quantities of coal, aluminum, and other strategic minerals. With such resources at his disposal, a warlord could create a mini-state generally independent from the rest of China.

Since the cornerstone of warlord authority hinged upon control of military force, a

---

[1] Qtd. in Jonathan D. Spence, *The Search for Modern China* (New York: W. W. Norton, 1999) 263.

[2] Formerly spelled Kuomintang and abbreviated as KMT, the Guomindang are also known as the Nationalists.

[3] Spence, *The Search for Modern China*, 284.

Warlords, 1925: Light-shaded areas represent major warlord coalitions; darker-shaded areas were controlled by the Guomindang and allied warlords.
(Courtesy of the United States Military Academy.)

warlord's first priority was to secure funds to pay and equip his soldiers. The size of these armies was not small. By the mid-1920s, nearly two million Chinese soldiers were under arms in warlord armies spread across the country.[4] Scholars estimate that in the years between 1917 and 1927, more than 600,000 people were killed in battles between warlords.[5] The cost of these armies outstripped the normal tax revenue of the provinces. Warlords, therefore, created new taxes on basic necessities like salt, established toll roads, or forced farmers to pay as many as twenty years' taxes in advance. Others turned to more criminal activities like reviving opium production or subdividing their territories to local criminals in return for payment

and military service. Many warlords took out large loans from foreign banks to shore up their positions in the rapidly shifting domestic alliances and intrigues that characterized the period. Little wonder that most political leaders and the general populace continued to believe that a politically unified China was the natural state to which honorable rulers should strive to return.

Intellectual Vitality

Yet, as in earlier periods of disunity in China, the turmoil of the Republican period sparked a great outburst of intellectual activity. The established elite and younger generations sought to find solutions to the country's dizzying array of problems in government and politics, culture and education, social organization and economics, and foreign relations and the military.

---

[4] By comparison, during the 1920s the U.S. Army had only 175,000 soldiers in its ranks.

[5] R.J. Rummel, *China's Bloody Century* (New Brunswick, NJ: Transaction Publishers, 1991). www.hawaii.edu/powerkills/NOTE2.HTM

The elimination of the imperial exam system left Chinese writers and students open to explore much more freely than under the Qing.[6] They drew upon the deep well of Chinese philosophy and political thought as well as the many currents of European, American, and Japanese ideas that were circulating in translated articles and books, in university and school classrooms, and through interaction with European and American businessmen, missionaries, and teachers stationed in the treaty ports.

Chinese men and women also traveled and studied abroad in large numbers. Many studied in Japan, which was held up as a model of an Asian nation that had avoided domination by foreign powers and modernized its institutions and society. Others studied in the United States or Europe, where they were exposed to the heated intellectual debates among socialists, communists, fascists, feminists, labor union activists, progressives, anarchists, liberal democrats, and capitalists that characterized the early twentieth century outside of China as well. Among those who traveled to Europe were 100,000 Chinese men who served as laborers supporting Allied forces in France against Germany in World War I. Upon their return to China, some of these students, laborers, and travelers became schoolteachers, translators, newspaper editors, writers, and political and social activists who tried to apply the ideas they had absorbed in their travels to the challenges that China confronted.

New Publications

Those who did not travel abroad benefited through the development of new schools and small local newspapers that published articles on political and social issues. Often these journals were short-lived, as their radical views eventually brought the unwelcome attention of the local warlords. But as quickly as they could be shut down, new papers would spring up to replace them. The new journalism created a constant flow of information that stirred people's minds and hearts with new ideas, stimulated discussions of deep-seated cultural and political problems, and inspired hope for rejuvenating the nation before it collapsed under the many internal and external pressures pushing and pulling against it.

Even the warlords themselves, as they constructed their regimes to govern their territories, were drawn into the intellectual currents of the day. Yan Xishan of Shanxi Province believed he had created a flawless ideology for governing his region by combining the best features of "militarism, nationalism, anarchism, democracy, capitalism, communism, individualism, imperialism, universalism, paternalism, and utopianism."[7] In many ways, the chaotic and bloody Republican period echoed the era of the "One Hundred Schools of Thought" (百家争鸣) from which Confucianism (儒家) and Daoism (道家) had emerged in the sixth century B.C.E.

The May Fourth Movement (五四运动)

The events of May 4, 1919, galvanized intellectuals and the general populace throughout China as people recognized the desperate need for radical change to Chinese society. Three days earlier, news had reached Beijing that at the Paris Peace Conference to end World War I, the Allied Powers had awarded Japan all of Germany's colonial possessions in China's Shandong Province (山东省).[8] This was in exchange for the naval assistance the Japanese had provided against the Germans. Students in Beijing's major universities marched to the homes of several prominent politicians to

---

[6] A series of increasingly difficult exams had served as the system whereby government officials would ideally be appointed on merit rather than family status and connections. (See Chapter 2.) As a man passed each exam, he would become eligible for a position of greater authority. From the Song dynasty (960 C.E.) on, the exams were based on mastery of four key Confucian books, including the *Analects*, and five ancient classics. These exams were abolished under the Qing in 1905.

[7] Qtd. in Spence, *The Search for Modern China*, 284.

[8] The Treaty of Versailles was signed at the conclusion of the conference.

protest the treaty. Soon thereafter, outraged students, teachers, workers, and businessmen in nearly one hundred cities around China protested against the settlement. In Paris, Chinese students and workers surrounded the Chinese delegation's quarters, preventing the representatives from signing the Treaty of Versailles.

These initial protests evolved into a wide range of actions and organizations all over the country, including the formation of student and labor unions, boycotts of foreign (particularly Japanese) goods, and the printing of radical newspapers, magazines, and books. The May Fourth Movement is considered to be the most important intellectual period in twentieth-century China.

Out of the protests, study groups, and unions formed in the May Fourth Movement, the leaders of China's resurgence would eventually emerge. Its future political leaders, such as Mao Zedong (毛泽东), Chiang Kai-shek (蒋介石), Zhou Enlai (周恩来), and Deng Xiaoping (邓小平), were all deeply influenced by the May Fourth Movement and its reaction against warlords and foreign imperialism. China's most creative writers and thinkers of the century forged their craft in the pages of the newspapers and journals that circulated through the nation during this era. Lu Xun (鲁迅), considered to be the founder of modern Chinese literature, wrote many of his most famous works in the years immediately surrounding the May Fourth Movement. Ba Jin (巴金), Lao She (老舍), Mao Dun (茅盾), and Hu Shi (胡适) were among the famous writers of novels, short stories, poems, and plays who found their voice in this turbulent period.

All sought to make sense out of their lives and foresee a hopeful future for their country, even as the crows and vultures of warlordism and imperialism descended upon the corpse of the imperial tradition. While terribly chaotic and dangerous to live through, the Republican period produced writers and leaders who, through their accomplishments, laid the foundation for a new China that today is a resurgent world power.

Primary Sources

DOCUMENT 8.1: "Medicine," a short story by Lu Xun, first published in *Xin Qingnian* (*New Youth* magazine), May 1919

"You know, that little bastard was really too much—even tried to get the jailer to rebel against the emperor!"

"Aiya! Have you ever heard the likes of that?" A man in his twenties is filled with overweening righteous indignation.

"Well, it was like this. Redeye Ah-yi went to question him and find out whatever he could, but the Xia kid acts as though it's just a regular conversation and starts tellin' Redeye how the Great Manchu Empire belongs to all of us. Now stop and think for a second, does that sound like talk you'd expect out of a human being? Redeye knew right from the start there was no one in the kid's family except his old mother, but he never imagined he could be *that* poor – couldn't squeeze a single copper out of him. Now that means Ah-yi is pissed off to begin with, right? Then the Xia kid's gotta go rub salt in the wound by talkin' *that* kinda stuff. Well Ah-yi gave him a couple good ones right across the mouth!... Gettin' hit didn't faze that punk one little bit. His only comeback was to say, 'Pitiful, pitiful.'"...

SOURCE: Lu Xun, *Diary of a Madman and Other Stories*, trans. William A. Lyell (Honolulu: University of Hawaii Press, 1990) 55.

 The complete story is available on the CD-ROM.

DOCUMENT 8.2: Excerpts from Act 2 of *Teahouse*, a play by Lao She, 1957

FOURTH ELDER CHANG: I was arrested by you gentlemen here in 1898, and spent more than a year in prison for saying that "the Great Qing Empire is about done for."

SONG ENZI: You have a remarkable memory. Life treating you well these days?

FOURTH ELDER CHANG: Thanks to you, yes. I got out of prison just before the year 1900, and joined the Boxers to help the dynasty oust the foreigners.[9] We did battle with the foreigners a few times; but despite all our efforts the Great Qing Empire collapsed in the end. Well, it deserved to collapse. I'm a Bannerman myself, but I must speak the truth.[10] Now, every day I'm up at dawn and get together two baskets of vegetables, and by mid-morning I have them all sold. Because I earn my own keep I'm healthier than ever. If the foreigners ever venture to attack again, I'll be ready for them. I'm a Bannerman. Bannermen are Chinese too! And how've you two been keeping?

WU XIANGZI: We muddle along. When there was an emperor, we served the emperor; when Yuan Shikai became president, we served President Yuan Shikai. And now... Song Enzi, how would you put it?

SONG ENZI: Now we serve whoever puts food in our bellies....

SOURCE: Lao She, *Teahouse*, trans. John Howard-Gibbon (Hong Kong: Chinese University Press, 2004) 78.

 The full text of Document 8.2 is available on the CD-ROM

---

[9] The Boxer Uprising took place in 1900; see Chapter 7.

[10] As the Manchus invaded China in the early 1600s, they organized their forces into eight military units known as "banners" that consisted of soldiers and their family members. The system remained in place until the Qing dynasty ended in 1912.

DOCUMENT 8.3: Table of Contents from *Xin Qingnian* (*New Youth magazine*), Vol. 6 No. 5, May 1919

New Youth Magazine
Vol. 6 No. 5
(Eighth Year of the Republic; Published in May 1919)

Marxism.. Gu Zhaoxiong pp. 450–465
Criticism on Marxism...................................... Ling Shuang pp. 466–469
The Philosophical Foundations of the Russian Revolution, Part 2 of 2
Qi Ming (translator)... pp. 470–478
Medicine... Lu Xun pp. 479–484
Poems:
A Little Star... Hu Shi p. 484
Sending Ren Shuyong Back to Sichuan................................ Hu Shi p. 485
Birds... Chen Weizhe pp. 485–486
Gypsies Returning Home.. Chen Weizhe p. 487
Why I Write Poems in the Vernacular............................ Hu Shi pp. 488–499
Studies of Marx:
1: Marx's Objective View of History and the Issue of Chastity
   Chen Qixiu... pp. 500–505
2: Marx's Objective View of History........................... Run Quan pp. 505–509
3: Marx's Life of Persistent Endeavor........................ Run Quan pp. 509–516
Biography of Karl Marx.. Liu Binglin pp. 517–520
My View on Marxism Part 1 of 2.......................... Li Dazhao pp. 521–537
Biography of Bakunin... Ke Shui pp. 538–541
Laozi's Political Philosophy.................................... Gao Yihan pp. 542–548
Random Thoughts:
(56) (57) (58) (59).................................... Tang Si pp. 549–552
(60) .... Zhang Chi pp. 552–554

SOURCE: *Xin Qingnian* (New Youth magazine) 6.4 (1919). Trans. Diana Lin.

DOCUMENT 8.4: Excerpts from "Why I Write Poems in the Vernacular" by Hu Shi, in *Xin Qingnian* (*New Youth* magazine), May 1919

I clearly stated that "Classical Chinese is a half dead language and should not be taught using a methodology used to teach a live language." I also stated that "so-called live language is a language that is used in daily life, such as English, French and vernacular Chinese. The so-called dead languages, such as [ancient] Greek and Latin, are not used daily, in other words, they're dead....

[T]he literary revolution that I propose is based on the current situation of Chinese literature and has little to do with the new literature movements in Europe and America. The reason that I sometimes quote Western literary history, (specifically the part when European authors began to write in their native languages three or four hundred years ago), is only because the need for vernacular literature in China today is very similar to the need in Europe then. If we study what those countries accomplished, we will reduce our conservatism and increase our courage....

SOURCE: Hu Shi, "Why I Write Poems in the Vernacular," *Xin Qingnian* May 1919: 488–499. Trans. Nan Ye.

 The full text of Document 8.4 is available on the CD-ROM.

DOCUMENT 8.5: Excerpts from "My View on Marxism" by Li Dazhao, in *Xin Qingnian* (*New Youth* magazine), 1919

I have not done much research on Marxism; therefore it is bold of me to attempt to talk about Marxism here. However, ever since the Russian Revolution, Marxism is about to sweep through the world. Countries such as Germany, Austria, and Hungary started their revolutions one after another following Marxist ideology. While Marxism caught people's attention around the world and stirred up great changes, it also generated many misunderstandings and misinterpretations.

Although our study of Marxism is slight, there has been a great deal of interest in, and criticism of, his works in various countries as a result of the 100th anniversary [of Marx's birth] in 1918. We have collected and edited these writings to introduce them to our readers in this Marxism edition of *New Youth* magazine. I believe it is not without benefit for readers to gain some insight into this world-altering theory through our discussions. If there are any errors due to the authors' limited knowledge of Marxism, we hope our dear readers will offer their corrections.

SOURCE: Li Dazhao, "My View on Marxism," *Xin Qingnian* May 1919: 521–537. Trans. Nan Ye.

 The full text of Document 8.5 is available on the CD-ROM.

DOCUMENT 8.7: Excerpts from a memoir by Li Xiuwen (1890–1992), describing the political turmoil of the 1920s

In the war years,[11] we moved often from city to city. We couldn't eat and sleep peacefully. Suddenly an order would be given by army headquarters to move. The families would hurry to pack and follow the army by boat or by sedan chair. Sometime we heard the noise of cannons. Sometimes the enemy advanced behind us. It was hard for a woman to take these adverse conditions.

Whenever we arrived in a new city, we rented a place to live, or we stayed in the barracks. There wasn't much discipline in the army. The people were terrorized by the soldiers. When the army came into a city, people locked their doors. The shops stopped doing business. Some stores had their doors half open. If the merchants got

[11] between 1912 and 1927

paid for their merchandise, they would open their doors wide and continue to do business....

SOURCE: Li Xiuwen, unpublished memoir.

 The full text of Document 8.7 is available on the CD-ROM.

Activities

ACTIVITY 1: Examining the common people

After reading the introductory essay, read the story "Medicine" (8.1) and discuss the following questions either as a class or in small groups.

1. The blood-soaked bun is the symbolic key to understanding the story. For what reasons did revolutionaries like the Xia boy shed their blood? For what reasons did the Hua family purchase the blood? How would Lu Xun, the author, account for the differences in the purposes between revolutionaries and more ordinary people like the Hua family?

2. Why did the Xia boy feel sorry for Redeye? Why did the people at the teahouse feel sorry for the Xia boy?

3. Do you think Mother Xia understands her son's cause? Give two reasons to support your opinion.

4. Reread the section at the end of the story about the red-and-white wreath placed on the revolutionary's grave. Here you can almost hear the author's voice. Who do you think placed the wreath at the revolutionary's grave? Why?

5. What do you learn about life in China in 1919 from this short story?

6. What do you think might be the author's purpose for writing the story? How do you think the story might have influenced the May Fourth Movement?

7. What other literature do you know that has political overtones?

ACTIVITY 2: Examining the revolutionary

Part 1:

Working in small groups, develop a first-person narrative from the perspective of one of the characters in "Medicine": Little Bolt (the sick boy), Big Bolt (the boy's father), Uncle Kang (the executioner), Redeye (the prison warden), Mother Xia (the revolutionary's mother), or a teahouse customer. In your narrative, make sure you address the following issues in a fictionalized style.

- Your relationship to the Xia boy
- Your place in society
- Why the boy was executed and whether it was justified

- What the Xia boy would or should do differently if he were given a second chance to carry out his cause

Part 2:

Reconvene in new groups of five or six students in which each student represents a different character. Present your first-person narratives to the group.

Part 3:

Compile the narratives and create a third-person narrative introducing the Xia boy, the revolutionary.

ACTIVITY 3: The Republic and its people

Read Act 2 of Lao She's *Teahouse* (8.2) before class. In class, choose roles and perform the play. Then:

1. Analyze the different characters' philosophies and the strategies that they rely on to survive and adapt to the social changes during this period.
2. Categorize the characters according to their philosophies and survival strategies. Create a description of the general philosophy and strategy of each category.
3. What is your overall impression of the challenges that individuals faced during these uncertain times?
4. What do you learn about life in and around Beijing in 1922? How had things changed (or not) since 1919?
5. What do you think might have been Lao She's purpose in writing this play?

Creative extension:

Create a cartoon, a comic strip, or a poster that reflects a sense of the times as Lao She depicts them.

ACTIVITY 4: Analyzing the May Fourth Movement

After reading the table of contents of *New Youth*'s May 1919 issue (8.3) and two excerpts from that issue (8.4 and 8.5), discuss as a class:

1. How did publications like *New Youth* mobilize intellectuals to think, discuss, and debate about social, political, and literary issues in Chinese society?
2. What kind of new cultural ideas and thoughts did magazines like *New Youth* stimulate in young intellectuals who carried out the May Fourth Movement?

ACTIVITY 5: **Evaluating the writing system**

After reading excerpts from "Why I Write Poems in the Vernacular" (8.4), answer the following questions.

1. What might have been some of the reasons that motivated young intellectuals like Hu Shi to promote writing in vernacular Chinese?

2. What kind of challenges do you think they might have encountered in promoting writing (including poetry writing) in the vernacular?

3. From the proposed rules for writing in the vernacular, what can be concluded about writing in the traditional style using classical Chinese?

4. Who would benefit from such a literary revolution? Why?

5. List some immediate effects that writing in the vernacular could have on early twentieth-century Chinese society. What might be the long-term significance of the change?

6. How is this movement tied to the goals and ideology of the May Fourth Movement?

ACTIVITY 6: **Examining the intellectuals**

Look at the slide show "Duolun Road" (8.6), and use books and online sources to learn about the lives of Hu Shi, Li Dazhao, Lu Xun, and others. Discuss:

1. What did Hu Shi, Li Dazhao, and Lu Xun have in common? How were they different? What did all the individuals commemorated on Duolun Road have in common?

2. What ideologies did they embrace and what paths did they embark on as their lifelong careers?

3. What influence did they have on Chinese people and society in the long term?

ACTIVITY 7: **Political turmoil of the 1920s**

After reading excerpts from Li Xiuwen's memoir (8.7), consider:

1. What do you learn about the life of soldiers and their families during the early warlord era from this document?

2. How did the political turmoil affect people's lives both in the countryside and in cities?

3. The excerpt describes how people, the army and their families celebrated the 1925 unification in Guangxi, thinking there would be no war again. When did the "normal and safe life" they dreamed of eventually come?

4. What is the relationship between the Chinese perception of war and peace depicted in the memoir and the strong emphasis on political stability and economic prosperity by the current Chinese government?

ACTIVITY 8: Examining Westerners' perspective

After viewing the film clips from the Northeast Historic Film Archive (in Additional Resources on the CD), discuss as a class:

1. What surprised you in the film clips?

2. What do you see in Clip 1 that is similar to what you would expect to see in a wealthy family in the United States during the early 1930s? What strikes you as different?

3. In Clip 2, Westerners are shown riding their horses over farm fields. Based on what you know about Chinese traditional views on farming, what does this suggest about the relationship between the average foreigner in 1930s China and the average Chinese person? The mounds in the background of the shot are possibly ancestral gravesites, though it is hard to be 100 percent positive without excavating the site. Suppose the mounds are indeed grave mounds. Considering Chinese reverence for their ancestors, how might this affect the Chinese farmers' reaction to foreigners riding across their fields? What might be concluded about foreigners' attitude toward Chinese people in general, and peasants in particular?

4. In Clip 3, how would you describe the interactions the American family had with the local villagers? What do you think was the villagers' attitude toward the touring Westerners? What was the Westerners' attitude towards these villagers?

5. What conclusions can you draw from the three film clips?

6. These were homemade family films (like a modern-day home video). How does that affect the content? How might a homemade film be different from a documentary, for example?

Suggested Resources

Books

Buck, Pearl S. *The Good Earth.* New York: Washington Square Press, 1931.
This is often regarded as the best novel written by a non-Chinese author about life in China during the warlord period.

Dong, Stella. *Shanghai: The Rise and Fall of a Decadent City, 1842–1949.* New York: Harper Perennial, 2002.
Dong provides an enjoyable and readable history of the city at the center of China's turbulent revolutionary years.

Hahn, Emily. *The Soong Sisters.* New York: Doubleday, 1941.
Written by an American expatriate living in China, this biography offers insight into the inner workings of the Republican era.

Lao She. *Rickshaw.* Honolulu: University of Hawaii Press, 1979.
The main character is a rickshaw puller hoping to make a successful life for himself against the backdrop of revolution, warlords, and social chaos (see Chapter 10 for excerpts).

Lao She. *Blades of Grass: The Stories of Lao She,* trans. William Lyell. Honolulu: University of Hawaii Press, 1999.
A collection of very approachable short stories set in the era of the early Republic.

Lu Xun. *Diary of a Madman and Other Stories,* trans. William Lyell. Honolulu: University of Hawaii Press, 1990.

Spence, Jonathan, and Annping Chin. *The Chinese Century: A Photographic History of the Last Hundred Years.* New York: Random House, 1996.
An unparalleled collection of photographs from the period.

Websites

http://www.wsu.edu/~dee/MODCHINA/ MODCHINA.HTM Useful segments on Sun Yat-sen, the Republican Revolution, the Republic of China, warlords and other relevant topics.

http://www.talesofoldchina.com "Tales of Old China": Memorabilia from Shanghai and Beijing in the Republican era; photographs, cartoons, and even whole books published at that time by British and American expatriates in China.

http://www.thecorner.org/hist/china/warlords. htm "The Early Republic" in "The Corner of the World" is a detailed introduction to many aspects of the Early Republic.

http://afe.easia.columbia.edu/china/modern/ read2.htm#Chiang%20Kai-shek Columbia University's *Asia for Educators* site has several interesting activities with primary sources related to the New Life Movement and May Fourth Movement.

http://www.ibiblio.org/chineseart/contents/peop/ c05.html A photo of Chen Duxiu and Hu Shi in traditional-style long gowns; can also be accessed by going to www.ibiblio.org and entering "Chen Duxiu" in the search.

http://en.wikipedia.org/wiki/Yen_Hsi-shan For a photo of Shanxi Province warlord Yan Xishan

Films

China in Revolution, vol. 1 of *China: A Century of Revolution* (120 minutes, 1997)
This documentary offers riveting footage of the Republican Period and interviews with Chinese people who lived through the era.

The Last Emperor (162 mins; 1987)
The film poignantly captures the anachronism of a child-emperor coming to power in China in the early 20th century and the subsequent political turmoil. Directed by Bernardo Bertolucci.

■ A CLOSER LOOK

Chen Duxiu: In the Thick of Things

Chen Duxiu (1879–1942), the first party secretary of the Chinese Communist Party, had always been a nonconformist. Born in Anhui Province and tutored by his grandfather, Chen received a classical Chinese education, but in an informal setting. This, combined with his exposure to Western political and philosophical theories while studying in Japan, led Chen to critically examine conventional Chinese beliefs and practices.

When only twenty-five years old and still studying in Japan, Chen founded his first newspaper. This paper and all of his later publications would promote revolutionary ideas using Chinese vernacular language instead of the classical Chinese language used in most other publications. Upon his return to Shanghai in 1915, Chen established *New Youth*, the single most important journal of the Republican era. It was read eagerly by students, thinkers, and revolutionaries around the nation. People gathered in groups to read the precious articles and passed them around until the paper was in tatters.

During his early career, Chen was a strong supporter of the Republican government. But by 1919, Chen wrote, "A false signboard 'Chinese Republic' has been hanging for eight years now but it is still the old medicine which is being sold."[12]

Following the 1919 student protests in Beijing, Chen was at the center of the May Fourth Movement, which spread across the country in waves largely tuned to the circulation of issues of his *New Youth*.

Disillusioned with the workings of the supposedly democratic Republic, Chen searched for other means to address China's many fundamental political and social problems. As early as 1919, communism appeared to offer Chen an attractive alternative, one he saw as having demonstrated clear success in transforming Russian society. By early 1920, Chen was at the center of efforts by Chinese revolutionaries and Soviet agents to organize a Chinese Communist Party. In 1921, he was elected party secretary of the CCP at its founding meeting in Shanghai. Chen held this post until 1927, when he was forced to resign due to disputes with Soviet advisors and other CCP leaders. After his resignation Chen was imprisoned by the Guomindang for five years, after which he gradually faded from prominence among China's revolutionary leaders.

■ *Discuss publications that you believe have had an impact on people's views and on political activism. What role can and should the media play in politics?*

---

[12] Chen Duxiu, "Basis for the Realization of Democracy," *Xin Qingnian* (*New Youth* magazine), Vol. 1, 14, qtd. in Benjamin Schwartz, *Chinese Communism and the Rise of Mao* (Cambridge, MA: Harvard University Press, 1961), 13.

Primary Sources

DOCUMENT 9.1: "Hometown," a short story by Lu Xun, first published in *Xin Qingnian* (*New Youth* magazine), May 1921

DOCUMENT 9.2: Excerpts from "The Guidelines of New Life Movement" by Chiang Kai-shek, *Central Daily News*, May 15, 1934

DOCUMENT 9.3: Excerpts from "Report on an Investigation of the Peasant Movement in Hunan" by Mao Zedong, March 1927

DOCUMENT 9.4: "The Long March," a poem by Mao Zedong, 1935

DOCUMENT 9.5: "Jinsha Jiang" ("The River of Golden Sand"), an anonymous account describing this segment of the Long March, 1934–1935

DOCUMENT 9.6: "The Bridge of Iron Chains," an account describing crossing the Luding Bridge on the Long March, 1934–1935

DOCUMENT 9.7: "Jiajin Shan" ("The Great Snow Mountain"), an anonymous account describing a segment of the Long March, 1934–1935

DOCUMENT 9.8: Excerpts from "Political Mobilization for the War of Resistance," a lecture by Mao Zedong, May 1938

DOCUMENT 9.9: "Manifesto on the Seizure of Chiang Kai-shek," a telegram sent to the nation by General Zhang Xueliang, December 12, 1936

DOCUMENT 9.10: "The Rebellion in Xi'an," a report in the *Manchester Guardian Weekly*, July 16, 1937 (only on CD-ROM)

DOCUMENT 9.11a & b: Photographs at site of the seizure of Chiang Kai-shek outside Xi'an, 2006

DOCUMENTS 9.12a–c: Cartoons by Sapajou in *The North China Daily News*, 1936–1937

DOCUMENT 9.13: Photograph of Zhou Enlai, Mao Zedong, and Bo Gu, 1937

Supplementary Materials

ITEM 9.A: Guidelines for "Hometown" character interviews, Activity 1, part 3

ITEM 9.B: Map of the Long March

ITEM 9.C: Map of China under Chiang Kai-shek, 1928–1937

CHAPTER 9

United Fronts: The Guomindang vs. the Communists (1921–1937)

By Ryan Bradeen and Nan Ye

Chapter Contents

Organizing Idea

As the Republic of China frayed into competing warlord territories, two major forces emerged: the Guomindang led by Chiang Kai-shek and the Communist Party of China. Throughout the 1920s and 1930s, these two forces would twice form united fronts against common enemies; and twice these alliances would break apart in bitter feuds. The rivalry between the Guomindang and the Communists would define the era and determine the path of modern China.

Key Questions

How did the political situation that led to the First United Front compare to the one that led to the Second United Front?

How does the gap between urban China and rural China during this era reflect the political contest between the Guomindang and the Communists?

How did the Long March and the Xi'an Incident shape the future of the Chinese Communist Party?

How was the Chinese Communist Party able to survive this era against the economically, politically, and militarily superior Guomindang?

How did Japan's invasion of China affect the political situation between the Guomindang and the Communist Party?

Key Terms

feudal	soviet (as in Jiangxi Soviet, for example)
gentry	

Essay

In July 1921, thirteen men filtered secretly into a Shanghai girls' school shuttered for summer vacation. Over the next ten days, they would launch a national Chinese Communist Party (中国共产党) that unified the numerous small cells spread across the country. Chen Duxiu (陈独秀), editor of the revolutionary journal *New Youth* (《新青年》), was elected leader of the party.

Among those attending the meeting was a young Communist from Hunan Province, Mao Zedong (毛泽东). Born in 1893, Mao was the eldest son of prosperous farmers. He received a progressive education in a modern high school, and in 1918 was given a position as a clerk in Peking University's library.[1] There he began to study communism under the direction of Li Dazhao (李大钊), the university's head librarian and China's leading authority on communism. In December 1919, Mao returned to Hunan, where he became a teacher and a contributor to local political publications.

Delegates at the founding of the Chinese Communist Party (CCP) discussed the structure of the party, its goals, and how to achieve them. Their main priorities included: unifying the nation, addressing the exploitation of rural Chinese by landlords, eradicating foreign imperialism in China, and preparing the way for a socialist revolution. One of the most disputed topics was what attitude the CCP should take towards the Guomindang (国民党).[2] Some argued that Sun Yat-sen (孙逸仙) was just another warlord and should be resisted as such. Others believed that, although they did not agree with all of Sun's ideas, they should support his attempts to unify the nation. It would take another year for CCP leaders to agree to seek an alliance with the Guomindang in order to defeat the warlords.

[1] Peking is the former name of Beijing.

[2] Formerly spelled Kuomintang and abbreviated as KMT, the Guomindang are also known as the Nationalists.

Sun Yat-sen, the Guomindang, and the First United Front

After fleeing into exile in 1913, Sun Yat-sen had gradually rebuilt the Guomindang in Guangzhou, but his position remained fragile. The CCP, with its backing from the Soviet Union, was an attractive partner. In 1919, the newly founded Soviet Union had renounced its colonial privileges in China. The Russians offered advisors to help the Guomindang improve its governing ability, as well as military equipment and financial support. The Russians hoped that Sun would become a critical ally to hem in Japan's ambitions in Manchuria and Siberia. In early 1924, the Guomindang began to accept CCP members into its own ranks, forming the First United Front (第一次统一战线). Chen Duxiu, Li Dazhao, Mao Zedong, Zhou Enlai, and many other CCP members were given important posts within the Guomindang.

One of the immediate outcomes of the First United Front was the establishment of the Whampoa Military Academy in Guangzhou. The academy trained young recruits in modern military techniques based on Russian models and with Russian equipment. The commandant of the Whampoa Academy was a young officer named Chiang Kai-shek (蒋介石) who had just returned from training in Moscow.

Chiang Kai-shek was born in 1887 in the Yangzi Delta region to a family of upper-class salt merchants. After training in Japanese military academies, Chiang returned to Shanghai after the 1911 Republican Revolution and joined the Guomindang. In addition to his political work, Chiang learned to navigate Shanghai's seamy underside, where opium-running, dirty politics, revolution-making, and crime intersected with China's wealthiest business circles and foreign dignitaries. Chiang rose through the ranks of the military, becoming a trusted protégé of Sun Yat-sen. Following Sun's unexpected death in early 1925, Chiang Kai-shek, possessing the loyalty of the officers he had trained at Whampoa, became one of the highest-ranking members of the Guomindang.

Nationalist China 1928–37: Dark-shaded areas were regions under direct Guomindang rule; light-shaded areas were ruled by semi-autonomous major warlords or warlord coalitions; unmarked territories were in dispute or ruled by minor warlords.
(Courtesy of the United States Military Academy.)

The Northern Expedition

On July 1, 1926, the Guomindang army marched out of Guangzhou. As Chiang Kai-shek would later say, the moment had come for the Guomindang to prove "whether or not the Chinese nation and race [could] restore their freedom and independence."[3] This campaign, called the Northern Expedition (北阀战争), involved three thrusts against the warlords of southeastern China. Experienced CCP labor and peasant organizers—Mao Zedong among them—were sent ahead to arrange strikes and sabotage to weaken the warlords before the Guomindang army even arrived.[4] In many cases, warlord soldiers defected to the Guomindang side or fled when faced with their more disciplined and better-equipped forces. By early 1927, the Northern Expedition had overrun warlord opposition in seven provinces south of the Yangzi River, including the major cities of Shanghai, Nanjing, and Wuhan.

The Shanghai Purge (上海大屠杀)

Momentum, public support, and international opinion all pointed towards a rapid reunification of China under Guomindang leadership. But the success of the initial stage of the Northern Expedition revealed rifts in the alliance between the Guomindang and the CCP. Chiang Kai-shek, emboldened by his recent successes, decided to break with the Communists, whom he saw as a threat to China's tradition and economy.

[3] Qtd. in Spence, *The Search for Modern China* (New York: W. W. Norton, 1999) 329.

[4] Mao Zedong was the head of the Peasant Training Institute.

On April 12, 1927, soldiers loyal to Chiang attacked Communist party members and labor unions in Shanghai. Hundreds of CCP activists and sympathizers were killed and protests brutally put down. In the following months, Guomindang forces hunted down Communists all over China. Leaders fled for their lives, and the party itself was dispersed into small, disconnected cells. Mao Zedong, for example, escaped with a ragtag band of CCP soldiers and bandits to the mountainous border between Hunan and Jiangxi provinces. The First United Front was over. It had gone a long way towards achieving its goal of national reunification, but at great cost for the Chinese Communist Party.

The Nanjing Government and Japan

The stunning success of the Northern Expedition, combined with his elimination of the CCP leaders and their allies, left Chiang Kai-shek as the undisputed head of the Guomindang. By January of 1928, he had been named commander in chief of the Guomindang, as well as chairman of the Central Executive Committee.

Chiang, however, did not have long to enjoy his triumph. Despite the new government's wide popularity, the Guomindang was desperately short of money. From his new capital in Nanjing, Chiang reactivated many of his contacts in the Shanghai underworld, who helped the Guomindang strong-arm the Shanghai business community into giving the government massive "loans," ostensibly to fund the next stage of the reunification campaign.

By early 1928, the Guomindang had raised enough money to send its armies into the field again. Guomindang forces, allied with several warlords including Yan Xishan of Shanxi Province (see Chapter 8), crossed the Yangzi River headed towards Beijing. Beijing was controlled by Zhang Zuolin, another powerful warlord who also ruled Manchuria in China's northeast.

As Guomindang troops moved into North China, however, they entered an arena in which Japanese business interests and the Japanese army were major power brokers.[5] Zhang Zuolin, for example, had built his powerful army with Japanese advisors, equipment, and funds.

In May 1928, Japanese soldiers stationed in Shandong Province clashed with Guomindang troops, forcing Chiang Kai-shek to reroute his army. Weeks later, with Chiang poised to defeat Zhang Zuolin and capture Beijing, Japan pressured Zhang to retreat to Manchuria, while Japanese troops committed to guarding the passes into Manchuria against a Guomindang advance. As Zhang's train approached Manchuria's capital, however, Japanese agents assassinated the warlord, hoping to provoke a wider war in North China that would give them an excuse to invade Manchuria. But Zhang's son, Zhang Xueliang (张学良), assumed his father's leadership of Manchuria and quickly pledged allegiance to the Guomindang. The Japanese would have to wait until 1931 to conquer Manchuria.

The Jiangxi Soviet

Chiang Kai-shek was reluctant to enter into a full-scale war with Japan. He was already facing a series of rebellions by warlords, and, more ominously from his point of view, the remnants of the Chinese Communist Party had regrouped and seized control of several large rural regions. Chiang established a policy of "internal pacification first, then external resistance." He intended to face Japan only when he had the full weight of a completely unified Chinese nation behind him. While perhaps tactically sound, this policy was hugely unpopular with the general populace.

In January 1931, Guomindang armies attempted to overpower the largest of the new CCP refuges, the Jiangxi Soviet (江西苏维埃). What had started in 1928 as a hideout for Mao and his small group of CCP followers had grown into a sizeable Communist enclave. Eventually covering an area larger than the state

---

[5] In 1919, the Treaty of Versailles transferred China's Shandong Province from the Germans to the Japanese. Japan had also colonized Korea in 1910.

Long March: Shaded areas were controlled by the Chinese Communist Party; darker line is the route of the First Front Army 1934-35; the lighter line represents the routes of minor CCP commands. *(Courtesy of the United States Military Academy.)*

of Massachusetts with a population of more than three million people, the Jiangxi Soviet declared itself an independent country and established its own government, currency, postal service, and army. Chiang's first four attempts to encircle and destroy this new Communist base were soundly defeated by Mao's skillful use of guerrilla tactics. But in 1933, employing ideas from his Nazi German advisors, Chiang's methodical Fifth Encirclement Campaign gradually whittled down CCP territory by blockading the entire region with tightening rings of roads, barbed wire fences, and block houses armed with machine guns, as well as air cover provided by Italian airplanes and pilots. The military campaign was accompanied by a political program called the New Life Movement (新生活运动), which was designed to counter Communist social reforms by reinvigorating the populace's Confucian values and nationalistic sentiment. Chiang founded

an organization called the Blueshirts,[6] strident anti-Communist partisans, who acted as enforcers of the public morals emphasized in the New Life Movement. In skirmish after skirmish, Chiang's troops defeated the Red Army (红军) in 1934. Other CCP officials took over command from Mao, but they, too, were unable to break Chiang's noose. The days of the Jiangxi Soviet were numbered.

The Long March

In October 1934, 80,000 CCP personnel broke out of the Guomindang stranglehold. Over

---

[6] So named for the simple blue shirts worn by members and modeled on similar paramilitary organizations in Nazi Germany and in Mussolini's Italy: the Brownshirts and the Blackshirts.

the next fourteen months, the Communists doggedly marched west and north, sometimes in circles, to avoid the pursuing Guomindang armies in what became known as the Long March (长征). CCP leaders fiercely debated the causes of their defeat in Jiangxi and how to carry on their fight after the Soviet Union's withdrawal of support. Those who had pushed Mao Zedong out of power were demoted, and Mao assumed command of the Long March. He successfully kept the tattered Communist forces together, despite relentless Guomindang pressure and the rugged terrain and climate of western China. The losses were staggering: only one in ten of those who had set out from Jiangxi made it to Yan'an (延安), a town in China's northwestern Shaanxi Province where a small Communist base had survived. In the end, they had marched farther than the distance from the northern tip of the state of Maine to Key West, Florida, and back again.

The Xi'an Incident and the Second United Front

While the weary Long March survivors recuperated in northwestern China, Chiang Kai-shek maneuvered to wipe out this last Communist base and also to contain Japan's most recent advances into Chinese territory. To confront the Communists, Chiang assigned General Zhang Xueliang, the Manchurian warlord, to move his troops to Xi'an and destroy the Yan'an Soviet. With the CCP finally destroyed, Chiang believed, a fully unified nation could concentrate its forces against the Japanese, who in late 1935 had moved south of the Great Wall to annex eastern Hebei Province around Beijing. Protests against Guomindang inaction

had spread across all of China's major cities, calling for an end to the civil war and for united action against the Japanese.

Zhang Xueliang, from his post in Xi'an, was caught in conflicting currents. He was loyal to Chiang Kai-shek, but he and his soldiers, all Manchurian, were reluctant to fight other Chinese given that the Japanese had killed Zhang's father and occupied their homeland. When Communist leader Zhou Enlai approached Zhang about forming a second united front against the Japanese, Zhang took action.

In December 1936, Chiang Kai-shek flew to Xi'an to inspect Zhang's preparations for what he believed would be the last campaign against the Communists. After several days of tense debates, electrified by student protests calling for a united front, Zhang Xueliang seized the Guomindang leader and placed him under house arrest. Zhang and his generals issued a nationwide call for a united front to ally the Guomindang, the CCP, and all warlords against the Japanese.

The Xi'an Incident (西安事变), as it was called, paralyzed the nation and was monitored with consternation by governments around the world. Among the Communists, some, including Mao Zedong, believed that Chiang should be publicly tried and executed, eliminating their archenemy once and for all. But others in Yan'an and Moscow, including Joseph Stalin himself, worried that there was no one else of Chiang Kai-shek's stature who could hold together a unified front against the Japanese. After two weeks of intense negotiations, General Zhang released Chiang Kai-shek. Immediate deliberations to establish a Second United Front (第二次统一战线) with the Communists began, and open war with Japan loomed on China's horizon.

Primary Sources

DOCUMENT 9.1: "Hometown," a short story by Lu Xun, first published in *Xin Qingnian* (*New Youth* magazine), May 1921

It was Runtu. Although I recognized him right off, he was not at all the Runtu who lived in my memory. He seemed twice as tall now. The round and ruddy face of yesteryear had already turned pale and grey, and it was etched with deep wrinkles. The rims of his eyes were swollen and red just like his father's. I knew that most farmers who worked close to the sea got that way because of the wind. He was wearing a battered old felt hat, and his cotton clothes were so thin that he was shivering. His hands held a paper package along with his pipe. They were not the smooth and nimble hands that I remembered. Now they were rough, clumsy, and as cracked as pine bark.

I was beside myself with enthusiasm, but didn't know how to begin and simply said, "Brother Runtu, you've come..."

There was so much I wanted to say. There were so many words waiting to gush out one after the other like pearls on a string: hornchicks, jumperfish, Guanyin hands, *zha*—but at the same time I was aware of something damming them up inside me, so that they simply swirled around in my brain without a single one coming out.

As he stood there his expression was a mixture of happiness and melancholy. His lips began to move, but not a single word came out. Finally he assumed a very respectful attitude and addressed me in a loud clear voice: "Master!"

I shuddered as I realized what a wretched thick wall now stood between us. I too was at a loss for words....

SOURCE: Lu Xun, *Diary of a Madman and Other Stories*, trans. William Lyell (Honolulu: University of Hawaii Press, 1990) 96.

 The full text of Document 9.1 is available on the CD-ROM.

DOCUMENT 9.2: Excerpts from the "Guidelines of the New Life Movement," by Chiang Kai-shek, *Central Daily News*, May 15, 1934

There are two kinds of people who are skeptical of the New Life Movement. One [kind] considers *li, yi, lian, chi* [propriety, righteousness, modesty, and a sense of shame] no more than some polished behaviors. They argue that if our knowledge and technology are below other nations, no matter how beautiful and benevolent our behavior may be, our country still would not be saved. This kind of argument is a result of reversing the importance of moral conduct with that of knowledge and technology, because knowledge and technology are by-products of the pursuit of perfect moral conduct. Otherwise, knowledge and technology will be used for ill purposes, harming others and not necessarily benefiting oneself. Therefore, *li, yi, lian, chi* can not only save the country, but also strengthen our country....

 The full text of Document 9.2 is available on the CD-ROM.

DOCUMENT 9.3: Excerpts from "Report on an Investigation of the Peasant Movement in Hunan," by Mao Zedong, March 1927

[T]he rise of the peasant movement is a colossal event. In a very short time, in China's central, southern and northern provinces, several hundred million peasants will rise like a mighty storm, like a hurricane, a force so swift and violent that no power, however great, will be able to hold it back. They will smash all the trammels that now bind them and rush forward along the road to liberation. They will sweep all the imperialists, warlords, corrupt officials, local tyrants and evil gentry into their graves. Every revolutionary party and every revolutionary comrade will be put to the test, to be accepted or rejected as they decide. There are three alternatives. To march at their head and lead them? To trail behind them, gesticulating and criticizing? Or to stand in their way and oppose them? Every Chinese is free to choose, but events will force you to make the choice quickly....

SOURCE: *Selected Works of Mao Zedong* (Beijing: Foreign Languages Press, 1967).

 The full text of Document 9.3 is available on the CD-ROM.

DOCUMENT 9.4: "The Long March," a poem by Mao Zedong, 1935

The Red Army fears not the trials of the Long March,
Holding light ten thousand crags and torrents.
The Five Ridges wind like gentle ripples
And the majestic Wumeng roll by, globules of clay.
Warm the steep cliffs lapped by the waters of Golden Sand [River],
Cold the iron chains spanning the Dadu River.
Minshan's thousand *li* of snow joyously crossed,
The three Armies march on, each face glowing.

SOURCE: Mao Zedong, *Mao Zedong Poems* (Beijing: Foreign Language Press, 2003) 37.

DOCUMENT 9.5: "Jinsha Jiang" ("The River of Golden Sand"), an anonymous account describing a segment of the Long March, 1934–35

Nearer and nearer we drew to the shore. The outline of the town was now visible and the lights became brighter. Shadows could be seen moving about and shouts were audible. A fierce battle was impending. My heart tightened. Grabbing my Mauser I looked intently at the approaching town. As the boat drew up along the bank, I pushed lightly the two sitting next to me who quickly jumped ashore and mounted the stone steps holding their rifles.

"Hey! You, why have you come back so late?" said a cracked voice in a Yunnan accent.

The two made no immediate response. Then we heard one say quietly: "Don't move!"

As soon as I heard that, I led the others up the steps, and before they knew a thing, the two enemy sentries were captives. The depositions of the captives were more or less like the boatmen's. I ordered the 1st Platoon to go up the street and attack the Guomindang regular troops and the 2nd Platoon to attack the police. I stayed on the jetty. They were to report back to me. The boats were sent for reinforcements. According to plan, I made the messenger gather some rushes and burn them by the riverside as a signal that our company had succeeded in crossing.

SOURCE: *Stories of the Long March* (Beijing: Foreign Languages Press, 1958) 35–50.

 The full text of Document 9.5 is available on the CD-ROM.

DOCUMENT 9.6: "The Bridge of Iron Chains," an account describing crossing the Luding Bridge on the Long March, 1934–35

The next day we received an order reading as follows: "Our Left Route Army has been given until the 25th to take the Luding Bridge. You must march at the utmost speed and act in the shortest possible time to accomplish the glorious mission. We are confident you can do it. Are preparing to congratulate you on your victory." Below was the forceful signature of General Lin Biao....

We couldn't stop. Time was too precious. As we marched we held a meeting of military and political officers to discuss what we should do. First we issued a number of rallying cries: "The 4th Red Regiment has a glorious battle record. We must complete our mission and preserve our glory!" "Emulate the 1st Red Regiment, which captured Anshunchang. Compete with them and take the Luding Bridge!" "Our mission is glorious but very difficult. We can pass the test!" We set six the following morning as the deadline for reaching our objective....

To cross the Wild Tiger Mountain you have to go up some forty *li*, then come down the same distance. It is a dangerous climb, with the Dadu River on the right, high cliffs on the left, and the path just a narrow twisting trail. People say it's the neck of the road between Anshunchang and the Luding Bridge, and that's no exaggeration in the least....

SOURCE: Yang Zhengwu, "The Fight at Luding Bridge," *Stories of the Long March* (Beijing: Foreign Languages Press, 1958) 61–76.

 The full text of Document 9.6 is available on the CD-ROM.

DOCUMENT 9.7: "Jiajin Shan" ("The Great Snow Mountain"), an anonymous account describing a segment of the Long March, 1934–35

By nightfall we had crossed, at an altitude of 16,000 feet, and that night we bivouacked in a valley where there was no sign of human life. While most of us were stretched out exhausted, General Zhu De came around to make his usual inspection. He was very weary, for he had walked with the troops. Yet nothing ever prevented him from making his rounds. He gave me half of a little dried beef, which he had in his pocket. He encouraged everyone and said we had crossed the worst peak, and it was only a few more days to Mougong.

To avoid enemy bombers, we arose at midnight and began climbing the next peak. It rained, then snowed, and the fierce wind whipped our bodies, and more men died of cold and exhaustion.

The last peak in the range, which we estimated to be eighty *li* [twenty-seven miles] from base to summit, was terrible. Hundreds of our men died there. They would sit down to rest or relieve themselves and never get up. All along the route we kept reaching down to pull men to their feet only to find that they were already dead....

SOURCE: "Across the Snow Mountain," *Stories of the Long March* (Beijing: Foreign Languages Press, 1958) 79–84.

 The full text of Document 9.7 is available on the CD-ROM.

DOCUMENT 9.8: Excerpts from "Political Mobilization for the War of Resistance," a lecture by Mao Zedong, May 1938

The mobilization of the common people throughout the country will create a vast sea in which to drown the enemy, create the conditions that will make up for our inferiority in arms and other things, and create the prerequisites for overcoming every difficulty in the war. To win victory, we must persevere in the War of Resistance, in the united front and in the protracted war. But all these are inseparable from the mobilization of the common people. To wish for victory and yet neglect political mobilization is like wishing to "go south by driving the chariot north," and the result would inevitably be to forfeit victory.

What does political mobilization mean? First, it means telling the army and the people about the political aim of the war. It is necessary for every soldier and civilian to see why the war must be fought and how it concerns him. The political aim of the war is "to drive out Japanese imperialism and build a new China of freedom and equality;" we must proclaim this aim to everybody, to all soldiers and civilians, before we can create an anti-Japanese upsurge and unite hundreds of millions as one man to contribute their all to the war....

The richest source of power to wage war lies in the masses of the people. It is mainly because of the unorganized state of the Chinese masses that Japan dares to bully us. When this defect is remedied, then the Japanese aggressor, like a mad bull crashing into a ring of flames, will be surrounded by hundreds of millions of our people standing upright, the mere sound of their voices will strike terror into him, and he will be burned to death....

SOURCE: *Selected Works of Mao Zedong, Volume II* (Beijing: Foreign Languages Press, 1967).

 The full text of Document 9.8 is available on the CD-ROM.

DOCUMENT 9.9: "Manifesto on the Seizure of Chiang Kai-shek," a telegram sent to the nation by General Zhang Xueliang, December 12, 1936

Generalissimo Chiang Kai-shek, surrounded by a group of unworthy advisers, has forfeited the support of the masses of our people. He is deeply guilty for the harm his policies have done the country. We, Zhang Xueliang and the others, undersigned, advised him with tears to take another way; but we were repeatedly rejected and rebuked….

The Military and Civilians in the Northwest unanimously make the following demands:

1. Reorganize the Nanjing Government, and admit all parties to share the joint responsibility of saving the nation.
2. Stop all kinds of civil wars.
3. Immediately release the patriotic leaders arrested in Shanghai.
4. Release all political prisoners throughout the country.
5. Emancipate the patriotic movement of the people.
6. Safeguard the political freedom of the people to organize and call meetings.
7. Actually carry out the Will of Dr. Sun Yat-sen.
8. Immediately call a National Salvation Conference….

SOURCE: Rpt. in James Bertram, *First Act in China: The Story of the Sian Mutiny* (New York: Viking Press, 1938) 126–127.

 The full text of Document 9.9 is available on the CD-ROM.

DOCUMENT 9.10: "The Rebellion in Xi'an," a report in the *Manchester Guardian Weekly*, July 16, 1937

> *The* Guardian's *reporter wrote the article based on Mme. Chiang's (Soong Meiling's) account, which she published under the title* Xi'an: A Coup D'Etat.

 The full text of Document 9.10 is available on the CD-ROM.

DOCUMENT 9.11a & b: Photographs at site of the seizure of Chiang Kai-shek outside Xi'an, 2006

The poster reads: "National Historical Red Tourist Site: Xi'an Incident Site in commemoration of the 70th anniversary of the Xi'an Incident." From left to right, the photographs are of Chiang Kai-shek, Zhang Xueliang, and Yang Hucheng.

This meeting room was in the suite of rooms Chiang used before he was placed under house arrest.
(Photos by Liz Nelson)

DOCUMENTS 9.12a–c: Cartoons by Sapajou in *The North China Daily News*, 1936–1937

THE NORTH-CHINA DAILY NEWS, MONDAY, DECEMBER 14, 1936

SABOTAGE IN SHENSI

By SAPAJOU

The other two cartoons are on the CD-ROM.

DOCUMENT 9.13: Photograph of Zhou Enlai, Mao Zedong, and Bo Gu, 1937

The three men were key figures in the Chinese Communist Party. *(Peabody Museum of Archaeology and Ethnology, Harvard University/Lattimore Foundation.)*

Activities

ACTIVITY 1: Evaluating the New Life Movement

Part 1:

After reading the introductory essay, read Lu Xun's short story "Hometown" (9.1) and consider the following:

1. What tone is set at the outset of the story?
2. What words does the narrator use to describe "life" (see page 9 of the story)?
3. What feelings does the narrator express?
4. What kind of "new life" do you think the narrator is proposing toward the end of the story?

Part 2:

After reading Chiang Kai-shek's "Guidelines of the New Life Movement" (9.2), discuss:

1. What were the central concepts in Chiang's New Life Movement?
2. In what spheres of life did he suggest they should be applied?
3. Do Chiang's guidelines echo any other philosophical or religious approach to living?
4. Which guidelines to New Life do you agree with? Why? With which do you disagree? Why?
5. What role can or should government play in people's personal behavior?

Writing extension:

Consider the statement, "Strong morals must be the foundation of all learning. Basic needs, such as food and clothing, and accumulation of knowledge and technology, are secondary." Write a response piece agreeing or disagreeing. Give specific examples to support your position.

Part 3:

Read Mao Zedong's report on the peasant associations (9.3) and consider the questions:

1. What were the peasant associations doing?
2. How had power shifted in the rural areas Mao describes?
3. What was Mao's attitude toward violence?
4. Compare Mao's approach to "new life" to Chiang Kai-shek's.

Creative extension:

Consider the impact of Chiang's New Life Movement and Mao's peasant actions on Chinese people by imagining how three major characters (the narrator, Runtu, and Second Sister Yang) in Lu Xun's story "Hometown" (9.1) might have responded to each. Assume the roles of media hosts/interviewers and one of Lu Xun's characters. Conduct live interviews with the characters or videotape interviews outside of class. (See Item 9.A on the CD-ROM for guidelines.)

Part 4:

In reality, Mao's peasant revolution eventually overthrew Chiang's government and led to the establishment of People's Republic of China in 1949. Chiang's New Life Movement failed to gain momentum at the time, but lived on in Taiwan after 1949.

1. List three reasons to explain the success of Mao's call for peasant revolution. Use specifics from Lu Xun's story and the documents to illustrate your point.

2. List three reasons to explain the failure of the New Life Movement at the time. Use specifics from the story and the documents to illustrate your point.

ACTIVITY 2: Analyzing accounts of the Long March

Part 1:

Read Mao Zedong's poem "The Long March" (9.4) and discuss:

1. What is the tone of the poem?

2. For what purpose might Mao have written this poem and other poems during the Long March?

3. Mao's poems are written in a traditional Chinese style that echoes that of much-loved poets of the Tang dynasty, particularly Li Bai (701–762 c.e.). Why might Mao have chosen this style as opposed to a more modern poetic form influenced by European or American writers?

Part 2:

Read the three accounts describing the Red Army's experience at three famous landmarks: "The River of Golden Sand," "The Bridge of Iron Chains," and "The Great Snow Mountain" (9.5. 9.6, and 9.7) and answer the following questions:

1. What is the tone of each account? Are they similar? How?

2. What impression do you get of the Red Army soldiers? How are Guomindang soldiers portrayed?

3. What are the highlights in each account?

4. How do they differ in perspective from Mao's "Long March" poem?

5. Whose account of events appears to be more authentic, Mao's or the soldiers'?

6. Whose account would have been more useful to the Communists' efforts to build support among the populace? Why?

ACTIVITY 3: Transforming narratives into news reports

Part 1:

Form three groups. Each group is responsible for one of the three landmarks (Golden Sand River, the Bridge of Iron Chains, or the Great Snow Mountain). Identify the location of the site on the map (Item 9.C). To get a sense of the terrain over which the Red Army marched, look at a topographic map in Additional Resources on the CD or use Google Earth to look up the locations. Based on information given in the accounts as well as supplemental research from text and online sources, develop a written or oral "news report" (such as a newspaper article, a "live" newscast, or a recorded audio or video news report) that describes the Red Army's experiences at the landmark. Each report should be five minutes in length (or roughly 1.5 pages) and contain the following information:

1. Describe the topographical characteristics of the area in which the landmark is located and the challenges the topography posed to Red Army troops.

2. Describe the other challenges that the Red Army encountered in this area, such as Guomindang troops, climate, disease, scarcity of food, or other obstacles.

3. List the advantages and strengths the Red Army possessed when they faced these obstacles.

4. Describe the strategies the Red Army used to overcome the obstacles.

Part 2:

Read or take notes on the three news reports at key junctures along the Long March. Write a paragraph summarizing the key elements that eventually contributed to the Red Army's success in completing the Long March.

Part 3:

These three accounts were among many published in 1958. Discuss as a class:

1. How might the time span between when the Long March took place (1934–35) and the date of publication affect the narratives?

2. What other factors, such as the political conditions in 1958 (see Chapter 13), might have affected the narratives?

3. Even though the Long March was essentially a retreat from superior Guomindang forces, it has taken on mythic proportions since the PRC was founded in 1949. Why might this event be viewed as so important?

4. Are there similar achievements or events in other countries that compare to the Long March? How do other countries remember or commemorate events they consider pivotal in their histories?

ACTIVITY 4: Examining political mobilization for the anti-Japanese National United Front

Part 1:

Read Mao Zedong's "The Japanese War and Peasant Nationalism" (9.8) and create a Chinese Communist Party propaganda leaflet to convince Guomindang officers and soldiers to support a United Front with the CCP to resist the Japanese invasion. The leaflet should include key wording from Mao's lecture and achieve the following aims:

- instill patriotism and confidence in the officers and soldiers for resisting Japanese invasion;
- encourage Guomindang officers and soldiers to mobilize civilians such as workers, peasants, merchants, and students to support the United Front.

Part 2:

Read Zhang Xueliang's telegram to the nation explaining the kidnapping of Chiang Kai-shek (9.9) and review the information in the introductory essay. Write an editorial on General Zhang's seizure of Chiang for either a CCP newspaper or a Guomindang newspaper. The editorial should:

- outline the political circumstances under which the incident happened;
- explain Zhang's motive in taking the action;
- predict possible outcomes of the incident and suggest a solution to the situation;
- call on the readers to take steps to help achieve the best solution.

ACTIVITY 5: Analyzing the Xi'an Incident

Read General Zhang's telegram (9.9) and "The Rebellion in Xi'an" (9.10) and complete the following assignment.

Part 1:

Discuss as a class:

1. How do the perspectives of these two accounts of the same incident differ from each other?
2. Of the eight demands presented to Chiang Kai-shek by force, which ones did he refuse and which ones did he comply with? Why?
3. In 1946, Chiang ordered Yang Hucheng, the other general involved in the kidnapping, to be executed along with his whole family, but he put Zhang under house-arrest instead. Why do you think he spared Zhang's life? Why did he wait until after the end of World War II to have General Yang's death sentence carried out?

4. After the Long March, the Xi'an Incident is considered "a historical turning point for China."[7] What might be the significance of the Xi'an Incident in the ultimate success of the CCP?

5. Examine the photos of the site where Chiang was captured and where the negotiations took place (9.11a & b). How has the Chinese government chosen to memorialize the Xi'an Incident?

6. General Zhang Xueliang lived under house arrest in Taiwan and later, after Chiang's death, lived in Hawaii, where he died at the age of 101. Why do you think that despite repeated invitations, he never returned to mainland China?

Part 2:

Divide into two groups (one takes the perspective of Zhang Xueliang, the other of Chiang Kai-shek) and debate the pros and cons of cooperation with the Communists against Japanese invasion.

ACTIVITY 6: Perspectives on the Xi'an Incident

Examine the three cartoons from the *North China Daily News* (9.11a–c) and answer the following questions:

"Sabotage in Shensi [Shaanxi Province]," December 14, 1936

1. The two figures depicted in the cartoon are actual people involved in the Xi'an Incident. Who are they?

2. What is the artist's attitude toward the figure in the plane?

3. The *North China Daily News*, the paper in which these cartoons ran, was owned by British businessmen in Shanghai. Explain why this paper would have had this perspective.

"Who Did It?" December 17, 1936

1. The two figures depicted here represent two countries with a keen interest in the events at Xi'an. They are placed in geographically accurate positions to China's northwest and northeast. What countries do the figures represent?

2. Why might they be interested in the development of the Xi'an Incident? What stake do they have in the outcome?

3. How does this cartoon reflect the international perspective on the political situation in China at this time? Would European and American governments be as likely to watch the events of the Xi'an Incident as the countries depicted in the cartoon? Why or why not?

"Don't Do It, Sister!" January 24, 1937

1. The two figures depicted here represent generalized images of China and Spain. What events in "Madrid" would make that city a sister to "Sian"?[8]

---

[7] Wording used at the museum created at General Zhang's headquarters in Xi'an.

[8] "Sian" is an older spelling of "Xi'an."

2. What is the message that "Madrid" tries to convey to "Xi'an"? In other words, don't do what?

3. What is the tone of this cartoon? How does it differ from the first two?

Overall:

1. How did the cartoons change over the course of about six weeks? Why might that have been?

2. Among all the key players in the Xi'an Incident, whose voice is not depicted in the cartoons? Why?

3. Based on your understanding of the artist's perspectives reflected in these cartoons, describe the artist's likely response to the outcome of the Xi'an Incident and the resulting change in the political situation in China.

ACTIVITY 7: **What can a photograph tell us?**

Examine the photograph of Zhou Enlai, Mao Zedong, and Bo Gu (9.13) and consider the following questions:

1. What are your impressions of the three Chinese Communist Party leaders depicted in the photo? Describe each person's attitude, expression, and appearance, using two or three adjectives for each category.

2. How do your impressions of these individuals differ from your expectations of CCP leaders prior to seeing this photo?

3. This photo was taken in June 1937, nearly two years after the successful but devastating Long March. In what ways do you think the experience affected the men's appearance as well as their attitude?

4. Pay close attention to their clothing and point out two differences between Mao's attire and that of the others. Do these differences suggest Mao's leadership within the Party? What else could they suggest?

5. Do these men, especially Mao and Zhou, look approachable? How would that have affected their ability to work with and recruit peasants?

6. The fourth person in the photo was not identified. Assuming he is a junior assistant to Mao, how would you interpret the way he gazes at Mao? In other words, what could be going through his mind at such a moment in history?

Use a search engine or look in books to find a photograph of Chiang Kai-shek from the 1930s. Describe his attitude, expression, and appearance. Compare it to that of the CCP leaders in the 1937 photograph.

Suggested Resources

Books

Dong, Stella. *Shanghai: The Rise and Fall of a Decadent City, 1842–1949*. New York: Harper Perennial, 2002.
Provides an engrossing and readable history of the city at the center of China's turbulent revolutionary years.

Gray, Jack. *Rebellions and Revolutions: China from the 1800s to the 1980s*. New York: Oxford University Press, 1990.
A concise and accessible introduction to China's recent history, written for non-experts.

Hahn, Emily. *The Soong Sisters*. New York: Doubleday, 1941.
Written by an American expatriate in China, the biography offers insight into the inner workings of the Republican era.

Lu Xun. *Diary of a Madman and Other Stories*. Trans. William Lyell. Honolulu: University of Hawaii Press, 1990.

Snow, Edgar. *Red Star Over China*. New York: Grove Press, 1994.
Snow, an American journalist, interviewed Mao and other Communist leaders in the years following the Long March, providing some of the most intimate reportage of the period. He was, however, quite enamored of the Communist cause, so his work should be treated as biased.

Spence, Jonathan D., and Annping Chin. *The Chinese Century: A Photographic History of the Last Hundred Years*. New York: Random House, 1996.
An unparalleled collection of photographs from the period.

Yu Hua. *To Live*. Trans. Michael Berry. New York: Anchor, 2003.
This acclaimed contemporary novel chronicles the life of the son of a wealthy family who gambles away his family fortune, survives war and famine, and manages to endure the myriad twists and turns of the Guomindang and Communist periods. See also Films.

Websites

Maps

http://users.erols.com/mwhite28/longmarc.htm A map of the Long March together with a timeline.

http://www.dean.usma.edu/history/default.htm The history department at the United States Military Academy provides links to atlases and excellent maps of China's Civil War.

http://earth.google.com/ to download Google Earth (a free download)

Founding of Chinese Communist Party

http://www.wsu.edu/~dee/MODCHINA/MODCHINA.HTM

http://www.thecorner.org/hist/china/may4th.htm "Intellectual Revolution" in *The Corner of the World*

http://www.china.org.cn/english/features/45954.htm "An Illustrated History of the Communist Party of China" contains some interesting photos from important moments in the early history of the CCP.

http://www.marxists.org/reference/archive/mao/selected-works/index.htm *The Selected Works of Mao Zedong* online includes Mao's most important political works, as well as his poetry and writings on military strategy.

http://www.talesofoldchina.com/default.cfm "Tales of Old China": Memorabilia from Shanghai and Beijing in the Guomindang period: photographs, cartoons, and even whole books published at that time by British and American expatriates in China.

http://www.talesofoldchina.com/sapajou/sapajou1.php "Sapajou" in "Tales of Old China": A biography and selection of work from the famous Shanghai cartoonist.

http://www.marx2mao.com/Mao/SCKS36.html "A Statement on Chiang Kai-shek's Statement" by Mao Zedong, December 28, 1936; Mao's response to Chiang's "Admonition to Zhang Xueliang and Yang Hucheng."

http://www.newsgd.com/pictures/construction/ **200312260045_8051.gif** A photograph of Mao Zedong in 1921, the year that the First National Conference of the Communist Party in China took place.

http://www.lib.umich.edu/govdocs/text/mchiang. **htm** Madame Chiang's appeal to the United States Congress, 1943

Films

China in Revolution, vol. 1 of *China: A Century of Revolution* (120 minutes, 1997)
This documentary offers riveting footage of the contest between the Guomindang and the Communists as well as interviews with Chinese who lived through the era.

To Live (133 minutes, 2003) In Chinese with subtitles. *The best of the films that span China's revolutionary years,* To Live *follows the son of an elite family through the hardships of the Guomindang and Communist periods. Based on the novel by Yu Hua. Directed by Zhang Yimou.*

The Last Emperor (162 mins; 1987)
The film poignantly captures the anachronism of a child-emperor coming to power in China in the early 20th century and the subsequent political turmoil. Directed by Bernardo Bertolucci.

Writers and Revolutionaries (60 mins; 1992)
Volume IV of the ten-part Pacific Century series focuses on the role of intellectuals in the rise of twentieth-century nationalism and progressivism in the East. Written and produced by Alex Gibney and Steve Talley.

■ **A CLOSER LOOK**

The Soong Sisters: "One loved money; one loved power; one loved China"

In 1878, twelve-year-old "Charlie Soong" (Sung Yaoju) moved to Boston, Massachusetts to begin his apprenticeship with a Chinese merchant family. He didn't last long and soon signed up as a crew man on a U.S. Revenue Service cutter. The vessel's captain and his wealthy friends in North Carolina helped arrange for Charlie to be educated as a Methodist missionary at Trinity College (later Duke University). In 1886, he returned to China to preach. He shifted from missionary work to the printing of Bibles and then opened a noodle factory, equipped with the latest Western machinery. A firm supporter of Sun Yat-sen's Revolutionary Alliance (see Chapter 7) and the need to modernize China, Charlie Soong wanted his three daughters as well as his three sons to be proficient in English and college-educated. The girls initially attended a private American school in Shanghai before traveling to the United States to pursue college degrees.

Soong Ailing, the eldest, left home when she was fourteen to study at Wesleyan College for Women in Georgia—the first Chinese woman to do so. After graduating, she would return to China, work briefly for Sun Yat-sen, and then marry H. H. Kung, a prominent banker and direct descendant of Confucius.

Madame Sun Yat-sen

Soong Qingling, born in 1893, joined her older sister in Georgia in 1908, where she, too, earned a degree from Wesleyan. In 1913, she returned to China and took over from Ailing as Sun Yat-sen's personal secretary. Two years later, as her family was arranging a marriage for her, Qingling and Sun Yat-sen (her senior by twenty-eight years) eloped. Her parents were appalled; Charlie Soong considered himself betrayed by his close friend. Sun Yat-sen continued his efforts to unify China as a republic but died prematurely in 1925. After Chiang Kai-shek routed the Communists and their supporters in Shanghai in the spring of 1927, Soong Qingling broke with the Guomindang and gave her support to the Chinese Communist Party. As a result of her dramatically different political views, Qingling became estranged from her sisters.

In the 1930s, with the Japanese threatening to occupy more and more of China, she supported a united front. In 1939, Soong Qingling founded the China Defense League, an organization that gathered donations and medical supplies from abroad. In later years, the organization became the China Welfare Institute, dedicated to providing maternal and infant medical care and promoting education. After the founding of the People's Republic of China in 1949, she held a number of government posts, includ-ing vice-chairperson of the PRC and vice-chairperson of the National People's Congress. She represented China on many occasions, traveling to several countries, among them the USSR, India, and Indonesia. She also wrote *The Struggle for New China* and founded and contributed to the magazine *China Reconstructs* (now known as *China Today*). Soong Qingling died in Beijing in 1981. Her home has been declared a historical landmark.

Madame Chiang Kai-shek

Soong Meiling had insisted on going to Georgia with Qingling in 1908, even though she was just ten years old. For several years she was privately tutored before she began at Wesleyan. In 1913, since both her sisters had returned to Shanghai, Meiling transferred to Wellesley College in Massachusetts to be close to a brother who was at Harvard. She graduated with a degree in English literature in 1917.

Meiling first met Chiang Kai-shek in 1922. Several years would pass before they married, since Chiang already had two wives,[9] and the Soong family insisted he divorce them and convert to Christianity.

Madame Chiang Kai-shek played an active role in the Guomindang government and in promoting the New Life Movement, which she helped develop. Described as a "dazzling and imperious politician,"[10] she helped negotiate a peaceful resolution to the Xi'an Incident. She is probably best remembered as China's eloquent and elegant "ambassador" to the United States during China's War of Resistance against Japan (see Chapter 11). She traveled across the Pacific several times to raise awareness of China's plight, and in February 1943, seeking financial aid, she was the first Chinese individual and only the second woman to address a joint session of Congress. That November, she served as Chiang's interpreter at the Cairo Conference with President Roosevelt and Winston Churchill, the British prime minister. Twice she appeared on the cover of *Time* magazine.

After the Allies defeated Japan and China's civil war resumed (see Chapter 12), Madame Chiang again sought financial assistance from the U.S. President Truman refused. "They're thieves, every damn one of them," he would insist later, referring to Guomindang leaders and the rampant corruption. It appears likely that the extended Soong family had siphoned hundreds of millions of dollars of U.S. aid intended for the war.[11] Soong Meiling was in the States when the PRC was founded; she joined her husband in

[9] Polygamy, marrying more than one woman, was legal in China at the time and common among wealthy or prominent men.
[10] "Madame Chiang Kai-shek, a Power in Husband's China and Abroad, Dies at 105," *New York Times*, October 24, 2003.
[11] "Madame Chiang Kai-shek...Dies at 105," *New York Times*, October 24, 2003.

Taiwan in 1950. After Chiang Kai-shek's death in 1975, when Chiang's eldest son by his first wife took over as president, she left Taiwan.[12] She continued to play a role in organizations such as the International Red Cross Committee and the British United Aid to China Fund, but spent most of her remaining years in New York. Madame Chiang died in October 2003 at age 105.

■ *What factors might explain how these three women were all so central to the story of China's development in the 20th century?*

---

[12] Neither Soong Qingling nor Soong Meiling had children.

CHAPTER 10

Challenges to Tradition in the Early Republic

By Cara Abraham

Chapter Contents

Challenges to Confucian Tradition

Reform Efforts

The Lives of Women

Rural China

The Urban Working Poor

Organizing Idea

The early years of the Republic were marked by both firm attachment to tradition and revitalized efforts by individuals to bring about social change in China.

Key Questions

What traditional customs were Chinese men and women practicing in the first thirty years of the twentieth century?

What were some of the ways in which reformers sought to bring about change?

What factors impeded social change?

To what extent did reformers work within the existing social structure to bring about change?

How much change took place for women, peasants, and the urban working poor?

How far did the changes go in creating a basis for a "modern" society?

Key Terms

concubine

Confucian hierarchy

foot binding

indentured servitude

mission schools

modernization

reform

rickshaw

"save face"

Essay

In the first decades of the twentieth century, at a time of significant political instability, China underwent important social change. In addition to reformers who published literature and essays in new political journals (see Chapter 8 for examples), there were individuals "in the field" studying social issues and implementing reforms. They sought to reduce the gap between the rich and poor. Many also worked to advance health care and to improve the lives of women. There were renewed efforts to simplify the Chinese script and extend educational opportunities to the greater populace.

Following the Boxer Uprising (义和团起义) of 1900, the Qing government had to pay indemnities to Western nations (see Chapter 7). The American government used these payments to provide scholarships for Chinese students to study in the United States. More than a thousand young Chinese took advantage of a work-study program in France, Zhou Enlai (周恩来) and Deng Xiaoping (邓小平) among them. Protestant and Catholic congregations funded Christian mission schools in China, which were instrumental in extending education to girls. Chinese students returned from overseas studies and themselves started many new schools.

The Qing (清) dynasty had abolished the civil service examination system in 1905; now many of the younger generation of the scholar-official and literati class led reform movements.[1] Increased literacy led to an explosion in print media, in which authors challenged old ways of thinking about marriage, family, and success. Increasing numbers of poor women worked outside the home, followed later by educated women. This period marked stronger efforts to end foot binding and indentured servitude. Reformers challenged the Confucian hierarchy. To a lesser degree, they questioned the practice of arranged marriages.

---

[1] See Chapter 2 to learn about the traditional role of the educated elite in Chinese society.

Rural China

The hope and promise of the 1911 Nationalist Revolution (*Xinhai geming*, 辛亥革命) quickly came face to face with the political realities of early twentieth-century China. In the late 1920s and early 1930s, Chiang Kai-shek's Guomindang (国民党) government enacted measures to bring about social change, but age-old institutions and problems often compromised the efforts. Challenged by warlords, the Chinese Communist Party (中国共产党), and encroaching Japanese (see Chapter 9), the Guomindang leaders were unable to create an effective administration in rural areas. Constantly strapped for funds, Chiang's weak central government barely responded to the effects of the worldwide depression or to natural disasters, both of which disrupted food production and resulted in hundreds of thousands of peasants' dying from starvation. Reform, when it happened, came primarily as a result of dedicated individuals such as James Yen and the Mass Education Movement he began.

Many impoverished peasants moved to the cities, hoping to find steady work. As various warlords continued to fight over Chinese territory, families trying to escape the violence were often separated. Young men with no other prospects joined militias or were involuntarily conscripted into them. The instability worsened the lives of villagers, who depended upon a steady source of labor and fixed social units in order to cultivate their land. Despite the chaos, those who remained in the countryside continued to live lives centered on their extended families and traditional festivals.

Urban Life

People living in coastal cities generally fared better during the Republican era. The wealthier Chinese urban residents, in particular, had increasing access to a sophisticated blend of foreign and Chinese culture. Travel on newly-paved roads, fast trains, and later even airplanes opened new avenues for national and international exchange. Cinemas, radios, and mass advertising competed for residents' attention and surplus income. Chinese reformers often found a more welcoming atmosphere in these urban centers. Shanghai (上海), in particular, was an international city in the 1920s and 1930s, home to foreign concession areas where French, English, Japanese, American, and Italian businessmen and their families—among others —resided. Their interests were protected by 22,000 of their own troops and police and 43 warships, ready for use should foreigners feel their interests were under threat.[2] The expatriates lived a comfortable life largely separated from the impoverished Chinese masses.

The years 1912 to 1937 were filled with chaos and dislocation; nevertheless, Chinese people in all walks of life continued to provide for their families and make plans for the future. Many of the reformers' efforts may be credited with paving the way for the dramatic changes that took place after Liberation in 1949.

Primary Sources

DOCUMENT 10.1 Excerpts from *Tell the People: Talks with James Yen about the Mass Education Movement*, by Pearl S. Buck, 1945

You remember those symbols, five of them, which are enshrined in practically every Chinese home? They are, you remember, these five characters: heaven, earth, emperor, parent, teacher. Teacher, as you see, is ranked side by side with heaven and earth. The teacher shares the homage and worship of the people with heaven and earth as well as parent and emperor. That tradition, as you know, accounts for the great reverence that the Chinese people, a farmer or laborer, have for the scholar, the teacher. So with an educational atmosphere prevailing in the community, everybody wants to learn, and also to teach....

SOURCE: Pearl S. Buck, *Tell the People: Talks with James Yen About the Mass Education Movement* (New York: The John Day Company, 1945) 44.

 The full text of Document 10.1 is available on the CD-ROM.

---

[2] Jonathan D. Spence, *The Search for Modern China* (New York: W. W. Norton, 1999) 334.

DOCUMENT 10.2 Photograph of Five Character Plaque in Lijiang, April 2006

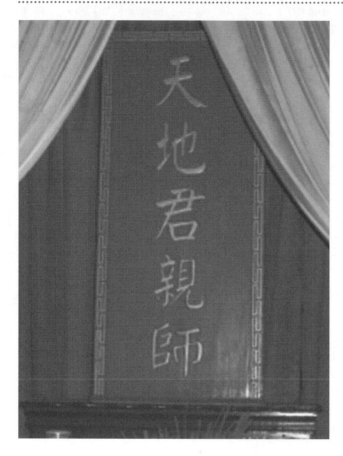

天
地
君
親
師

From top to bottom, the characters read "heaven, earth, emperor, parent, teacher." *(Photo by Cara Abraham)*

DOCUMENT 10.3: Excerpts describing the founding of schools from *Tell the People: Talks with James Yen About the Mass Education Movement* by Pearl S. Buck, 1945

"It required weeks of 'social calls' and group meetings to set the atmosphere. Then the campaign went on almost of itself. A big meeting of the townspeople elected a council to take charge of it. Schools were drawn in, and students volunteered to serve on recruiting teams. Events led up to a mass meeting and parade all around the town to the gaping astonishment of the villagers who had come in to town for market day. There was hardly anyone left unaware of the literacy campaign, what it meant, what it stood for. The recruiting teams went from house to house, and there was no peace for a family until every illiterate between twelve and twenty-five had signed up...."

SOURCE: Pearl S. Buck, *Tell the People: Talks with James Yen About the Mass Education Movement* (New York: The John Day Company, 1945) 17–18.

 The full text of Document 10.3 is available on the CD-ROM.

DOCUMENT 10.4: Excerpts describing the Fellow Scholar Association from *Tell the People: Talks with James Yen About the Mass Education Movement* by Pearl S. Buck, 1945

The creation of a People's Literature was approached scientifically; the writers were trained in the use of language and they studied at first hand the people for whom they were to write. The subjects were stories from Chinese history, general information about modern China, lives of great men and women of China and other nations, simple accounts of scientific discoveries, descriptions of methods of improving agricultural production, information about common ailments and other health knowledge, plays, poems and songs…. We made a special research study of folk songs and folk literature. These are the real living literature of the people. Never written down, but passed on from generation to generation. We had to get those who were familiar with them to recite or sing them while our writers took them down, word for word. Studies of this sort helped to bring our writers to a better understanding of the culture of our race. In folk literature they found a great deal that was fine and true and representative of the best qualities of the Chinese….

SOURCE: Buck, Pearl S. *Tell the People: Talks with James Yen About the Mass Education Movement* (New York: The John Day Company, 1945) 55–56.

 The full text of Document 10.4 is available on the CD-ROM.

DOCUMENT 10.5 Photograph, "Shanghai Street," 1937

(Getty Images/Hulton Archive/Getty Images)

DOCUMENT 10.6d: Photographs taken on an Ohio man's summer tour of China, 1913

A busy street

 The remaining photographs are on the CD-ROM.

DOCUMENT 10.7: Excerpts from *Family* by Ba Jin, 1931

In contrast to the older generation, Juemin took active measures concerning his marriage. Without the least shyness, he made inquiries about the proposed match. Juehui became his scout. Together with Qin the two brothers formed a committee of three. They discussed tactics—how to block the match with old man Feng's niece, how to publicize the relationship between Juemin and Qin.

As the opening stage of the battle, Juemin made his attitude plain to his Big Brother. Juexin replied that it was not up to him. Juemin requested his stepmother to cancel the match. But Juemin couldn't approach the old man directly and he could find no one with influence to help him. In this family, the Venerable Master Gao [Juemin's grandfather] passed final judgment....

After the preliminary skirmish ended in total failure, Juemin began the second phase of his tactics. He spread the story that unless the family respected his wishes, he would take drastic measures. Since this threat was never permitted to reach the old man's ears, it did not produce any results either.

Then Juemin learned that his horoscope and that of his proposed bride were about to be exchanged, after which a date would be set for the engagement. He heard this news only two weeks after the Venerable Master Gao's birthday. It was then that Juexin had given the old man some indication of Juemin's feelings, but to no avail.

"How dare he disagree?" the patriarch had retorted angrily. "What I say is final!"

SOURCE: Pa Chin, *Family*, trans. Sidney Shapiro (Boston: Cheng & Tsui, 1999 edition).

 The full text of Document 10.7 is available on the CD-ROM.

DOCUMENT 10.8: Excerpts describing view of family from *A Daughter of Han: The Autobiography of a Chinese Working Woman* by Ida Pruitt, 1945

My daughter was a good girl until she was twenty-eight. When she said a word it was a true word, and she did what I told her to do. I was out all day, but while her father lived she was good and safe....But after he died and her husband went away and never returned she learned bad ways from the neighbors in the court....

My daughter had always been a good girl and listened to my words. But now she reproached me for her life. She said that I had spoiled it. The new neighbors in our court became very friendly with my daughter. The woman painted her face. She cut her hair above her temples. It hung over her face in long, parted bangs. She talked all day with my daughter about pleasure. She talked and laughed pleasantly but she was not good. The things she talked about to my daughter were not good.

One day when I came home I found that my daughter had cut her front hair in the same long uneven bangs. I was very angry. I seized the bangs and said that I would tear them out, that only a lewd woman wore such. Good women combed their hair straight back and sensibly. My daughter answered me back and said that she was a married woman now and that she no longer needed to obey me. It was the first time she had ever answered me....

SOURCE: Ida Pruitt, *A Daughter of Han: The Autobiography of a Chinese Working Woman, from the Story Told Her by Ning Lao T'ai-t'ai* (New Haven: Yale University Press, 1945) Chapters 17, 20.

 The full text of Document 10.8 is available on the CD-ROM.

DOCUMENT 10.9: Excerpts from "On Freeing Slave Girls," in *Funü zazhi (Women's Magazine)*, January 1920

This article in the popular magazine was written by Hu Huaican, a man.

[T]his essay is written for women with new ideas who I am hoping will carry out this liberation movement without help from men. In reality, it is easier for women to liberate slave girls than prostitutes and concubines, so we might as well begin with the simplest....

[W]hat is to be done after they are given their freedom? This is indeed a great problem. In my opinion, the best course is to take them into your family as your daughters. You should send the younger girls to school to be educated, and in their after-school hours they should be taught to work around the house. They should be encouraged to do any work which they are fitted to do, which would benefit the whole family, and which would not injure their health. As for the older girls, you could arrange marriages for them or if you keep them at home, you should teach them housework as well as the ways of the world....

[I]f the same thing is done by many people, others consider it perhaps worth doing and opposition is slight. Therefore I suggest that if women are to liberate slave girls, it would be best to organize a society. If all unite and work together then this would be a simple thing to do. The society might adopt these rules:

1. The society shall be called the Society to Free Slave Girls.
2. Member of the society must all be female.
3. The duty of each member is to free slave girls she owns and to persuade others to free ones she does not own.
4. The society has no other business....

SOURCE: Hu Huaican, "On Freeing Slave Girls," trans. Nancy Gibbs. In *Chinese Civilization: A Sourcebook*, Patricia Buckley Ebrey, ed. (New York: Free Press, 1993) 346–347.

DOCUMENT 10.10: Excerpts from a memoir by Li Xiuwen (1890–1992), describing growing up female

In those days, there were many interesting old formalities and customs in the farming community when a young girl was getting married. The most impressive custom in my memory was the songs-blessing-the-new-bride party. This party given by the bride's female relatives was held the night before the bride left her home. At the party, the ladies took the opportunity to show off their talents and skill making up songs on the spur of the moment. They also took the occasion to amuse and enjoy themselves.

The purpose of the party was a gathering where the female relatives gave praise, congratulations, advice, and good wishes to the bride in songs made up by the participants. First, they brought the bride—a good and obedient girl—to her parents, then to her brothers and sisters. Then they congratulated her for having found a good husband, and they advised her to be an obedient wife and a good daughter-in-law. Finally the songs expressed wishes that she would bear many sons and that she would have a happy and prosperous family.

After the lady relatives finished singing, the bride would sing the songs expressing her sorrow at leaving home and her worries about going to the new family. She hoped her husband would love her and her in-laws would like her....

SOURCE: Li Xiuwen, unpublished memoir.

 The full text of Document 10.10 is available on the CD-ROM.

DOCUMENT 10.11 Excerpts from the Peking United International Famine Relief Committee's Report on the North China Famine, 1922

The famine of 1920–21 has been a real one. Workers in Shandong [Province] report intense privation. In Zhanhua County, 50 percent of the people in 250 villages were absolutely destitute. In Yucheng, the young crops died close to the earth in the fields which were as dry as the roads, and the starving poor were known to go out and dig up the wheat sprouts, still in the ground, in the fields of the more prosperous neighbors. In Linyi County, where throughout the last six years there had been but one year of good crops, there were in the entire county, but a few pecks of grain and those had been imported. Even chaff had been brought in from other regions. From the province of Hebei, similar reports are made. In the district about Chengde one third of a population of 1,093,000 were in direct need and there were 31,286 deaths from hunger and cold....

SOURCE: Peking United International Famine Relief Committee, *Report on the North China Famine*, 1922, rpt. in Pei-kai Cheng, Michael Lestz, and Jonathan D. Spence, *The Search for Modern China: A Documentary Collection* (New York: W. W. Norton, 1999) 247.

 The full text of Document 10.11 is available on the CD-ROM.

DOCUMENT 10.12: Excerpts from a memoir by Li Xiuwen (1890–1992), describing life in the village where she grew up, early 20th century

Usually farmers ate rice cooked with sweet potatoes or white potatoes with one dish of home-grown vegetables three times a day. Meat, mixed with vegetables, appeared at the table only on the New Year. People thought of eating melon or vegetables as producing cold in the body, so they ate hot peppers to counteract it. Therefore each family had a hot pepper stone grinding bowl in the house. Some nights, the farmers, after their hard day's work, went out to the river to catch fish, shrimp, and frogs. They would eat the frogs, and dry the fish to save for meals in later days. In the busy farming season, farmers usually ate a little better. At dinner, they added a dish of fried soybeans, cooked dried fish, vegetables, and they might even drink some rice wine. Only the male workers drank rice wine, not female workers. Usually the men and women ate separately. The men's table had better food than the women's table....

SOURCE: Li Xiuwen, unpublished memoir.

 The full text of Document 10.12 is available on the CD-ROM.

DOCUMENT 10.13: Excerpts from "Agrarian Problems in China," in *Peasant Life in China* by Fei Xiaotong, 1946

There was another dilemma in the Chinese land problem. The national [Guomindang] government with all its promises and policies on paper was not able to carry out any practical measures owing to the fact that most of the revenue was spent on its anti-communist campaign, while, as I have pointed out, the real nature of the communist movement was a peasant revolt due to their dissatisfaction with the land system. Despite all kinds of justification on either side, one thing is clear: that the conditions of the peasants are getting worse and worse. So far no permanent land reform has been accomplished in any part of China since the recovery of the Red Area [Jiangxi Soviet] by the government.

It must be realized that a mere land reform in the form of reduction of rent and equalization of ownership does not promise a final solution of agrarian problems in China. Such a reform, however, is necessary and urgent because it is an indispensable step in relieving the peasants. It will give a breathing space for the peasants and, by removing the cause leading to "revolt," will unite all forces in finding the way to industrial recovery.

SOURCE: Fei Xiaotong, *Peasant Life in China: A Field Study of Country Life in the Yangtze Valley* (New York: Oxford University Press, 1946) 284–285.

 The full text of Document 10.13 is available on the CD-ROM.

DOCUMENT 10.14: Excerpts from the novel *Rickshaw* by Lao She, 1936

[Xiangzi] had to save all he could; otherwise he couldn't get his own rickshaw soon. Even if he bought one today and lost it tomorrow, he still had to buy one. This was his ambition, his hope, even his religion. It would simply be a waste of his life if he didn't buy a rickshaw. Thoughts of becoming an official, getting rich, buying property, these were all beyond him. Pulling a rickshaw was all he was good for. To be able to buy a rickshaw was the only reliable hope he could have. He could not face himself if he didn't buy a rickshaw. This hope filled his mind all day long as he counted and recounted his money. Should a day come when he forgot it then he would have forgotten himself and would know he was only a beast of burden, running along the streets without any promise and without any manhood....

SOURCE: Lao She, *Rickshaw: The Novel Lo-t'o Hsiang Tzu*, trans. Jean M. James (Honolulu: University of Hawaii Press, 1979) 39.

 The full text of Document 10.14 is available on the CD-ROM.

DOCUMENT 10.15: Excerpts describing working life, from *A Daughter of Han: The Autobiography of a Chinese Working Woman* by Ida Pruitt, 1945

But the worst trouble I had with her was the trouble of the eyeglasses. I asked for time off to go down town to have mine mended. She said that that was not necessary. The cook could take them to town the next time he went, and I could wear hers. She took them out of her pocket and gave them to me. They were a very fine pair of bifocals. It was a pleasure to wear them.

The next day I was not feeling well. I had a headache, and so I went to a neighbor's to have my temples cupped for my headache. While there, lying on the bed, I felt the glasses in my pocket, so I took them out, fearing that I would lie on them and break them. The cupping took a long time and we talked about many matters. I forgot the glasses.

After I left, the little boy of the house, a boy of about nine, saw them and said to his mother, "Mother, let me take these to auntie." The children of the family called me auntie. As he was running along the street after me, calling me and the holding the glasses up in his hand, he met a man who stopped him and said, "Let me see them. What is it?" He took them in his hands, put them in his pocket, and ran away. As he had long legs he was soon out of sight. I heard the wails of the child calling me and turned.

"He took the glasses, he took the glasses." Then I was frightened. What should I do? The man was gone. He could not be caught. It was Sunday afternoon. I knew that Miss Mason had gone to church. I went to her house and waited at the gate for her return. When she saw me she said, "Oh, amah. It is Sunday. What are you doing here?" And she was all smiles and pleasant. But when I told her, her face changed. "They were a very valuable pair of glasses. You are a naughty amah. You do not need to come anymore."

So I went home and was very miserable indeed. She did not believe that the glasses had been stolen. She thought that I had sold them or kept them for myself. I felt pressed down till I could not breathe. I had offered to pay for them, but where could I find the money?...

SOURCE: Ida Pruitt, *A Daughter of Han: The Autobiography of a Chinese Working Woman* (New Haven: Yale University Press, 1945) 215.

 The full text of Document 10.15 is available on the CD-ROM.

Activities

ACTIVITY 1: Researching the Mass Education Movement

Part 1:

Read the statements by James Yen (10.1) and examine the Five-Character Plaque (10.2).

1. How does the use of the word "laboratory" reflect a modern approach to education?

2. How might this attitude affect the success or failure of an educational movement like James Yen's?

3. How would you answer the questions Yen poses?

4. What is the significance of the Five-Character Plaque? Yen writes that such plaques used to be present in "every Chinese home." What does this suggest about traditional values in China?

Part 2:

To get a sense of life in China's rural areas in the 1920s and 1930s, review the materials in Chapter 1. Then read about James Yen's efforts to start schools (10.3). Review your original answers to Yen's questions (from 10.1) and adjust your responses based on this additional reading.

1. What inspired James Yen to start educating illiterate Chinese workers?

2. What needed to be done in order to successfully start a modern school in a rural village?

3. Who were the key people who truly made a difference in the campaign to establish schools?

4. How and when were schools set up in your community? How does that compare to Yen's work?

Part 3:

Read about James Yen's Fellow Scholars Association (10.4).

1. How did the Fellow Scholars Association work? What was expected from Fellow Scholars?

2. How did education influence other aspects of a Chinese peasant's life?

3. What was the significance of having text be written in the vernacular?

4. What challenges did Yen take on beyond improving literacy? Why?

Creative extensions:

Choose from among the following:

- Write an article for a community newspaper describing James Yen's work in rural China.
- Create a poster that compares Yen's work to another reform or development effort elsewhere in the world.

ACTIVITY 2: Life in Shanghai, the "Paris of the East"

Examine the photograph "Shanghai Street" (10.5) and complete the analysis worksheet (Item 10.A). Discuss the Western influences that you see. Go online and view photos from the Hutton-Getty Archive (see Item 10.B) and other collections to compare and contrast Shanghai and Paris in the 1920s and 1930s. Use a Venn diagram or other graphic organizer to note your observations. Then decide to what extent Shanghai could have been called the "Paris of the East."

ACTIVITY 3: Examining an American's perspective

Divide the photographs taken by an American tourist in 1913 among the class (10.6a–e). Use the photograph analysis sheet (Item 10.A) to help you note all the details in the images. As the class views each photo on a screen, report on the ten details you consider most important. Discuss as a class:

1. The photographs were taken by an American tourist. How does that affect what is shown? Would a Chinese traveler have taken these same photographs? Why or why not?
2. What have you learned about China in 1913 from these photographs?
3. What issues arise when you generalize about a country roughly the size of the United States based on five photographs?
4. What do you find most striking about the images?
5. What conclusions can you draw about relationships between people in the photos?

Extended research:

Search online or in a library to find photographs taken in other countries around the same time. Compare those images to the ones from China.

ACTIVITY 4: Comparing rural with urban China

After viewing the film clips from Northeast Historic Film Archive (in Additional Resources on the CD-ROM), discuss as a class:

1. How is the rural landscape different from the urban ones you have seen?
2. What kind of work did people do in the rural areas? What jobs did people do in the cities? How do the differences reflect the economy?

3. What are the primary means of transportation in the cities depicted in the films?

4. How do rural people and urban people respond differently to foreigners filming them?

ACTIVITY 5: Contrasting perspectives

Part 1:

Write your answers to these preliminary questions. (You will refer back to them after you complete the reading for this activity.)

1. What traditional values are upheld by the older generation in your family?

2. What modern values are you, the younger generation, pursuing in your family?

3. Have you ever gone against the wishes of your family? What happened? If not, would you ever go against the wishes of your family? Why or why not?

Part 2:

Literature of this period reflects many historical truths about the lives of the people. Read the selections from Ba Jin's *Family* (10.7) and answer the questions for each part (Item 10.C). Imagine yourself as one of the main characters. How does he or she fit into the family?

Writing extension:

Working in small groups, write new plot lines or letters of advice to resolve issues faced by each character (Juexin and his arranged marriage; Juexin and his new job; Juexin taking over his family's affairs; Juemin facing an arranged marriage; Juehui handling his feelings for Mingfeng; Mingfeng facing an arranged marriage as a concubine; Juehui writing for the journal *Dawn*; Qin writing for the journal *Dawn*; Qin entering a coed school; Qin cutting her hair).

Part 3:

Recall your answers to the preliminary questions and discuss your answers to these questions with your classmates.

1. What were the traditional values being upheld by the older generation in the Gao family?

2. What were the modern values being pursued by the younger generation in the Gao family?

3. To what extent were the members of the family in control of their destinies? Were they overwhelmed by the established order of life? Were they swept up by the events of the time?

4. What skills and knowledge would you need to set out on a "new road" like some of the characters in the story?

5. Why do you think the author, Ba Jin, wrote this novel?

6. To what extent could this novel be used by reformers to bring about change? Can you think of any novels or movies today that seem to be created with the goal of bringing about change?

Extension activity:

Contrast the Gao family with the rural family in Pearl Buck's *The Good Earth*. Though told from the perspective of the father, *The Good Earth* also explores the upheaval of this time period and the changes the younger generation tries to make.

ACTIVITY 6: **Research for and planning of social activism**

The changes in Republican-era China affected different people in different ways. Women, peasants, and the urban working poor all faced challenges in surviving and prospering in a changing China. Our information about these people comes from varied sources, as well. Consider the source when reading each selection. Does the type of source make the information more or less reliable?

You may want to read all the documents, or the class can be divided into "expert groups." If the class splits into groups, your expert group will read the documents about either women, peasants, or the urban working poor. Then you will complete a mobilization campaign to change ancient traditions in order to modernize China. Be sure to refer back to the information presented in the documents when presenting your group's work to the class.

Group One: Women's Lives

Read about women's lives in "On Freeing Slave Girls" (10.8), the excerpts from Ida Pruitt's *Daughter of Han* (10.9), and Li Xiuwen's memoir (10.10) and answer questions about each document (Item 10.D). Then, in small groups, discuss:

1. What was women's traditional status in society?

2. What physical restraints and social barriers kept women there?

3. What reforms were being proposed to liberate women?

4. What conditions and resources would need to be in place for reform efforts to succeed?

Within your group, organize a public event to advocate for one of the following changes in women's lives:

- Ending foot binding
- Ending arranged marriages
- Ending indentured servitude/slavery

You may want to create a series of slogans to appear on placards and posters. Will you have supporters march in a parade or meet at a rally, or both? Will you have public speakers? Draft a short speech or two that argues persuasively for the changes that your group wants.

Group Two: Peasants' Lives

Read about peasants' lives in the "Report on the North China Famine, 1922" (10.11), Li Xiuwen's memoir (10.12), and Fei Xiaotong's report (10.13) and answer questions about each document (Item 10.E). Then, in small groups, discuss:

1. What were the benefits and hardships in a Chinese peasant's life at this time?
2. What recourse did peasants have when natural disasters, corrupt tax collectors, or harsh landlords reduced their ability to provide enough food for the family?
3. What reforms would you propose to help peasants?
4. What conditions and resources would need to be in place for reform efforts to succeed?

Within your group, plan a new peasants' association to address the ecological, economic, and political problems faced by farmers in the early twentieth century. What will you call your new association? How will you encourage people to join? Will you have public speakers? Draft a short speech or two that argues persuasively for the changes your group wants. (Note: Refer back to Document 9.3 to find out about the Peasant Associations that Mao Zedong observed in 1927.)

Group Three: Lives of Urban Working Poor

Read about the lives of the urban working poor in Lao She's *Rickshaw* (10.14) and Ida Pruitt's *Daughter of Han* (10.15) and answer questions about each document (Item 10.F). Then, in small groups, discuss:

1. What did Xiangzi and Ning Lao do to survive?
2. How were Xiangzi and Ning Lao treated by their respective employers?
3. Do you think each would have been better off with or without an extended family?
4. What could each have done to improve his or her life?

Within your group, organize a public event to advocate for one of the following changes in the lives of the Chinese urban working poor in the 1920s and 1930s by:

- Establishing an minimum wage
- Organizing a labor union

You may want to create a series of slogans to appear on placards and posters. Will you have supporters march in a parade or meet at a rally, or both? Will you have public speakers? Draft a short speech or two that argues persuasively for the changes your group wants.

ACTIVITY 7: **Constructing a newspaper**

In the 1920s and 1930s, newspapers and journals were distributed and read in China's cities and towns by officials, politicians, educators, students, businessmen, and professionals. They contained important information about the affairs of the day and issues of concern. As a class, produce a newspaper that will serve the same purpose—informing others about the important issues in China, 1912–1937. You may publish one or more newspapers depending on the size of your class. Each newspaper should contain the following sections:

1. "On the street" interviews with people (students, women, peasants, individuals from the urban working poor) with a picture and a one-to-two sentence caption commenting on the state of China from their particular perspective

2. Reports on activities by the women's movement, labor movement, peasant movement, and student movement

3. Articles that review earlier material (from Chapters 8 and 9) and summarize national political news and international news

4. International updates about what is happening in Japan, Russia, France, Great Britain, and the United States with regard to movements to improve the condition of women, labor, peasants, and/or students (will require additional research)

5. Lyrics (actual or student-invented) to new patriotic songs

6. Op-ed page with letters supporting and opposing current government policies and China's position in the international community

7. Images; for example, the national flag, important people, city street scenes, rural village scenes

8. Want ads seeking the ideal teacher to work in Yen's education efforts

9. Advertisements for consumer products and services appropriate to the period

Suggested Resources

Books:

Buck, Pearl S. *The Good Earth*. New York: Washington Square Press, 1931.
The novel tells the story of a farmer and his growing family confronted by new practices that threaten to wash away old traditions. It includes the themes of women's rights, the importance of family, class conflict, spiritual and moral trials, and the hardships of the modern world. Pearl S. Buck won the Pulitzer Prize for this work, and in 1938, she won the Nobel Prize in Literature. The Good Earth became a Broadway play and motion picture. Chapters 1, 8, and 25 are especially relevant to the material in this lesson.

—. *East Wind: West Wind*. Wakefield, RI: Moyer Bell, 1930.
Buck's first novel tells the story of a Chinese sister and brother who give up old traditions such as foot binding and arranged marriages. Through the narration of the sister, it describes how difficult it is to accept change after growing up in a culture where these traditions have been practiced for hundreds of years. The novel includes the themes of a generation gap and adult independence from one's parents. Chapters 3, 4, and 5 are especially relevant to the material in this lesson.

Chang, Jung. *Wild Swans: Three Daughters of China.* London: Globalflair Ltd, 1991.
   This sweeping tale of three generations of women in China spans the twentieth century. Chapters 1 and 2 are relevant to the material in this lesson.

Li, Leslie. *Bittersweet.* Rutland, VT: Charles E. Tuttle Co., Inc.,Tuttle, 1999.
   Based largely on the memoir used in this lesson, Bittersweet *recounts the life of the author's grandmother, Li Xuewen, who lived to the age of 101. The novel spans the twentieth century and provides insights into Chinese traditions and values. The book is out of print, but signed copies are available from the author, who may be contacted at leslieli@sover.net.*

Liu, Aimee. *Cloud Mountain.* Lebanon, IN: Grand Central Publishing, 1998.
   Liu based this historical novel on her grandparents' story. Set in the early decades of the twentieth century, Cloud Mountain *is a compelling love story between a young man raised in China's upper class and an American woman. Their story begins in California and then moves to China. The history is accurate and the settings filled with evocative detail.*

Shen Congwen. "Xiaoxiao." Trans. Eugene Chen Eoyang. *The Columbia Anthology of Modern Chinese Literature.* Ed. Joseph S.M. Lau and Howard Goldblatt. New York: Columbia University Press, 1995. 97–110. See annotation for the film *Girl from Hunan.*

Spence, Jonathan D., and Annping Chin. *The Chinese Century: A Photographic History of the Last Hundred Years.* New York: Random House, 1996.
   An unparalleled collection of photographs from the period.

Tsukiyama, Gail. *Women of the Silk.* New York: St. Martin's Press, 1991.
   Set in rural China in the 1920s and 1930s, this is a story of girls whose families "give them to silk work" in factories. The beautifully written novel is filled with details of Chinese traditions and values.

Websites:

http://editorial.gettyimages.com Search for additional photos from the Hutton-Getty Archive (see also Item 10.G)

http://www.talesofoldchina.com "Tales of Old China" offers short text documents, excerpts from English language periodicals, photos, and other images such as advertisements from Shanghai, Beijing, and Hong Kong from the years 1840 to 1950.

Films:

Girl from Hunan (1986, 110 mins.**)** *In Chinese (Mandarin) with English subtitles. Directed by Xie Fei and U Lan. An adaptation of the short story "Xiaoxiao," by Shen Congwen, this movie includes good scenes of the traditional arranged marriage ceremony and familial bonds. A teenage girl is sent to marry a toddler in a remote Chinese village. As she matures, she enters into an illicit love affair and has to face the consequences.*

Rickshaw Boy (1982; 120 mins.) *In Chinese (Mandarin) with English subtitles. Directed by Ling Zifeng. An adaptation of Lao She's famous novel* Rickshaw, *the film captures the grim realities of life for the urban working poor in 1920s China.*

■ A CLOSER LOOK

Fei Xiaotong, Sociologist and Anthropologist

Fei Xiaotong (1910–2005) was recognized in China and the United States as a leading expert on China's agricultural society. Educated at Christian mission schools and a graduate of Yenching and Tsinghua universities, he earned his doctorate from the London School of Economics in 1936. Fei originally wanted to become a physician, but like Lu Xun he decided that "China's problem was not sickness, not a medical problem. It was a social problem and a political problem. So I went into the social sciences."

He conducted research in rural areas, studying everything from kinship to religion to marriage customs, but mostly focusing on economics. He discovered that farmers relied upon local industries such as growing silkworms to make a living. His proposal to revive the economic viability of rural areas as the key to reviving China itself was first developed in the 1930s, but was not adopted in China until the 1980s. In the 1950s, Fei also studied ethnic minorities in Guizhou and Guangxi provinces. He taught hundreds of college students in China and lectured at many universities in the United States during World War II. In China, he joined the Democratic League in 1944, an alternative to the Guomindang and Communists.

A few years after the Communists came to power in 1949, Fei was denounced during the Anti-Rightist Campaign (1957) and again during the Cultural Revolution (1966–1976). He was forbidden to teach, stripped of his official posts, and after he was sent to the countryside to be a farm laborer, many of his papers were destroyed. He returned to Beijing in 1972 and was politically rehabilitated. In 1994, he was awarded the prestigious Ramon Magsaysay Award for Community Leadership established by the Rockefeller Brothers Fund.

■ *For more about Fei and his work, refer to Chapter 1. Document 1.2 has additional excerpts from his book* Peasant Life in China. *Discuss: What was the significance of Fei Xiaotong's research in China's villages? What lessons did he learn?*

Primary Sources

DOCUMENT 11.1: "Military Door Gods," a print by Huang Yao, late 1930s

DOCUMENT 11.2: "Study," a wood block print by Jing Yun, 1937–1945

DOCUMENT 11.3: Excerpts from a memoir by Li Xiuwen (1890–1992), describing life under Japanese invasion and occupation

DOCUMENT 11.4: Interview with Hsu King-Ming, May 2007

DOCUMENT 11.5: Excerpts from the diary of John Rabe, a witness to the Nanjing Massacre, 1937

DOCUMENT 11.6: The Empire of Japan's 66th Regiment 1st Battalion Report, December 13, 1937

DOCUMENT 11.7: Photo at Nanjing Massacre Museum, 2006

DOCUMENT 11.8: Excerpts from "Snow Falls on China's Land," a poem by Ai Qing, 1937

DOCUMENT 11.9: Excerpts from "New Faith," a short story by Ding Ling, 1939

DOCUMENT 11.10: Excerpt from *Shanghai Diary: A Young Girl's Journey from Hitler's Hate to War-Torn China* by Ursula Bacon, 2002

DOCUMENT 11.11: General Joseph Stilwell bust outside the Stilwell Museum, Chongqing

DOCUMENT 11.12: Excerpts from *Red Star Over China* by Edgar Snow, 1968

DOCUMENT 11.13: "Chinese germ warfare victims call for just ruling by Japanese Supreme Court," in *China Daily*, June 26, 2006

Supplementary Materials

ITEM 11.A: Map of occupied China, 1940

CHAPTER 11

China Occupied and Splintered, 1937–1945

By Rachel Zucker

Chapter Contents

Escalating War

The Nanjing Massacre

International Involvement

The Impact of War

Biological Warfare

Organizing Idea

Between 1937 and 1945, the Chinese fought what they refer to as the "War of Resistance Against Japan," a war that caused extraordinary hardship for the vast majority of Chinese citizens. At the same time, both the Communists and the Guomindang laid the groundwork for a future confrontation.

Key Questions

How can a nation divided the way China was in the 1930s defend itself against an aggressive invading force?

Are there rules in warfare? Why? What are they, and how can they be enforced?

What is the impact of warfare and occupation on the lives of ordinary citizens?

What was China's role in World War II?

Key Terms

biological warfare

collaborator

Communism

nationalism

occupation

Essay

After the Japanese took over Manchuria (满洲) and Inner Mongolia (内蒙古) in 1931 and 1936, Japan and China engaged in minor conflicts until July 1937, when the Marco Polo Bridge Incident (near Beijing) finally ignited full-scale war between the two countries. Both countries used this small skirmish between Japanese soldiers, who claimed they were being attacked, and Chinese soldiers, who fiercely resented Japanese presence, as a reason to escalate violence.

Escalating War

As the Japanese advanced further south, Chinese troops fled Beijing (北京) on July 28, 1937. The Japanese subsequently captured Tianjin (100 km southeast of Beijing) and then attacked Shanghai, the financial center, on August 13. There began a three-month siege, which cost the Chinese approximately 270,000 of their best-trained men. Generalissimo Chiang Kai-shek (蒋介石) appealed to the League of Nations, and on October 6, 1937, the League condemned Japanese incursions into China, but the countries that made up the League were cautious about offending the Japanese; they provided no assistance. The confrontation ended with the Guomindang[1] (国民党) troops withdrawing to Nanjing (南京).[2] China's capital was to be defended "to the last man," insisted Chiang. But in the face of the approaching Japanese bombers and troops, the disorganized Chinese forces held the city for four days and then fled. On December 13, 1937, Nanjing fell to the Japanese.

The Nanjing Massacre (南京大屠杀)

The battle-wearied Japanese troops initially killed approximately 90,000 Chinese soldiers who had surrendered. They then continued to slaughter men who they suspected were soldiers disguised as civilians. The violence escalated further as Japanese soldiers raped an estimated 20,000 women and girls. Over a seven-week period, the Japanese soldiers massacred between 150,000 and 300,000 men, women, and children. Historians have attempted to explain the appalling violence as the culmination of dehumanizing hand-to-hand combat experienced by Japanese soldiers in the earlier Battle of Shanghai, or as the result of the soldiers' frustration and hunger caused by Chinese scorched-earth tactics and rumors of Chinese torture of Japanese prisoners of war. Additionally, Japanese Emperor Hirohito's failure to direct his soldiers to adhere to existing international laws concerning the treatment of prisoners of war implied that human rights did not apply to the Chinese.[3] It is frequently claimed by Chinese journalists, but difficult to verify, that Emperor Hirohito's uncle, Prince Yasuhiko Asaka, Commander of the Central China Area Army, issued a secret directive to "kill all captives." While the exact number of people killed is now a nationalistic point of debate between the two countries, no historian questions the magnitude of the horror.

A Fractured China

Initially, no foreign power came to China's defense. In June 1937, a desperate Chiang Kai-shek ordered the Huang He (黄河, Yellow River) dikes blown up. This slowed the Japanese offensive by three months, but the resulting floods killed an unknown but large number of Chinese peasants. The Japanese soon occupied

---

[1] Spelled Kuomintang (KMT) in Taiwan. The Guomindang were also known as the Nationalists.

[2] China's capital after Chiang Kai-shek came to power in 1927.

[3] Herbert Bix, *Hirohito and the Making of Modern Japan* (New York: HarperCollins, 2000) 360.

Shaded area in eastern China was under Japanese occupation.
(Courtesy of the United States Military Academy.)

the wealthier, more developed coastal areas and the most fertile land. After the fall of Nanjing, the Guomindang had retreated to Wuhan (武汉). In October 1938, they moved their capital deep into China—to Chongqing (重庆) in Sichuan Province (四川). In an extraordinary human feat, they dismantled and transported factories, universities, and the entire imperial art collection. Hundreds of thousands of men, women, and children walked hundreds of miles to escape occupied regions. The Japanese established several puppet or collaborationist governments in areas they held or which were under the control of local warlords. External and internal forces had splintered China.

The Communists Grow Stronger

In 1941, the United Front (统一战线), which had been loosely cobbled together with help from the Russians, fell apart, and the Guomindang and Communists (共产党)

fought the Japanese separately. In several instances, Guomindang troops attacked Communist soldiers rather than focusing on their mutual enemy. Those favoring greater resistance to the Japanese joined the Communists in their stronghold closer to the front at Yan'an (延安) in Shaanxi Province (陕西) (see Chapter 9). This Yan'an Period, from 1937–1945, was a time of regrouping for the Communists. Mao Zedong (毛泽东) had the opportunity to read Marx and adapt aspects of Communist thought to his perception of what China would need to recover from decades of conflict. The two pillars of Maoism—land reform and revolutionary nationalism—were designed to recruit peasants who sought power after generations of disenfranchisement. The lure of land ownership and resistance against the Japanese fueled the growing Communist forces. Membership in the Party rose from 40,000 in 1937 to 800,000 in 1940 and to 1.2 million by 1945.[4]

---

[4] Jonathan D. Spence, *The Search for Modern China* (New York: W.W. Norton, 1999) 436, 456.

International Involvement

While the conflict between Chinese and Japanese forces was reported in the Western press, European countries were coping with the German invasion, occupation, and bombing. An ambivalent United States maintained its official isolationist position.[5] When Japan bombed Pearl Harbor in December 1941, however, everything changed. Great Britain, the Soviet Union, and the United States recognized that by refusing to surrender, the Chinese were tying up two-fifths of Japan's armed forces, preventing them from waging war elsewhere. Western allies began to extend massive loans to the Guomindang government, and to send equipment and fuel via India. At the Cairo Conference of 1943, the Allied powers vowed to eventually defeat Japan and to restore to China all occupied land. They also pledged not to (re)establish their own imperial control in China.

President Franklin Delano Roosevelt sent General Joseph Stilwell to serve as a liaison with Chiang Kai-shek and commander in chief of the American forces in the China-Burma-India region (see A Closer Look at the end of the chapter). Despite many setbacks, gradually the course of the war began to shift. In August 1945, after the United States dropped the second nuclear bomb on Nagasaki, Japan finally surrendered.

Biological Warfare

The Chinese citizenry had endured enormous hardships under Japanese occupation. The Communists' guerrilla tactics and attempts to organize local opposition often met with brutal reprisals: Japanese soldiers eradicated entire villages. In addition, Japanese researchers conducted extensive experiments on prisoners of war and civilians.[6] The most notorious center for these experiments was Unit 731, which had been built outside Harbin (哈尔滨) in Heilongjiang Province[7] (黑龙江) in 1932. Japanese doctors and their medical staff deliberately infected people with bubonic plague, cholera, anthrax and dozens of other pathogens. They experimented with ways to manage burns, frostbite, and bullet wounds after first causing the physical trauma. They also conducted "field tests" by dropping plague bombs on several Chinese cities. It is extremely difficult to determine how many people died as a result of this biological warfare. Estimates range from at least 3,000 at Unit 731 alone to more than 200,000 when the germ warfare field experiments are included.

The guerilla fighting by the Communist Red Army (红军) and the tactical attacks by the Guomindang mired two-fifths of the Japanese Army in a costly and unproductive conflict, contributing to Japan's defeat in 1945. However, when the almost decade-long War of Resistance Against Japan (抗日战争) ended, fighting continued in China, over who would ultimately govern the nation.

---

[5] Nevertheless, the Roosevelt administration authorized the United States Army Air Force to recruit "volunteer" pilots. The "Flying Tigers" fought against the Japanese in China.

[6] In addition to Chinese people, Koreans, Russians, and Mongolians were also victims of this experimentation.

[7] At that time known as Manchuria

Primary Sources

DOCUMENT 11.1: "Military Door Gods," a print by Huang Yao, late 1930s

Huang Yao, a famous cartoonist of the 1930s from Shanghai, fled to Chongqing to escape the Japanese. His images adorned doors in Guomindang areas throughout the war. The banners say "Defeat Japan, revive China" and the children hold discs that proclaim, "Those who have money should donate money, those who have strength should give strength." The sun emblem was on the Guomindang flag. *(Private collection.)*

DOCUMENT 11.2: "Study," a wood block print by Jing Yun, 1937–1945

Jing Yun was among those who escaped from eastern China to Yan'an, the head-quarters of the Communist forces and the setting for this print. While wood block is a traditional form of printing, this composition reflects both European influence and Chinese elements, such as use of line and uncluttered or white space. *(Courtesy of the Picker Art Gallery, Colgate University [1968.93].)*

DOCUMENT 11.3: Excerpts from a memoir by Li Xiuwen (1890–1992), describing life under Japanese invasion and occupation

At the beginning of the war, people left their homes in the war zones and came to Guilin for their safety. Those who were wealthy immediately bought houses and properties in the city for them to live in. Some could only afford to rent a house or a few little rooms and some just built the simplest living space with wooden boards and bamboo outside the city....

The city population increased from under 100,000 to 300,000. Government and business offices and civilian organizations moved in and spread all over the city. More new business offices, stores, hotels, restaurants and teahouses were opened. There was a teahouse every block, a restaurant on every other block....

[T]here was an interesting open market where people bought and sold second-hand clothes, personal belongings, furniture and everything that one could think of. The majority of the customers were refugees from other parts of the country. When they arrived in Guilin, they couldn't find work right away. When their savings were exhausted, they had to sell their clothes and belongings for food. Some sold the things that they had no use for anymore, and some reduced their belongings for convenience in traveling. However, when they needed something cheap, they went there to buy. This marketplace was very busy and crowded. When the enemy came close to Guilin, the people sold their belongings and turned them into money to escape from the city....

SOURCE: Li Xiuwen, unpublished memoir.

 The full text of Document 11.3 is on the CD-ROM.

DOCUMENT 11.4: Interview with Hsu King-Ming, May 2007

Despite the war, those were our happiest times. We were children. We played despite the Japanese bombing every night. A lot of things didn't seem unbearable. [To escape the Japanese occupation,] we walked from Shanghai to Xi'an, the four of us, (uncles and dad) and hired a person to pull a two-wheeler to pull bedding, no clothes. China still had floods then. Some places we would walk on high ground; sometimes we would take boats. We would eat where we could. Once at an inn after the meal, my father inquired about the meat, and they told us we had eaten human flesh. That is what they told me; I really do not know. Mostly it was steamed buns made of sorghum flour, not white. We stayed in inns. Not many others were traveling because we were supposed to stay in a small group to not gather attention. My family was eight children. We left the youngest three behind in Shanghai to be sent for later....

SOURCE: Hsu King-Ming, interview with Rachel Zucker, May 2007.

 The full text of Document 11.4 is on the CD-ROM.

DOCUMENT 11.5: Excerpts from the diary of John Rabe, a witness to the Nanjing Massacre, 1937

Our Chinese servants and employees, about 30 people in all including immediate families, have eyes only for their "master." If I stay, they will loyally remain at their posts to the end....

The rest of the poor servants, most of whom are actually from northern China, simply don't know where to go. I wanted to send off the women and children at least, offered their husbands money for the trip, but they don't know what to do. They want to go back home to the north, but there's war there, too; and so they would rather just huddle here around me. Under such circumstances, can I, may I, cut and run? I don't think so. Anyone who has ever sat in a dugout and held a trembling Chinese child in each hand through the long hours of an air raid can understand what I feel....

Times are bitterly hard here in the country of my hosts, who have treated me well for three decades now. The rich are fleeing; the poor must remain behind. They don't know where to go. They don't have the means to flee. Aren't they in danger of being slaughtered in great numbers? Shouldn't one make an attempt to help them? Save a few at least? And even if it's only our own people, our employees?...

SOURCE: Erwin Wickert, ed., *The Good Man of Nanking: The Diaries of John Rabe* (New York: Vintage, 2000) 5–6.

 The full text of Document 11.5 is on the CD-ROM.

DOCUMENT 11.6: The Empire of Japan's 66th Regiment 1st Battalion Report, December 13 1937

Battalion report: At 2:00 (P.M.) received orders from the Regiment commander: to comply with orders from Brigade commanding headquarters, all prisoners of war are to be executed. Method of execution: to divide the prisoners into groups of a dozen. Shoot to kill separately. It is decided that the prisoners are to be divided evenly among each company…and to be brought out from their imprisonment in groups of 50 to be executed. The vicinity of the imprisonment must be heavily guarded. Our intentions are absolutely not to be detected by the prisoners. Every company is to complete preparation before 5:00 P.M. Executions are to start by 5:00 and action is to be finished by 7:30.

SOURCE: Chang, Iris. *The Rape of Nanking: The Forgotten Holocaust of World War II* (New York: Penguin, 1998) 41.

DOCUMENT 11.7: Photo at Nanjing Massacre Museum, 2006

(Photo by Liz Nelson)

DOCUMENT 11.8: Excerpt from "Snow Falls on China's Land," a poem by Ai Qing, 1937

Snow falls on China's land;
Cold blockades China....

On the river of this snowy night,
One small oil lamp drifts slowly
In a rickety boat with a black canopy.
Who sits in there
In the lamplight, head bowed?

–Ah, it's you,
Tousle-haired and grubby-faced young woman.
Wasn't it
Your home
–Warm and happy nest!
That was burnt to the ground
By the brutal enemy?
Wasn't it
A night like this
Bereft of the protection of a man
That, in the terror of death,
You were teased and poked by enemy bayonets?

On such cold nights as tonight,
Our countless
Aged mothers
Huddle together in homes not theirs—
Like strangers
Not knowing
Where tomorrow's wheel
Will take them.
And China's roads
Are so rugged
And so muddy.

Snow falls on China's land;
Cold blockades China....

SOURCE: Ai Qing, "Snow Falls on China's Land," trans. Marilyn Chin, *The Columbia Anthology of Modern Chinese Literature*, ed. Joseph S. M. Lau and Howard Goldblatt (New York: Columbia University Press, 1995) 519–520.

 The full text of Document 11.8 is on the CD-ROM.

DOCUMENT 11.9: Excerpts from "New Faith," a short story by Ding Ling, 1939

He'd left it five days before. Around dawn he'd heard a burst of gunfire coming from just outside the village. He'd leaped out of bed. His wife was already up, and his fifteen-year-old daughter, Jingu, ashen faced, came bursting into the room. Everybody knew what was happening. "Run!" he said. "Get to Granny's house by the back route on the other side of the hill."

"Daddy, oh, Daddy! If we have to die, let's die together."

"Where's my sheepskin vest?"

"Don't worry about your things now! The Japs are nearly here…"

He'd dragged out his bound-foot wife with one hand, his pretty young daughter with the other. Jingu ran crazed with panic. Her face looked hideous, disguised with smears of soot and dirt. They ran ahead of the crowd and soon reached the top of the hill. But then his wife started sobbing. Had their second daughter and their son gotten away? And what about Chen Xinhan's fifty-seven-year-old mother? So leaving the women to flee with the crowd, he slipped off and went back toward the village. People grabbed him, saying, "Don't turn back! Run for your life!" but he didn't know the meaning of fear because his only concern was to rescue his mother. He searched the sweeping tide of people shouting her name…

The village was in total chaos. Bullets flew around his head, people screamed for help. The outlying houses were in flames, and white smoke rolled into the village. There wasn't a soul at his house, just a few chickens darting around the courtyard screeching. He nearly walked right into a hail of bullets. With a shout, he dodged back. He could hear hoofbeats bearing down on him but couldn't risk the time to glance at his rear. The skies were falling, the earth splitting behind him. Crushed, people hadn't the time to draw their next breath; only the sounds of a sharp cry, gasps….

Source: Ding Ling, "New Faith," trans. Jean James and Tani E. Barlow. *I Myself Am a Woman: Selected Writings of Ding Ling,* ed. Tani E. Barlow and Gary J. Bjorge (Boston: Beacon Press, 1989) 283.

 The full text of Document 11.9 is on the CD-ROM.

DOCUMENT 11.10: Excerpt from *Shanghai Diary: A Young Girl's Journey from Hitler's Hate to War-Torn China* by Ursula Bacon, 2002

Barely avoiding a collision with a wildly weaving, rattly old automobile, our driver suddenly turned away from the harbor side and entered the web of crowded, narrow, intersecting streets of inner Hongkou. Finally, we came to a stop at a large, run-down building that squatted in an equally run-down courtyard, where a handful of refugees had gathered to greet the new arrivals.

A dark-haired lady in a simple cotton dress stepped forward when the truck squealed to a stop, and with a friendly smile welcomed us in a heavy, unmistakable Viennese dialect. We climbed down from the truck, grabbed our suitcases, and on unsteady sea legs, followed her into the building. A blending of fried onions, stewed cabbage, and a hint of 4711 Cologne greeted us when we entered a large hall-like room. Several rows of rough wooden tables and benches for eating and meeting occupied the center of the hall. The rest of the area was divided into cubicles equipped with two to four cots, which were separated from each other by flimsy sheets or thin blankets hung on clotheslines in an attempt to provide a semblance of privacy....

SOURCE: Ursula Bacon, *Shanghai Diary: A Young Girl's Journey from Hitler's Hate to War-Torn China* (Milwaukie, OR: Milestone Books, 2002) 36.

 The full text of Document 11.10 is on the CD-ROM.

DOCUMENT 11.11: General Joseph Stilwell bust outside the Stilwell Museum, Chongqing

(Photo by Liz Nelson)

DOCUMENT 11.12: Excerpts from *Red Star Over China* by Edgar Snow, 1968

Bao'an, July 19, 1936

On Land Distribution

SNOW: What is the foremost internal task of the revolution, after the struggle against Japanese imperialism?

MAO: The Chinese revolution, being of bourgeois-democratic character, has as its primary task the readjustment of the land problem—the realization of agrarian reform. Some idea of the urgency of rural reform may be secured by referring to figures on the distribution of land in China today. During the Nationalist Revolution, I was secretary of the Peasant Committee [department] of the Guomindang and had charge of collecting statistics for areas throughout twenty-one provinces.

Our investigation showed astonishing inequalities. About 70 percent of the whole rural population was made up of poor peasants, tenants or part-tenants, and of agricultural workers. About 20 per cent was made up of middle peasants tilling their own land. Usurers and landlords were about 10 per cent of the population. Included in the 10 per cent also were rich peasants, exploiters like the militarists, tax collectors, and so forth. The 10 per cent of the rich, peasants, landlords, and usurers together owned about 70 per cent of the cultivated land.

SOURCE: Edgar Snow, *Red Star Over China: The Classic Account of the Birth of Chinese Communism* (New York: Grove Press, 1968) 445.

 The full text of Document 11.12 is on the CD-ROM.

DOCUMENT 11.13: "Chinese germ warfare victims call for just ruling by Japanese Supreme Court," in *China Daily*, June 26, 2006

A group of 180 Chinese who were victims or whose family members were killed by Imperial Japanese Army's germ warfare program, filed a lawsuit with the Tokyo District Court in 1997, demanding 10 million yen each and an apology from the government.

Ichinose Keiichiro, a Japanese lawyer for the plaintiffs, said germ warfare victims had appealed for compensation according to law, and the Japanese court should require the Japanese government to apologize and compensate the victims. Acknowledging the plaintiff's request was the way to realize the rule of justice, said the Japanese lawyer.

"We are not just demanding an apology and compensation from the Japanese government, we are also defending the dignity of the Chinese people," said Lou Xian, another Chinese lawyer for the victims....

SOURCE: Xinhua, "Chinese germ warfare victims call for just ruling by Japanese Supreme Court," *China Daily*, June 26, 2006.

 The full text of Document 11.13 is on the CD-ROM.

Activities

ACTIVITY 1: Interpreting propaganda art

After reading the introduction, examine the two prints (11.1 and 11.2).

Huang Yao's "Military Door Gods": The purpose of Door Gods, which remain popular decorations, is to protect homes from evil spirits. List the many details in the image. Then consider:

1. How are these Door Gods like and unlike traditional Door Gods? (Consider color, pose, and symbols.) You can consult page 152 of *The Enduring Legacy of Ancient China* for examples of traditional Door Gods.

2. These Door Gods express one artist's views about his world. What is his perspective? What evidence do you see to illustrate this? How does Huang add to the traditional design of Door Gods as guardians?

3. Why might an artist, especially one who had studied abroad, choose to use traditional folklore figures to express himself?

Jing Yun's "Study": Working in small groups, discuss the setting, the people, and the activities depicted in the woodcut. Then consider the following questions:

1. Looking at how the students and teacher are arranged, what kind of learning is taking place here?

2. What are the workers in front of the cave dwellings doing? What was the artist trying to convey? What is your evidence?

3. Why might a twentieth-century artist choose to use a traditional Chinese form of printing to express himself?

4. What may have been Jin's purpose in creating this piece of art?

5. Both images are political works in support of two different and opposed political groups. How are these two artists' works similar and different?

Creative Extension:

Create a pair of Door Gods with symbols and ideas that make your own statement about what you want to guard against and perhaps what you want to "let in" to your life. Explain why you chose the symbols and images that you did. Alternatively, after reading Documents 11.3 and 11.4, design Door Gods from the perspective of Li Xiuwen or Hsu King-Ming. How would their Door Gods be unique?

ACTIVITY 2: Examining war's impact on civilians

Part 1:

Read the excerpts from Li Xiuwen's memoir (11.3) before class. Working in small groups, examine the map of occupied China (Item 11.A) and identify all the major Chinese cities under Japanese control. Find Chongqing, Yan'an, and Guilin. Compare the map to a topographical map of China (see Suggested Resources). What areas did Japan target for occupation? Why? Then discuss the memoir:

1. What did you notice about Li Xiuwen's narrative? What new insights did you gain?

2. Do you think Li gives a trustworthy account of the time period? Why? How do historians verify memoirs and other sources such as diaries, articles, letters, etc.?

3. How would life in your community be different if tens of thousands of people fled from urban centers to your area? What resources would be in short supply? What would be the biggest challenges? What would be the benefits, if any?

4. When Japan's surrender is described, why do you think Li doesn't mention the U.S. bombings of Hiroshima and Nagasaki? How might the end of the war have been viewed in China as compared to the United States or Australia, for example?

As a class:

1. Discuss how the Japanese occupation of coastal China affected civilian life.

2. Create a list of changes and debate which changes would be most important.

Part 2:

Read Hsu King-Ming's account of his family's escape (11.4). In small groups, consider:

1. Hsu was a teenager when he left his home in Shanghai. What can you determine about him and his family from this reading? (For example: class, education level, traditional or non-traditional values, etc.)

2. How can a person be scientifically trained and at the same time believe deeply in the powers of fortune-tellers? Are these beliefs contradictory or can they co-exist?

3. How had the areas that Hsu's family traveled through been affected by the collapse of Chinese control and the influx of westward migrants?

4. Looking at the map (Item 11.A), how do you think Hsu and his family got from Shanghai to Xi'an? What physical barriers did they have to cross?

5. Explain Hsu's father's reaction to finally reaching Xi'an. How far had they traveled, and what did "free China" mean to him?

As a class, compare Li's and Hsu's descriptions of leaving their homes.

1. What surprised you in either document? Why?

2. Which events in the accounts are most memorable and what do they illustrate?

3. If you had to leave your home, knowing that it would be occupied by an invading army, what would you take with you? What would you need for the road?

4. How are Li's and Hsu's experiences similar to or different from other materials you have read or seen about war-torn countries?

5. How does the flight of Chinese from occupied regions compare to migrations that are not a result of war? (For example, in the United States consider the Great Western Migration of immigrants in the 1850s, that of African Americans in the South who migrated north to urban areas in the twentieth century, or the Irish migration to the United States during the Great Famine in the 1840s.)

Creative extensions:

Select one scene described by Li Xiuwen or Hsu King-Ming and respond to it with a piece of art: for example, a drawing, sculpture, poem, collage, or piece of music.

ACTIVITY 3: Reflecting on the Nanjing Massacre

Part 1:

Begin by considering the old saying "All's fair in love and war." Write a response that addresses "All's fair in war." What does this mean? Is it true or should there be rules for warfare? Share your responses. Then come up with and record a possible list of rules that might be effective or necessary in times of war. Some students might believe that no rules are needed or possible. They should explain and defend their position in writing as well.

   Read the excerpts from John Rabe's diary (11.5). Rabe wrote on December 24, 1937 that he "wanted to see these atrocities with [his] own eyes" to be able to speak as an eyewitness later.

1. Why did he think people would need to know about this? What did he expect from the international community?

2. Why did John Rabe stay in Nanjing to protect Chinese people after sending his family away and being told by his employer to flee immediately?

3. What, if anything, surprises you about this diary?

4. How does it challenge your understanding of members of the Nazi Party?

5. How does Rabe's diary deepen your understanding of the war in China?

6. What happened after Rabe returned to Germany?

7. Why do you think Rabe firmly believed that the Nazi Party, which he had joined in 1933, would be interested in and capable of stopping this violence? (See http://www.fordham.edu/halsall/mod/25points.html for the 25 founding principles of the Nazi Party.)

8. Compare the Battalion Report (11.6) to Rabe's diary entries. (Examine style, content, and purpose, for example.)

9. Why are the Japanese officers who wrote the Battalion Report so concerned with concealing the executions from Chinese soldiers? If they truly believed that the executions were permissible, why conceal them?

Part 2:

Why do humans appear to have such a need to commemorate loss? Together as a class, create a list of all the memorials and monuments you can think of. Then star those memorials or monuments that were or are considered controversial because of either the event being memorialized or the design. Some examples might include the Vietnam Veterans Memorial in Washington, D.C.; the National Slavery Past Monument in Amsterdam, the Netherlands; and the Monument to the Murdered Jews of Europe in Berlin built on the grounds of the former Nazi headquarters. Hypothesize why these might have been controversial.

Look at the photograph taken at the Nanjing Massacre Museum in Nanjing (11.6). How does this part of the museum convey the loss of hundreds of thousands of lives? Do you think it's effective? Why or why not? Examine additional photographs of memorials at the museum at http://www.nj1937.org/english/default.asp. How does a memorial compare to the Battalion Report (11.6) or Rabe's diary (11.5)?

Working in groups, brainstorm what factual information and emotions you would want to convey in a memorial to the victims of biological warfare or medical experiments. Sketch your design ideas.

ACTIVITY 4: Analyzing literature of the occupation

After reading excerpts from the poem, the short story, and the memoir (11.8–11.10) consider the following questions:

"Snow Falls on China's Land," by Ai Qing

1. What do you think Ai Qing is trying to convey in this poem?

2. What does the last line mean? Can poetry help people cope with the terrible experiences described here? How?

3. To whom is the poem directed?

"New Faith," by Ding Ling
Before answering the questions, read about Ding Ling's life in A Closer Look at the end of the chapter.

1. What images dominate parts 1, 2, and 3 of the story? What images dominate the rest of the story? What is the significance of these images?

2. How does the grandmother change from the beginning of the story to the end? (Consider her role, how people view her, and how she views herself.)

3. Why do you think the grandmother had to share her stories? Many people would be silent about a rape, but she forced everyone to listen to what had happened to her. How did her unusual reaction affect her family and the community?

4. What is the author trying to communicate about traditional and newly emerging roles for women? How does this reflect Communist ideology?

5. Based on this story, how did the Communists work to get people to join their movement?

6. Where was Ding Ling when she wrote this short story? Do you think the story was well received by the Communist Party leaders? Why?

Shanghai Diary: A Young Girl's Journey from Hitler's Hate to War-Torn China, by Ursula Bacon

1. How did Ursula feel about leaving home? Why? How would you have felt or reacted in her position? Why?

2. How was China different from Europe in Ursula's experiences? What surprises you about her account?

3. Ursula wrote that her childhood ended. Today, many young people want to stop being a "child" as soon as possible. What are the advantages to being a child or young adult, specifically in times of great upheaval?

4. What similarities and differences exist between Bacon's account and Hsu's (11.4)? Given that they were of similar ages, is this surprising?

5. What issues may be involved when someone speaks or writes about traumatic events that took place many years earlier?

Creative extension:

Write a postcard that captures what was going on in one or more of the lives of the women in "Snow Falls on China's Land." This short greeting should be addressed to either one of the characters in Ding Ling's short story "New Faith," or Ursula Bacon as she arrives in Shanghai. Exchange cards among members of the class, and then write a return postcard, including a drawing of some aspect of your character's life during the occupation.

ACTIVITY 5: A Western journalist reports

After reading the excerpts from Edgar Snow's book (11.12), A Closer Look on General Joseph Stilwell, and looking at the photograph (11.11), discuss:

1. Why did the United States choose to support Chiang Kai-shek and the Guomindang but not the Communists, even when both parties were fighting the Japanese?

2. Chiang was storing American resources to fight the Chinese Communists in the future. Why did this frustrate Stilwell?

3. In 1936, Mao told Snow that "the seizure of power is not our (immediate) aim. We want to stop civil war, create a people's democratic government with the Guomindang and other parties, and fight for our independence against Japan" (*Red Star Over China*, 445). List these goals in order of priority for Mao, for Stilwell, and for the Chinese peasants. Why and how might these lists be different?

4. Snow asked Mao to list his goals for China after defeating Japan. What were these goals, and what parts of the population was Mao trying to win over to support his ideas?

5. In this interview with Snow, whom did Mao blame for the problems facing China?

ACTIVITY 6: Debate: Are reparations the answer?

Read the news article describing the victims' lawsuit seeking reparations from the Japanese government (11.13). Conduct further research online and in books to learn more about the extent of medical experiments done on people during the Japanese occupation of Manchuria; Unit 731; biological warfare conducted in China; the U.S. response to what Japanese researchers had done in North China; and the most recent developments in the legal case. Half the class will take the stand that reparations are a necessary next step, and half the class will argue that they are not.

EXTENDED RESEARCH:

Conduct further research using books and online sources and present your findings in a paper, or an electronic presentation such as a PowerPoint® or Photo Story 3® slide show.
   Suggested topics:

- The Burma Road
- The Flying Tigers
- Unit 731
- U.S. treatment of Japanese individuals involved in biological warfare
- The Nanjing Massacre
- Japanese and Chinese textbook coverage of the war and/or the Nanjing Massacre and other war crimes
- The effects of Japanese war crimes on Chinese-Japanese relations today
- Chiang Kai-shek
- Madame Chiang's role and her speech to the United States Congress
- Compare and contrast the situation of survivors of Japanese biological warfare with that of other groups seeking reparations, such as the descendents of slaves in the United States, Holocaust survivors, and slave wage laborers in Latin America.

Suggested Resources

Books

Bix, Herbert. *Hirohito and the Making of Modern Japan.* New York: Harper Perennial, 2000.

Chang, Iris. *The Rape of Nanking: The Forgotten Holocaust of World War II.* New York: Penguin, 1998.

Harris, Sheldon H. *Factories of Death: Japanese Biological Warfare, 1932–1945, and the American Cover-Up.* New York: Routledge, 2002.

Honda, Katsuichi, and Frank Gibney. *The Nanjing Massacre: A Japanese Journalist Confronts Japan's National Shame.* Armonk, NY: M.E. Sharpe, 1999.

Includes many primary source materials and maps.

Zhao, Yali, and John D. Hoge. "Countering Textbook Distortion: War Atrocities in Asia, 1937–1945." *Social Education* 70 (2006): 424–432.

Websites

Maps

http://www.dean.usma.edu/history/web03/atlases/chinese%20civil%20war/chinese%20civil%20war%20index.htm Map of Japanese occupation of China.

or go to **http://www.dean.usma.edu/history/default.htm** and follow the links to "Our Atlases," "Go to Atlases," "The Chinese Civil War," and number 4, "Japanese Occupation, 1940."

http://www.askasia.org/teachers/maps/map.php?no=43&era=&grade=&geo and **http://www.askasia.org/teachers/maps/map.php?no=43&era=&grade=&geo** Topographical maps of China.

http://wsu.edu/~dee/MODCHINA/OCCUP.HTM An overview of Japan's occupation of China.

http://www.lib.umich.edu/govdocs/text/mchiang.htm Madame Chiang's appeal to the United States Congress, 1943.

http://www.fordham.edu/halsall/mod/25points.html A summary of the 25 principles of the National Socialist German Workers' Party (Nazi Party), 1920.

http://www.yale.edu/lawweb/avalon/imt/document/nca_vol4/1708-ps.htm Provides the complete set of Nationalist Socialist German Workers' Party principles, 1920.

The Nanjing Massacre

http://www.nj1937.org/english/default.asp The Nanjing Massacre Museum in Nanjing; includes additional information and a number of photographs of the memorials.

http://www.library.yale.edu/div/Nanking/ *The Nanking Massacre Project* from the Special Collections of the Yale Divinity School Library is a digital archive of documents and photographs from American missionaries who witnessed the atrocities.

http://www.fordham.edu/halsall/mod/nanking.html "All Captives Slain; Civilians Also Killed as the Japanese Spread Terror in Nanking," a report by F. Tillman Durdin, a *New York Times* correspondent, December 18, 1937.

http://www.cnd.org/njmassacre/

Japanese Germ Warfare and Unit 731

http://www.ww2pacific.com/unit731.html

http://centurychina.com/wiihist/germwar/germwar.htm Excerpts from "Unmasking Horror: Japan Confronting Gruesome War Atrocity," by Nicholas D. Kristof, *New York Times*, March 17, 1993. The full article is also available from the New York Times, www.nytimes.com (requires free subscription to the site).

Films

Shanghai Ghetto (2002, 95 mins.) *In English, German, and Chinese with subtitles. This documentary includes interviews with survivors and historians, photographs, and footage of the "Jewish ghetto" and synagogue, which remain in Shanghai today. A compelling portrayal of little-known history. Directed by Amir Mann et al.*

Nanking (2007, 90 mins.) *In English, Chinese, and Japanese with subtitles. The documentary based on Iris Chang's book relies exclusively on interviews with Chinese survivors and Japanese soldiers, and diaries, letters, or reports written by Westerners present during the 1937 atrocities. A powerful and deeply disturbing film. For more information, see http://www.nanking1937.com.*

■ **A CLOSER LOOK**

General Joseph Stilwell Enters the Fray

Born in 1883, Joseph Stilwell traced his roots to English settlers who arrived in New England in 1638. He was raised in Yonkers, New York and graduated from West Point in 1904. After serving in World War I, Stilwell divided his time between assignments in China, where he learned to speak fluent Chinese, and teaching Spanish, French, and English at West Point. His service in China included a post as military attaché to the United States embassy from 1935–1939. Independent-minded and blunt, he earned the name "Vinegar Joe." However, those who served under him also considered him a soldier's general. When President Franklin D. Roosevelt needed a liaison to Generalissimo Chiang Kai-shek, Joseph Stilwell was the obvious choice. Among

Stilwell's responsibilities was that of ensuring that Lend-Lease supplies from the United States reached Chongqing. He also oversaw the construction of the Ledo Road, which linked to the northern end of the Burma Road and was a vital supply route to landlocked Chongqing.

Stilwell and Chiang Kai-shek did not get along. Stilwell correctly believed that Chiang was hoarding the military supplies from the United States to use against the Communists in the future rather than the Japanese in the present. The American general wanted to reform the dysfunctional Guomindang army, a move that Chiang blocked because the upper ranks of his army supported his government. Concluding that Chiang and his government were corrupt, incompetent, and

timid, the four-star general routinely referred to him as "Peanut" in his official reports to Washington. In October 1944, presumably under pressure from Chiang, President Roosevelt recalled Joseph Stilwell. Of his years in China, the general said little except to note: "The trouble was largely one of posture. I tried to stand on my feet instead of my knees. I did not think the knee position was a suitable one for Americans." Joseph Stilwell died of liver cancer in 1946 at the age of 63. The Ledo Road now bears his name, and the Chinese Communist Party considers him a hero, honoring him with a museum in Chongqing, where the general's headquarters once stood.

■ *Why do you think the present Chinese government honors Stilwell?*

■ **A CLOSER LOOK**

Feminist Writer Ding Ling

Ding Ling is one of the most famous twentieth-century Chinese writers. She was born in Hunan Province in 1904 and educated with the help of her widowed mother. In 1920, sixteen-year-old Ding Ling joined other young intellectuals in Shanghai, in part to avoid the marriage her uncle had arranged. She became deeply involved in the May Fourth Movement (see Chapter 8) and in 1924 married poet Hu Yepin. Ding published her first short story in 1927, and a collection of her stories the following year. Her work, featuring women struggling with modernity, was extremely popular. In 1931, Ding Ling's husband, who had become active in the League of Left-Wing Writers, was arrested and executed by the Guomindang. Devastated, Ding Ling joined the Communist Party and devoted herself to the cause through her revolutionary writing.

In 1933, the Guomindang arrested her and placed her under house arrest, but she managed to escape three years later and made her way to Yan'an. In time, the Communist Party also tried to stifle her work, especially when she wrote about discrimination against women at Yan'an. *The Sun Shines Over the Sanggan River*, the politically correct novel she wrote in 1949, however, was highly praised. During the Anti-Rightist campaign in 1957, Ding Ling was once again a target. She was sent to be "reformed through labor" on a farm near the Siberian border. During the Cultural Revolution (see Chapter 14) she endured brutal beatings and was imprisoned from 1970 to 1975. Only after Deng Xiaoping took power did Ding Ling reappear in public. She was a changed woman who no longer spoke about feminist issues or freedom of expression. She died in 1986.

■ *Compare Ding Ling's life story with that of poet Ai Qing (11.8). How would you describe this period in history for writers who were politically inclined? What is the relationship between politics and art? (Consider the prints at the beginning of the chapter as well.)*

Primary Sources

DOCUMENT 12.1: Excerpt from *China's Destiny* by Chiang Kai-shek, 1943

DOCUMENT 12.2: Excerpt from "Manifesto of the Chinese People's Liberation Army" by Mao Zedong, 1947

DOCUMENT 12.3: Excerpt from General George Marshall's "Personal Statement by the Special Representative of the President," 1947

DOCUMENT 12.4: Letter to the Editor by Ding Keshan, March 30, 1948

DOCUMENT 12.5: Excerpts from a survey sponsored by the North American Chinese Students Christian Association, 1948

DOCUMENT 12.6: "Dead Water," a poem by Wen Yiduo, 1928

DOCUMENT 12.7: Excerpt from Wen Yiduo's speech at the memorial service for Li Gongbu, 1946

DOCUMENT 12.8a–c: Wood block prints by Li Hua, 1946–1948

DOCUMENT 12.9: Excerpts from reports and writings related to land reform leading up to the founding of the People's Republic of China, 1946–1948

DOCUMENT 12.10: "The People's Liberation Army Captures Nanjing," a poem by Mao Zedong, 1949

Supplementary Materials

ITEM 12.A: Further information and questions related to wood block prints (Activity 7)

CHAPTER 12

War Continues, 1945–1949

By Philip Gambone

Chapter Contents

The Roots of the Civil War
U.S. Attempts at Mediation
Civil War
The Communist Victory

Organizing Idea

The Chinese Civil War resulted from a fundamental contradiction between the political objectives of the Guomindang and the Chinese Communist Party. While the Guomindang initially enjoyed international support and material advantages, a combination of their failures and the successful strategies of the Communists led to a Communist victory.

Key Questions

What were the respective strengths of the Guomindang and the Chinese Communist Party at the end of World War II?

What role did the United States play in trying to help the two factions form a coalition government? Why?

What attitudes on the part of the Guomindang and the Communists led to a failure to form a coalition government?

What was the military and political stratey of the Guomindang? What was the military and political strategy of the CCP?

Why did the Guomindang lose the war?

Key Terms

Chinese Communist Party (CCP)
class struggle
coalition
Democratic League
extremist
feudal

Generalissimo
Guomindang (GMD)
manifesto
propaganda
reactionary

Essay

With the Japanese surrender in August 1945, World War II came to a close. In China, this signaled the intensification of the struggle for power between the Guomindang (中国国民党) and the Chinese Communist Party (中国共产党) (CCP).[1] During the War of Resistance Against Japan (抗日战争) (1937–1945), the two rivals had joined together in an uneasy, bitter alliance. (See Chapter 11.) Deeply antagonistic, their "coalition" was marked more by suspicion, betrayal, and hostility than by cooperation. Therefore, it is not surprising that as soon as the war was over, each side speedily mustered its forces to try to be the first to receive the surrender of the Japanese, and take possession of their weapons.

Each party enjoyed certain advantages. Under the leadership of Chiang Kai-shek (蒋介石), the Guomindang controlled the major urban areas in unoccupied China. Meanwhile, the Communist forces had grown dramatically during the war against Japan and had the advantage of proximity to Northeast China (Manchuria, 满洲), where a strong guerrilla resistance already existed. Mao Zedong (毛泽东) dismissed Chiang as "China's fascist ringleader, autocrat and traitor to the people."[2] The Communists controlled much of the countryside in North China, where the peasants, who numbered about 100 million, saw the CCP as far more sympathetic to their plight.

In an effort to prevent a Communist takeover, the United States ordered the Japanese to surrender only to the Guomindang. The United States further helped the Guomindang by moving half a million men into the areas in North China formerly occupied by the Japanese. The Chinese Communists also received foreign assistance. Though its help was not as substantial as the aid provided to the Guomindang by the United States, the Soviet Union lent its support to the CCP by turning over weapons, artillery, aircraft, and combat vehicles, which it had confiscated from the Japanese in Manchuria. Furthermore, Japanese prisoners of war were used to train the Communist armed forces.

In the first weeks after World War II, the Guomindang looked to be in the better position. Their armed forces outnumbered that those of the CCP (2.7 million to 1 million), and they had more weapons. The Guomindang quickly regained control of most of the major cities in East, Central, and South China. Nevertheless, the Communists did not yield their hold of North China. They used their huge stockpiles of Japanese weapons and advanced into Manchuria, a region rich in minerals and forests. Mao's strategy was to maintain Communist bases in the countryside. From these strongholds, he would mount guerrilla-style attacks and eventually take over the cities.

Attempts at Reconciliation

On August 28, 1945, Mao, escorted by U.S. Ambassador Patrick Hurley, flew to Chongqing (重庆), the wartime capital, for talks with Chiang. Many hoped that civil war could be averted, and at first, a positive outcome seemed a real possibility. The two leaders issued a joint communiqué that acknowledged the importance of peaceful postwar reconstruction. Mao agreed to pull his remaining forces from South China, and the two leaders further agreed to form a unified national army and to resume discussions about China's long-range future. But behind the scenes, the two leaders' distrust of each other festered. Chiang Kai-shek was determined to destroy the Communists. In November 1945, he launched a huge military assault. Mao dug in. He hoped that through ideological work and continued land reform,[3] he would prevail.

---

[1] Guomindang (abbreviated GMD) was spelled Kuomintang (KMT) in the older Wade-Giles system of transcription and was also known as the Nationalist party.

[2] Mao Zedong, "Chiang Kai-shek is Provoking Civil War" in *Selected Works of Mao Zedong*, vol. 4. (Beijing: Foreign Languages Press, 1967), 27.

[3] See Chapter 9, Document 9.3.

In December 1945, U.S. President Harry Truman sent the much respected wartime leader General George Marshall to mediate the dispute. Many in China and the United States were eager to bring the two parties together because they feared the excesses of one-party rule from either side. Twice in 1946, Marshall arranged a truce between the Guomindang and CCP. Talks began about forming a coalition government, but within weeks both sides had violated the truce.

By this time, Mao did not trust the United States. He told an American correspondent: "I doubt very much that the policy of the U.S. government is one of 'mediation.' Judging by the large amount of aid that the United States is giving Chiang Kai-shek to enable him to wage a civil war on an unprecedented scale, the policy of the U.S. government is to use the so-called mediation as a smoke-screen for strengthening Chiang Kai-shek in every way and suppressing the democratic [Communist] forces in China...."[4] Guomindang leaders took measures to ensure that neither the Communists nor the other major opposition party, the Democratic League (民主同盟), participated in the National Constitutional Assembly, which met toward the end of 1946 to adopt a new Constitution. In effect, they packed the Assembly with Guomindang supporters, locking out other voices in the formation of China's fledgling "democracy." In January 1947, a deeply frustrated Marshall abandoned his efforts at mediation. Blaming both parties, he wrote, "The greatest obstacle to peace has been the complete, almost overwhelming suspicion with which the Chinese Communist Party and the Guomindang regard each other."[5] China dissolved into civil war.

The Civil War

Early on, most of the battles were won by the Guomindang. Yan'an (延安), an important Communist stronghold, fell to the Guomindang. "How long can the Communist Party keep on?" an American correspondent asked Mao in August 1946. "We can fight to the finish," Mao confidently replied. "We have only millet plus rifles to rely on, but history will finally prove that our millet plus rifles is more powerful than Chiang Kai-shek's aeroplanes plus tanks."[6]

In 1947, the Communists took the offensive in Manchuria. To meet the Communist advance, Chiang committed a half a million men to the campaign and airlifted massive aid to Manchuria's cities. This proved to be a disastrous mistake. The Communists controlled the countryside, and the cities in which the Guomindang were based quickly became isolated from each other. The Communists took Manchuria in November 1948. In the process, Chiang lost some 470,000 of his best troops, in addition to weapons and equipment. With the North firmly in his pocket, Mao turned south.

Communist Victory

Despite the fact that Chiang's army was still superior in terms of equipment and air power, morale within the army and among the civilian populace began to erode. The troops were poorly paid and huge numbers defected. Moreover, some of the Communist military leaders were brilliant strategists; they had a keen understanding of local conditions. Chiang stubbornly refused to listen to better advice from his generals. Pushing his men forward, he exposed them to the superior military tactics of the CCP forces.

On the civilian front, too, there was growing discontent with the Guomindang. Inflation was out of control and the government was riddled with corruption. Many educated Chinese opposed the Guomindang. They pointed to farcical elections, poor leadership, and violations of civil liberties, including the imprisonment, torture, and assassination of

---

[4] Mao Zedong. "The Truth About U.S. 'Mediation' and the Future of the Civil War in China," *Selected Works of Mao Zedong*, vol. 4. (Beijing: Foreign Languages Press, 1967) 109.

[5] Department of State Bulletin, January 19, 1947.

[6] *Selected Works of Mao Zedong*, vol. 4, 97–101.

critics of the government. "The Government cares for nothing but itself," wrote Zhu Anping, the editor of a popular weekly. "The people have nothing to eat, does it care? It does not.... The Government only protects the wealthy and cares nothing for the poor."[7]

Others, especially the older intellectuals, wanted to reform the Guomindang. They argued that their chances for a democratic society were better with a Guomindang government than one headed by the CCP. Many Chinese were alarmed by the extreme methods the Communists used to address the needs of the peasantry. Beatings, mass killings of landlords, total seizures of land and property—such were the methods peasants adopted, often at the instigation of Communist Party agents.

By the middle of January, first Tianjin (天津) and then Beijing (北京) fell to Communist General Lin Biao (林彪), and on January 21,

1949, Chiang was forced to resign. The new president tried to negotiate with the Communists, but Mao was not interested. His generals continued pushing south and west. Toward the end of April, Communist troops crossed the Yangzi River (长江) and took Nanjing (南京). Shanghai (上海) fell in May, Changsha (长沙) in August.

By early fall, it was clear beyond a doubt that the Communists had won the Civil War. On October 1, 1949, addressing an uproarious crowd at the Gate of Heavenly Peace in Beijing, Mao announced the creation of the People's Republic of China. "China has stood up!" he proclaimed. Two months later, remnants of the Guomindang forces fled to Taiwan, where Chiang Kai-shek and a substantial Guomindang military force were already established. The Civil War for political supremacy had ended.

Primary Sources

DOCUMENT 12.1: Excerpt from *China's Destiny* by Chiang Kai-shek, 1943

....

Every Chinese citizen has the right as well as the duty to become a member of the Guomindang. As the central organ directing the work of revolution and reconstruction, the Party treats the people, be they members or non-members, on an equal footing, without the slightest discrimination. It assumes the responsibility of guiding and training the people so that everyone may have the opportunity and the ability to work for the success of the National Revolution, the realization of the Three Principles, the rebuilding of the state and the revival of the nation. It entertains no bias in favor of or against any profession or class. Furthermore, the Guomindang seeks to take care of and give training to every citizen, and does not deny any qualified person his opportunity of service. It welcomes each and every patriotic citizen to join it in a common struggle for the completion of its mission....

SOURCE: Chiang Kai-shek, *China's Destiny*, trans. Wang Chung-hui (New York: Macmillan, 1947) 99–100.

 The full text of Document 12.1 is available on the CD-ROM.

---

[7] Qtd. in Suzanne Pepper, *Civil War in China: The Political Struggle, 1945–1949* (Berkeley: University of California Press, 1978) 144–145.

DOCUMENT 12.2: Excerpt from "Manifesto of the Chinese People's Liberation Army" by Mao Zedong, 1947

We are the army of the Chinese people and in all things we take the will of the Chinese people as our will. The policies of our army represent the urgent demands of the Chinese people and chief among them are the following:

1. Unite workers, peasants, soldiers, intellectuals and businessmen, all oppressed classes, all people's organizations, democratic parties, minority nationalities, overseas Chinese and other patriots; form a national united front; overthrow the dictatorial Chiang Kai-shek government; and establish a democratic coalition government.

2. Arrest, try and punish the civil war criminals headed by Chiang Kai-shek.

3. Abolish the Chiang Kai-shek dictatorship, carry out the system of people's democracy and guarantee freedom of speech, of the press, of assembly and of association for the people.

4. Abolish the rotten institutions of the Chiang Kai-shek regime, clear out all corrupt officials and establish clean government.

5. Confiscate the property of the four big families of Chiang Kai-shek, T.V. Soong, H.H. Kung and the Chen Li-Fu brothers, and the property of the other chief war criminals; confiscate bureaucrat-capital, develop the industry and commerce of the national bourgeoisie, improve the livelihood of workers and employees, and give relief to victims of natural calamities and to poverty-stricken people.

6. Abolish the system of feudal exploitation and put into effect the system of land to the tillers.

7. Recognize the right of equality and autonomy of the minority nationalities within the borders of China.

8. Repudiate the traitorous foreign policy of Chiang Kai-shek's dictatorial government, abrogate all the treasonable treaties and repudiate all the foreign debts contracted by Chiang Kai-shek during the civil war period. Demand that the U.S. government withdraw its troops stationed in China, which are a menace to China's independence, and oppose any foreign country's helping Chiang Kai-shek to carry on civil war or trying to revive the forces of Japanese aggression. Conclude treaties of trade and friendship with foreign countries on the basis of equality and reciprocity. Unite in a common struggle with all nations, which treat us as equals....

SOURCE: *Selected Works of Mao Zedong*, vol. 4 (Beijing: Foreign Languages Press, 1967) 149–150.

 The full text of Document 12.2 is available on the CD-ROM.

DOCUMENT 12.3: Excerpt from General George Marshall's "Personal Statement by the Special Representative of the President," 1947

[T]he greatest obstacle to peace has been the complete, almost overwhelming suspicion with which the Chinese Communist Party and the Guomindang regard each other.

On the one hand, the leaders of the Government are strongly opposed to a communistic form of government. On the other, the Communists frankly state that they are Marxists and intend to work toward establishing a communistic form of government in China, though first advancing through the medium of a democratic form of government of the American or British type.

The leaders of the Government are convinced in their minds that the Communist-expressed desire to participate in a government of the type endorsed by the Political Consultative Conference last January had for its purpose only a destructive intention. The Communists felt, I believe, that the government was insincere in its apparent acceptance of the PCC [Political Consultative Conference] resolutions for the formation of the new government and intended by coercion of military force and the action of secret police to obliterate the Communist Party....

SOURCE: Department of State Bulletin, January 19, 1947: 83–85, rpt. in Immanuel C.Y. Hsü, *Readings in Modern Chinese History* (New York: Oxford University Press, 1971) 543–546.

 The full text of Document 12.3 is available on the CD-ROM.

DOCUMENT 12.4: Letter to the Editor, by Ding Keshan, March 30, 1948

[T]he Guomindang's candidate for the National Assembly representative was Dong Xiuming; and there were a few others also seeking election. One cold cloudy afternoon, Dong Xiuming gave a public election speech in the open-air theater... In order to learn something about democracy, I braved the cold wind to listen. When I arrived, except for a few shop apprentices, all those seated in the audience were peddlers from off the nearby streets.... [They said] the police had told them to come.... Then three or four officers brought in over two hundred men who were said to be just then undergoing military training. Only then were all the seats filled. Mr. Dong's speech was very simple and contained no election principles at all... After Mr. Dong had concluded his speech, the *xian* [district] magistrate, Wang Yifang, took over and began to talk. To the "voters" in the audience he said: "I order you to elect Mr. Dong Xiuming. This order is the same as the order telling you that you should go to do repair work on the defense installations. It is wrong for anyone to disobey...." After the meeting, [word went out] to every household: "The *xian* magistrate has spoken. Whoever does not vote for Dong Xiuming will have to go out and work on the defense installations when they need repairs in the future." The result of the election was, of course, that Dong Xiuming received the most votes.

Today is the big opening of the National Assembly and I suppose Mr. Dong Xiuming is already sitting securely in a representative's seat.... Really what a joke it is.

SOURCE: Qtd. in Suzanne Pepper, *Civil War in China: The Political Struggle, 1945–1949* (Berkeley: University of California Press, 1978) 139–140.

DOCUMENT 12.5: Excerpts from a survey sponsored by the North American Chinese Students Christian Association, 1948

QUESTION 3: *I feel that peace in China must be sought by:*

	(% of those responding)
no answer	1.8
the Nationalist Government should eliminate the Communist Party	18.0
the organization of a coalition government to include the CCP, the Democratic League, other parties and Independent elements	51.1
The adoption of a federal system	17.9
The division of the country into independent areas	3.2
national rule by the CCP	2.7
let the United Nations arbitrate	1.1
other	4.2

SOURCE: *Kuan-ch'a (The Observer)*, July 17, 1948: 8–9, rpt. in Suzanne Pepper, *Civil War in China: The Political Struggle, 1945–1949* (Berkeley: University of California Press, 1978) 90–92.

 The complete survey is available on the CD-ROM.

DOCUMENT 12.6: "Dead Water," a poem by Wen Yiduo, 1928

Here is a ditch of hopeless water,
The fresh breeze would not even raise half a ripple.
One might as well throw in a few more tins and scraps of metal
And why not pour in your left-over food and gravy.

Perhaps the green of the copper will turn into emerald,
Rust on the tin cans emerge as petals of peach blossom;
Then let grease weave a layer of patterned muslin,
And bacteria brew vapours of coloured clouds.

Let the dead water ferment into a gully of green wine,
Floating pearl-like crowds of white foam;
The laughter of small pearls will change them to large pearls
Broken by mosquitoes to steal the alcohol.

Even a ditch of hopeless dead water
Can boast of some ornaments.
If the green frogs can't bear the silence,
Then we can say that the dead water can sing.

Here is a ditch of hopeless dead water,
This cannot be a place where beauty lives,
Better let ugliness cultivate it,
And see what kind of world comes of it.

SOURCE: Wen I-to, "Dead Water," *Red Candle: Selected Poems by Wen I-to,* trans. Tao Tao Sanders (London: Jonathan Cape, 1972) 34.

DOCUMENT 12.7: Excerpt from Wen Yiduo's speech at the memorial service for Li Gongbu, 1946

We all know that, only a few days ago, the most despicable, the most shameless incident occurred in Kunming. What crime had Li Gongbu committed to deserve such an ending in unconscionable hands!... Today I want to know if there are more secret agents here, right here. Step up, you, tell us, why you killed Li Gongbu...

You reactionaries, you try so hard to alienate us from our friends. What shame! You think now that Lianda [University] has moved away and the students have dispersed for the summer, you think we are powerless now. But, secret agents, you are wrong! Look at the thousand and more young people gathered here, our arms linked together. We, the young generation of Kunming, shall not tolerate your reckless action.... We are not afraid of death; we are constantly ready to follow in Li Gongbu's footsteps. The moment we step out of this door, we don't think of stepping back!

SOURCE: Rpt. in Kai-yu Hsu, *Wen I-To* (Boston: Twayne Publishers, 1980) 173.

DOCUMENT 12.8a & b: **"Soldiers and People Working Together" and "After the Guard in Charge of Grain Has Gone (Victory)," wood block prints by Li Hua, 1946–1948**

Li Hua (1907–1994) was among the many wood block print artists who were active during the Chinese Civil War. He drew inspiration from socialist authors like Lu Xun, who was an admirer of wood block prints as a vehicle for social protest. Li used his art as a way to capture people's lives and to inspire the oppressed to take action.

(Courtesy of the Picker Art Gallery, Colgate University [1968.43, 1968.35])

 An additional wood block print by Li Hua is on the CD-ROM.

DOCUMENT 12.9: Excerpts from reports and writing related to land reform leading up to the founding of the People's Republic of China, 1946–1948

The National Land Conference of the Communist Party of China was held in September 1947 in Hubei Province. The law written at the conference was published by the Central Committee of the Communist Party of China on October 10, 1947. It stipulated the following:

Abolish the land system of feudal and semi-feudal exploitation and put into effect the system of land to the tillers.

All the land of the landlords and the public land in the villages is to be taken over by the local peasant associations and, together with all other land there, is to be equally distributed among the entire rural population, regardless of sex or age.

The peasant associations of the villages shall take over the draught animals, farm tools, houses, grain, and other property of the landlords, requisition the surplus of such property of the rich peasants, distribute all this property among the peasants and other poor people who are in need of it and allot the same share to the landlords.

SOURCE: *Selected Works of Mao Zedong* (Beijing: Foreign Languages Press, 1967). Transcribed by the Maoist Documentation Project, revised 2004 by Marxist.org. http://www.marxists.org/reference/archive/mao/selected-works/volume-4/mswv4_24.htm#bm4

 The full text of Document 12.9 is on the CD-ROM.

DOCUMENT 12.10: "The People's Liberation Army Captures Nanjing," a poem by Mao Zedong, 1949

Over Zhongshan swept a storm, headlong,
Our mighty army, a million strong, has crossed the Great River.
The City, a tiger crouching, a dragon curling, outshines its ancient glories;
In heroic triumph heaven and earth have been overturned.
With power and to spare we must pursue the tottering foe
And not ape Xiang Yu the conqueror seeking idle fame.
Were Nature sentient, she too would pass from youth to age,
But Man's world is mutable, seas become mulberry fields.

SOURCE: *Mao Zedong Poems* (Beijing: Foreign Languages Press, 1998) 49.

Activities

ACTIVITY 1: A reading from Chiang Kai-shek

After reading the excerpt from *China's Destiny* (12.1), discuss:

1. What is the overall tone of the first passage? What kinds of appeals does Chiang Kai-shek make to the Chinese population? How effective do you think this passage was in inspiring the Chinese to join the Guomindang cause?

2. In the first passage, Chiang does not specifically mention the Communists. Nevertheless, are there subtle ways in which he expresses criticism of the Communists? Why do you suppose he did not actually name the Communists?

3. In the second passage, Chiang is much more explicitly attacking the Communists. What are some of his criticisms?

4. What does Chiang mean when he refers to the Guomindang cause as the "National Revolution"? What was revolutionary about the Guomindang cause?

5. Taking into account what you have learned about some of the Guomindang tactics, what do you think of Chiang's claim that his party "entertains no bias in favor of or against any profession or class"?

6. Does a political party have a duty to fairly represent itself and competing parties? Why or why not?

ACTIVITY 2: Analyzing a manifesto by Mao Zedong

After reading Mao Zedong's manifesto (12.2), divide into two groups. One group will be responsible for making a chart of all the phrases Mao uses against Chiang Kai-shek and his government; the other group should make a chart of all the phrases Mao uses to describe the Communist cause. Display both charts and hold a discussion comparing the picture that emerges of the two sides in the Civil War.

1. According to Mao, what are the aims of the Communists and their army? In what ways are these aims different from the aims of the Guomindang as expressed by Chiang Kai-shek in Document 12.1? In what ways are the Communists' aims similar to those of the Guomindang? Could the two groups have cooperated?

2. Both Chiang Kai-shek and Mao Zedong claimed to be working for the good of "the people." Did they have the same "people" in mind? Which groups would more likely have been attracted to Chiang's cause? Which groups would have gravitated toward Mao's? Why?

3. How would you describe Mao's style of writing and speaking? What is propaganda? Is this manifesto an example of propaganda? Is Chiang's piece an example of propaganda? Debate these questions.

ACTIVITY 3: Evaluating General Marshall's assessment

After reading General Marshall's analysis (12.3), consider:

1. How would you assess Marshall's statement? Does he support the Guomindang, the Communists, or is his account even-handed?

2. Marshall wrote that the greatest obstacle to establishing peace between the two factions was "almost overwhelming suspicion." Why do you think this was so? What did each side have to be suspicious about?

3. On the Guomindang (Nationalist) side, Marshall singled out "reactionaries" who were opposed to a coalition. What is a reactionary? What are the political disadvantages of a reactionary stance? Are there times when a reactionary stance is appropriate?

4. What does Marshall see as the faults of the Communist side in the breakdown of negotiations? You might want to make a chart comparing and contrasting the faults, as Marshall listed them, on each side.

5. Toward the end of his report, Marshall expressed his hope for the end of "one-party rule." Would the Guomindang have been more successful if they had allowed the Communists and other political groups to participate in the government? Why or why not?

Creative extension:

Write a script or dialogue between three characters—Chiang Kai-shek, Mao Zedong, and George Marshall—in which they try to negotiate a coalition. Use some of the actual words from the first three documents. Give a live or recorded performance acting out your script.

ACTIVITY 4: Letter to the editor

After reading Ding Keshan's letter to the editor (12.4), discuss:

1. What picture of democracy under the Guomindang does this letter give?

2. What is the writer's tone?

3. How do these types of election tactics fit into your definition of "democracy"?

Later on, in Chapter 14, when you read about how the Communists ran "struggle meetings" and other assemblies, return to this letter and compare the accounts.

ACTIVITY 5: Analyzing a survey

Present the answers in the survey (12.5) in a pie graph or bar graph to illustrate in a more visual way the distribution of opinions on each question.

1. Look at the responses to Question 1. What is the difference between a cooperative farm and a collective farm? Why do you suppose these students favored cooperatives over collectives?

2. What does "nationalization" mean? Why do you think that over half the students favored nationalization of heavy industry (machinery, manufacturing, etc.) and public utilities? Do you think that other groups in China would have been so supportive of nationalization? What areas of the economy in your country are nationalized?

3. From the students' responses to Question 3, we see that over half of them favored a coalition government, while only 18 percent thought the Guomindang (Nationalist) government should eliminate the Communists. Are students likely to be more "liberal" than other segments of a society? Why? Do you think a coalition could have worked?

4. What do you make of the students' answers to Question 4 and 5? How much confidence did they have in the Guomindang government? Why?

Writing extension:

Pretend you are a Chinese student studying in the United States in 1948. Write a letter home expressing your views of the situation in China. Use ideas that you gather from the survey results and the documents in this chapter.

Debate what role intellectuals, and especially students, have in political affairs. Have you ever participated in any political activity? If so, what did you do? Did you feel you made a contribution? What kind of contribution?

ACTIVITY 6: Listening to the voice of dissent

Part 1:

Choose four adjectives to describe the tone of the poem by Wen Yiduo (12.6). Discuss:

1. What does the "dead water" stand for in this poem?

2. What are some of the other strong images in the poem? What does the poet's attitude seem to be about the possibilities for progress in China?

Classical Chinese poetry uses very few words to evoke meaning. Characters in Chinese poetry often cannot be precisely translated because the meaning changes subtly depending on the context. This translation is by Tao Tao Sanders. The final stanza of the poem is translated somewhat differently by Kai-yu Hsu in *Wen I-To*:

Here is a ditch of hopelessly dead water—
a region where beauty can never reside.
Might as well let the devil cultivate it—
see what sort of a world it can provide.

3. How is this different from and similar to Tao Tao Sanders's translation? Whom might Wen Yiduo have identified as the "devil" in the next-to-last line?

Part 2:

Read the excerpt from Wen Yiduo's speech at the memorial service for his friend Li Gongbu (12.7)

1. In the eighteen years between Wen's poem "Dead Water" and this speech, what changes do you detect in his attitude, his writing style, and his subject matter? What might account for the changes?

2. Do you think Wen was aware of the danger of speaking out so boldly?

3. Kai-yu Hsu writes in his biography of Wen Yiduo, "He regarded patriotism as being as important in literature as 'love, the ephemeralness of beauty, the approach of death, and all universal sentiments suggested by nature'" (Kai-yu Hsu, *Wen I-To*, 100–101). Is "Dead Water" a patriotic poem?

4. Do you think that artists—writers, painters, musicians, actors, etc.—should become involved in politics? Should they create art for political purposes?

5. What artists do you know in other countries who used or use their art to express political beliefs? What effect did the artists' work have on the political process?

ACTIVITY 7: Analyzing political art

Begin by reading a short introduction to the New Woodcut Movement at http://depts.washington.edu/chinaciv/graph/9polwood.htm. Working in small groups, examine the three wood block prints (12.8a–c). (Note: Refer to Item 12.A on the CD for additional information and questions specific to each print.)

1. Describe the people, things, and place depicted in the print.

2. What is happening? Why?

3. What may have been the artist's purpose in creating this image?

4. What message, if any, is the print communicating?

Then as a class discuss:

1. Many of Li Hua's woodcuts were given as traditional New Year pictures (*nianhua*), images that would be pasted on doors during the festival, and often would remain up all year. What effect do you think these images had on the peasants and other people who received and displayed them?

2. Does visual art have the power to change people's thinking? Can you think of examples from today?

Creative extension:

Create a piece of art (e.g. a sculpture, poem, song, cartoon, or painting) expressing your view on a political or social issue about which you feel strongly. Give it a title, and write a two- to three-sentence caption for your work if it is a visual piece. After everyone has had chance to see everyone else's work, discuss the challenges of this assignment.

ACTIVITY 8: Analyzing efforts at land reform

Land reform was a central tenet of the CCP. Read excerpts describing the efforts (12.9) and discuss:

1. What was at the heart of the land reform movement?
2. Why did the Party insist that the rights of "middle peasants" be protected?
3. How did land reform change over this period of time?
4. How was land reform related to the success of the CCP in winning the war?
5. What alternate methods might a government use to address rural poverty?
6. Compare the CCP's land reform programs with Fei Xiaotong's recommendations for alleviating rural poverty (Chapter 10, Document 10.13).

ACTIVITY 9: Interpreting a poem by Mao Zedong

1. What is the overall mood of the first four lines of Mao Zedong's poem (12.10)?
2. Who is the "tottering foe" (line 5)?
3. Find out who Xiang Yu was. How did he seek "idle fame"? What comparison is Mao making here?
4. In Mao's view, what has passed from youth to age with this victory? (Keep in mind that the Chinese honor age over youth.)
5. How do you interpret the final line of the poem? Is it a positive image? How so? Find out what the leaves of mulberry trees are used for in China.

Chinese leaders—including emperors, other members of the court, and scholar-officials—were often accomplished poets. (See Chapter 2.)

6. Do you see Communist leader Mao Zedong's poetry as part of this tradition?
7. Does it seem unusual to you that he would indulge in an activity that was so closely tied to the imperial system of government? What might be his reasons for doing so?
8. Can you think of leaders in other countries who were also creative artists?

ACTIVITY 10: A debate: How did the Communists win the war?

At the beginning of her book *Civil War in China*, historian Suzanne Pepper asks: "Did the Chinese Communists win a genuine mandate to rule, or were they primarily the beneficiaries of Guomindang mistakes and Japanese excesses?" (p. 6) Debate the question in class. Alternatively, answer the question in an essay.

Suggested Resources

Books

Chiang Kai-shek. *China's Destiny*. Translated by
Wang Chung-hui. New York: Macmillan, 1947.
*Written in 1943, while China was still fighting
the Japanese, this is Chiang's vision for his
country.*

Selected Works of Mao Zedong. Beijing: Foreign
Languages Press, 1967.
*Volume 4 covers the period of the Civil War. This
series includes many interesting, provocative
speeches and essays. Writings of Mao are also available online at* http://www.marx2mao.com/Mao/
Index.html

Pepper, Suzanne. *Civil War in China: The Political
Struggle, 1945–1949*. Berkeley: University of
California Press, 1978.
*For those more interested in the political and
intellectual aspects of the Civil War, this is a
first-rate account.*

Spence, Jonathan D. *Mao Zedong*. New York:
Viking, 1999.
*A good short biography by one of the finest China
scholars writing today.*

Websites

Maps

http://www.dean.usma.edu/history/web03/
atlases/chinese%20civil%20war/chinese%20civil
%20war%20index.htm The West Point history
department has five maps detailing the events of the
Civil War.

The Civil War

http://en.allexperts.com/e/c/ch/chinese_civil_
war.htm A general history of the Chinese Civil
War.

http://news.bbc.co.uk/2/shared/spl/hi/pop_
ups/03/asia_pac_0life0_in_civil_war_china/
html/1.stm An interesting collection of photographs documenting life during the Chinese Civil
War.

http://en.wikipedia.org/wiki/Chinese_Civil_
War A detailed account of the Civil War with good
photographs.

http://www.pbs.org/wgbh/amex/china/timeline/
timeline1nf.html This site from PBS provides an
excellent timeline of China's foreign relations during
the Civil War (and beyond).

Woodcuts

http://depts.washington.edu/chinaciv/graph/
9polwood.htm

http://www.artgallery.sbc.edu/exhibits/00_01/
chinesewoodblock/ "Half a Century of Chinese
Woodblock Prints," from an exhibition at Sweet
Briar College.

http://kaladarshan.arts.ohio-state.edu/exhib/
gug/intr/modintro.html

Film

China, A Century of Revolution, Part 1: *China in
Revolution: 1911–1949* (1997 & 2001; 120
mins.) *The first of three PBS films documenting the
economic and political development of
China since 1911. (Ambrica Productions/
Zeitgeist Films)*

■ A CLOSER LOOK

Edgar Snow (1905–1972): Journalist and Activist

In 1937, Edgar Snow ended "Red Horizon," the final chapter in his ground-breaking book *Red Star Over China*, by writing: "The movement for social revolution in China might suffer defeats…but it will not only continue to mature; in one mutation or another it will eventually win, simply because the basic conditions which have given it birth carry within themselves the dynamic necessity for its triumph." It turned out to be a prophetic statement.

By the time he met with Mao Zedong in 1936, Edgar Snow had worked as a foreign correspondent and traveled widely in China for seven years. He spoke some Chinese and was friends with numerous Chinese intellectuals in Beijing and Shanghai. Soong Qingling, the widow of Sun Yat-sen (see A Closer Look in Chapter 9), helped arrange for Snow to travel to Yan'an. Once there,

Snow stayed for four months, conducting extensive interviews with leaders of the CCP; he was the first Western journalist to do so.

In 1937, he published *Red Star Over China*, which he described as the "first authentic account of the Chinese Communist Party and the first connected story of their long struggle to carry through the most thorough-going social revolution in China's three millenniums of history."[11] Snow's largely sympathetic account of the Communists introduced the Western world to a movement and individuals about which little was known. During the McCarthy-era anti-Communist persecutions of the 1950s, Snow was blacklisted in the United States and was only able to sell his articles to foreign journals. He returned to China several times and was the only American journalist given

frequent access to interview CCP leaders. In 1970, on his final visit, Premier Zhou Enlai entrusted Snow with a message for the U.S. government: the "door is open" for improving relations between the two countries. Snow died in February 1972, at almost the same time that President Richard Nixon arrived in China (see Chapter 15).

■ *Discuss: What combination of factors enabled Snow to write his pivotal book? What was the ultimate impact of all of Snow's visits to and writing about China? (For excerpts from Snow's first book, see Chapter 11.)*

■ *Review the chapters in this unit and then consider Snow's prediction quoted in the first paragraph. What conditions was he referring to that gave birth to the social revolution and would ensure its triumph?*

---

[11] Snow, 16.

UNIT FOUR

The People's Republic of China
(1949–2000)

UNIT OVERVIEW

By Kenneth Hammond

In the autumn of 1949 the leaders of the **Chinese Communist Party** (CCP) and the Red Army found themselves in command of much of the territory of China. They faced immense challenges in completing the process of military control, and in bringing order and stability to the country. On October 1, 1949, the **People's Republic of China** (PRC) was formally proclaimed by Party Chairman **Mao Zedong**, in Beijing, which became the capital of the new regime.

Over the ensuing months and years, the CCP pursued a wide range of policies that rapidly restored the domestic economy and launched China on a program of development as a socialist state. For the first decade of the PRC's existence, the **Soviet Union** provided significant aid and served as a model for many aspects of China's new system. But the relationship with the Soviets was always a tense one, and by 1960 it broke down as China took a path that the Russians viewed as irrational.

Among the immediate tasks that the CCP undertook were the transformation of the rural economy through **land reform,** the nationalization of major urban businesses and industries, and the restructuring of family life through the **Marriage Law of 1950**, which gave women equal rights in marriage and divorce. These policies yielded immediate results, as the ravages of decades of war and division were healed and China began to grow into a more stable and prosperous society.

In carrying through the early policy reforms, the CCP also faced an internal challenge. When the Party came to power in 1949, there were only around two million members. With a vast and populous country to manage, the Party had to expand its ranks quite rapidly, and this resulted in many new members who were not necessarily devoted to the ideals of socialism, but who saw the Party as a path to security and advancement. This complicated the political landscape and led to an expanding gap between the Party and the people.

Once the initial stage of economic and political transformation was completed, the PRC embarked on a path of socialist modernization, which involved the **collectivization of the agricultural economy** and building up a state-owned industrial sector. Farming was the foundation, and the expansion of grain production in the early and mid-1950s generated revenue for the government, which was used to **invest in factories and infrastructure** like railroads and communications networks. But there were divisions among the leaders

NE

1949: Mao Zedong announces the founding of the People's Republic of China

1949: Chiang Kai-shek and Guomindang forces retreat to Taiwan

1949: India adopts a constitution

1950: Agrarian Reform Law and Marriage Law are enacted

1950: People's Liberation Army enters Tibet

1950-1953: Korean War begins with North Korea's invasion of South Korea; in late 1950, China enters war on behalf of North Korea

1953–present: Republic of Korea (South Korea) and Democratic People's Republic of Korea (North Korea) are separated by the 38th parallel

1950s: Senator Joseph McCarthy launches the second "Red Scare" in the U.S.

1953: First Five-Year Plan put into effect

1956: Hundred Flowers Campaign

1957: Anti-Rightist Campaign

1958–1961: Great Leap Forward

1959: PLA represses Tibetan uprising; Fourteenth Dalai Lama leaves Tibet

1960: Soviet Union withdraws all its experts from China

1965–1973: Second Indochina War between the Democratic Republic of Vietnam and the United States; known in the U.S. as the Vietnam War

1966–1976: The Great Proletarian Cultural Revolution

1970: United States begins bombing raids in Cambodia

1971: The People's Republic of China joins the United Nations; Taiwan loses the "China seat" at the UN

1972: President Richard Nixon visits China

1972: Japan and China normalize relations

1972: Park Chung-hee, president of the Republic of Korea (South Korea), declares martial law; he continues as president with control over parliament until his assassination in 1979

1975–1979: Khmer Rouge are in power in Cambodia

regarding how best to manage this process. Some, led by Mao Zedong, believed the best way to develop the country rapidly was through voluntarism and popular political mobilization. Others, led by President Liu Shaoqi and top economist Chen Yi, and including a junior member of the top leadership, Deng Xiaoping (later to become the leader of the CCP), thought it made more sense to develop a corps of technical experts who could use the most advanced and up-to-date technologies and methods to build the new economic order. These divisions deepened as time went on and ultimately led to violent confrontations between Party factions.

In the mid- to late 1950s the agricultural sector was the scene of the greatest upheavals. The process of collectivization, in which farming communities were encouraged to share resources and labor to achieve greater production, was pushed into high gear by Mao Zedong in 1957–1958. Wanting to build on early successes, and to unleash the enthusiasm he believed was pent up within the rural villages, he called for a **Great Leap Forward**. But a combination of bureaucratic resistance and incompetence, along with natural disasters in 1959 and the withdrawal of Soviet aid and advisors in 1960, led to massive drops in grain production, widespread hunger, and even

1975: **Chiang Kai-shek dies in Taiwan; his son assumes power**

1976: **Mao Zedong dies September 9**

1976: Socialist Republic of Vietnam founded

1978: **Deng Xiaoping promotes Four Modernizations**

1978: Vietnam invades Cambodia to drive out Khmer Rouge

1979: **January 1, the People's Republic of China and the United States formally recognize each other**

1979: **Deng Xiaoping is the first Chinese leader to visit the United States**

1979: **One-Child Policy implemented**

1980: **Special Economic Zones established**

1980s: Japan has the world's second largest economy

1988: **The first two-party elections held in Taiwan**

1989: **Tiananmen Square protests**

1989: **Mikhail Gorbachev, head of state of the Soviet Union, visits China**

1989: In November, the Berlin Wall is demolished

1990: October 3, East and West Germany are reunited

1991: Communist Party loses power in the Soviet Union; the country breaks up into a number of independent states

1991: First Gulf War

1992: The first civilian in thirty years is elected president of the Republic of Korea

1997: **China regains control of Hong Kong from the United Kingdom**

1999: **China regains control of Macao from Portugal**

2000: Leaders of North and South Korea meet for the first time since the end of the Korean War

2001: **China becomes a member of the World Trade Organization**

starvation. Deep conflicts within the leadership led to Mao Zedong's being relegated to a secondary role in the day-to-day affairs of the Party, and to a retreat from the policies of mass mobilization that he had championed.

China's economy recovered from the trauma of the Great Leap Forward in the early 1960s, but by 1965 new tensions within the leadership led to renewed conflict. In 1966 the **Great Proletarian Cultural Revolution** broke out, in which Mao and his allies sought to root out what they saw as the bureaucracy and elitism of some leaders within the CCP. But the Cultural Revolution soon became a struggle for power within the Party, and by 1969 a stalemate had set in that paralyzed many aspects of Chinese life for the next decade.

At the same time a shift was underway in China's foreign policy, away from the role as promoter of world revolution and towards a more pragmatic model. The relationship with the Soviet Union had become openly antagonistic, and the CCP, under the guidance of Zhou Enlai, moved toward establishing **relations with the United States.**

The stalemate within the Party over domestic policy was only broken by Mao's death in September 1976. A few weeks later, a coalition of forces within the Party brought down Mao's allies. By 1978 **Deng Xiaoping** emerged as the dominant figure within a new, technocratic elite that now controlled the CCP. This group moved carefully over the next few years to dismantle many aspects of the Maoist economic and social model, and began to move China in the direction of a market economy. Mao's fear that China would "take the capitalist road" was about to be realized.

In the 1980s China went through a period of increasingly **rapid transformation** and development. The agricultural economy was reformed to give private family farms priority, and this led to an immediate jump in production. The reform of the industrial sector and encouragement of private business generated a huge growth in urban incomes and the development of a consumer economy. But the benefits of this growth were not shared in an equal way. While Deng Xiaoping sought to buffer this inequality by arguing that "to get rich is glorious," others saw the accumulation of wealth by individuals with close ties to the Party and government as evidence of widespread corruption. By 1989, frustration and resentment over corruption and the limited opportunities for participation in political affairs resulted in the outbreak of mass protests in Beijing and other cities. The situation grew beyond the control of either the government or the original protest leaders, and eventually resulted in an armed crackdown. Units of the People's Liberation Army (PLA) fought with citizens in the streets around **Tiananmen Square**, killing hundreds of people.

In the wake of 1989, many feared China would turn away from reform and engagement with the outside world. But instead, China renewed its commitment to developing a market economy while retaining features of the socialist state and the leadership of the Chinese Communist Party.

Primary Sources

DOCUMENT 13.1: Excerpts from The Common Program of the Chinese People's Political Consultative Conference, September 1949

DOCUMENT 13.2: Excerpt from Lu Dingyi's speech "Let Flowers of Many Kinds Blossom, Diverse Schools of Thought Contend!" May 26, 1956

DOCUMENT 13.3: Excerpt from "The Masses Can Do Anything," speech by Mao Zedong, September 29, 1958

DOCUMENT 13.4: Excerpts describing urban living arrangements, from *Growing Up in the People's Republic: Conversations Between Two Daughters of China's Revolution* by Ye Weili and Ma Xiaodong, 2005

DOCUMENT 13.5: Excerpt from Mao Zedong's speech "On the Policies of Our Work in Tibet," April 6, 1952

DOCUMENT 13.6a–d: Propaganda posters, 1957–1959

CHAPTER 13

The Early Years of the People's Republic of China, 1949–1966

By David Green

Chapter Contents

The Founding of the PRC

Reforms

The Hundred Flowers Campaign

The Great Leap Forward

Foreign Relations

Organizing Idea

The Chinese Communist Party and Chairman Mao Zedong were driven by revolutionary zeal to transform China into a modern industrialized and proletarian nation. Controversial reforms and campaigns resulted in rapid and widespread change.

Key Questions

What steps were taken by the Chinese Communist Party and Mao Zedong to reorganize and reform China after decades of chaos?

What was the purpose and impact of the Hundred Flowers Campaign?

How did the Great Leap Forward affect China's industry, agriculture, and population?

What characterized the relationship between China and the Soviet Union in the 1950s?

Why did Mao begin to lose favor within the Communist Party?

Key Terms

agrarian	dictatorship	reform
bourgeois	imperialism	rural
cadre	inflation	socialist
collective	proletarian	struggle session
commune	propaganda	

Essay

On October 1, 1949, Mao Zedong (毛泽东) stood atop the Gate of Heavenly Peace (*Tiananmen*, 天安门), looking over what is now Tiananmen Square, and proclaimed the founding of the People's Republic of China (PRC) (中华人民共和国). The challenges facing any government at this point in China's history were staggering. Years of warfare, incessant flooding, extremely low industrial output, and rampant inflation had wreaked havoc on China's people. The Chinese Communist Party (CCP) (中国共产党), often with Chairman Mao leading the way, exacted radical and often autocratic policies that brought profound change to China's culture, economy, and political organization.

Shortly before proclaiming the PRC, Party leadership had adopted the "Common Program for China" (《共同纲领》), which defined and framed the Chinese Communist Party's goals. It outlined a "New Democratic" state that was anti-imperialism, anti-feudalism, and anti-capitalism, one that would empower China's workers and huge peasant population.

The People's Republic of China's communist government was distinct from that of the Soviet Union since it was defined as a "Democratic Dictatorship" (民主专制), based on four coexisting social classes: workers, peasants, and two levels of bourgeoisie. At lower levels of government, popular assemblies voted for higher-level representatives. Authority, as the Common Program made clear, lay in the hands of the central government: "All local people's government...shall obey the Central People's Government," giving locally-elected representatives virtually no power. Most governing power was in the hands of the Chinese Communist Party. CCP committees established at the local level sent delegates to committees on the county or provincial level, who, in turn, sent representatives higher still. The top three levels of the Party were the Central Committee (with forty-four members in 1949), the Politburo (with a dozen members) and the Standing Committee (of five[1]). Within the Standing Committee, Mao Zedong was the unchallenged ideologist.

Reforms

The CCP had issued a People's Currency (*renminbi*, RMB 人民币) in May 1949 and immediately upon taking control, worked tirelessly to stabilize prices, wages, and lines of communication. As a result, inflation, which had plagued Chiang Kai-shek's government (see Chapter 12), quickly abated.

Land reform continued as a top priority.[2] The 1950 Agrarian Reform Law (土地改革法) gave Party teams and peasant associations the authority to redistribute some 115 million acres of land from landlords to over 300 million peasants. This was a tense and sometimes violent process, as the repressed hostilities beneath the surface of village life broke out in struggle sessions in which landlords were denounced, beaten, and sometimes killed.[3] In order to rapidly increase agricultural production, the farms were soon grouped into cooperatives.

The urban economy presented major difficulties to the PRC leaders. Production had almost ground to a halt; drugs and prostitution were widespread. Between 1949 and 1952 the new authorities carried through a series of steps to bring factories, banks, and major retail operations under state management. Drug dealers were dealt with harshly, and prostitutes were rounded up and given vocational training to suit them for new employment.

The Marriage Law of 1950 gave men and women equal rights to enter into marriage, banned arranged marriages, and allowed either partner to sue for divorce. In the following two

---

[1] In 1949, the Standing Committee included Mao Zedong (chairman of the CCP), Liu Shaoqi, Zhou Enlai, Zhu De, and Chen Yu.

[2] See Chapter 12, Document 12.9 for information about earlier efforts.

[3] Jonathan Spence estimates that an estimated 1 million people were killed. Jonathan Spence, *The Search for Modern China* (New York: W. W. Norton, 1999), 492.

years many couples divorced, and the great majority of people quickly remarried, often to people with whom they had secretly been in love for a long time. In the countryside, the effects of the Marriage Law were reinforced by the granting of land to women as well as men.

In 1953, the Chinese government, using the Soviet Union as a model, put into effect its First Five-Year Plan (一五计划). An energized, fiercely patriotic populace threw itself into the work of rebuilding China, and industrial output soared between 1953 and 1957.

Continued Revolution and the Hundred Flowers Campaign

The first decade of life in the People's Republic of China was characterized by one campaign after another. Among them was the Hundred Flowers Campaign (百花齐放) in 1956. Party leadership was split over whether to include intellectuals, who weren't necessarily staunch communists, in efforts to transform the nation. But Mao was feeling upbeat about the initial successes, and he urged a "campaign of criticism and self-criticism" to keep the revolution alive. China's intellectuals had hesitated to speak their minds; now they did. Posters, magazine articles, campus demonstrations, rallies, and letters communicated great dissatisfaction. The critics wanted, among other things, an end to corruption among Communist Party cadres and an end to artistic censorship; they wished for a higher standard of living. Within weeks, Mao abruptly changed course. Joining Party leaders who had never backed the campaign, he branded critics as "Rightists" (右派) who opposed the Party. More than half of China's intellectuals—social scientists, economists, writers, scientists—lost their jobs; many were imprisoned or sent to the countryside for re-education. China effectively lost its educated urban professional elite—a loss that would, among other things, seriously affect future economic planning.

The Great Leap Forward

After traveling throughout China in 1956, Mao had come to the conclusion that "the masses can do anything." During the First Five-Year Plan, the nation's industrial output had risen 18.7 percent per year, agricultural production by 3.8 percent. Within fifteen years Mao wanted China to surpass industrial production in the United Kingdom, but much higher agricultural production was essential to pay for this planned industrial growth. In 1958, overruling more cautious long-term planners in the Party, Mao rallied the populace into another campaign: the "Great Leap Forward" (大跃进). Cadres were sent into rural China to exhort peasants to work ever harder. A bumper crop in the summer of 1958 inspired the central government to reorganize about 740,000 farm cooperatives— 99 percent of the rural population—into 26,000 centralized People's Communes. Each commune included about 5,000 families.[4] In order to maximize production and ensure efficiency, the communes provided schools, rudimentary healthcare, kitchens, and banks.

The central government also launched a drive to create some 600,000 backyard furnaces throughout the country in order to meet greatly expanded steel production targets. The government encouraged everyone, regardless of his or her job, to melt down all household metals, from woks to utensils.

Unfortunately, as a result of the euphoria and revolutionary passion, local rural cadres filed exaggerated forecasts for grain production. The pig iron produced by overworked peasants in backyard furnaces proved to be unusable. When the Huang He (黄河, Yellow River) flooded in 1959 and unrelenting drought afflicted other parts of China, Mao Zedong refused to revise his expectations. He dismissed a famous general who had warned of a growing crisis and cowed Party officials into following his mass revolutionary line. Local cadres, fearing punishment, continued to grossly exaggerate the amount of grain being produced

---

[4] Spence, *The Search for Modern China*, 549.

in the countryside. As a result, too much grain was removed from the countryside, leaving farming families with little. Rather than respond to concerns over shortfalls, Mao insisted provincial leaders meet the established goals.

By 1961, as a result of government policies, floods, drought, and insect infestations, conditions in the countryside had become catastrophic and the government began to import far more grain than it exported.[5] Though the numbers are difficult to certify, demographers and historians estimate that approximately 20 million people, about half of them children, died of starvation between 1959 and 1962.[6] The period is still mutely called the "Three Hard Years."

Foreign Relations Through 1960

The CCP and Mao wanted the world to see that China was a nation worthy of respect. They viewed the humiliations of past wars, foreign incursions, and civil conflict as relics of the past, and they were ready to assert new leadership throughout Asia and among the developing countries of the world. The Soviet Union was a significant source of empowerment for Mao, and his first trip abroad to Moscow in 1949 resulted in a multifaceted alliance. Although the relationship was characterized by mutual distrust, Chinese leaders saw the alliance as critical to their economic plans. Utilizing over $300 million in Soviet loans and thousands of Soviet experts on technology, military, and infrastructure, the CCP oversaw construction of new roads, railways, and radio networks that reached all corners of an evolving China.

Party leadership saw China's territorial integrity and the protection of its spheres of influence as high priorities. The actual territory of the PRC after 1949 was not significantly different than what the Guomindang (国民党) government had claimed for itself in the 1930s.[7] While the island of Taiwan (台湾) was a point of contention, U.S. naval protection of Taiwan throughout the Korean War (朝鲜战争) in the early 1950s prevented mainland China from claiming it.

The People's Republic of China sent one million "volunteers" to fight United Nations forces in North Korea when UN troops under General Douglas MacArthur's command pushed north of the 38th parallel. The addition of Chinese forces to the conflict reversed the trajectory of the war and ultimately cost China between 700,000 and 900,000 casualties.[8]

Beginning in 1950, the CCP reasserted its control over Tibet (西藏), further demonstrating that the Party was not afraid to use its military power. The staggering losses in Korea, however, led Chinese military leaders to conclude that they needed to modernize the PLA (People's Liberation Army, 人民解放军).

In late 1958, even before the worst of the famine caused by the Great Leap Forward had devastated rural China, members of Mao's own party had lost confidence in his leadership. The most notable, Liu Shaoqi (刘少奇), was among the Party leaders who pushed for Party discipline, economic retrenchment, and a greater emphasis on technology. When Mao accepted some responsibility for the disasters and "retired" from his position, Liu Shaoqi became chairman of the PRC and together with Secretary General Deng Xiaoping (邓小平) took charge of China's economic recovery. However, it was quite clear that Mao, with his remarkable ability to mobilize the

---

[5] Denis Crispin Twitchett and John King Fairbank, eds., *The Cambridge History of China*, vol. 14 (New York: Cambridge University Press, 1978) 381.

[6] Spence, *The Search for Modern China*, 553; Patricia Ebrey, *The Cambridge Illustrated History of China* (Cambridge, UK: Cambridge University Press, 1996) 312.

[7] The Guomindang was also known as the Nationalist Party and in the past was spelled Kuomintang (KMT).

[8] Close to 3 million Koreans died in the war, as well as more than 35,000 UN troops, 33,629 of whom were from the United States.

country's long-suffering and angry populace, continued to have strong influence. Few dared speak out against him, as increasingly Mao positioned it so that speaking out against him was the same as speaking out against the Party itself.

Primary Sources

DOCUMENT 13.1: Excerpts from the Common Program of the Chinese People's Political Consultative Conference, September 1949

Article 1. The People's Republic of China is a New Democratic or a People's Democratic state. It carries out the people's democratic dictatorship led by the working class, based on the alliance of workers and peasants, and uniting all democratic classes and all nationalities in China. It opposes imperialism, feudalism and bureaucratic capitalism and strives for independence, democracy, peace, unity, prosperity and strength of China....

Article 5. The people of the People's Republic of China shall have freedom of thought, speech, publication, assembly, association, correspondence, person, domicile, change of domicile, religious belief and the freedom of holding processions and demonstrations....

Article 7. The People's Republic of China shall suppress all counter-revolutionary activities, severely punish all Guomindang counter-revolutionary war criminals and other leading incorrigible counter-revolutionary elements who collaborate with imperialism, commit treason against the fatherland and oppose the cause of people's democracy. Feudal landlords, bureaucratic capitalists and reactionary elements in general, after they have been disarmed and have had their special powers abolished, shall, in addition, be deprived of their political rights in accordance with law for a necessary period. But, at the same time, they shall be given some means of livelihood and shall be compelled to reform themselves through labor so as to become new men. If they continue their counter-revolutionary activities, they will be severely punished....

SOURCE: *The Important Documents of the First Plenary Session of the Chinese People's Political Consultative Conference* (Beijing: Foreign Languages Press, 1949).

 The full text of **Document 13.1** is available on the CD-ROM.

DOCUMENT 13.2: Excerpt from Lu Dingyi's speech "Let Flowers of Many Kinds Blossom, Diverse Schools of Thought Contend!" May 26, 1956

To artists and writers, we say, "Let flowers of many kinds blossom." To scientists we say, "Let diverse schools of thought contend." This is the policy of the Chinese Communist Party. It was announced by Chairman Mao Zedong at the Supreme State Conference....

If we want our country to be prosperous and strong, we must, besides consolidating the people's state power, developing our economy and education and strengthening our national defence, have a flourishing art, literature and science. That is essential. If we want art, literature and science to flourish, we must apply a policy of letting flowers of many kinds blossom, letting diverse schools of thought contend....

"Letting flowers of many kinds blossom, diverse schools of thought contend" means that we stand for freedom of independent thinking, of debate, of creative work; freedom to criticize and freedom to express, maintain and reserve one's opinions on questions of art, literature or scientific research.

SOURCE: Lu Ting-yi, "Let Flowers of Many Kinds Blossom, Diverse Schools of Thought Contend!" (Beijing: Foreign Languages Press, 1957) 3–35.

 The full text of **Document 13.2** is available on the CD-ROM.

DOCUMENT 13.3: Excerpt from "The Masses Can Do Anything," speech by Mao Zedong, September 29, 1958

During this trip, I have witnessed the tremendous energy of the masses. On this foundation it is possible to accomplish any task whatsoever. We must first complete the tasks on the iron and steel fronts. In these sectors, the masses have already been mobilized. Nevertheless, in the country as a whole, there are a few places, a few enterprises, where the work of mobilizing the masses has still not been properly carried out, where mass meetings have not been held and where the tasks, the reasons for them, and the methods have still not been made perfectly clear to the masses or discussed by the masses. There are still a few comrades who are unwilling to undertake a large-scale mass movement in the industrial sphere. They call the mass movement on the industrial front "irregular" and disparage it as "a rural style of work" and "a guerrilla habit." This is obviously incorrect.

However, while devoting ourselves to iron and steel production on a large scale, we must not sacrifice agriculture... The 1959 task in agriculture is to achieve a leap forward even greater than that of 1958. Consequently, we must organize the industrial and agricultural labour force effectively and extend the system of people's communes throughout the whole country....

SOURCE: Mao Zedong, "The Masses Can Do Anything," 29 Sept. 1958, transcribed by the Maoist Documentation Project.

DOCUMENT 13.4: Excerpts describing urban living arrangements from *Growing Up in the People's Republic: Conversations Between Two Daughters of China's Revolution*, by Ye Weili and Ma Xiaodong, 2005

YE WEILI: I grew up in Xinhua compound in downtown Beijing.[9] The entire compound occupied more than 70 *mu* of land (about 12 acres). It was divided into work and residential areas.... I don't know how the adults felt about the closeness of the living arrangement. With hindsight I realize they might not have liked it that much, especially when there was a political campaign going on. After a criticism meeting in the office, they would have wanted to avoid their colleagues in the living quarter and privacy would have been desirable. But for us kids who had little sense of the adult world, this living arrangement was great....

Without leaving the compound, one could get almost every type of service. The service was not free but it was cheaper than what would have been charged outside. Besides, you also didn't have to wait in long lines. My parents deposited their money at the compound bank and mailed their letters in the compound post office. When I didn't feel well, I would go to the compound clinic. My parents joined a medical program for children so I didn't need to bring any cash with me. I knew every doctor and nurse there and would try to avoid the ones with a poor reputation.

My favorite places were the library and the auditorium. I spent a lot of time in the library, doing homework in the reading room and browsing the many journals and newspapers on the shelves....

SOURCE: Ye Weili and Ma Xiaodong, *Growing Up in The People's Republic: Conversations Between Two Daughters of China's Revolution* (New York: Palgrave Macmillan, 2005) 33–37.

 The full text of **Document 13.4** is available on the CD-ROM.

DOCUMENT 13.5: Excerpt from Mao Zedong's speech "On the Policies of Our Work in Tibet," April 6, 1952

We must do our best and take proper steps to win over the Dalai [Lama] and the majority of his top echelon and to isolate the handful of bad elements in order to achieve a gradual, bloodless transformation of the Tibetan economic and political system over a number of years; on the other hand, we must be prepared for the eventuality of the bad elements leading the Tibetan troops in rebellion and attacking us, so that in this contingency our army could still carry on and hold out in Tibet. It all depends on strict budgeting and production for the army's own needs. Only with this fundamental policy as the cornerstone of our work can we achieve our aim....

SOURCE: Mao Zedong, "On the Policies of our Work in Tibet," 6 April 1952. Transcribed by the Maoist Documentation Project.

 The full text of **Document 13.5** is available on the CD-ROM.

---

[9] Xinhua is the Chinese government's official news service; everyone who worked for the news service lived and worked together in the *dayuan* (compound).

DOCUMENT 13.6a–d: Propaganda posters, 1957–1959

Propaganda posters played a significant role in communicating the goals of the CCP and of Mao himself. They captured the essence of CCP ideology and permeated all levels of Chinese society. The text at the bottom of this 1959 poster reads, "The commune is like a gigantic dragon; production is visibly awe-inspiring." (*Collection Stephan R. Landsberger at the International Institute for Social History, Amsterdam, the Netherlands. http://www.iisg.nl/~landsberger*)

 Additional posters are on the CD-ROM.

Activities

ACTIVITY 1. Examining the Chinese Communist Party's founding principles

Working in small groups, read the preamble and articles of the Common Program (13.1) carefully. Each group will then discuss and vote on the three most poignant articles and justify their choices. Regroup as a class to discuss findings and address the following questions:

1. What is the overall tone of the document, and what are some striking examples of that tone based on the three articles your group chose?
2. What strikes you about the language used in the preamble?
3. Compare this preamble to the one in the Constitution of the United States of America. Where are the similarities and differences?
4. Compare the complete text of the Common Program to the U.S. Constitution and the Bill of Rights.
5. How does the document hold up as a provisional constitution for the early PRC? Does it feel like a constitution to you? Why or why not?
6. What aspects of this document will clearly serve the people of the PRC? To what extent might it be injurious?
7. What, if anything, would you add or take away? Why?

ACTIVITY 2: Analyzing the Hundred Flowers Campaign

Read the excerpt from Lu Dingyi's speech (13.2) and consider the following questions:

1. What is the tone of the speech?
2. Who is delivering the speech and what is his position?
3. What are the main themes of the speech?

Assume the identity of an artist, poet, or scientist who has just heard this speech. Write a letter to a relative living abroad in which you discuss your response to it. Be sure to compare your understanding of the speech to your observations of what is going on around you in 1956 China.

Review the explanation in the introductory essay of what happened after the campaign.

1. Why do you think the Party and Mao reacted in this way to the criticism?
2. How might removing half of the educated professionals affect society?
3. What does this suggest about Mao's attitude toward highly educated individuals? Do you know of other politicians who have shared Mao's attitude?

ACTIVITY 3: Responding to a speech by Mao Zedong

Read the excerpt of Mao's speech "The Masses Can Do Anything" (13.3), carefully evaluating the language and imagining the audience response. Writing from the perspective of an audience member living in Beijing, create a journal entry in which you react to the speech. Take into consideration the context of the time period, and be sure to make specific reference to detailed aspects of the speech. Now, assume the persona of a formerly wealthy Chinese land owner in western China. Write another journal entry that assumes that point of view. Before writing, assess the ways in which the two journal writers will differ and perhaps be alike in their perspectives.

ACTIVITY 4: Comparing perspectives on growing up in 1950s and 1960s China

Imagine what it would be like to be a child or student as China profoundly transformed. What might be the experiences of youth in China during the 1950s and early 1960s? Read the description of growing up in Beijing by Ye Weili and Ma Xiaodong (13.4) and consider the following questions:

1. How were the two girls' experiences similar and different?

2. What aspects of China's reforms seemed to affect the girls the most?

3. What was most striking about the girls' experiences? Why?

4. Did the girls' experience match any of your guesses about what children and teens would experience in China during the 1950s and early 60s?

5. Do you relate to any of the experiences described in this reading?

6. What challenges do youth face growing up now? Are there any parallels to the two girls' narratives?

ACTIVITY 5: Analyzing Mao Zedong's speech on Tibet

The topic of Tibet incites controversy both within and outside of China. Citing historical precedence, Mao advocated strongly for incorporating Tibet into the borders of the PRC, a goal that was eventually realized.

After reading the overview of Tibet's history (in Additional Resources on the CD-ROM), read the excerpt from Mao's speech "On the Policies for Our Work in Tibet" (13.5) and take brief notes on the following issues:

1. What are the main components of the speech?

2. What is Mao's general attitude toward Tibet?

3. What are Mao's concerns about Xinjiang and Tibet?

4. How does the topic of diversity fit into your understanding of this speech?

5. Why might Mao be singling out Tibet as the focus of this speech?

Working with a partner, look at an outline map of China and place both Tibet and Xinjiang. Together, address the following:

1. Go back to the speech and try to identify why Mao might hold such specific attitudes about Tibet.

2. What is geographically interesting and challenging about Tibet's location? Where might this appear in the speech?

3. Answer the same questions for Xinjiang.

4. Given their locations, how would China benefit from exerting influence in Tibet and Xinjiang?

5. What are the disadvantages of exerting such influence?

(An outline map as well as further information on Xinjiang are available in Additional Resources on the CD-ROM. Chapter 20 also looks at issues related to Xinjiang and Tibet.)

ACTIVITY 6: Examining posters as propaganda tools

Part 1: Methods of propaganda

Before examining the posters, as a class define the word "propaganda." Discuss different avenues of propaganda and offer examples from your daily life. Then consider ways in which a populace could be mobilized in a time when there was no Internet, e-mail, widespread television or radio, and literacy rates were low.

1. What would you expect a propaganda poster to look like and why?

2. What would be the key components of an effective propaganda poster?

Examine "Chairman Mao provides us with a happy life" (13.6a)

1. What is most striking to you and why?

2. List ten details and explain their significance.

3. What surprised you the most about this poster? Why?

4. Does this poster remind you of any other visual materials you've seen? What are they? How do they compare?

Part 2: Analyzing propaganda posters from the 1950s

Work in small groups with one poster (13.6b, c, or d). Examine it carefully and discuss the following:

1. What do you see?

2. What is the visual message communicated by this poster?

3. Is this an effective propaganda poster? Why might it successfully mobilize people, or not?

4. What aspect of the CCP's and/or Mao's ideology is being communicated? How do you know?

Present the poster to the rest of the class and share the group's observations.

Creative extension:

Create your own propaganda poster based on an issue currently in the news. The poster must demonstrate an understanding of the Chinese style and genre of the 1950s and 1960s. (For additional examples of propaganda posters, check the websites listed in Suggested Resources.)

ACTIVITY 8: Analytical writing

Part 1: China's place in the world

Research the ways in which countries such as the United States, the Soviet Union, England, France, India, or others reacted to the immense changes in China during the 1950s and 1960s. How did they analyze and react to the creation of the PRC, the Hundred Flowers Campaign, the Great Leap Forward, and Mao Zedong's leadership? Write an essay that captures some of the foreign attitudes toward a China undergoing enormous change.

Part 2: Changes for women

Read the PRC's Marriage Law of 1950 (available online at http://www.isop.ucla.edu/eas/restricted/marriage.htm) and conduct research in books and online to learn about women's traditional roles and rights prior to Liberation. (See also Chapter 1, Document 1.2.) Write an essay that highlights the changes for women brought about by this law. Alternatively, capture the changes in a piece of visual art.

Suggested Resources

Books

Cheek, Timothy. *Mao Zedong and China's Revolutions: A Brief History with Documents*. Boston: Bedford/St. Martin's, 2002.
An excellent collection of essays on Mao and the Chairman's own writing or speeches.

Landsberger, Stefan. *Chinese Propaganda Posters: From Revolution to Modernization.* Amsterdam: The Pepin Press, 1998.
Text and images detail the role of posters in the PRC.

Spence, Jonathan D. *Mao Zedong*. New York: Viking, 1999.
A good short biography by one of the finest China scholars writing today.

Websites

On Mao Zedong

http://www.time.com/time/time100/leaders/profile/mao.html An essay by Jonathan Spence.

http://www.oxfordreference.com/pages/samplep-02 A brief biography by Maurice Meisner.

http://www.marx2mao.com/Mao/Index.html Translations of *Selected Works of Mao Zedong*, volumes 1–5.

http://news.bbc.co.uk/hi/english/static/special_report/1999/09/99/china_50/iron.htm "China's Communist Revolution, a Glossary" includes short definitions of multiple terms related to the early decades of the PRC.

http://www.iisg.nl/~landsberger/glf.html An excellent site by Stefan R. Landsberger, professor of Contemporary Chinese Culture at the University of Amsterdam. Includes posters from the full Mao era and beyond, with translations of slogans, a narrative, and information about the artists.

http://depts.washington.edu/chinaciv/graph/9prcmain.htm More information on posters in the Mao era.

http://www.isop.ucla.edu/eas/restricted/marriage.htm The PRC's 1950 Marriage Law.

Films

All Under Heaven (58 mins; 1986) *Part of the* One Village in China *series, this documentary by Carma Hinton and Richard Gordon captures the various ways in which the CCP has tackled the challenge of land reform and gives insight into rural traditions.*

The Blue Kite (138 mins; 1993) *In Chinese (Mandarin) with subtitles. The film captures how the turbulent political times affected the lives of everyday people. The Chinese Ministry of Broadcast, Film and Radio prohibited the film from being shown in China and barred director Tian Zhuangzhuang from making any further films in China. The Blue Kite won the "Best Film" award at the Tokyo Film Festival.*

To Live (133 mins; 1994) *In Chinese (Mandarin) with subtitles. The film spans four turbulent decades of China's 20th century. The film tells the story of Fugui and Jiazhen and their two children as they struggle to survive the constantly changing political climate. Winner of the Grand Jury Prize and Best Actor awards at the Cannes Film Festival. Directed by Zhang Yimou. It is also very interesting to note what is* not *told about the Great Leap Forward and the Cultural Revolution.*

■ A CLOSER LOOK

Liu Shaoqi: Mao's Second in Command

Referred to by some as "the other chairman," Liu Shaoqi (1898–1969) left an indelible mark on China's development in the mid-twentieth century. On October 1, 1959, the tenth anniversary of the People's Republic, the newly appointed chairman reflected on the progress of his country: "The first decade has been dedicated to reform. The second should be devoted to reconstruction." Tragically, the opposite occurred.

Liu Shaoqi was born and raised in Yinshan, Hunan Province, not far from Shaoshan, the childhood home of Mao Zedong. Though such beginnings were coincidental, Liu Shaoqi's life paralleled Mao's in many respects. As the theoretician for the CCP, Liu was considered Mao's heir apparent, and he served as chairman of the People's Republic from 1959 to 1966. After briefly attending college in Moscow in the early 1920s, Liu Shaoqi organized several successful labor movements back in his homeland, particularly among coal miners. After being elected to the Central Committee of the CCP in 1927 and the Politburo in 1934, Liu became head of the North and Central China bureaus of the Central Committee between 1936 and 1942. In this capacity, Liu Shaoqi faced the daunting challenge of promoting communist ideology in the face of Guomindang efforts to eliminate the Communist Party. His successes as an organizational leader and theorist during this time consolidated his position as a top leader of the CCP.

Liu's seminal work *How to Be a Good Communist* became a central text for the Party. Its unique combination of Confucian and Marxist ideals were appealing to readers of many socio-economic classes, and in 1949, Liu became second vice-chairman of the government and general secretary of the CCP.

The split between Mao and Liu came into the open during the Great Leap Forward and grew increasingly wide as news of the appalling famine began to trickle in from the countryside. Liu and Deng Xiaoping took over government and Party management, but Mao continued to insist that any perceived Party weakness should be open to the "masses" for discussion and debate. As Mao's Cultural Revolution took form and evolved (see Chapter 14), re-establishing Mao as the central figure in Chinese politics and daily life, Liu Shaoqi became the target of an immense campaign to vilify him. In 1967, he and his wife were put under house arrest. Liu died two years later after succumbing to repeated interrogations, physical abuse, and medical neglect.

■ *Find out more about Liu Shaoqi and/or read excerpts from his book* How to Be a Good Communist *(online at http://www.marxists.org/ reference/archive/liu-shaoqi/1939/how-to-be/ index.htm). Discuss or write about how Liu's and Mao's visions for China differed.*

■ **A CLOSER LOOK**

The Dalai Lama Living in Exile

The Dalai Lama is the central figure in both Tibetan Buddhism and Tibetan government. Tibetan Buddhism views the position of the Dalai Lama as a lineage of reborn leaders extending back centuries. The current Dalai Lama, Tenzin Gyatso (born in 1935), is the fourteenth individual to hold the position. He was installed as Tibet's head of state in 1950, one year after Mao Zedong announced the creation of the PRC and sent Chinese armed forces into Tibet. The Dalai Lama met with Mao Zedong in 1954 when he attended a meeting of the National People's Congress in Beijing. However, tensions between the Chinese government, which considered Tibet a part of China, and Tibetans, who wanted independence, kept increasing, until in 1959 the Tibetans staged a major uprising. The Chinese military responded forcefully. Fearing for his life and the future of the Tibetan government, the fourteenth Dalai Lama left his summer residence secretly and was escorted by loyal guards across the Himalayas to safety in India, where he has lived ever since.

As the leader of the Tibetan government in exile, he has made several appeals for autonomy, acknowledging the highly unlikely chances for independence from China. The Dalai Lama's emphasis on ethics, non-violent conflict resolution, spirituality, and simple living has won him widespread support throughout the world and beyond the Tibetan cause. He has traveled to forty-six countries, speaking in front of large audiences to discuss topics as diverse as Tibetan Buddhism, environmental responsibility, and morality. In 1989, as a result of his unfaltering global efforts, the Dalai Lama was awarded the Nobel Peace Prize.

Difficult questions simmer below the surface: what will happen when the fourteenth Dalai Lama passes away? Some Chinese politicians insist that China's government will select the next Dalai Lama. However, most Tibetans, including the present Dalai Lama himself, have suggested that the next reincarnation will be identified outside of Tibet. In the meantime, the Dalai Lama remains a notable figure for many groups of people for many different reasons.

■ *Search the Internet for an account of a recent appearance by the Dalai Lama. What was at the heart of his speech? Why does he continue to draw such large audiences?*

For further information about Tibet's history, see Additional Resources on the CD-ROM. Tibet is also discussed in Chapter 20.

CHAPTER 14

The Cultural Revolution, 1966–1976

By David Green

Chapter Contents

Tensions in the Early 1960s
The Great Proletarian Cultural Revolution
Sent-Down Youth
The Death of Mao Zedong

Organizing Idea:

The Cultural Revolution grew out of disagreements among the Chinese Communist Party's leaders over how to energize the populace and to continue to develop the nation's economy. The destruction unleashed by this movement affected every element of life in China.

Key Questions

What were some of the factors that led to the "Great Proletarian Cultural Revolution"?

How did the role of the Red Guards change over the course of the Cultural Revolution?

What are some different ways in which Chinese youth was affected by the Cultural Revolution?

Other than Mao Zedong, who were the significant political figures during the Cultural Revolution and why were they important?

What are some views of the Cultural Revolution in retrospect?

Key Terms

bourgeoisie	nationalism	re-education camp
cadre	purge	sent-down youth (*zhiqing*)
Gang of Four	radical	struggle meetings
Little Red Book	reactionary	"victim literature"
Mandate of Heaven	Red Guard	

Essay

At the height of the Mao cult in the late 1960s, prior to their communal meals, villagers would recite "We respectfully wish a long life to the reddest sun in our hearts, the great leader Chairman Mao…Having been liberated by the land reform we will never forget the Communist Party, and in revolution we will forever follow Chairman Mao!"[1] It was a symbol of how under the stress of the Cultural Revolution, loyalty to China, the Party, and Mao Zedong (毛泽东) had fused into one.

Tensions in the Early 1960s

Many leading Party members felt that the Great Leap Forward (大跃进) of 1958 was a complete disaster, and Mao himself even admitted to some general errors (see Chapter 13). Communist veterans such as Liu Shaoqi (刘少奇)[2] tried to diminish the personality cult increasingly surrounding Mao, but Mao still had powerful followers. Opposing Liu Shaoqi's efforts was Lin Biao (林彪), whom Mao had appointed minister of defense and head of the People's Liberation Army (PLA) (人民解放军). In 1963, Lin Biao ordered everyone in the armed forces to read the newly printed *Little Red Book* (红宝书), filled with "Mao Zedong Thought" (毛泽东思想). The booklet that could fit into the palm of one's hand would influence a generation of young and impressionable people.

The Great Proletarian Cultural Revolution Begins

There are many differing explanations as to why the Cultural Revolution occurred and how to judge its impact. One thing appears clear: a serious breakdown had occurred among the top leaders over how the transformation of China should continue. Liu Shaoqi and Deng Xiaoping (邓小平), who had taken charge of economic recovery after the Great Leap Forward, favored a pragmatic conventional approach. To spur production, they suggested higher salaries and bonuses, which to the radical left sounded like capitalist incentives. Liu and Deng wanted educated experts to lead the way. Mao Zedong, on the other hand, believed economic planning should stay in the hands of those with strong communist convictions. Frustrated by what he saw as slow economic gains, he believed the Party needed to revitalize nationalism and communist ideology. In *The Rise of Modern China*, Immanuel Hsü writes, "Mao wanted to re-establish the supremacy of his authority, his line of revolution, his work-style, to revitalize the youth, politicize the masses and combat old customs, old habits, old culture, and old thinking—and to do so with a single, immediate expurgation."[3]

The trigger for the Cultural Revolution (文化大革命) appears to have been an allegorical play that was a thinly veiled critique of the government. Accusing the play of having "traditionalist" content, Mao's estranged wife, Jiang Qing (江青), attacked it as an "anti-socialist poisonous weed." Jiang Qing and other extreme leftists wanted to purify art by having it serve political purposes only.

During the early part of 1966, the disputing sides maneuvered to shore up their positions. On May 25th, a radical philosophy professor at Beijing University wrote a "big-character poster" (*da zi bao*, 大字报) accusing other professors and university administrators of being anti-Party. Mao backed the poster and broadcast its message throughout China. Liu Shaoqi attempted to quell the resulting unrest at the university, but his actions were perceived as

---

[1] Qtd. in Anita Chan, Richard Madsen and Jonathan Unger, *Chen Village: The Recent History of a Peasant Community in Mao's China* (Berkeley: University of California Press, 1984) 170.

[2] Liu Shaoqi had temporarily taken Mao's place as chairman of the CCP.

[3] Immanuel Hsü, *The Rise of Modern China*, 4th ed. (New York: Oxford University Press, 1990) 697.

another strike against already embittered students and faculty. Revolutionary spirit spread from universities to secondary schools, where groups of students, calling themselves "Red Guards" (红卫兵), donned armbands and pledged allegiance to Mao Zedong and this new revolution. Schools shut down, and Mao further encouraged this youthful revolutionary zeal by making train travel anywhere in China free for students.

The Revolution Spreads and the Role of the Red Guard

In August 1966, the Central Committee of the Chinese Communist Party put forth the "Decision Concerning the Great Proletarian Cultural Revolution" or "The Sixteen Points." It called for "all forces to strike at the handful of ultra-reactionary bourgeois Rightists and counter-revolutionary revisionists, and expose and criticize to the full these crimes against the Party, against socialism, and against Mao Zedong's thought."[4] This spawned a massive outbreak of violence and destruction. "Revolutionaries," bent on isolating and eliminating those who were not in step with Mao's extreme policies, attacked thousands of individuals.

The Cult of Personality

Together with Mao's wife, Jiang Qing, Minister of Defense Lin Biao promoted Mao Zedong as an infallible genius, "our great teacher, great leader, great supreme commander, and great helmsman."[5] All of this was done with Mao's blessing. As August wore on, Mao Zedong and Lin Biao made ten appearances at the Gate of Heavenly Peace (天安门) to address vast throngs of Red Guards, who made the pilgrimage to Tiananmen Square waving Mao's *Little Red Book* of quotations in adulation of their leader.

On a more planned level, for Mao Zedong, Jiang Qing, and Lin Biao, the revolution centered on consolidating and reclaiming power in the Party for Mao and his supporters. They initiated purges, which escalated to the highest level with the removal and humiliation of Liu Shaoqi and Deng Xiaoping. Hundreds of cadres were disgraced publicly, imprisoned, beaten, and often exiled to the countryside.

Mao called on Red Guards to undo China's "Four Olds" (old customs, old habits, old culture, and old thinking). Teens and young adults interpreted this as a blank check to attack anything deemed Western, archaic, or anti-revolutionary. Uncontrolled violence erupted as students attacked their teachers, school administrators, parents, and known intellectuals. A stunning destruction of Chinese heritage erupted. In the name of revolution, Red Guards destroyed temples, art, innumerable historical manuscripts, archaeological sites, libraries, sculptures, and artifacts, and anything remotely "Western." In addition, cultural minorities living in China such as Tibetans, Koreans, and Uyghurs were harassed, attacked, and often killed.

Factions of the Red Guard soon began to compete with one another to demonstrate loyalty to Mao, using radical behavior as the measure of that loyalty. Youthful Red Guards brought their purges to all corners of the country, and extremism reached its peak in 1967 when a radical group attempted to attack the People's Liberation Army (PLA). Several major confrontations between the Red Guard radicals and the PLA at Wuhan (武汉) in the summer of 1967 resulted in numerous casualties. One faction of the Red Guard even managed to take over the Ministry of Foreign Affairs, an attack on the upper echelons of China's government that threatened the functions of China's foreign ministry. Even radical leaders on the far left agreed that something had to be done to check the Red Guard and control the chaos. However, it took over a year for order to be restored.

---

[4] Qtd. in Michael Schoenhals, ed., *China's Cultural Revolution, 1966–1969: Not a Dinner Party*, (Armonk, NY: M. E. Sharpe, 1996) 37.

[5] Qtd. in Jonathan D. Spence, *The Search for Modern China* 575.

New Purges

Mao launched the "Campaign to Purify Class Ranks" to isolate the "bad elements" in China's population. He created investigation teams to locate and re-educate these "bad elements," which included those perceived to be intellectuals, capitalists, and Western sympathizers. Ironically, Mao's list now included and affected many members of the Red Guard. As Mao isolated and purged top cadres, their children were labeled as having a "bad background" or coming from "bad elements." In many cases, this process denied these children and young adults access to basic services and education. "Re-education camps," where authorities combined hard labor with intense study of Mao's writings and thoughts, sprang up across rural China. Living conditions were deplorable. From 1967 to 1969, up to two million people, including prominent members of the Party—dedicated Communists—were investigated, sent to be re-educated, and subjected to all manner of physical and mental torture. Unknown numbers of people were killed. Others, humiliated beyond endurance, committed suicide. Many of those who survived grew exhausted and embittered by their ordeals.

Lin Biao's Demise

In 1969, Mao designated Lin Biao as his successor, but Lin soon began to fall out of favor. By 1970, Mao viewed Lin Biao as an obstruction to Party power and a potential threat to his own power. As a result, Mao began to undermine him by blocking his ascension to higher Party positions. In September 1971, Lin Biao fled China with his family, apparently headed for the Soviet Union. His plane crashed in Mongolia under suspicious circumstances, killing all aboard, and when the news was made public (a year later), the government claimed that Lin had hatched a plot against Mao that failed. Lin Biao's death had a profound impact on the Cultural Revolution. As Jonathan Spence describes it, "the credulity of the Chinese people had been stretched beyond all possible boundaries as leader after leader had first been praised to the skies and then vilified."[6]

The Gang of Four, Zhou Enlai, and Deng Xiaoping

Mao, deeply shaken by what he believed were Lin Biao's plots against him, reenlisted separately the help of Deng Xiaoping and Premier Zhou Enlai (周恩来). However, Mao's wife Jiang Qing and her closest supporters viewed Deng Xiaoping and especially Zhou Enlai as threats, and they attempted to turn the people against Zhou. The move failed. By the mid 1970s, the populace was exhausted, utterly unable to support another set of purges and protests.

After four years of struggling with cancer, Zhou Enlai died on January 8, 1976. People across China mourned the leader who was seen by many as one of the most selfless and talented members of the CCP. (See A Closer Look at the end of Chapter 15.) On July 28, a massive earthquake, among the worst in China's historical record, shook Hebei Province (河北). This devastating event is officially reported to have killed almost a quarter of a million people and seriously injured another 160,000. It destroyed the city of Tangshan (唐山) and caused serious damage in Tianjin and Beijing. Many saw the disaster as a signal that Mao had lost the Mandate of Heaven (天命).[7]

Finally, Mao Zedong himself died on September 9, 1976, and with his passing, what little remained of the Cultural Revolution ground to a halt. Many people, even those whose lives were ravaged by Mao's policies,

---

[6] Spence, *The Search for Modern China*, 586.

[7] For millennia, Chinese tradition dictated that a leader/emperor had to have legitimate authority from the gods—the Mandate of Heaven—in order to rule the country. Huge natural disasters or civil disorder were seen as signs that a ruler had lost this mandate.

could hardly believe that their leader could have died. His cult of personality, his thoughts, and even his image had permeated every facet of Chinese society. But all this adulation no longer protected his associates. Within a month, his wife and her three closest colleagues—the "Gang of Four" (四人帮) —were arrested by military forces and accused of one crime after another. It was now their turn to languish in jail while their victims, some of whom had been confined for ten years or more, were at long last released.

Reflections on the Cultural Revolution

Different people experienced the Great Proletarian Cultural Revolution in different ways. Ye Weili, who experienced the revolution as a teenager, writes in her introduction to *Growing Up in The People's Republic* that "the texture of everyday life and the multiple shades of grey" are utterly lost in the sea of "victim literature" that permeates our understanding of the Cultural Revolution. She further cautions: "Traumatic as the Cultural Revolution was for us, our history did not begin or end with it. Nor did our life experiences always revolve around politics."[8] While the disastrous elements of this period are undeniable, also important are the family dynamics, conversations, traditions, and resilience that saw the majority of China's population through its crises.

On October 1, 1979, the thirtieth anniversary of the founding of the PRC, Marshal Ye Jianying stated, "Leaders are not gods. It is impossible for them to be free from mistakes or shortcomings. They should definitely not be deified." A year later, he said, "We can occasionally slap our own faces, but we cannot, nor do we have time to, start from scratch.... If we want to trace the responsibility to the end, we will find that it lies not with Mao alone. It lies in all of us."[9]

Primary Sources

DOCUMENT 14.1: Excerpts from "One Hundred Items for Destroying the Old and Establishing the New," created by Red Guards at the #26 Middle School, Beijing, August 1966

Students at Beijing No. 26 Middle School created a list of 100 instructions for how the Great Proletarian Cultural Revolution should be carried out. They also renamed their school the Maoism School.

1. Under the charge of residential committees, every street must set up a quotation plaque; every household must have on its walls a picture of the Chairman plus quotations by Chairman Mao....

5. With a copy of the *Quotations from Chairman Mao* in the hands of everyone, each must carry it with him, constantly study it, and do everything in accord with it....

[8] Ye Weili and Ma Xiaodong, *Growing Up in The People's Republic of China: Conversations Between Two Daughters of China's Revolution* (New York: Palgrave Macmillan, 2005) 5.

[9] Qtd. in Hsü 782.

11. Every school and every unit must set up highest directive propaganda teams so that everyone can hear at any time the repeated instructions of the Chairman....

24. You landowners who still rode on the people's heads and drank the people's blood after the Liberation, we order you bastards to hurry up and turn over all your private holdings to the state. In a socialist state we absolutely cannot allow you vampires to exist.

25. In a proletarian society, private enterprise cannot be allowed to exist. We propose to take all firms using joint state and private management and change them to state management and change joint state and private management enterprises into state-owned enterprises....

41. Heads of families are not allowed to educate their children with bourgeois ideology. The feudal family-head system will be abolished. No more beating or scolding of children will be tolerated. If the child is not of one's own begetting, no mistreatment is allowed. Children will be consistently educated in Mao Zedong Thought....

SOURCE: Michael Schoenhals, ed., *China's Cultural Revolution, 1966–1976: Not A Dinner Party* (Armonk, NY: M.E. Sharpe, 1996) 212–217.

 The full text of **Document 14.1** is available on the CD-ROM.

DOCUMENT 14.2: "The Red Guards Cut Your Mother's Hair," an excerpt from *Growing Up in the People's Republic: Conversations Between Two Daughters of China's Revolution* by Ye Weili and Ma Xiaodong, 2005

Ma Xiaodong's father spoke of his wife's experiences.

Hewen was forty-two in 1966. She was in the prime of her life, well educated, experienced at work and in good health. But then came the Cultural Revolution. Schools, especially secondary schools, were the first to be turned upside down. Hewen became a black gangster at her school.[10] She was confronted at numerous meetings, where she was spat at, hit by stones, had her body bent in the "jet airplane" position and was forced to don a heavy board over her neck and a dunce hat on her head. She tried her very best to endure all these abuses.

The worst finally came on August 24th when, at a meeting in the school, Hewen was severely beaten along with five other former leaders of the school. Two died on the spot. Hewen's life was spared, but her hair was shaved and wounds covered all her body. When she came back from school, all I could do was to clean the blood from her body. While dressing her wounds, I cried and asked myself why she had to suffer

---

[10] During the Cultural Revolution, the term "black gangster" was used to brand anyone accused of being anti-Party or anti-socialist. Top administrators in schools, industry, and government were the most likely targets. The label was a reference to criminals who worked in the underworld before the founding of the PRC.

like this. I was afraid that after this horrendous experience Hewen would not want to live anymore. We stayed up the whole night and I tried my best to comfort her and to discourage any thought of suicide....

SOURCE: Ye Weili and Ma Xiaodong, *Growing Up in the People's Republic: Conversations Between Two Daughters of China's Revolution* (New York: Palgrave Macmillan, 2005) 89.

 The full text of **Document 14.2** is available on the CD-ROM.

DOCUMENT 14.3: Excerpt from "On the Bridge to Mama's School," a poem by Chun Yu, 2005

Chun Yu was born in China in 1966, the year the Cultural Revolution began. In her book Little Green, *she tells her story of growing up during that period in poetic form.*

There were two political groups in Mama's school:
the "rebels" who wanted to
"down with" everything, and
the "emperor protectors" who wanted to
"down with" only some things.
Mama didn't belong to either of them,
which made her life difficult.

The head of the rebellion group
was a young sports teacher.
Born into a family of three generations of peasants,
he proclaimed his roots were the most revolutionary of all.
Mama told me that
after the Cultural Revolution began,
instead of teaching, this man held struggle meetings,
calling teachers onto the stage and
deciding their fate according to his wishes.
He also organized a propaganda team.
With red bands on their arms
they performed "loyalty dances" to Chairman Mao every day.
They threw one arm up to Mao's picture;
With the other arm they held Mao's *Little Red Book*
pressed against their chests.
I couldn't help thinking that
the head of the rebellion group looked like a puppet,
not a man.

Like many teachers in the school,
my mama avoided him as much as she could....

SOURCE: Chun Yu, *Little Green: Growing Up during the Chinese Cultural Revolution* (New York: Simon & Schuster, 2005) 33–34.

DOCUMENT 14.4: Excerpt from *Wild Swans: Three Daughters of China* by Jung Chang, 1991

The Rebels' denunciation meetings became more brutal, even though my father was still allowed to live at home. One day he came back with one of his eyes badly damaged. Another day I saw him standing on a slow-moving truck, being paraded through the streets. A huge placard hung from a thin wire that was eating into his neck, and his arms were twisted ferociously behind his back. He was struggling to keep his head up under the forceful pushing of some Rebels. What made me saddest of all was that he appeared indifferent to his physical pain. In his insanity, his mind seemed to be detached from his body....

We watched my father deteriorate mentally and physically with each passing day. My mother went to ask [an acquaintance] for help again. He promised to see what he could do. We waited, but nothing happened: his silence meant he must have failed to get [those in power] to allow my father to have treatment....

SOURCE: Jung Chang, *Wild Swans: Three Daughters of China* (New York: HarperCollins, 1993) 464, 468.

 The full text of **Document 14.4** is available on the CD-ROM.

DOCUMENT 14.5: Excerpts describing the personal experiences of Nathan Hu during the early stages of the Cultural Revolution, written in 2006–2007

Mao encouraged Red Guards to bring revolutionary zeal to different schools, factories, and governments at all ranks. We could go to any city through free transportation. Our boarding and food were all free. Mao's purpose was to paralyze all the party and government administrations and put power into those people who would follow his political ideology.

I left the middle school when classes were no longer being held, and I returned to my home at my father's university. Children like I, we followed the college students whom we called Big Red Guards. We helped them to print brochures, to write Big-character Posters. Students from the school were divided into two parts. One we called the revolutionary part. The other was called the conservative part. The revolutionaries followed Mao's teachings exactly. They wanted to act against the school leaders. The other side—the conservatives—they tried to protect school leaders. In almost any institution, universities and schools, people divided into these two factions. Sometimes even into three, four, five factions, but generally speaking the two. "Rebellion" was considered a very good word. We called the other group, "protect the emperor group." I was on the side of the revolutionaries, the radicals. I followed the older students....

SOURCE: Hu, Nathan. Unpublished memoir; interview with Liz Nelson, June 2007.

 The full text of **Document 14.5** is available on the CD-ROM

DOCUMENT 14.6a & b: Posters from the Cultural Revolution

The slogan on the right side of the poster reads: "Go to the Countryside; Go to the Borderland; Go to the Places Where the Motherland Needs You." On the red cloth, the text says "Become educated by the once poor and low middle class peasants; take roots in the countryside for the Revolution." The poster was created in February 1970 (*Collection Stephan R. Landsberger at the International Institute for Social History, Amsterdam, the Netherlands. www.iisg.nl/~landsberger*).

This poster shows Dazhai, a village that from 1964 until the late 1970s was held up as a model of success to be copied, regardless of widely varying growing conditions (*Collection Stephan R. Landsberger at the International Institute for Social History, Amsterdam, the Netherlands. www.iisg.nl/~landsberger*).

DOCUMENT 14.7: "I Now Knew the Face of Poverty," an excerpt from *Growing Up in the People's Republic: Conversations Between Two Daughters of China's Revolution* by Ye Weili and Ma Xiaodong, 2005

Ye Weili describes her experience as a zhiqing, *one of 12 million "sent-down youth" sent to the countryside between 1968 and 1975 to be re-educated by the peasants.*

It was unsettling to see the poverty surrounding us. There were three scenes I will never forget. One occurred in late fall. By then I had lived in the village for a number of years. Our team harvested potatoes earlier that day. In the evening we were going to divide up the potatoes so that each household would get its share—we received all our grains and vegetables this way. After supper I took a wicker basket to collect my share. When I came out of our alleyway, I saw a scene that has been forever frozen in my mind. Under the yellow streetlight, people from my team stood by a pile of potatoes. They were shivering in the cold wind in their shabby clothes. How they resembled a group sculpture of beggars! It was as though I was seeing my fellow team members for the first time. I now knew the face of poverty....

SOURCE: Ye Weili and Ma Xiaodong, *Growing Up in the People's Republic: Conversations Between Two Daughters of China's Revolution* (New York: Palgrave Macmillan, 2005) 115.

 The full text of **Document 14.7** is available on the CD-ROM.

DOCUMENT 14.8: "Singing Our Turbulent Youth," an excerpt from *Growing Up in the People's Republic: Conversations Between Two Daughters of China's Revolution* by Ye Weili and Ma Xiaodong, 2005

With or without books, people continued their pursuit of knowledge. One boy was a physics nut. He often adjusted the angle of his hoe at the end of the day, applying his knowledge of mechanics to make his hoe more labor efficient. Another boy was interested in international affairs. His hobby was to gather every piece of information he could find about a foreign country; climate, geography, population, and so on. The data primarily came from *The People's Daily*—the only paper available to us. His newspaper clippings eventually filled several thick columns of used magazines. He liked to challenge us to test him about any country in the world, the more obscure the better.

There was no electricity when we first arrived in the village. In the third year the area was connected to a power plant. By then we had become accustomed to physical labor and we needed release for our surplus energy, especially during the long winter months when there was little work in the field. Some of us began to make systematic study plans. My brother finished studying senior high math and physics on his own. Nobody knew if colleges would ever be open again, but the desire for learning was too strong for us to care about its practical value. Several people decided to study English and it was fun to join them. Many of us had short-wave radios. It was amazing how easily we could receive foreign broadcasts such a VOA (Voice of America), BBC [British Broadcasting Corporation], and Radio Moscow in this remote region....

SOURCE: Ye Weili and Ma Xiaodong, *Growing Up in the People's Republic: Conversations Between Two Daughters of China's Revolution* (New York: Palgrave Macmillan, 2005) 122.

 The full text of **Document 14.8** is available on the CD-ROM.

DOCUMENT 14.9: Excerpts describing the personal experiences of Nathan Hu as a "sent-down youth," written in 2007

The majority of us were happy to go to the countryside because we thought that it was a test to our generation—the leaders of the People's Republic of China in the future. First of all, we really believed what Mao said. He said the world belonged to us, also, the world belongs to you—the youth. You're like the morning sun; the future will be created in your hands. We saw it as Mao offering us a chance to go to the countryside to be re-educated. The education we received before in school was a *bourgeoisie* education and now we needed to go to the countryside to get a farmer's education. This would be a good education. So we said, "OK, yes, why not? We'll go there."

In some ways we felt very superior to the farmers. They were considered the bottom [of the social hierarchy]. We were from the city; naturally we felt superior. Even though we were supposed to receive an education from the farmers, mentally, psychologically we felt higher than them. We were cheerful, optimistic about going to the countryside. We were excited about going to a new environment. We felt it was like a test that we needed to pass. We would gain strength....

> *In 1991, forty-year-old Nathan Hu came to the United States to continue his studies. After completing his course work toward a doctorate, he worked full time while he wrote his dissertation. In 2005, he received his Ph.D. from the University of Massachusetts in Amherst.*

SOURCE: Hu, Nathan. Unpublished memoir; interview with Liz Nelson, June 2007.

 The full text of **Document 14.9** is available on the CD-ROM.

DOCUMENT 14.10: Descriptions of two women's reactions to the Cultural Revolution, an excerpt from *Growing Up in the People's Republic: Conversations Between Two Daughters of China's Revolution* by Ye Weili and Ma Xiaodong, 2005

MA XIAODONG: My enthusiasm at the beginning of the Cultural Revolution also reflected my yearning for more thrills in life. I had always wished to be born during the time of war. Now my turn had finally come. My spirits were very high. I was busy making revolution and often didn't go home for days. At night we put a few desks together as beds and slept in the classroom. I was so excited that I didn't need much sleep.

YE WEILI: I shared some of your excitement. I was captivated by the full name of the Cultural Revolution: the Historically Unprecedented Great Proletarian Cultural Revolution. It sounded galvanizing. I felt I was participating in the making of history. It was a grand feeling. I was in this mood when we marched in a parade hailing the launch of the Cultural Revolution after the publication of *The People's Daily* editorial. We just walked around the school campus, shouting slogans and so forth. The parade was led by school administration even though the campus was now covered with posters denouncing them....

SOURCE: Ye Weili and Ma Xiaodong, *Growing Up in the People's Republic: Conversations Between Two Daughters of China's Revolution* (New York: Palgrave Macmillan, 2005) 73.

 The full text of **Document 14.10** is on the CD-ROM.

DOCUMENT 14.11: A peasant's reflection on Mao Zedong, from an interview conducted in the early 1980s

Fifty-four-year-old Zhang Yuxi lived in a village in Shandong Province at the time of this interview. He described the effects of the frequently changing policies under Mao, spoke of how "things were going wrong" under the co-op system, and of how hard he cried when in 1964 he was forced to cut down an orchard of peach trees he had grown from scratch because it was a "capitalist activity." "Life got harder and harder after that," he continued. "It was so hard to get by those days that...I can't find the words." Nevertheless, he had the following to say about Mao Zedong:

Life has been better the last couple of years. I'm still hoping to get the money together for a trip to Beijing to have a look round. Before I die, I want to see what Chairman Mao really looked like. I know about the mistakes in his last years. But they weren't his mistakes. Sitting there in his dragon palace, he couldn't possibly have known what was happening to us peasants. It was the people under him who were bad. They kept him in the dark and did all sorts of terrible things in his name. Chairman Mao had wealth and greatness written all over his face. He had the look of a real emperor, but he was better than an emperor. No emperor ever saved the poor. Chairman Mao was the savior of the poor from the moment he was born. If he hadn't been, would we be missing him now?

SOURCE: Zhang Xinxin and Sang Ye. W. J. F. Jenner and Delia Davin, eds., *Chinese Lives: An Oral History of Contemporary China* (New York: Pantheon, 1987) 117.

DOCUMENT 14.12: Poster depicting people swimming across the Yangzi River, emulating Mao's crossing ten years earlier, 1976

万里长江横渡

Mao Zedong was a strong proponent of swimming as a form of exercise. In 1966 (at age 73), he swam in the Yangzi ostensibly to promote the sport but also to show his own well-being. The event was covered extensively by the Chinese press. This poster by Wei Yang was created to commemorate that event. The words at the bottom read: "Crossing the 10,000 li Yangzi River, 1976." (*Collection Stephan R. Landsberger at the International Institute for Social History, Amsterdam, the Netherlands. www.iisg. nl/~landsberger*)

DOCUMENT 14.13: Photograph of people waiting to visit Mao Zedong's mausoleum, Beijing, May 2006

Even on extremely hot and humid summer days, hundreds of people still wait in line for the opportunity to go inside the mausoleum and to walk past Mao Zedong's coffin. (*Photo by Liz Nelson*)

Activities

ACTIVITY 1: Assessing student goals during the Cultural Revolution

After reading the introductory essay, examine the "One Hundred Items for Destroying the Old and Establishing the New" (14.1). Consider the following questions:

1. Who wrote the rules?
2. What is the overarching tone of the rules and regulations?
3. What language or phrases are particularly striking and why?
4. As a list of rules, how does this compare to other lists or sets of rules that you may have encountered? What are the similarities? The differences?
5. What would it be like to live under rules of this sort?

ACTIVITY 2: Examining individual experiences of the Cultural Revolution

Part 1:

Working in small groups, read one of the documents describing experiences during the Cultural Revolution (14.2–14.5). In your group, discuss the reading and then take notes in response to the following questions:

1. What is the tone of the excerpt you read?

2. In what format has the author chosen to tell of his or her experiences? How does it affect what you learn from the writing?

3. How would you summarize the author's experiences?

4. What did you find most striking about the document? What surprised you?

5. From the account you read, what can be concluded about the state of affairs in China during the mid-1960s?

6. In what ways could individuals respond to the events unfolding around them? What were the likely consequences to the choices they had?

Part 2:

Groups will then present a summary of their excerpt and their discussion. This activity could be done in a three-way Socratic format as well. (See Item 14.A on the CD-ROM for guidelines for a Socratic discussion.) Discuss as a class:

1. What do these accounts tell us about the Cultural Revolution?

2. What were some of the effects of the Cultural Revolution on children, adults, and families?

3. How do the accounts compare to each other?

4. What role did justice play?

5. How does the span of time between when the experiences took place and when the individual wrote or spoke about them affect the document?

Part 3:

Look at the two posters (14.6a & b) on the CD-ROM, where they are in color. For 14.6a, discuss:

1. What is the overall impression you get from this poster?

2. What is the primary color? Why? What is the significance of this color in traditional Chinese culture?

3. What aspect or aspects of the Cultural Revolution does the poster capture?

For 14.6b, discuss:

4. What do you see in the poster?

5. What is your general impression of the poster?

6. How does this poster express propaganda? What is it trying to say?

7. Given what you read in the introductory essay and additional primary sources, what strikes you about the poster?

8. How do you think people reconciled the discrepancies between the imagery of Dazhai and what, in fact, was actually unfolding throughout China?

Extension activity:

With appropriate permission, interview an adult about his or her views on a revolutionary movement that occurred in his or her country. Compare and contrast your subject's comments to those of any one of the accounts in this chapter (14.2–14.5). Write a short essay that analyzes the most salient points of similarity and difference. What influences the interviewee's recollections the most?

ACTIVITY 3: From the city to the countryside

Working in small groups, divide up documents 14.7–14.9 so that each group is reading one account. Discuss in your group:

1. How does the individual feel about his or her experience as a sent-down youth?

2. How does the account match the image on the poster (14.6a)?

3. Why did Mao put this huge program into action?

4. What did the individual gain from the experience? What did he or she lose?

Reconvene in groups that include readers of each document. Share what you learned and discuss the varied experiences.

1. What stands out the most?

2. What would your reaction be if you were told you had to move to a distant rural part of the country to work on a farm? How did these three individuals react? Why?

3. What might be the lasting effects of millions of teens having lived and worked with peasants in rural China? (These individuals are now in their early- to mid-50s.)

ACTIVITY 4: Reflecting on the chaos and violence

Read document 14.10, in which Ye Weili and Ma Xiaodong reflect on the Cultural Revolution. Discuss:

1. How do the two authors compare in their views of the Cultural Revolution?

2. What explains the differences in the authors' accounts?

3. Why do both authors express a degree of excitement they felt during this turbulent time in China?

4. What specific factors most strongly affected the authors' opinions of the Cultural Revolution?

5. What accounts for the complex emotions the authors experienced during the Cultural Revolution?

6. As middle-aged adults, how might the authors' feelings about what they experienced have evolved or changed since the 1960s?

Creative extensions:

- In response to all that you've learned about people's experiences during this very difficult period, create a piece of visual art (such as a sculpture, collage, poster, painting, or cartoon strip.) Write a brief caption to go with your work.

- Write a poem in response to any one of the experiences about which you read.

- Explore posters and other propaganda from the Soviet Union, especially under Joseph Stalin. Write a short essay that describes parallels and differences between Russian propaganda and that of the Cultural Revolution. Evaluate the similarities and try to determine what themes and issues are consistent and why this might be the case. Explain what might account for the differences.

ACTIVITY 5: **Exploring Mao Zedong's legacy**

Read the excerpt from the interview with a peasant (14.11) and the final paragraph of the introductory essay. Next, look at the poster on the CD-ROM (14.12), and the photograph taken in Beijing (14.13).

Interview:

1. Why might the man hold these opinions about Mao?
2. What does the excerpt teach us generally about the impact of Mao Zedong?
3. What does the excerpt teach us about Mao's "cult of personality"?
4. How does the man's view of Mao Zedong fit with the official's statement?

Poster:

1. What is the overriding color in the poster? Why?
2. What emotions does the poster convey?
3. How does this poster depict Mao's cult of personality?
4. How does this poster help explain the far-reaching impact of Mao on many Chinese people?

Photograph:

1. What surprises you about the photograph?
2. How long does this queue appear to be?
3. Why do thousands of Chinese citizens stand in line for hours to see the mausoleum?
4. How does this contribute to your understanding of Mao Zedong's legacy?

ACTIVITY 6: Analytical thinking and writing

Conduct further research before choosing one of the following:

- Write an essay in which you assess the effectiveness of Mao Zedong's leadership. Did he change China for the better or were the costs too high? Support any claims with evidence drawn from both primary and secondary sources.
- Assess the same question in the form of an in-class debate.
- Write an essay in which you assess the consequences of the Cultural Revolution.
- Assess the same topic but in the form of an in-class Socratic discussion (see Item 14.A for guidelines).
- Write an essay in which you analyze and compare the views of three different firsthand accounts of the Cultural Revolution. What are the common threads? What aspects stand out as being strikingly different? What could account for these similarities and differences?
- Write an essay comparing China's Cultural Revolution to periods of social and political upheaval elsewhere in the world in the twentieth century (e.g. to the McCarthy Era in the United States or to Stalin's purges in the 1930s). Where do the similarities begin and end? What accounts for the similarities and differences?
- Research the Khmer Rouge regime and its impact on the people of Cambodia in the 1970s. This government claimed to be heavily influenced and supported by Maoist communism. Write an essay that evaluates the impact of Maoist China in Cambodia. Alternatively, write an essay comparing the ideas and actions of the Khmer Rouge with those of the Red Guards during the Cultural Revolution.

Suggested Resources

Books

Cheek, Timothy. *Mao Zedong and China's Revolutions: A Brief History with Documents.* Boston: Bedford/St. Martin's, 2002.
An excellent collection of essays on Mao and the Chairman's own writing and speeches.

Cheng, Nien. *Life and Death in Shanghai.* New York: Grove Press, 1987.

Francis, Gregory and Stefanie Lamb. *China's Cultural Revolution.* Stanford Program on International and Cross-Cultural Education (SPICE), 2005.
An extensive curriculum.

Jiang Yarong and David Ashley. *Mao's Children in the New China: Voices from the Red Guard Generation.* New York: Routledge, 2000.
A collection of interviews with former Red Guards, who talk about the effects of the Cultural Revolution on themselves and their experiences in the "New China" of the past two decades.

Landsberger, Stefan. *Chinese Propaganda Posters: From Revolution to Modernization.* Amsterdam: The Pepin Press, 1998.
Text and images detail the role of posters in the PRC.

Liang Heng and Judith Shapiro. *Son of the Revolution.* New York: Alfred A. Knopf, 1983.
Liang Heng engages young adults in his own and his family's experiences living with the erratic policies of Mao Zedong.

Dai Sijie. *Balzac and the Little Chinese Seamstress.* Translated by Ina Rilke. New York: Alfred A. Knopf, 2001.
A beautifully written and translated autobiographical novel about two teenage boys' time as "sent-down" youth being re-educated in a Sichuan mountain village. Highly recommended for teens and adults.

Spence, Jonathan D. *Mao Zedong.* New York: Viking: 1999.
A good short biography by one of the finest China scholars writing today.

Ye Weili and Ma Xiaodong. *Growing Up in The People's Republic: Conversations Between Two Daughters of China's Revolution.* New York: Palgrave Macmillan, 2005.
A highly readable and thoughtful exploration of the two women's experiences and the legacy of the Cultural Revolution.

Yu, Chun. *Little Green: Growing Up During the Chinese Cultural Revolution.* New York: Simon & Schuster, 2005.
Written in poetic form from a child's perspective, a poignant account of the experiences of one family.

Websites

http://www.iisg.nl/~landsberger/crc.html This site managed by Stefan R. Landsberger, professor of Contemporary Chinese Culture at the University of Amsterdam, includes posters from the full Mao era, with translations of slogans, a narrative, and information about the artists.

http://kaladarshan.arts.ohio-state.edu/exhib/poster/exhibintro.html "Picturing Power: Posters of the Cultural Revolution," an online exhibit hosted at the Ohio State University. Curated by Harriet Evans, Senior Lecturer in Chinese Studies, University of Westminster, London, and Jeffrey Wasserstrom, Associate Professor of History, Indiana University.

http://depts.washington.edu/chinaciv/graph/9wenge.htm Information and posters from the Cultural Revolution.

http://news.phoenixtv.com/photo/history/200708/0821_1398_196612_1.shtml Photos from the Cultural Revolution.

http://www.wellesley.edu/Polisci/wj/China/CRSongs/crsongs.htm A small but effective collection of songs (in MP3 format) from the Cultural Revolution. Compiled by Bill Joseph of Wellesley College.

http://hua.umf.maine.edu/China/culturr.html An extensive bibliography of sources on the Cultural Revolution.

http://faculty.washington.edu/yomi/CR.html This syllabus lists a wide variety of literature and films pertaining to the Cultural Revolution.

Films

The Blue Kite (138 mins; 1993) *In Chinese (Mandarin) with subtitles. The film captures how the turbulent political times affected the lives of everyday people. The Chinese Ministry of Broadcast, Film and Radio prohibited the film from being shown in China and barred director Tian Zhuangzhuang from making any further films in China. The Blue Kite won the "Best Film" award at the Tokyo Film Festival.*

Morning Sun (120 mins; 2003) *Produced and directed by Carma Hinton, Geremie Barmé, and Richard Gordon. This documentary provides a multi-perspective view of a tumultuous period as seen through the eyes of a generation born at the time the PRC was founded. Companion website:* ***http://www.morningsun.org/film/index.html***

To Live (133 mins; 1994) *In Chinese with subtitles. Based on the novel by Yu Hua, the film spans four turbulent decades of China's 20th century. The film tells the story of Fugui and Jiazhen and their two children as they struggle to survive the constantly changing political climate. Winner of the Grand Jury Prize and Best Actor awards at the Cannes Film Festival. Directed by Zhang Yimou. It is also very interesting to note what is* not *told about the Great Leap Forward and the Cultural Revolution.*

■ **A CLOSER LOOK**

Lei Feng and His Diary

The 22-year-old PLA soldier died helping a comrade in trouble, the public was told. And he left behind a diary. *The Diary of Lei Feng*, published in 1963, expressed the young man's love for the revolution, his country, his comrades, and especially Chairman Mao. I work to "make the world more beautiful every day," Lei had written in his diary. In the 1960s, Lei Feng became a household name, and his face was instantly recognized on multiple posters that soon appeared across China. Study of his diary became standard practice in Chinese schools, and Mao himself endorsed the book by adding his calligraphy to the title page. The journal suggested that young people "learn from Comrade Lei Feng," and included an honor code and list of duties not unlike that of the Boy Scouts. Lei Feng "spent all his spare time and money helping the needy," wrote the *People's Daily* on the fortieth anniversary of his death. The diary was meant to inspire thousands to follow in Lei's selfless footsteps, to live simple, honest lives.

The diary, however, was a work of fiction, created by PLA writers, though there had been a real Lei Feng. Orphaned when he was seven, he joined the PLA at age 20 as a soldier in a transportation unit. He had been killed by a falling telephone pole, which had been accidentally hit by a truck, but that fact came to light years later. Lei Feng's image is still common throughout China, his picture sometimes found at the entrance to primary schools. March 5 has been designated "Learn From Lei Feng Day," a time for students to engage in community service. According to the *People's Daily Online*, the Lei Feng Memorial Hall in Fushun has been visited by 64 million people since it opened in 1964.

■ *To see the many posters of Lei Feng, visit http://www.iisg.nl/~landsberger/lf.html. Discuss why Lei Feng's diary and his story became so inspirational. What stories of everyday good deeds are part of the histories of other countries? How and why do some stories, such as the one about George Washington and the cherry tree, take on a life of their own?*

Primary Sources

DOCUMENT 15.1: Joint Communiqué of the United States of America and the People's Republic of China, February 28, 1972

Supplementary Materials

ITEM 15.A: Chart for analysis of the Joint Communiqué (Activity 4)

ITEM 15.B: Map of Asia

CHAPTER 15

Overtures Between East and West

By Liz Nelson

Chapter Contents

The Sino-Soviet Rift

China and the United States in the 1950s and 1960s

Steps Toward Diplomatic Relations

Organizing Idea

Complex relations among the United States, China, and the Soviet Union set the stage for U.S. President Richard Nixon's groundbreaking visit to China in 1972. The presidential visit led to significantly increased contact between China and the United States.

Key Questions

What were the relationships like among China, the Soviet Union, and the United States in the period leading up to President Richard Nixon's visit to China?

Why did the United States and China want to establish diplomatic relations?

What were the most important impediments to resuming relations?

What were the results of President Nixon's visit?

Key Terms

diplomacy

"Ping Pong diplomacy"

Essay

With the founding of the People's Republic of China (PRC) (中华人民共和国), the Chinese Communist Party (中国共产党) leadership and the majority of the Chinese populace wanted to re-establish their international prestige. Premier Zhou Enlai (周恩来), a skilled and experienced negotiator, directed the government's foreign policy (see A Closer Look at the end of the chapter). By the mid 1950s, Zhou had established warm relations with India's fledgling government. He also sought ties with twenty-nine Asian and African nations whose delegates attended the Bandung Conference in Indonesia in 1955. The most critical relationships that Chinese leaders needed to manage, however, were those with the two world superpowers at the time: the Soviet Union and the United States.

Sino-Soviet Rift

After a working partnership in the very early years of the PRC (see Chapter 13), China's relationship with the Soviet Union began to change following Joseph Stalin's death in 1953. Under Nikita Khrushchev, who led the Soviet Union beginning in 1953, Soviet citizens began to criticize the brutal former dictator. Since Stalin and Mao had forged a working relationship, the implications for the CCP were problematic. In *The Search for Modern China*, Jonathan Spence explains: "Behind the Soviet-Chinese disagreements that emerged in the late 1950s lay a tangled history of friendship and distrust."[1] The CCP was distressed by Khrushchev's policies in Eastern Europe, his friendlier attitude toward capitalism and the United States in particular, and his unwillingness to share nuclear technology with China. Tensions escalated until in September 1960, the Soviet Union removed all of its 1,390 experts on technology, military, and infrastructure from China. Shortly after, when the Russians

called a meeting of the Communist parties from eighty-one countries, Mao declined the invitation.

China and the United States in the 1950s and 1960s

The relationship between China and the United States turned frigid during and after the Korean War (朝鲜战争). The U.S. government was extremely suspicious of China's intentions and fearful of the ability of China's leadership—as demonstrated in that war—to mobilize hundreds of thousands of men to fight as needed. While managing the Cold War with the Soviet Union dominated U.S. foreign policy, its approach to China consisted of isolating, demonizing, and containing the Communist regime. McCarthyism raged in the United States in the 1950s, further escalating anti-Communist sentiment.[2] The Chinese government, on the other hand, saw U. S. involvement in Korea (and later Vietnam) as proof of Washington's intent to dominate Asia.

By the early 1960s, China's relationship with the Soviet Union was in shambles; its relationship with the United States was hostile. Despite Zhou Enlai's early efforts to partner with other developing nations, anti-Chinese riots broke out in Indonesia and a territorial dispute arose with India. The PRC began a decade of isolation, imposed both from within and by the rest of the world. As the Cultural Revolution (文化大革命) took hold (see Chapter 14), China's closest friend was Albania.

When the Soviet Union invaded Czechoslovakia in 1968 to assert its dominance, Chinese leaders feared China might be next. In March 1969, two incidents on the border between the two countries resulted in heavy casualties and added to the tension between the former allies.

---

[1] Spence, *The Search for Modern China*, 584.

[2] Senator Joseph McCarthy launched the second Red Scare in the early 1950s. Thousands of individuals were accused of being Communists or Communist sympathizers, and many were investigated by the House Committee on Un-American Activities.

"We must have relations with Communist China"

In November 1968, U.S. citizens had elected Richard Nixon to be their next president. The following summer, the Nixon administration eased some travel and trade restrictions with China and stopped U.S. Navy patrols of the Taiwan Straits (台湾海峡), sending signals that the United States wished to improve relations. On the other side of the Pacific, members of the Chinese leadership, recognizing China's need for Western technology in order to move the economy forward, advocated a more pragmatic approach to foreign policy. Early in 1970, Chinese and American diplomats resumed talks in Warsaw, Poland.[3] As the year progressed, the ways in which the government-controlled Chinese press wrote about the United States began to change. At the end of the year, President Nixon announced at a press conference that the United States "must have relations with Communist China," and Mao Zedong notified Edgar Snow (see Chapter 11) that he would be happy to talk to Nixon.[4]

One cautious step after another, Washington and Beijing came closer to some kind of formal relations. In July 1971, following National Security Advisor Henry Kissinger's secret meeting with Premier Zhou Enlai in Beijing (北京), Nixon announced that he would soon visit China. Later that year, the United States withdrew its opposition to China joining the United Nations, and on October 25, 1971, the General Assembly gave the "China seat" to the People's Republic of China, concurrently taking it away from Taiwan (台湾). Finally, after years of careful maneuvering, in February 1972, President Nixon flew to Beijing and met with Zhou Enlai and Mao Zedong. China and the United States signed a Joint Communiqué (联合公报) frankly stating their views, agreeing that there should be "one China," (which would include Taiwan), and pledging to eventually normalize relations.

Domestic issues in the United States (including the Watergate scandal) and the death of Zhou Enlai in January 1976, followed by Mao's death in September, delayed the normalization process. But after further refinement of their respective stances regarding Taiwan, on March 1, 1979, the United States finally recognized the People's Republic of China as the government of China. The two countries set up embassies in each other's capitals and sent ambassadors to help manage diplomatic relations. A new era began.

---

[3] High-level diplomats from China and the United States had been quietly meeting since August 1, 1955. At first they met in Geneva, Switzerland; after 1958, the periodic meetings took place in Warsaw. It was the only contact between the two countries for sixteen years.

[4] Warren I. Cohen, *America's Response to China: A History of Sino-American Relations* (New York: Columbia University Press, 2000) 197.

Primary Source

DOCUMENT 15.1: Excerpts from the Joint Communiqué of the United States of America and the People's Republic of China, February 28, 1972

1. [T]he two sides stated that: Progress toward the normalization of relations between China and the United States is in the interests of all countries. Both wish to reduce the danger of international military conflict. Neither should seek hegemony in the Asia-Pacific region and each is opposed to efforts by any other country or group of countries to establish such hegemony. Neither is prepared to negotiate on behalf of any third party or to enter into agreements or understandings with the other directed at other states....

2. The two sides reviewed the long-standing serious disputes between China and the United States. The Chinese side reaffirmed its position: the Taiwan question is the crucial question obstructing the normalization of relations between China and the United States; the Government of the People's Republic of China is the sole legal government of China; Taiwan is a province of China which has long been returned to the motherland; the liberation of Taiwan is China's internal affair in which no other country has the right to interfere; and all U.S. forces and military installations must be withdrawn from Taiwan. The Chinese Government firmly opposes any activities which aim at the creation of "one China, one Taiwan," "one China, two governments," "two Chinas," an "independent Taiwan," or advocate that "the status of Taiwan remains to be determined."

3. *The U.S. side declared*: The United States acknowledges that all Chinese on either side of the Taiwan Strait maintain there is but one China and that Taiwan is a part of China. The United States Government does not challenge that position. It reaffirms its interest in a peaceful settlement of the Taiwan question by the Chinese themselves. With this prospect in mind, it affirms the ultimate objective of the withdrawal of all U.S. forces and military installations from Taiwan....

SOURCE: http://usinfo.state.gov/eap/Archive_Index/joint_communique_1972.html

 The complete Joint Communiqué is available on the CD-ROM.

Activities

ACTIVITY 1: Understanding the motives of the key players

Read the introduction to the lesson. Then check your textbook and online resources to get a detailed sense of the foreign policy goals of the United States, the People's Republic of China, and the Soviet Union during the late 1960s and early 1970s. (PBS's "Nixon's China Game" at http://www.pbs.org/wgbh/amex/china/ is an especially useful site.) Create a diagram (or a cartoon or comic strip) that demonstrates the relationships among the three countries. Discuss as a class who wanted what and why.

ACTIVITY 2: "Ping Pong diplomacy" and the role of sports

Use a search engine to learn more about the Ping Pong diplomacy that took place in April 1971. You can also find information at http://www.pbs.org/wgbh/amex/china/peopleevents/pande07.html and http://www.china.org.cn/english/features/olympics/100660.htm
In small groups:

1. Compare the Chinese and American accounts of the opening of relations between China and the United States, and the accounts of how the Ping Pong (table tennis) players came to play in China. Are the differences between the accounts significant? Why?

2. Why would the Chinese government choose to invite Ping Pong players as the first group of Americans to enter China since 1949?

3. Which sports events come to mind when you think of international relations? What role do these events play?

ACTIVITY 3: Stories in photographs

View the collection of photographs of President Nixon's visit to China taken by White House photographers and the China News Agency at http://www.gmu.edu/library/specialcollections/nixon_in_china.
Choose among the following options:

- Write a letter from President Nixon to Premier Zhou Enlai as a follow-up to the visit.

- Write an essay in which you explain why the Chinese leaders chose to include these particular destinations and events as part of Nixon's visit.

- Take on the role of a reporter traveling with the president, and write a diary based on the photographs.

Discuss in class what your overall impressions are of this presidential visit. Use specific details from the photographs to make your points.

ACTIVITY 4: Analyzing a formal agreement

After reading the Joint Communiqué between the U.S. and China (14.1), work in small groups to fill in a chart (Item 15.A on the CD), which will identify China's and the United States' views of themselves and each other, the issues as stake, and each country's goals. First, go through the communiqué again and highlight adjectives and other descriptive words. Then fill in the chart.

As a class, discuss:

1. On which issues did China and the United States agree? On which issues did they disagree?

2. What was the most important point in the Communiqué? Why?

Note: for an overview of Taiwan's history see Additional Resources on the CD-ROM. Chapters 16 and 20 include further information on U.S.-Taiwan-China relations and the "one China" issue.

ACTIVITY 5: An essay: Did the visit change the world?

After his visit to China in 1972, Richard Nixon said, "This is the week that changed the world." Write an essay in which you take a stand: the visit did or did not "change the world."

EXTENDED RESEARCH

Write a paper, create an electronic presentation using, for example, PowerPoint ® or Photo Story 3 ®, or work with a partner to write and perform an interview on one of the following topics:

- Richard Nixon
- Henry Kissinger
- *Nixon in China*, the opera by John Adams
- present-day relations between China and Russia
- the role of China in the Vietnam War
- the Chinese invasion of Vietnam in 1979

Suggested Resources

Books

MacMillan, Margaret. *Nixon and Mao: The Week that Changed the World*. New York: Random House, 2007.
An accessible history of Nixon's visit to China, including many archival documents and photographs that help shed light on the complex events leading up to the Joint Communiqué.

Websites

http://kaladarshan.arts.ohio-state.edu/exhib/poster/PictPow1.html Several posters at this online exhibit give an excellent sense of how China was aligning itself with oppressed peoples in Asia, Africa, and Latin America.

http://www.history.com/exhibits/fifties/mccarthy.html and http://en.wikipedia.org/wiki/McCarthyism For more information on the McCarthy era of the 1950s in the United States.

http://www.pbs.org/wgbh/amex/china/ "Nixon's China Game," an *American Experience* website, with background information, an interview with Henry Kissinger, timelines, and teacher resources.

http://www.pbs.org/wgbh/amex/china/timeline/timeline6nf.html PBS *American Experience* site. with excellent timeline of U.S.–China relations, 1945–1979.

http://www.china.org.cn/english/features/olympics/100660.htm An introduction to ping pong diplomacy.

■ **A CLOSER LOOK**

Zhou Enlai: Dedicated Communist

Virtually no one in the top tier of the PRC government emerged from the first quarter century of brutal politics unscathed. However, Zhou Enlai did. Most Chinese adults continue to speak of him with great admiration and affection.

Zhou was born in 1898 in Jiangsu Province to a poor gentry family. Since he was the eldest son and eldest grandson, his extended family ensured that he would receive an excellent education. After graduating from a prestigious school in Tianjin (funded by American missionaries), he continued his education in Japan. In 1920, he returned briefly to China, where he became involved in student activism. Later that year, Zhou left for France to participate in a work-study program. It was there that he dedicated himself to the communist cause.

In the summer of 1924, Zhou Enlai returned to China and quickly assumed leadership positions in the as yet nascent Chinese Communist Party. Three years later, he was elected to the CCP Central Committee and its Politburo. Throughout the 1930s, Zhou would be the Party member who skillfully tackled delicate negotiations, chief among them forming the United Front against Japan with the Guomindang, and as the CCP's chief representative to the hostile Guomindang government in Chongqing (see Chapter 11).

With the founding of the PRC, Zhou Enlai became the nation's premier (or prime minister), a position he held until his death. As premier, he managed the immense bureaucracy, but he was also the architect of China's foreign policy, where he became renowned the world over for his diplomatic skills. Though his power was curtailed by Mao Zedong and the Gang of Four during the chaotic years of the Cultural Revolution (see Chapter 14), he was a moderating influence on its worst excesses. It is widely believed that he protected some of the oldest historic sites from destruction by Red Guards and several military and government leaders from recurring purges. Deeply devoted to communist ideals, Zhou was a pragmatic statesman. In the mid 1970s, well aware of Mao Zedong's failing health as well as his own, Zhou helped maneuver Deng Xiaoping into position to take over leadership.

Zhou Enlai's death in January 1976 brought an outpouring of grief by a people desperate for the balance, moderation, and ethics the premier had come to represent.

■ *You can read some of Zhou Enlai's writing, including "Guides for Myself," (1943) at http://www.marxists.org/reference/archive/zhou-enlai/index.htm. Discuss: What characteristics should a statesman have?*

Nixon's Visit to China

http://video.google.com/videoplay?docid=308955 9250589214196&hl=en Brief video footage.

http://www.gmu.edu/library/specialcollections/nixon_in_china

http://www.gwu.edu/~nsarchiv/nsa/publications/DOC_readers/kissinger/nixzhou/ Declassified records of historic talks between Richard Nixon and Zhou Enlai, 1972.

http://news.xinhuanet.com/english/2007-02/20/xinsrc_03202042107585151517201.jpg A

photograph of Mao Zedong and Richard Nixon.

Nixon in China, the Opera

http://www.eno.org/src/nixon_teachers.pdf Background information on the opera and a synopsis of each act.

http://video.google.com/videoplay?docid=192867 5857440280503&hl=en A video clip from the original 1987 production.

CHAPTER 16

Socialism with Chinese Characteristics

By Todd Whitten

Chapter Contents

The Four Modernizations
The One-Child Policy
The Fifth Modernization
Foreign Affairs
The Tiananmen Square Confrontation

Organizing Idea

During the 1980s, Deng Xiaoping began to move China out of the rubble of the Cultural Revolution and Mao's economic policies toward modernization. This process rapidly moved into realms beyond the economic. The Party began to confront the social and political consequences of liberalization, which culminated in the events in and around Tiananmen Square in 1989.

Key Questions

What is the relationship between economic liberalization and political freedom? Does one necessitate the other?

If an organization of people (a nation, a political party, or another group) is to grow and advance, is dissent useful or distracting? Why? How should a ruling group manage different perspectives and opinions?

Under what circumstances can a revolutionary regime transition into an authoritarian but stable system and ultimately into a democracy?

How did Deng Xiaoping's leadership differ from that of Mao Zedong?

What happened in and around Tiananmen Square between April and June 1989, and why did the government eventually respond with violence? Was this response inevitable?

How did the relationships among the People's Republic of China, the United States, and Taiwan change during this period?

Key Terms

big character poster	communism	dissent	Republic of China
cadre	counter-revolution	Politburo	socialism
capitalism	Democracy Wall	propaganda	

A gradual shift in power occurred after Mao Zedong's death in 1976. By 1980, Deng Xiaoping (邓小平) and his protégés Hu Yaobang and Zhao Ziyang held key posts in both the government and the Chinese Communist Party. Deng inherited a People's Republic of China (中华人民共和国) (PRC) with a domestic economy in tatters, a populace deeply traumatized by the Cultural Revolution (文化大革命), a fractured relationship with the Soviet Union, and a forward-looking, but as yet undefined, relationship with the United States.

The Four Modernizations (四个现代化)

In 1978, Deng launched the modernization campaign that Zhou Enlai had first proposed in a 1975 speech. Modernization would focus on four priorities: industry, agriculture, national defense, and science and technology. Deng's overriding vision for China was to concentrate on these four areas in the hopes that they would bring stability, unity, discipline, and economic progress to the people of the PRC.

Deng faced significant challenges in his effort to make his ideas reality, and many of his peers were openly skeptical. An attempt to work on all of these areas would incur massive bills that had to be paid; where would the money come from? The knowledge base to adapt or create modern technology required a new level of education; who would be educated? Where would this education occur? Infrastructure would have to be created, from roads to schools to factories to ports to airports.

Deng compiled a comprehensive financial plan that included significant foreign investment. He set as a goal the quadrupling of the gross national product (GNP) by the end of the century, from $250 million to $1 trillion. One result of such a leap in GNP would be that more money would be available for reinvestment. Deng reached out to other nations for technological assistance, and he made it easier for Chinese college students to study abroad. The idea was that they would then return to China with the knowledge and skills needed to move agriculture, technology, and industry forward.

Rural Reform

Deng's brilliance had a simple foundation: China needed first to better feed itself. If the people had enough to eat, he believed, then they could look to new horizons beyond survival. To this end, Deng made the rural areas of China his first priority for reform. He set about dismantling the commune system (the People's Commune; see Chapter 13) and encouraged local leaders to shift from collective farming to the household responsibility system. Within a few years almost all communes were dismantled, and by 1987 rice and wheat yields had risen 50 percent over those of years under the commune system.[1] This process was not totally smooth, and it took time to get the farmers to accept yet another change, but with support from the top, steady progress was made.

Education

China simultaneously embarked on a campaign to improve and expand its educational system. The government established eighty-eight additional universities throughout China and increased the number of technical colleges. More visas were issued, inviting foreign experts to China and permitting students to leave China to study at top universities in Japan and the United States. Chinese students abroad usually studied the hard sciences and agriculture, though more and more went to learn languages—essential for work with foreign businesses that would be vital for the much-needed infusion of capital.

---

[1] Immanuel Hsü, *The Rise of Modern China* (New York: Oxford University Press, 1990), 845.

Special Economic Zones

Deng oversaw a revision of the Chinese Constitution that was approved in March 1978. This allowed for the establishment of four Special Economic Zones (经济特区) the following year (in Shenzhen, Zhuhai, Shantou and Xiamen). In these zones, foreign companies like Yamaha and Motorola could build factories, conduct business in a "capitalist fashion," and take advantage of cheap labor. To further joint business ventures, fourteen coastal cities opened to foreign investment in 1984.

Foreign Affairs

As a part of his campaign to expand foreign investment in China, Deng made a concerted effort to reach out to the outside world in a way China had never done. Several years after U.S. President Richard Nixon's 1972 visit to China (see Chapter 15), the People's Republic of China and the United States formally recognized each other on January 1, 1979. At the same time, the United States ended its formal ties with Taiwan. Shortly thereafter, Deng traveled to the United States as a guest of President Jimmy Carter. In 1984, an agreement was reached with the United Kingdom to hand over Hong Kong (香港) in 1997; the Portuguese would return Macao (澳门) to China two years later. The government also indicated a willingness to resolve the issue of Taiwan's eventual reunification peacefully. Investment from the United States, Japan, and Taiwan was flowing into China at a rapid rate, thus funding both directly and indirectly the establishment of a new Chinese infrastructure for industry and technology.

The One-Child Policy

Mao Zedong had paid little attention to the potential negative impact of population growth, and had encouraged couples to have large families. This attitude, together with a dramatic decline in infant mortality and rise in life expectancy, had caused China's population to significantly increase. The population of China was 594 million in 1953, 695 million in 1964, and 1 billion by 1982.[2] In addition, the population was very young, with a huge number of young women entering their childbearing years. Chinese leaders in the late 1970s faced a formidable challenge: without some sort of controls, the sheer number of people would cancel any material gains in the country's economy and standard of living. Initially, the CCP encouraged later marriage and childbearing, longer spacing between children, and fewer children. But when the ambitious goals of the Four Modernizations were announced, officials decided that stronger measures had to be taken and in 1979 implemented the One-Child Policy (一个中国政策), which made it illegal for a married couple to have more than one child. This policy ran directly counter to Chinese tradition, whereby sons cared for their parents as they aged. Program workers and village cadres were under pressure to enforce the policy, and forced sterilizations and abortions were widely reported. However, according to official accounts, without this policy in place, it is estimated that China's population today would be even larger, by approximately 400 million people.[3]

The Fifth Modernization

The process of economic liberalization was not without its critics. Many in China worried at the seeming destruction of both Communist and traditional Chinese values. Others insisted that Deng Xiaoping wasn't doing enough. Almost immediately after Deng launched the Four Modernizations, Wei Jingsheng, a young man who worked as an electrician, proposed a

---

[2] http://www.allcountries.org/china_statistics/4_4_basic_statistics_on_national_population.html

[3] A number of experts believe the effect of the One-Child Policy is exaggerated. They argue that modernization has also played a significant role in reducing the birth rate, as it has in other countries.

Fifth Modernization (第五个现代化): democracy. Echoes of the May Fourth Movement (五四运动) (see Chapter 8) began to be heard as students, intellectuals, and eventually workers agitated for greater freedom and a voice in the nation's decision-making. At first, Deng tolerated and even encouraged the Democracy Wall (民主墙) movement as he was trying to win popular support for post-Mao reforms, but when his economic reform programs encountered strong resistance from the conservative forces within the party, Deng decided to crack down on the Democracy Movement in order to please and pacify the conservative forces. In March 1979, officials arrested Wei on the grounds that he had leaked state secrets and sentenced him to fifteen years.

The Tiananmen Square Confrontation

Student discontent sparked again in 1986, and then grew increasingly vocal in the spring of 1989. College students organized protests around the goals of increased democratic participation, an end to corruption, and improved university buildings. They used the death of Hu Yaobang to stage demonstrations of mourning similar to those that occurred when Zhou Enlai had passed away thirteen years earlier. The government responded by forbidding public gatherings, which only served to fan the flames. Students and others gathered by the thousands in Tiananmen Square (天安门广场) in Beijing, then went on a hunger strike at the exact time that the Soviet Union leader Mikhail Gorbachev was making his first visit to China's capital.

At first it seemed that the government was going to tolerate the students' actions, but as time went on, the original protesters left, other students took their place, and then the movement began to spread to other sectors of Chinese society. While groups of workers and even writers for the official newspaper the *People's Daily* joined the protests, members of the Politburo sharply disagreed about how to respond. Many who had witnessed the chaos of the Cultural Revolution argued for shutting down the protests. The liberal faction that favored allowing the protest, led by Zhao Ziyang, lost the debate to hard-liners like Li Peng, and the decision was made to have the People's Liberation Army (中国人民解放军) quell the uprising by whatever means necessary. On the night of June 4, 1989, they did just that, and Beijing crackled with sounds of gunfire. In the aftermath, protesters were arrested, tried, and either given prison sentences or executed. Several of the organizers of the movement managed to flee to Hong Kong and beyond, some surfacing in the United States. The overall pattern of the changes since 1978 suggests that Chinese leaders will not allow economic liberation and political changes to jeopardize the power of the ruling party and social stability.

Primary Sources

DOCUMENT 16.1: Quotations from Karl Marx, Mao Zedong, and Deng Xiaoping

Karl Marx:

(1848): When, in the course of development, class distinctions have disappeared, and all production has been concentrated in the hands of a vast association of the whole nation, the public power will lose its political character. Political power, properly so called, is merely the organized power of one class for oppressing another. If the proletariat during its contest with the bourgeoisie is compelled, by the force of circumstances, to organize itself as a class; if, by means of a revolution, it makes itself the ruling class, and, as such, sweeps away by force the old conditions of production, then it will, along with these conditions, have swept away the conditions for the existence of class antagonisms and of classes generally, and will thereby have abolished its own supremacy as a class.

In place of the old bourgeois society, with its classes and class antagonisms, we shall have an association in which the free development of each is the condition for the free development of all.

Source: Karl Marx and Friedrich Engels, *The Communist Manifesto*, trans. Eric Hobsbawm (London: Verso, 1998).

Mao Zedong:

(November 1938) Every Communist must grasp the truth: Power grows out of the barrel of a gun.

(1955) In order to build a great socialist society it is of the utmost importance to arouse the broad masses of women to join in productive activity. Men and women must receive equal pay for equal work in production.

Sources: Mao Zedong, "Problems of War and Strategy," in *Selected Works, Volume 1* (Beijing: Foreign Languages Press, 1965) 224.

Mao Zedong, "Women Have Gone to the Labour Front" 1955 in *The Socialist Upsurge in China's Countryside*, Vol. 1 (Beijing: Foreign Languages Press, 1965).

Deng Xiaoping:

It doesn't matter if the cat is black or white as long as it catches mice.

Poverty is not socialism. To get rich is glorious.

Reform is China's second revolution.

Sources: "Cat" qtd. in William R. Doerner "The Comeback Comrade," *Time*, January 6, 1986.
"Poverty" from a speech in 1978;
"Reform" from "Reform is China's Second Revolution," a speech in March 1985.

DOCUMENT 16.2: Excerpts from Deng Xiaoping's speech "Emancipate the Mind, Seek Truth from Facts and Unite as One in Looking to the Future," December 13, 1978

When people's minds aren't yet emancipated and their thinking remains rigid, curious phenomena emerge....

People whose thinking has become rigid tend to veer with the wind. They are not guided by Party spirit and Party principles, but go along with whatever has the backing of the authorities and adjust their words and actions according to whichever way the wind is blowing. They think that they will thus avoid mistakes. In fact, however, veering with the wind is in itself a grave mistake, a contravention of the Party spirit which all Communists should cherish. It is true that people who think independently and dare to speak out and act can't avoid making mistakes, but their mistakes are out in the open and are therefore more easily rectified.

Once people's thinking becomes rigid, book worship, divorced from reality, becomes a grave malady. Those who suffer from it dare not say a word or take a step that isn't mentioned in books, documents or the speeches of leaders: everything has to be copied....

SOURCE: Pei-kai Cheng, Michael Lestz, and Jonathan D. Spence, *The Search for Modern China: A Documentary Collection* (New York: W. W. Norton, 1999) 448–451.

 The full text of **Document 16.2** is available on the CD-ROM.

DOCUMENT 16.3: Excerpts related to the "Pan Xiao" discussion on the meaning of life, from *China Youth* magazine, May 1980– December 1980

"The Path of Life: Why Is It More Narrow?" Pan Xiao's first letter

I turned 23 this year. You could say that my life has only just begun, and yet all of life's mysteries and attractions don't appeal to me anymore. It seems like I've already reached the end. When I look back upon the path I've already taken, the road changes from red-violet into grey, from hope to disappointment. It is a path of despair. It is a river flowing from a source of selflessness and purity into a self-centered end.

In the past, I cherished high hopes and fantasies about life. In elementary school, I had heard stories like "How to Build Iron and Steel" and *The Diary of Lei Feng*.[4] Although I didn't completely grasp the concepts, the heroic adventures excited me so much that night after night I couldn't sleep a wink. I thought, "My father, my mother, and my grandfather are all good Communists. Of course I am a Communist, too, and in the future, I want to be a member of the Party—no doubt about it."

After I had enrolled in elementary school for some time, the Cultural Revolution began and the currents grew increasingly fierce. I was a bit confused, and I began to think that perhaps life around me wasn't as attractive as it was described in the books.

---

[4] See A Closer Look in Chapter 14 for the story of *The Diary of Lei Feng*.

I asked myself, "Should I believe what these books tell me or what I see with my own eyes?"…

Source: *China Youth*, May–December 1980. Trans. Diana Lin.

 The full text of **Document 16.3** is available on the CD-ROM.

DOCUMENT 16.4: Description of a visit to a rural school in the 1980s by Ma Xiaodong

This was the only middle school in the region, and the majority of the students were children of local peasants…. They were shy in front of a stranger and they looked at me with curiosity. To make conversation, I asked to see where they slept and they took me into their dorm, which was a deep cave room. It was already dark and there was no electricity. Under the dim light I saw a long *kang* from one end of the cave to the other. It must have been very crowded at night for the many boys. In the dorm, each boy kept a small box for cooked food. I asked them what food their parents had prepared for them. By now it was completely dark and I was unable to see anything. The kids competed with each other to invite me to feel their food. So I used my hand to touch. I didn't think I touched anything better than bread made of corn and millet.

Source: Ye Weili and Ma Xiaodong, *Growing Up in The People's Republic: Conversations Between Two Daughters of China's Revolution* (New York: Palgrave Macmillan, 2005) 145–146.

 The full text of **Document 16.4** is available on the CD-ROM.

DOCUMENT 16.5: Excerpts from the 1979 "U.S.–PRC Joint Communiqué on the Establishment of Diplomatic Relations" and the (U.S.) Taiwan Relations Act of 1979

Joint Communiqué

1. The United States of America and the People's Republic of China have agreed to recognize each other and to establish diplomatic relations as of January 1, 1979.
2. The United States recognizes the government of the People's Republic of China as the sole legal government of China….

Separately, the United States issued a statement on Taiwan.

Taiwan Relations Act

1. On that same date, January 1, 1979, the United States will notify Taiwan that it is terminating diplomatic relations and that the Mutual Defense Treaty between the United States and the Republic of China is being terminated in accordance with the provisions of the Treaty. The United States also states that it will be withdrawing its remaining military personnel from Taiwan within four months.
2. In the future, the American people and the people of Taiwan will maintain commercial, cultural, and other relations without official government representation and without diplomatic relations.

3. The United States is confident that the people of Taiwan face a peaceful and prosperous future. The United States continues to have an interest in the peaceful resolution of the Taiwan issue and expects that the Taiwan issue will be settled peacefully by the Chinese themselves.

SOURCE: http://usinfo.state.gov/eap/Archive_Index

 The full text of **Document 16.5** is available on the CD-ROM.

DOCUMENT 16.6: Excerpts from "The Fifth Modernization" by Wei Jingsheng, December 5, 1978

People should have democracy. When they ask for democracy, they are only demanding what is rightfully theirs. Anyone refusing to give it to them is a shameless bandit no better than a capitalist who robs workers of their money earned with their sweat and blood. Do the people have democracy now? No. Do they want to be masters of their own destiny? Definitely, yes. This was the reason for the Communist Party's victory over [the] Guomindang. But what then happened to the promise of democracy? The slogan "people's democratic dictatorship" was replaced by the "dictatorship of the proletariat." Even the "democracy" enjoyed by the infinitesimal portion—one among tens of millions—was abolished and replaced by the autocracy of the "Great Leader"....

SOURCE: http://www.echonyc.com/~wei/Fifth.html

 The full text of **Document 16.6** is available on the CD-ROM.

DOCUMENT 16.7: Excerpts from *A Higher Kind of Loyalty* by Liu Binyan, a Chinese journalist and activist writing about democracy, 1990

Evidently, these bloodthirsty rulers stake everything on the force of arms. They have lost all ability to understand the people, whom they fear and despise at the same time. They assume that the people, in the eighties, are just as submissive as they were in the twenties and thirties to the bloody rule of the warlords of the time, or just as responsive to the rallying calls and lying propaganda of the Communist Party as they were in the fifties and sixties.

On the surface, the rulers have attained their objective. Under the all-encompassing terrorism, China seems to have been cowed into silent submission. But this will actually create a bigger nightmare for them than if they had made some compromise.

The peaceful demonstration at Tiananmen Square was crushed, but it lit a flame in the hearts of countless people. The long-suffering Chinese people, after repeatedly being bullied and cheated, have finally given up their last illusions about the Chinese Communist Party....

I gave up my youth for the Communist Party in its struggle to seize state power. And now a handful of tyrants have betrayed the Party, turning themselves into enemies of the people in the real sense of the word. My generation has thrown itself into the struggle led by the Communist Party in the hope that our children will lead a better life, and now it is precisely the best and brightest of their generation who have died at the butchers' hands, or are fugitives fleeing from arrest.

Source: Liu Binyan, *A Higher Kind of Loyalty: A Memoir by China's Foremost Journalist,* trans. Hong Zhu (New York: Pantheon, 1990) 282.

 The full text of **Document 16.7** is available on the CD-ROM.

DOCUMENT 16.8: Excerpt from *Deng Xiaoping: My Father* by Deng Maomao, 1995

Deng Xiaoping was already seventy-five years old [in 1977] when he was reinstated the third time. He did not change his tenacious work style, which he had had for decades, his bold way of thinking, or his firm convictions. His conviction was that a new path of development, suited to China, could be blazed by taking a realistic and scientific approach and by making use of a multitude of assets and strengths, both ancient and modern, both Chinese and foreign. His conviction was that the Chinese people could lead a prosperous life and that China could become a strong and prosperous country....

Deng Xiaoping has held that the Chinese should build socialism with Chinese characteristics. Under his guidance, China has been trying to discover its own path of development and marching forward steadily. More than fifteen years have elapsed since 1978. China has made progress and achievements that are universally acknowledged. There is a popular view that the next century will be the century of the Asia-Pacific countries, and that among them China will attract the greatest attention. China is proud of this expectation....

In 1989 Deng Xiaoping resigned and retired. He retired so as to abolish the feudal life tenure system in China and to promote younger people to the leading posts.... At the advanced age of eighty-eight, he still goes around calling for further development of China.

Source: Deng Maomao, *Deng Xiaoping: My Father* (New York: Basic Books, 1995) 469–470.

DOCUMENT 16.9: Excerpts from "Deng Xiaoping" by George J. Church, *Time*, January 6, 1986

Politically and culturally, that fight [over how much to engage in trade with the West] has waxed and waned. China is still a one-party dictatorship and Deng has no intention of letting it become anything else. Rights taken for granted in the U.S., such as freedom of speech and assembly, are strictly controlled; some limited freedom of religion has been granted. Even so, a revised constitution adopted in 1982 marked a step toward making China a society governed by law rather than the whim of party officials.

In other ways, too, the dictatorship is less oppressive. Deng has permitted a popular press to spring up. Hundreds of new publications have appeared all over China; they cannot criticize policy, but they print lurid exposes of prostitution, pornography, corruption and black-marketeering by party officials (indeed, they sometimes seem to report little else). Culturally, Deng in 1983 permitted officials to start a crackdown on writers and artists, in the guise of a campaign against "spiritual pollution," probably as a gesture toward conservatives concerned that the pace of change was too rapid. But Deng speedily announced that the campaign had gone too far and called it off, leaving citizens and party officials alike in a quandary over just what is permitted and what is not.

SOURCE: George J. Church, "Deng Xiaoping," *Time* 6 January 1986.

Activities

Preliminary activities: Read the unit overview and the introduction to the lesson. To get a sense of how interconnected the government and the Communist Party are, you may also want to check the *CIA World Factbook* at https://www.cia.gov/library/publications/the-world-factbook.

ACTIVITY 1: Comparing the ideas of Marx, Mao, and Deng

Read Document 16.1, and paraphrase each quote. Working in small groups with large sheets of paper illustrate an evolutionary path for the change between one ideology and the next. Refer to a phylogenetic tree of the evolution of *Homo sapiens sapiens* as an example of this type of "evolutionary diagram." Take no more than three minutes for discussion, then complete the rest of the activity without speaking to each other. You may write or draw what you want, but no oral communication should take place. Then discuss the process of communicating in this method, and close with presentations of the illustrations to the larger group.

ACTIVITY 2: Analyzing Deng Xiaoping's proposals

Read and discuss the speech by Deng Xiaoping (16.2), focusing on the following questions:

1. What is your general impression of the speech?
2. Deng Xiaoping was walking a thin line in his speech. What pitfalls did he appear to be avoiding?
3. What problems did Deng highlight?
4. What criticisms were implied in the speech? Why were they implied and not stated openly?
5. What changes did he insist had to happen?
6. What general impression does this 1978 speech give regarding China's future?

7. If you were a person hearing this speech, how would you react to it?

8. If the president of the United States were to give a speech like this, how might it be received by the public, Congress, the press, or other countries?

9. Given the trends in the history of the Communist Party, how big a risk was this speech for Deng? What if it had not been well received?

ACTIVITY 3: **Examining the impact of change**

Read the letter by Pan Xiao (16.3) and discuss the language used. Summarize the points that Pan Xiao is trying to make. Write a response to Pan Xiao. Do you sympathize with her? Have you ever felt the same way? Discuss:

1. How might a school newspaper or national youth magazine with which you are familiar respond to a letter like this?

2. What does Pan Xiao's letter have to do with the economic and social changes taking place in China during this time?

Next, read two of the responses and discuss the contents.

1. What is the tone of these letters?

2. Do they offer any practical suggestions to Pan Xiao?

3. Pan Xiao's letter generated an extraordinary response. What does this tell us about the impact of change on individuals?

4. Examine copies of advice columns from current newspapers. Compare these samples to the Pan Xiao series.

5. What is similar and what is different in tone and content?

6. What are the differences in the meaning of life in China and in these samples?

Creative extension

Read the selection from Ma Xiaodong's article about a school in rural China (16.4). Compose a series of three journal entries as though you are a child in the middle school described by Ma Xiaodong. Working in groups of three, discuss the entries, then report to the class:

1. What are the recurrent or common themes in the journals?

2. How do you feel about life in rural China after reading this account and creating the diary entries?

3. Do you agree with Deng Xiaoping that modernization was needed in the areas he stressed? (See Activity 2, Document 16.2.)

4. Do you think it is possible to modernize a society rapidly enough to reach these children during their school years? Why or why not?

5. Do you think this is a typical or atypical report of a rural Chinese school? Why?

For homework, read related segments in Chapter 19 and research the current status of rural education in China. Did Deng's reforms reach the rural areas? What has changed in rural China in the past twenty-five years, and what has remained the same?

ACTIVITY 4: Debating changes in international relationships

First, read the overview of the history of Taiwan (on the CD-ROM in Additional Resources) to understand the context of these diplomatic documents. Then read excerpts from the communiqué (16.5).

1. Discuss the language used in this document. What is clear and what is ambiguous?
2. What do the two parties agree to do?
3. What is meant by the phrase "there is but one China and Taiwan is part of China"?

Then read the Taiwan Relations Act, which the U.S. Congress enacted the following year. Discuss:

1. What is the United States obligated to do for Taiwan under this Act?
2. Why might the U. S. government have proposed and passed this legislation?

Write briefly about how these two documents contradict each other. Divide the class into three groups. One group represents the PRC, the second represents the U.S. Congress, and the third represents Taiwan. The "PRC" should describe its response to the Taiwan Relations Act. "Congress" then states why it is in favor of this act. "Taiwan" should then present its position. Can the class resolve the differences? Write about or discuss the benefits of ambiguity in international politics. Does it help or hurt a delicate diplomatic situation to be vague?

ACTIVITY 5: The One-Child Policy: a debate

Examine population statistics for China (available on http://afe.easia.columbia.edu/china/geog/population.htm) and conduct research to learn more about the One-Child Policy and the way it was implemented. Create two teams. One team will take the position that the One-Child Policy is a necessary and proper policy for China to continue to pursue. The other will take the opposite stand. As you conduct your research, be aware that government policies have changed in recent years. Take those changes into account as you plan the debate.

To prepare for the debate, research:

- What are the traditional views regarding children in Chinese society?
- What is the current ratio of males to females in China?
- How popular are ultrasound machines?
- How widely available are abortions in China?

- What were the penalties for having more than one child? Was the policy enforced uniformly across China? Why?

- What, if anything, has changed in the ways the One-Child Policy is enforced?

- What was the rate of growth of China's population at ten-year intervals from 1950 to the present? Compare these rates to those in countries around the world.

- What are the consequences of spiraling population growth?

ACTIVITY 6: Essay examining Wei Jingsheng's "Fifth Modernization"

Review the Four Modernizations Deng Xiaoping proposed and his speech "Emancipate the Mind" (16.2). Discuss whether or not democracy is needed to make these four changes happen. What rights need to be protected in order for individuals to be able to "emancipate [their] minds"? Then read Wei Jingsheng's big character poster (16.6). Address in an essay: Given the nature of power in Chinese politics, is Wei's text threatening to the Chinese government? Why or why not and what would you do about it if you were in charge? For example, from a position of power, is it better to bring your adversary in, or to marginalize or arrest him or her?

ACTIVITY 7: Dissent and intellectuals

The intellectual class of China has often been at the forefront of calls for reform. Read the selections by Fang Lizhi and Liu Binyan (16.7). Role-play or compose a dialogue between the two writers, or between the two writers and a CCP cadre, in which Fang and Liu are accused of counter-revolutionary activity and have to defend themselves. In an essay, compare their actions and words with those of the intellectuals of the May Fourth Movement (see Chapter 8). Are Fang Lizhi and Liu Binyan's actions in keeping with this tradition? Why?

Alternatively, compose an essay about the proper role of the intellectual in fostering change in a nation. Should scientists stick to science, for example, or should they become involved in public affairs? Are these intellectuals qualified to talk about what political changes are needed? What are the benefits and/or drawbacks to society of their political involvement?

ACTIVITY 8: Tiananmen Square

Access online the picture of the civilian halting the line of tanks, or watch the prologue to *The Tank Man* (see Suggested Resources). Write a response to what you see happening, and imagine what could be going through the heads of both the civilian and the driver of the tank. Role-play, add thought balloons, or compose a dialogue to articulate this situation.

1. Who do you think the civilian was? Was he the type of person you would expect to take a stand? Why?
2. What role can an individual play to bring about change?
3. Why do some individuals take a stand and others not?
4. Argue one side: Was what this man did effective? How? Why?
5. What has this photo come to represent?

ACTIVITY 9: Will the real Deng Xiaoping please stand up?

Deng Xiaoping was an authoritarian leader, an economic liberalizer, and *Time* magazine's "Man of the Year" in 1985. He charmed the American public when he wore a ten-gallon hat and delighted the business community when he opened up the Chinese market to foreign investors. At the same time, he ruled the Party with a combination of political savvy and defensiveness. Research the many facets of Deng through his own words and the descriptions of his biographers. Work in teams of three to create a presentation in which you a) present Deng Xiaoping as having had a negative influence on China, b) present Deng Xiaoping as having had a positive influence on China, or c) illustrate the complexity of being the leader of China. After the class views each other's presentations, discuss what choices you had to make in order to meet the terms of the assignment. Do documentarians, biographers, and journalists make similar choices? What is the significance of these choices?

EXTENDED ACTIVITIES:

- Watch the film *All Under Heaven* (see Suggested Resources) about the economic life of one small village north of Beijing. Capture the essence of the documentary in a poster, collage, sketch, poem, or sculpture.
- Explore how Deng Xiaoping and the Politburo approached the topic of Mao Zedong's legacy.
- Learn about how the Chinese government dealt with the aftermath of the Cultural Revolution. What was the "literature of the wounded"? What purposes did it serve?
- Compare and contrast the Chinese leadership's approach to addressing the horrors and tragedies of the Cultural Revolution to the way other nations have confronted tragedies in their recent history (for example, South Africa, Rwanda, Cambodia, Serbia, Brazil, or Chile).
- Compare China's original constitution of 1954 to the revised one it adopted in 1982. (See Suggested Resources.)
- Research information about Wei Jingsheng. Read opinions regarding the justice (or lack thereof) of his first imprisonment. What is Wei Jingsheng doing today? Consider: Did he inherit the legacy of the May Fourth Movement, or was he an innovator?

- Learn about one of the leaders of the democracy movement in 1989: Chai Ling, Wu'erkaixi, Wang Dan, Cui Jian, or Feng Congde. Make a campaign poster for the leader as if he or she were running for office. What would their slogan be? What would their campaign promises be? For a follow-up discussion, research the post-1989 lives of these individuals and discuss where they are now, what they are doing, and whether they have come close to attaining their goals.

- Watch Frontline's documentary *The Tank Man* and Carma Hinton's documentary *The Gate of Heavenly Peace*, both of which examine the Tiananmen Square confrontation. (See Suggested Resources.) Compare and contrast the two documentaries.

- After watching *The Gate of Heavenly Peace*, hold a class discussion. Consider how the protest and leadership changed over the two-month period, why tensions escalated, and why the Chinese government responded with violence. What other options were there? Why were they not pursued?

- Write an essay addressing how China's turbulent twentieth-century history and the leaders' experiences during the Cultural Revolution might have affected the response of the government to the protests.

Suggested Resources

Books

Link, Perry. *Evening Chats in Beijing*. New York: W.W. Norton, 1992.
A compilation of discussions that the author, an American scholar of Chinese literature, had with many people from different walks of life in China about the reform activities that were happening throughout Chinese society in the 1980s.

Lord, Betty Bao. *Legacies: A Chinese Mosaic*. New York: Alfred A. Knopf, 1990.
In her memoir, the wife of a former U.S. ambassador to China interweaves news headlines with her perspectives on Chinese society and culture during the demonstrations of 1989.

Schell, Orville. *The Mandate of Heaven*. New York: Simon and Schuster, 1994.
A comprehensive overview of the events surrounding and including the Tiananmen Square incident of 1989.

Shambaugh, David. *Deng Xiaoping: Portrait of a Chinese Statesman*. New York: Oxford University Press, 2006.
A collection of essays that show many different parts of Deng's life and work.

Zhang Xinxin and Sang Ye. *Chinese Lives: An Oral History of Contemporary China*. New York: Pantheon Books, 1987.
An extraordinary collection of interviews with people from all walks of life. All were facing the challenges of the changes Deng Xiaoping had put in motion, and many were taking advantage of the opportunities.

Websites

https://www.cia.gov/library/publications/the-world-factbook/geos/ch.html#Govt CIA World Factbook

http://english.people.com.cn/constitution/constitution.html The Chinese constitution, amended in 1982

http://www.washingtonpost.com/wp-srv/newsweek/tiananmen.htm A 1998 retrospective that includes the photograph of the Chinese man standing in front of a tank in Tiananmen Square.

Rural Education

http://www.ruralchina.org/site/ The Rural China Education Foundation, a nongovernmental organization, includes information about present-day rural education in China with links to current initiatives and development campaigns.

One-Child Policy

http://www.overpopulation.com/faq/Population_Control/one_child.html A blog that gives an unofficial overview of what China has done and invites readers to discuss their responses to the information. Also links to other population control efforts around the world.

http://www.irmgard-coninx-stiftung.de/fileadmin/user_upload/pdf/roundtable07/Hao.pdf "Rethinking of China's Population Policy in Line with the Change in China's Development Strategy," by Dr. Yan Hao, August 2006.

http://www.cpirc.org.cn/en/eindex.htm This site from the China Population Information and Research Center includes China's "Ticking Population Clock" as well as many articles pertaining to population issues.

http://afe.easia.columbia.edu On the *Asia for Educators* website, go to "population."

http://www.allcountries.org/china_statistics/4_4_basic_statistics_on_national_population. html Various statistics on population.

Deng Xiaoping

http://library.thinkquest.org/26469/movers-and-shakers/deng.html A brief biography and summary of his career and accomplishments

http://english.peopledaily.com.cn/dengxp/ Selected Works

Online Lessons

http://afe.easia.columbia.edu/china/geog/population.htm Lessons on population growth and challenges.

Films

All Under Heaven (58 mins; 1986) *part of the* One Village in China *series, this documentary directed and produced by Carma Hinton and Richard Gordon captures the various ways in which the CCP has tackled the challenge of land reform and gives insight into rural traditions.*

The Gate of Heavenly Peace (189 mins, 1995) *directed by Carma Hinton and Richard Gordon. The detailed and balanced account of what led to the violent confrontation in June 1989 is the result of six years of research. The documentary links the student demonstrations to the legacy of student activism in twentieth-century China and captures the idealism as well as the confusion within the movement. "A deep, powerful and rivetingly complex study of Tiananmen," wrote Newsweek.*

The Tank Man (90 mins 2006), produced by PBS/ Frontline, can be viewed online at http://www. pbs.org/wgbh/pages/frontline/tankman/view/ It provides a simpler look at the events in and around Tiananmen Square on June 5, 1989.

■ **A CLOSER LOOK**

Zhao Ziyang: Economic Reformer

Zhao Ziyang was born in 1919 and began his career in Guangdong Province working for agricultural improvement. During the Cultural Revolution, he was purged and ridiculed as a "stinking remnant of the landlord class." He was later rehabilitated by Zhou Enlai and became the governor of Sichuan Province, where he revived the economy by implementing a series of reforms aimed at developing a market-based economy. Deng Xiaoping brought him into the central government, and Zhao became the premier of the Chinese State Council and eventually the secretary general of the Party. He was widely viewed as Deng Xiaoping's successor after the death of Hu Yaobang in March 1989.

Zhao was a reformer and a modernizer, and during the Tiananmen Square protests he attempted to find common ground with the student protesters. He actually appeared in the square and pleaded with the students to leave before it was too late. He then disappeared for a time, and later it was announced that he had been stripped of his titles and placed under house arrest, though he did get out to play golf in Beijing and was never expelled from the Party. He died in January 2005.

■ *Look online to see how Zhao's death was marked in China, and compare that to the death of Hu Yaobang in 1989. Why was Zhao's death dealt with in this way?*

Li Peng: Promoting Social Control

Li Peng was born in 1928 and was just seven when the Guomindang government executed his father for being a Communist sympathizer. A few years later, Zhou Enlai adopted him and in 1948 sent Li to the Soviet Union to study. "He was carefully groomed for leadership," writes Jonathan Spence in *The Search for Modern China* (688). In 1982, he joined the Central Committee, and in 1987, he became a member of the Politburo.

In 1988, Deng Xiaoping picked Li Peng to become premier, succeeding Zhao Ziyang. Li emphasized stability over reform, and he became one of the leading voices for social control as the economy liberalized. When the student protests broke out, he advocated for a crackdown. Li met with a group of students protesting with a hunger strike and was chastised on television by students who accused him of being out of touch. Some believe that this interaction led Li to orchestrate the PLA action as a response to such insolence. Li held on to the post of premier for a second term before stepping down. He remains a shadowy presence in the government, and his actual authority is unknown at this point.

■ *Read the transcript of the televised interaction between the students and Li Peng, available at: http://www.tsquare.tv/ chronology/May18mtg. html (or watch The Gate of Heavenly Peace, directed by Carma Hinton). What kind of interactions was Li probably accustomed to as a leader in the CCP? Does this exchange make Li's response acceptable? What other reasons might Li have had for advocating a hard-line approach?*

UNIT FIVE

Contemporary China

UNIT OVERVIEW

By Liz Nelson

China in the first decade of the twenty-first century is a vastly different country than China in the first fifteen years after Mao Zedong founded the People's Republic of China, or even the early years of Deng Xiaoping's reforms.

China's economy is the third largest in the world,[1] and since it became a member of the World Trade Organization (WTO) in 2001, its volume of trade has mushroomed: it is now the world's third largest. In 1978, foreign direct investment (FDI) in China was $0. By 2003–2004, it had reached a total of $448 billion.[2] China is a central figure in the global economy, and the benefits for Chinese citizens have been many.

As "socialism with Chinese characteristics" has unfolded, however, the shift away from state-owned enterprises and virtually guaranteed life-long employment and benefits (the "iron rice bowl") has made many middle-aged

workers feel extremely vulnerable. The extraordinary economic growth has also increased economic disparities. "Today…there are many 'Chinas,'" write the authors of *China: The Balance Sheet*: "rural and urban, wealthy and poor, educated and illiterate, international and isolated. Within this context of diversity and disparity, China's citizens and leadership are grappling with unprecedented domestic dynamism, coming to grips with globalization's challenges, and deliberating different political and economic futures."[3]

Most of the new economic prosperity has happened in coastal cities, while in the rural areas in particular, approximately 400 million people subsist on less than $2 a day. Even the rudimentary **healthcare** available during the first twenty years of the PRC is now gone, leaving people to travel considerable distances to access care and forcing them to pay for services out of pocket. Too often, the rural poor simply go without. These realities notwithstanding, it is important to note overall improvements in healthcare in China. In the 1950s, life expectancy in China was 35 years; in 2003, it was 71. Similarly, the rate of infant mortality has shown dramatic improvement.

---

[1] After the United States and Japan.

[2] Harry G. Gelber, *The Dragon and the Foreign Devils: China in the World, 1100 B.C. to the Present* (London: Bloomsbury, 2007) 401.

[3] C. Fred Bergsten et al., *China: The Balance Sheet: What the World Needs to Know Now About the Emerging Superpower* (New York: Public Affairs/Center for Strategic and International Studies/Institute for International Economics, 2006) 16.

As in healthcare, in **education** the disparities between urban and rural China are significant. Well-equipped, challenging "key" schools in the cities prepare students for universities. In many rural areas, on the other hand, students need to board at schools in the closest larger town in order to attend bare-bones middle schools. In 2007, the government launched new initiatives to address some of these inequities. Despite the ongoing problems, if one compares education before 1949 to the present, one sees stunning improvements in areas such as basic literacy: the Chinese have cut the number of people who cannot read or write by two-thirds, to 7 percent of the population.[4]

As a result of work opportunities in the cities, poverty in the countryside, and a relaxation of policies regulating people's ability to move, China is experiencing the largest **human migration** in history. More than 140 million people—about 20 percent of the working-age population—have left their homes in search of jobs. This is putting stress on housing and social services in the cities. However, the money those working in the city send home has helped to pull millions above the official poverty line.

The People's Republic of China faces **domestic political challenges**, too. The Chinese Communist Party's top priority is to manage a rapidly changing economy and society without losing political control. Recently, to offset growing consumerism, the Party has not only tolerated but encouraged the practice of traditional Chinese philosophies and religions, as long as the practitioners do not play any political role. Economic reforms and openness to the outside world have brought with them an exchange of views that was definitely not possible in the 1950s and 1960s. But the government continues to try—with limited success—to control Internet access. Finally, while the "rule of law" is making some inroads in China, civil liberties and protections, as the West knows them, are not something on which Chinese citizens can rely.

One of the gravest challenges Chinese leadership and citizens face is that of creating a sustainable economy, one that will not destroy **the environment**. "China's economic explosion has created an ecological implosion. Severe air and water pollution along with water shortages are threatening human health, industrial production, and crops. Land degradation and deforestation are exacerbating floods and desertification."[5] Though the central government has welcomed help from abroad and passed scores of laws and regulations to address the crisis, much of the responsibility for enforcing these is in the hands of local officials. Too often, their sole concern appears to be immediate profits rather than pollution control.

Long gone are Mao Zedong's antagonistic **foreign relations** with the West. Under Deng Xiaoping and the leaders who have followed, the PRC has moved back into a leadership role regionally. Furthermore, as a permanent member of the United Nations Security Council, China's is an important voice in world affairs—which is not to say that the relationships with foreign nations are always free of tension. After fifteen years of quite open hostility, the dialogue between China and Japan has begun to be productive. Both the People's Republic of China's and Taiwan's leadership appear to be comfortable maintaining the status quo. China's leaders seek to dispel concern over their increased military spending;[6] they insist that their intentions are to coexist in peace. The relationship between China and the United States is becoming increasingly complex and challenging. Chinese leadership watches the world superpower with few illusions, ever cautious about talk in Washington of "containing" China or in any way interfering in Chinese domestic affairs.

China, writes Harry Gelber in *The Dragon and the Foreign Devils*, is "emerging from two centuries of weakness and trauma…to tell the world… 'presume not that I am the thing I was.'"[7]

---

[4] Gelber 18.

[5] Gelber 53.

[6] Estimates of how much China is spending vary, but even using the highest number suggested by the U.S. Department of Defense, China's military budget is about one-tenth of that of the United States.

[7] Gelber 434.

CHAPTER 17

China Steps Back onto the World Stage

By Todd Whitten

Chapter Contents

Expanded Special Economic Zones
Regional Relations
WTO Membership
Army Modernizations

Organizing Idea

China's emergence as an economic world power since the 1990s has led to significant gains as well as increased tensions—domestically, regionally, and globally.

Key Questions

What is the purpose of China's Special Economic Zones? What effects have they had on China's economy and populace?

Why is unification with Taiwan so important to China?

What has been the impact of WTO membership for China?

What has been the impact of China's WTO membership on the global economy?

What have been the sources of tension between China and Japan?

Key Terms

Foreign Direct Investment (FDI)
Gross Domestic Product (GDP)
iron rice bowl
Special Economic Zones (SEZ)
World Trade Organization (WTO)

probrubly

Essay

As the twenty-first century approached, China began to reassert itself as a global economic presence. After the death of Deng Xiaoping (邓小平) in 1997, first Jiang Zemin (江泽民) and then, in 2003, Hu Jintao (胡锦涛) took over the reins of government. Both leaders continued and expanded Deng Xiaoping's policies: Special Economic Zones (SEZ) (经济特区), integration with the global economy, and modernization of the People's Liberation Army, together with the careful monitoring of political dissent. The economic reforms begun by Deng Xiaoping in 1978 have over time lifted some 200 million Chinese citizens out of poverty, made about 300,000 Chinese millionaires (in U.S. dollars),[1] and created conditions for an ever-expanding middle class. In the past few years, Chinese leaders have reached out to the global community by working with economic organizations such as the Association of Southeast Asian Nations (ASEAN) and joining the World Trade Organization (WTO), by pursuing a position of leadership in East Asia, and by exerting their authority as a permanent member of the United Nations Security Council.[2]

One China

In 1997, the British finally returned Hong Kong (香港) to China, a political and symbolic victory much celebrated across the country; this was repeated in 1999 when the Portuguese handed over Macao (澳门). Integrating the territories that had been under foreign control (see Chapter 5) into China as "one country, two systems" (一国两制) has required diplomatic skill. The PRC bears the responsibility for defending the territory and managing the foreign affairs of Hong Kong and Macao. However, Hong Kong is responsible for its own monetary,

legal, and immigration institutions, and for maintaining its police force and customs structure. Often at issue is the autonomy of the local governing body of Hong Kong: How independent is it? What are the limits on its decision-making? The questions brought up by the re-integration of Hong Kong and Macao suggest ways in which Taiwan may eventually be reunited with mainland China. At present, while Taiwan (台湾) continues to have de facto independence, both the People's Republic of China (中华人民共和国) and Taiwan's leadership seem willing to preserve the status quo, rather than Beijing pushing for immediate reunification or Taiwan's leaders suggesting independence, which Beijing has made clear it will not permit.

Relationship with Japan

China's relationship with Japan has undergone changes since Japan's occupation of significant areas of China between 1932 and 1945 (see Chapters 9 and 11). Beginning in the early 1990s and continuing for about fifteen years, the relationship was strained. The issues included China's role in East Asia, the security alliance between the United States and Japan, the ways in which Japan addressed the history with China, and territorial disputes. Yet at the same time, Japan and China have become increasingly linked economically. China is Japan's largest trading partner; Japan is China's third-largest trading partner (after the European Union and the United States). Neither country wishes to disrupt this vibrant economic relationship, and in 2007, leaders of the two countries began a more productive exchange.

WTO Membership

In 2001, China became a member of the World Trade Organization. This has caused significant changes in China's and the global economy. While some politicians in developed countries like to blame trade deficits and economic uncertainties on China's membership in the

---

[1] Bergsten et al., 3, 6.

[2] ASEAN's ten member countries are Brunei Darussalam, Cambodia, Indonesia, Laos, Malaysia, Myanmar, the Philippines, Singapore, Thailand, and Vietnam.

WTO, most economists note that the impact has generally been positive. For example, foreign investment in China has increased, but it also grew in the ten ASEAN countries, up to a record $37 billion in 2005.[3] China's factories assemble products—from toys to high-tech items—out of parts made elsewhere in the world. Many of the firms involved are foreign, so their stockholders benefit. Virtually all successful corporations around the world share the goal to have work done where it can be done most effectively and efficiently; this is not limited to assembly in China. The finished products are sold inexpensively around the world, which especially benefits anyone who has limited discretionary income. In addition, as China's economy continues to boom, the World Bank has predicted that Chinese *imports* would grow more than U.S. imports for the first time in 2007.[4]

The bi-polar world that existed in the second half of the twentieth century has transformed itself into a multi-faceted, interdependent one. China's relationship with its immediate neighbors and as a member of the global community is changing. These changing conditions call for flexible, thoughtful diplomatic approaches from everyone involved.

Primary Sources

DOCUMENT 17.1: Excerpt from a speech by former premier Zhao Ziyang on the purpose of Special Economic Zones, 1984

The special economic zones…[and open cities] are the bridgeheads in our opening to the outside world, and they should play the role of springboard. *On the one hand*, they should import advanced foreign technology, equipment, and management…absorb and digest them; apply them in innovations; and transfer them to the interior. *On the other hand*, they should send commodities produced in the coastal areas with foreign technology to the interior, and export the latter's raw materials and produce, with added value after processing… to the international market.

SOURCE: Foreign Broadcast Information Services, *Daily Report, China*, December 26, 1984. Qtd. in Christopher J. Smith, *China: People and Places in the Land of One Billion* (Boulder, CO: Westview Press, 1991) 106.

DOCUMENT 17.2: "Shenzhen: Showcase for China's Economic Growth," *China Daily*, February 4, 2002

Shenzhen City, one of China's five special economic zones, has had an annual gross domestic product (GDP) growth rate of 25 percent ever since the late Chinese leader Deng Xiaoping's tour to south China's Guangdong Province 10 years ago. On January 19–22, 1992, Deng Xiaoping, the architect general of China's reform and opening policy, visited Shenzhen and called for bold measures to accelerate reform and opening during his fact-finding and inspection tour of the south China city.

---

[3] "The export juggernaut," *The Economist*, 29 Mar. 2007.

[4] "The export juggernaut."

According to local sources, Shenzhen's GDP reached 190.82 billion *yuan* (about 23 billion U.S. dollars) last year [2001], compared with 31.73 billion *yuan* (about 3.82 billion U.S. dollars) in 1992. Over the decade the per capita consumption of urban residents in Shenzhen has shot up to over 20,000 *yuan* (about 2,409 U.S. dollars), from less than 5,000 *yuan* (about 602 U.S. dollars).

Shenzhen, which used to be a small town with about 20,000 residents, has grown into a boom city, which is now highly rated throughout the country as one of China's leading exporters and having won the most "garden-like city in the world " award in 2000....

SOURCE: "Shenzhen: Showcase for China's Economic Growth," *China Daily*, 4 February 2002.

 The full text of **Document 17.2** is available on the CD-ROM.

DOCUMENT 17.3: "China's WTO entry of great impact," *China Daily*, December 3, 2006

As the world's most populous nation marks the fifth anniversary of its entry into the global trade body, it is time for both the 1.3 billion Chinese themselves and the rest of the world to take stock of the changes. For the well-heeled resident of Beijing or Shanghai, the advantages of WTO membership are obvious: His imported Mercedes is cheaper; his local Citibank offers more services; his Wal-Mart sells a wider variety of products. But China's entry into the WTO has not just created winners. Reduced tariffs on agricultural produce have threatened the livelihoods of hundreds of millions of farmers.

Beyond affecting the individual lives of the Chinese, the WTO has also profoundly and irreversibly changed the Chinese economy as a whole....

"In this period of expanding trade, every country has to make some adjustments. Some of its industries expand and other industries tend to contract," said Dollar [World Bank country director for China]. "In China, for example, more than 100,000 people have been released from state-owned banks, as the state-owned banks adjust to this more competitive environment."...

China's entry into the WTO has brought about monumental changes in global trade flows that it will take a long time to absorb, according to Cliff Stevenson [a UK-based consultant].... "It's quite hard to predict when the transition will be over, because I don't think the world has ever seen anything like this before," he said.

SOURCE: "China's WTO entry of great impact," *China Daily*, 3 December 2006.

 The full text of **Document 17.3** is available on the CD-ROM.

DOCUMENT 17.4: Excerpt from "China on the Move" by the RAND National Defense Research Institute (U.S.), 2005

The changes in the international security environment have had a profound impact on the threat perceptions of the People's Liberation Army (PLA) and its civilian masters, creating bureaucratic and political support for accelerated military modernization. For the PLA, two of the most important perceived changes were the rise of dominant U.S. military power, as evidenced in Gulf Wars I & II, Kosovo, Afghanistan, and Iraq and the evident desire on the part of the sole remaining superpower to use that military power to pursue a global unilateral agenda.

These changes in PLA perceptions have also significantly shaped the trajectory of its military buildup and rapid acceleration of equipment upgrades and doctrinal revision that had heretofore been relatively gradual. Beginning in the early 1990s and accelerating after 1999, PLA modernization was elevated from a relatively low priority to a core element of national policy....

SOURCE: David C. Gompert et al., eds., *China on the Move: A Franco-American Analysis of Emerging Chinese Strategic Policies and their Consequences for Transatlantic Relations* (Santa Monica, CA: RAND Corp., 2005) viii.

 The full text of **Document 17.4** is available on the CD-ROM.

DOCUMENT 17.5: Excerpts from "Prime Minister's war shrine visits the issue that matters, Beijing tells Tokyo" in the *Australian*, November 2005

Ambassador Wang Yi made it clear yesterday that of all the recent frictions between Japan and China, the "historical problem" symbolized by the Yasukuni visits had done most to poison the bilateral relationship.

"We need to resolve the situation as soon as possible," said Mr. Wang. "This is not a situation we can simply avoid." Though he insisted that anti-Japanese riots that swept China in April were not sanctioned by the Beijing government, Mr. Wang pointedly declined to rule out further trouble....

Mr. Wang, one of China's most senior diplomats, dismissed [the Japanese prime minister] Mr. Koizumi's contention that he and China's top leaders should hold a summit to deal with other differences, while leaving the Yasukuni issue in abeyance. Those problems include a territorial dispute in the East China Sea covering potentially large gas fields, China's objection to Japan gaining a permanent UN Security Council seat, and the two countries' intense competition for influence in the rest of Asia.

SOURCE: Peter Alford, "PM's war shrine visits the issue that matters, Beijing tells Tokyo," *Australian* 25 Nov. 2005.

 The full text of **Document 17.5** is available on the CD-ROM.

DOCUMENT 17.6: "Japanese investment into China hits record high" by David Ibison, *Financial Times*, April 3, 2006

According to the Japan External Trade Organization, Japanese investment in China rose 19.8 percent to $6.5 billion in 2005. A Japanese official suggested that the business relationship between the two countries was strong enough to withstand political difficulties. He also pointed out that Japan's market is flat and the population is declining, so the Chinese market is very important for Japan. However, the historic issues remain.

Hu Jintao, China's president, said late last week he would only meet with Junichiro Koizumi, Japan's prime minister, if he stopped visiting the Yasukuni shrine in Tokyo, which commemorates Japan's war dead. In response, senior politicians in Japan criticised China and called into question increases in its military spending, saying China was becoming a threat to its Asian neighbours. This prompted Wen Jiabao, the Chinese premier, to say in Australia on Monday that China posed no threat and that its defence policy was "transparent."

SOURCE: David Ibison, "Japanese investment into China hits record high," *Financial Times* 3 Apr. 2006.

DOCUMENT 17.7: "Peace breaking out," *The Economist*, April 4, 2007

As for the Yasukuni shrine, to which [Prime Minister] Mr Abe has traditionally been a more committed visitor than has Mr Koizumi [his predecessor], the Chinese believe that they have an understanding from him that he will not go while he is prime minister. Afterwards, says one Chinese policymaker, he can even go and live at Yasukuni, for all the Chinese will care.

If this minimum requirement—no prime ministerial visit, or at least no public one, to Yasukuni—is met, then the Chinese government seems determined to build a new "strategic partnership." Japan seems inclined to reciprocate. In a surprisingly short time, a wide range of topics has come up: economic and environmental co-operation; mechanisms to ease territorial disputes in the East China Sea, complicated by possibly large deposits of gas and oil; even confidence-building measures between the two countries' armed forces.

Mr Wen's visit will formalise a new cabinet-level dialogue on economic co-operation. In addition, Japanese firms will be offered the chance to bid for nuclear-power projects, as well as for parts of proposed high-speed railway lines between Beijing and Shanghai, Beijing and Wuhan, and Dalian and Harbin in Manchuria—whose railways imperial Japan once controlled. Japanese investment and know-how will be sought for environmental projects, including on energy efficiency.

SOURCE: "Peace breaking out," *The Economist*, 4 Apr. 2007.

 The full text of **Document 17.7** is available on the CD-ROM.

Activities

ACTIVITY 1: Mapping and analyzing the Special Economic Zones

On a map of China, place the Special Economic Zones and cities open to foreign trade and investment, established by Deng Xiaoping (Item 17.A). Why were these cities chosen and why were the zones set up in these areas? Read Premier Zhao Ziyang's explanation regarding the SEZ and open cities (17.1). Next read the *People's Daily* article "Shenzhen, Showcase for China's Economic Growth" (17.2) and additional information on the "China in Brief" website (see Suggested Resources). Discuss what might be some of the advantages and disadvantages of placing all the SEZ near the coast. Then read the introductory essay.

Given their definition and purpose, write an essay arguing that the Special Economic Zones and "open cities" are either a positive or negative policy for the Chinese economy. Consider the impact on people of the shift toward capitalism in light of the guarantees of the "iron rice bowl." Discuss in class the challenges of taking a pro or con stance such as this.

ACTIVITY 2: Analyzing the impact of foreign retailers

Watch "Chapter 4: China's View of Wal-Mart: Big Partner," a selection from the Frontline documentary "Is Wal-Mart Good for America?" available at http://www.pbs.org/wgbh/pages/frontline/shows/walmart. Discuss:

1. Is Wal-Mart helpful or harmful for enhancing relations between the United States and the People's Republic of China? What are the pros and cons for each of the three sides (the United States, China, Wal-Mart)? Who benefits and in what ways?

2. If you were advising the leaders of the People's Republic of China or the United States, would you be for or against Wal-Mart's presence in China? Why?

ACTIVITY 3: Research: China joins the WTO

Read the introduction describing the World Trade Organization (WTO) at http://www.wto.org. Examine the statistics comparing China's economy in 2001 to 2006 (Item 17.B) and read "China's WTO entry of great impact," (17.3), written on the five-year anniversary of China's becoming a WTO member. Working with a partner, choose one of the following questions, research it, and prepare a three-minute presentation for your classmates that includes a handout of some kind.

1. Why was China interested in joining the WTO?

2. What was the position of one the following developed countries on China's accession to the WTO: Australia, Japan, the countries of the European Union, the United States?

3. Who was the most involved in the negotiations for including China? Why? What were that country's concerns?

4. In order to join the WTO, China agreed to meet a series of benchmarks. What are the benchmarks? Is China meeting them? What may happen if they are not met?

5. What have been the effects in China of WTO membership?

6. Describe the effects of China's membership on any one of the following: countries in the European Union, Australia, the United States, Japan, India, or countries in Central America.

Listen to the others' presentations and take notes using the handouts from the groups. Finally, complete the statement: "The effects of China becoming a member of the World Trade Organization have been _____." Write an essay providing details to support your position.

ACTIVITY 4: Weighing the modernization of the People's Liberation Army

Read the RAND Corporation analysis of further modernization in the PLA (17.4) and do additional research online to explore a range of views—Chinese and non-Chinese—on the topic of China's armed forces. Compare China's defense budget with those of the United States and Japan. (Note that Japan's post–World War II constitution prohibits it from maintaining armed forces for any purpose other than national defense.) Then write a position paper in which you analyze the PLA's relative strengths and weaknesses, and answer the question: Should China's neighbors feel threatened, or should China's statement that it is "pursuing economic development with peaceful intentions" be taken at face value?

ACTIVITY 5: Examining the shifting relationship between China and Japan

Begin by referring to Chapter 11 for information about Japan's eight-year occupation of much of China (1937–1945). Then read the 2005 news report about the Japanese prime minister's annual visits to the Yasukuni war memorial (17.5).

1. According to the article, what have been the issues between China and Japan?

2. Next, read the 2006 article from the *Financial Times* about record high Japanese investments in China (17.6).

3. Note the main points in the report.

4. Finally, read "Peace breaking out," reporting on events in 2007 (17.7).

5. What was changing between the two Asian nations and why?

6. What measures were the two countries putting in place, and why were they taking these steps?

7. Check a major international news source to learn what recent developments have taken place between China and Japan.

Discuss, as a class, what conclusions can be drawn from the shifting relationship. Come to consensus as to the advice diplomats should give to both countries (A good supplemental article on the subject of regional dominance is "China Influence in Asia Concerns Japan, Ministry Says" by Sachiko Sakimaki, at http://www.bloomberg.com/apps/news?pid=newsarchive&sid=aWAGMLS7iEew).

Creative extension:

Create a visual piece of art (poster, sculpture, cartoon, drawing, comic strip) that captures the relationship between China and Japan. Write a caption to go with it.

Suggested Resources

Books

Bergsten, Fred C., et al. *China: The Balance Sheet: What the World Needs to Know Now About the Emerging Superpower*. New York: Public Affairs/ Center for Strategic and International Studies/ Institute for International Economics, 2006.
A thoughtful balanced look at China's extraordinary economic growth and its many implications. The book is short and very readable.

Hessler, Peter. *Oracle Bones: A Journey Between China's Past and Present*. New York: Harper-Collins, 2006.
Chapters 2, 4, 7, 11, 17, and 22 will be of strong interest to students wishing to learn about the lives of young Chinese adults in the new economy.

Websites

https://www.cia.gov/library/publications/the-world-factbook/index.html The *CIA World Factbook* provides excellent statistics on China today.

http://www.china.org.cn/e-china/index.htm "China in Brief" includes multiple topics.

http://www.wto.org The official website of the WTO gives extensive information about many aspects of the World Trade Organization.

http://www.uschina.org/public/wto The website of the U.S.-China Business Council, an organization of U.S. companies doing business in China, has an archive of all its reports to Congress on the progress the PRC has made or not made in meeting its obligations as laid out in the accession to the WTO agreement. The oral testimony is extensive, but for the most part easily digested.

http://www.bbc.co.uk/politics97/hk Describes the 1997 handover of Hong Kong, including photographs, audio, and video resources.

http://english.people.com.cn/data/people/hujintao.shtml An official biography of China's President Hu Jintao.

Film

China Blue (88 mins; 2005) *In Chinese (Cantonese and Mandarin) with subtitles and explanatory text. The powerful and disturbing documentary captures the lives of teen girls in a Chinese factory that produces denim jeans. The film provides another perspective on what China's involvement in the global economy means to one segment of the population and the role Western corporations and consumers play.*

■ **A CLOSER LOOK**

Shanghai

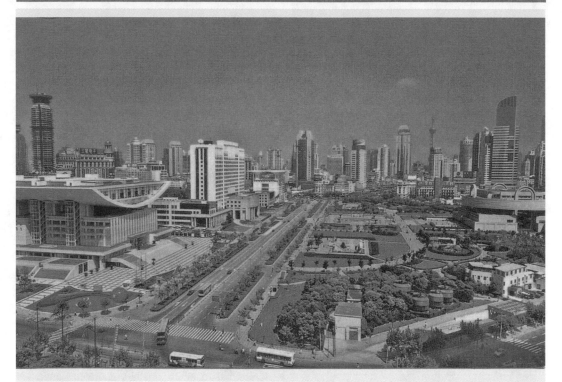

■ *Access the color image on the CD-ROM to view it in greater detail. List twenty details from the photograph. Next, working in small groups, create a master list of details. Compare Shanghai as shown in this photograph to cities you've seen. What does this suggest about China's modernization?*

CHAPTER 18

The Consequences of Modernization

By Michael Abraham

Chapter Contents

New Consumers
A Changing Economy
Changing Demographics
Religion and Politics

Organizing Idea

Modernization has affected different segments of China's population in very different ways. The extraordinary pace of economic development is leading people to adapt to dramatically altered living and working patterns.

Key Questions

How has the shift to a modern economy led to a rural-urban divide in Chinese society? Is this divide a new phenomenon?

How is the Chinese government responding to the pressures of a modern society?

What benefits and problems do Chinese people face, living in this era of change?

Key Terms

demographics
floating population
migrant worker
multinational company
state-run economy
yuan

Essay

One of the most interesting consequences of China's rapid pace of modernization has been the changing face of Chinese society. From the style of clothing Chinese people wear, to the increased quantities of food in the countryside, to the influx of foreign-owned companies, China today looks very different than it did a generation ago.

New Consumers

The face of a homogeneous, Maoist society where men and women all wear drab gray or blue tunic jackets, pants, and caps may soon become as much a remnant of the past as that of a society whose scholar-officials once wore silk robes. In the cities, in particular, increased capitalism and the growth of free enterprise have helped generate an abundance of consumer goods, such as DVDs and designer jeans. Young adults can now choose their own jobs and career paths. In the face of such change and opportunity, it is easy to understand why the generation that came of age under Mao Zedong (毛泽东) (see Chapters 13 and 14) might harbor resentment, particularly when some of those changes erode the previous guarantee of lifelong job security and social services.

The faces of China's industrial and market sectors have also changed. Today, private enterprises, foreign companies, and multinationals compete where state-run industries and factories once enjoyed monopolies. One does not have to walk far in a Chinese city before spotting a McDonald's, KFC, Starbucks, or Pizza Hut. Pedestrian malls and luxury auto dealerships now also dot the urban landscape. In addition, China's quest to modernize has resulted in large-scale investments in infrastructure, which has increased both the quantity and quality of roads, bridges, communications services, and high-rise housing units.

But while the standard of living has risen sharply during the reform era, the rise has been very uneven, especially when urban areas are compared to rural areas. By and large, incomes are higher and social services such as education and health care are better in the cities. (See Chapter 19 for information about educational disparities.)

Changing Demographics

China's total fertility rate[1] dropped dramatically from 5.8 in 1970 to 1.8 in the early 2000s. Experts credit modernization and improved living standards as well as the One-Child Policy.[2] In part as a response to protests charging human rights violations, the Population and Family Planning Law of 2001 called for far more flexibility in implementing the one-child goal and allows for a number of exceptions to the policy. While the One-Child Policy has met its goal to control population growth, it has resulted in several challenging side effects. The age distribution in the population is changing dramatically.[3] In addition, a gender gap exists; China's national census of 2000 showed 117 males for every 100 females. According to Chinese tradition, a son takes care of his parents in their senior years. Since farmers don't receive pensions, a son is, in effect, a couple's guarantee for security in their old age. (See Chapter 16 for additional information about the One-Child Policy.)

Another demographic change in China is the steady rise in the number of migrant laborers. While the great majority of China's population still makes its livelihood in agriculture, the opportunity to make more money in the cities

---

[1] The total number of children born per woman.

[2] Yan Hao, "Rethinking of China's Population Policy in Line with the Change in China's Development Strategy." International Working Paper/Essay Competition and Workshop of the Irmgard Coninx Foundation, the Social Science Research Center Berlin and Humboldt University Berlin. Wissenschaftszentrum Berlin für Sozialforschung, Berlin. 14–20 Feb. 2007.

[3] This demographic shift is a challenge for all developed countries. In China, experts estimate that in 2010, citizens 65 and older will make up 8.23% of the population. By 2050, they will constitute 24.25%.

has led to a "floating population" of workers, estimated at 140 million, moving from rural to urban areas. This phenomenon—a trend seen around the world—has put a strain on city services, as well as the fabric of the traditional Chinese family. In some cases grandparents are stepping in for absent parents and, beyond caring for children while their parents work, are actually raising them, at least for a few years.

The Changing Face of Religion and Politics

Religion was strongly repressed during the Mao years, but today the practice of religious beliefs is much more evident. Despite the more tolerant attitude, there have been clashes between the government and religious groups of different persuasions, including Buddhists in Tibet (西藏), Muslims in Xinjiang (新疆), and Christians. Any time one of these groups, or one such as the Falun Gong (法轮功), is able to organize its followers, the Communist Party becomes very nervous, fearing possible political activity.

The government continues its efforts to control the pace of political reform, but China in the twenty-first century is a dramatically different society than China in the 1950s and 60s. While today's calls for greater political openness and less state corruption have yet to match the high profile outcry of the 1989 Tiananmen (天安门) demonstrations (see Chapter 16), dissidents have proved effective at using the Internet to exchange and express their views. As a result, the government now restricts and censors the activities of Internet companies in China. At the same time, however, political reform is moving forward. For example, village self-government has been carried out since 1998. Entrepreneurs are now admitted into the CCP, and formal establishment of non-governmental organizations (NGOs) is permitted. In addition, there is a growing interest in recognizing the importance of the rule of law.

The Chinese government believes that human rights are important, but that for developing countries the communal rights to survival and economic development outweigh the rights to personal freedom of thought, expression, religion and organization. Nevertheless, in 2004, the Party added a new clause to the Constitution stating that "the State respects and protects human rights."

Primary Sources

DOCUMENT 18.1: Photographs taken in China, 2006

Plant vendor in Beijing

The Conference Center in Pudong district,
Shanghai
(*Photos by Liz Nelson*)

 The slide show "Contemporary China: A Study in Contrasts" is on the CD-ROM.

DOCUMENT 18.2: Excerpts from one of four individual stories from the "new China," 2005–2006

Zang Jianhe, born in Qingdao, Shandong Province, used to run a snack stall that sold handmade *jiaozi*[4] at the Wanchai Ferry in Hong Kong. In its heyday, customers would queue for more than an hour for a taste of Zang's *jiaozi*. "A competitive product is a must for any business to start with," says Zang. Today, Wanchai Ferry *jiaozi* come frozen in fine packaging at supermarkets and shopping malls in many large cities. Zang sees much growth in the market for frozen *jiaozi* and jokes, "If we are dedicated to the *jiaozi* business, it will prove to be even more profitable than real estate speculation." In 1996, she invested in a 1,200-square-meter workshop of international standards, putting the stamp of quality on her brand.

One feature of Zang's success has been her ability to know "when to say 'no' and when to say 'yes.'" After declining several proposals for joint-venture operations, Zang chose the 100-year-old United States-based Pillsbury Group for its rich experience in modern production, management expertise of Harvard elites and for being the first to adopt the Hazard Analysis Critical Control Points (HACCP) model which embodies a systematic approach to food safety.

SOURCE: Tang Yuankai, "Quick, Pass Me A Burger! A huge market and a keen ear to the ground keep fast food business tills ringing," *Beijing Review*, 14 Apr. 2005.

 The full text of Document 18.2 is available on the CD-ROM.

DOCUMENT 18.3: One of two stories of their families written by the children of migrant workers living and working in Beijing, 2007

My mother worried about us a lot, concerned that we wouldn't be able to handle everything ourselves [at home]. Then she brought us to Beijing and wanted us to go to school here. When I first came to Beijing, I couldn't adjust here at all, because everything in Beijing was so strange to me. They made me feel I was so tiny and insignificant and there was no place in the city for me to exist. Seeing my mother working so hard every day, I felt so empty and had no feeling for going to school. I knew the reason mother worked so hard was to support us so we could go to school and live a better life. But I couldn't do well in school; I would only be wasting money. Schools here were not cheap. Maybe mother saw through me. She said, "Just try your best. Don't worry about the rest."

SOURCE: Hu Yan, "Rebirth," 2007. Unpublished essay. Trans. Kongli Liu.

 The full text of Document 18.3 is available on the CD-ROM.

---

[4] *Jiaozi* are dumplings filled with meat and vegetables. Very popular in China, they take a long time to prepare.

DOCUMENT 18.4: Excerpt from "Bridge over the Digital Divide" by Rong Jiaojiao in *China Daily*, June 2006

"The ancient farmers' houses of these Zhuang minority groups have three floors. The first is for raising animals like pigs and hens, the second is for people and the third is for storing grain and corn.

"It's a pretty smart design because it saves space and is very environment-friendly," said 11-year-old Tang Zijun, a fifth-grader at Haizhuzhonglu Elementary School in Guangzhou and one of the provincial capital's 10 million residents.

Tang is talking about the PowerPoint photos she just received from Tong Jingyan, a student of Jingxi Pilot Elementary School of the Guangxi Zhuang Autonomous Region, 688 kilometres west of Guangzhou.

In the county town of Jingxi, where 99 per cent of the population of 580,000 is Zhuang minority, Tong is studying photos of ancient Guangdong farmhouses taken on Tang Zijun's recent school field trip....

This exchange forms just one small link in a United Nations Children's Fund (UNICEF) distance education project launched last year. The project involves fifteen primary schools in Guangxi and Chongqing Municipality, and seven schools in Guangdong and Anhui provinces and Shanghai. Students were divided into groups to conduct research on the same topic, exchange ideas and discuss their findings in a chat room at the project website (www.isnet.org.cn).

SOURCE: Rong Jiaojiao, "Bridge Over the Digital Divide," *China Daily*, June 2006.

 The full text of **Document 18.4** is available on the CD-ROM.

DOCUMENT 18.5: Excerpt from "Too Big, Too Fast" by Feng Jianhua in *Beijing Review*, October 27, 2005

In the 1980s, Shenzhen was supposed to hold 800,000 people. In the city's 10th Five-Year Plan (2001–05), the population capacity was limited to 4.8 million. Today, with 12 million people crowded into the city, crises loom ahead.

A major problem is the water supply. Shenzhen is listed as one of China's seven thirstiest cities, with its per-capita freshwater resources comprising a quarter of the national average. Even if the population decreases to 7.5 million in 2010, the city will still be facing a water shortage of 1.6 billion cubic meters a year. The local government is fully aware of the grave situation and warns Shenzhen's future development will collide with four major crises—diminishing land resources, water and energy shortages, overpopulation and weakening environmental sustainability.

Shenzhen, one of the earliest special economic zones in China, is a test balloon for the country's reform and opening-up policy. What the city is facing now may afflict other cities in the future. If and how Shenzhen will cope with its problems has great meaning to cities around the country.

SOURCE: Feng Jianhua, "Too Big, Too Fast," *Beijing Review*, 27 Oct. 2005.

 The full text of **Document 18.5** is available on the CD-ROM.

DOCUMENT 18.6: Excerpt from "Wealth Grows, but Health Care Withers in China" by Howard W. French in the *New York Times*, January 14, 2006

China's economic reforms have turned an almost uniformly poor nation into an increasingly prosperous one in the space of a mere generation. But the collapse of socialized medicine and staggering cost increases have opened a yawning gap between health care in the cities and the rural areas, where the former system of free clinics has disintegrated.

In the last several years China has experimented with reforms aimed at improving health care for peasants. The most important is an insurance plan in which participating farmers must make an annual payment of a little more than a dollar to gain eligibility for basic medical treatments. Many peasants have complained that even the dollar payment is too big a burden and… the coverage the plan theoretically provides is inadequate….

That China finds itself in this situation today is as remarkable as the country's economic takeoff and, paradoxically, is inseparably related to it. Until the beginning of the reform period in the early 1980s, China's socialized medical system, with "barefoot doctors" at its core, worked public health wonders. From 1952 to 1982 infant mortality fell from 200 per 1,000 live births to 34, and life expectancy increased from about 35 years to 68, according to a recent study published by The New England Journal of Medicine.

Since then, in one of the great policy reversals of modern times, China has dissolved its rural communes, privatized vast swaths of the economy and shifted public health resources away from rural areas and toward the cities.

SOURCE: Howard W. French, "Wealth Grows, but Health Care Withers in China," *New York Times*, 14 Jan. 2006.

DOCUMENT 18.7: Excerpt from "The Price of Health" by Tan Wei in *Beijing Review*, February 2, 2006

Liu is a farmer from Xinxiang, Henan Province, one of the biggest sources of labor in the country. Since 1999, he has been trying his luck in Beijing with several of his friends. A year-long, hard-earned wage from the farmland was about 1,000 yuan ($807)….

Liu lives on site in a temporary structure made of cardboard. Taking up most of the 15-square-meter floor space are six beds, some piled with washbowls, mess tins, bedding and luggage. The room is bitterly cold. According to Liu, most migrants cannot afford the costly medicine and hospitalization when they fall ill. They would rather grin and swallow medicine to help cure common diseases such as a cold. "We can't afford the time off to see a doctor, as we lose money," he complained….

SOURCE: Tan Wei, "The Price of Health," *Beijing Review,* 2 Feb. 2006.

 The full text of **Document 18.7** is available on the CD-ROM.

DOCUMENT 18.8: Excerpt from "Holiday Season" by Zhang Zhiping in *Beijing Review*, January 26, 2006

Christmas is becoming increasingly popular among the Chinese, although originally it was heavily promoted by businesses. For the holiday last month, in the bustling Xidan commercial district in downtown Beijing, a large shopping mall put up Christmas trees, welcoming visitors to write down their Christmas wishes and hang the notes on the trees. In just one or two days, the trees were filled with all kinds of Christmas messages, such as, "I wish those who love me and whom I love happiness in the next year," "May God bless my parents' health and happiness," or "I hope my girlfriend will be accepted at renowned universities."

Sociologists say the rising popularity of Christmas is due to the cheerful and bright colors associated with the holiday. Red is the most favored holiday color in China, representing harmony and indicating a happy event. On Christmas Day, people may find that Santa Claus and traditional red Chinese lanterns go well together.

SOURCE: Zhang Zhiping, "Holiday Season," *Beijing Review*, 26 Jan. 2006.

 The full text of **Document 18.8** is available on the CD-ROM.

DOCUMENT 18.9: Excerpt from "Still Brewing" by Lu Ling in *Beijing Review*, January 19, 2006

Teahouses in today's China have emerged to become fashionable. The old-style teahouse is becoming trendy, while newly built teahouses are adapting to the needs of modern society. "Tea drinking and tasting tradition was born along with China's folk culture and stamped with Chinese flavor," said Professor Wang Congren at the Shanghai Normal University. "Its recent rejuvenation is a signal showing that city people are searching for the tradition and roots of the nation, by exploring their peculiar social functions and meanings."…

Professor Wang analyzed that contemporary teahouses embrace at least three new functions. First, teahouses not only provide a chance to sip fine teas, but also provide a place for entertainment. Customers regard them as information distribution centers. The second lies in the matter of culture. Although people drink tea to satisfy their taste and thirst, there is also a healthy aspect on a psychological level and the aesthetic manner in which tea is drunk. Third, there are networking opportunities. Valuable business contacts are made in teahouses as they have always maintained the function of being communication hubs.

SOURCE: Lu Ling, "Still Brewing," *Beijing Review*, 19 Jan. 2006.

 The full text of **Document 18.9** is available on the CD-ROM.

DOCUMENT 18.10: Excerpt from "Quick, Pass Me A Burger!" by Tang Yuankai, *Beijing Review*, April 14, 2005

As lifestyles change, Chinese are taking to fast foods in a big way. Unlike earlier times, they too are hankering after speed, efficiency, convenience and taste. "More people, working under tight schedules, have no time for trivialities like cooking and dining," affirms Ying Hua [a lecturer at Beijing University]. Indeed, many a business is thriving on China's "fast food survival." The fact that it is lucrative has only ushered in more competition, leaving the fast food "connoisseur" spoilt for choice. Coming back to Ying and his classmate. They have a pleasant lunch [of frozen *jiaozi*] that took just 20 minutes to put together....

SOURCE: Tang Yuankai, "Quick, Pass Me a Burger!" *Beijing Review*, 14 April 2005.

 The full text of **Document 18.10** is available on the CD-ROM.

DOCUMENT 18.11: Excerpts from "Should a Lack of Filial Piety Be Penalized?" a Forum article in *Beijing Review*, February 23, 2006

At the end of January, as the Chinese traditional lunar New Year was drawing near, the local community office of Nanjingdonglu in Shanghai issued new rules requiring children to pay regular visits to their parents living in the community. According to the provisions, children must visit their parents or bring them to their own homes to spend a weekend every one or two weeks, and visit them on state stipulated holidays. If they do not have the time, they can send their spouse or children to visit instead.

Under these rules, if children fail to fulfill the requirements for one or two months, they will be given a friendly reminder. If they refuse to visit their parents after three months, however, they will be "blacklisted" by having their name posted on the community bulletin board. The community office also would send a letter to their workplace, detailing and criticizing their un-filial behavior.

SOURCE: Zhang Zhiping, "Should a Lack of Filial Piety Be Penalized?" *Beijing Review*, 23 Feb. 2006.

 The full text of **Document 18.11**, including samples of responses generated by this regulation, is on the CD-ROM.

DOCUMENT 18.12: "Wedding Bells?" by Lu Lin, *Beijing Review*, May 18, 2006.

For Chinese women, marriage has always been a blend of the bitter and the sweet, but as Chinese society advances, women's attitudes toward marriage are undergoing subtle changes. They are being encouraged to develop their own understanding of marriage and to seek a happy life for themselves....

Fan Fang, a senior translator in a foreign-invested company, holds a viewpoint that also is popular among young professional women. "At the age of 27, I still have quite a lot of things to do. I'm eager for opportunities to study further for my master's degree or to improve my work capability abroad, so why should I get married so early? There are many available young men around me, but I'm afraid that marriage and family life will block me from doing better in my work. To be frank, I won't sacrifice too much for marriage, especially when the ideal partner has not come yet."

SOURCE: Lu Lin, "Wedding Bells?" *Beijing Review*, 18 May 2006.

 The full text of **Document 18.12** is available on the CD-ROM.

DOCUMENT 18.13: "Governing Gender" by Lan Xinzhen in *Beijing Review*, March 23, 2006

On March 1, the research institution under the All-China Women's Federation published a green paper on Chinese women, the nation's first-ever paper by a research institution on the advancement of Chinese women and situation of gender equality in China. The paper is a collection of research results, ideas and practical experiences from experts, scholars and people working in fields related to women. It provides a general overview of the situation of women in China, and offers references for enhancing work on their advancement.

The paper points out that despite the increasing influence women have in politics, challenges are ahead. For example, the proportion of female cadres, especially in top government leadership, is still relatively small and most female cadres hold only deputy positions. The paper also notes that the proportion of female members of villagers' affairs committees is dropping.

Apart from the above-mentioned challenges, the shortage of female cadres poses a significant problem. Many female government officials are approaching retirement age, but the next generation of female cadres hasn't yet grown up. "Even organizations which are most obviously suitable for women, such as the All-China Women's Federation and Family Planning Office, face a shortage of female officials," Duan said.

SOURCE: Lan Xinzhen, "Governing Gender," *Beijing Review*, 23 Mar. 2006.

 The full text of **Document 18.13** is available on the CD-ROM.

Activities

NOTE: Many of the readings in this lesson mention figures in RMB or Chinese *yuan*. In some cases, the writer has given the dollar "equivalent." However, it is problematic to convert Chinese salaries to salaries in Europe, the United States and many other countries because the purchasing power of 1 dollar or 1 euro is much higher in China than in most Western countries. Dr. Zheng Shiping, an expert in comparative politics, explains that for a more accurate sense of what an RMB figure represents, one can consider that 4.7 *yuan* are roughly equivalent to a U.S. dollar in terms of what that money can buy. Another way to compare is to consider that an unmarried white-collar worker in his or her early twenties living in a large city in China earns about 5,000 *yuan* a month, and that this salary places him or her at the lower end of the emerging middle class. The "Big Mac Index" periodically published by the *Economist* is an excellent resource to get a sense of comparative purchasing power (see Suggested Resources).

ACTIVITY 1: Writing about China based on photographs

View the slide show of photographs taken in China in the past few years. Choose one (see image index on the CD-ROM) and write a one-paragraph news bulletin to go with the photograph, along the lines of the very brief reports that appear in newspapers. Post the photographs and the accompanying news stories around the classroom for everyone to examine. Discuss in class: what are the overall impressions you get of present-day China from the photographs?

NOTE: Chapter 1 includes an additional slide show of China's rural landscape.

ACTIVITY 2: Individual stories from "the New China"

After reading the introductory essay, create teams of three or four. Divide the four excerpts in Document 18.2 among members of the group. After reading the assigned accounts, report back to the group:

- The name and gender of a key individual(s) from your story.
- A summary of the account as well as an explanation of how economic changes in China have affected the individual in your account.

Discuss in your group how these accounts fit with your image of China. What is the meaning of the phrase "the American dream"? Do any of these stories reflect a "Chinese dream," and how would you define *that* dream? What changes in Chinese society have made this possible?

ACTIVITY 3: Reading teenagers' narratives

Begin by reading the stories written by children of migrant workers living and working in Beijing (18.3). Discuss as a class:

"Hard Life"

1. What factors caused the family to split up?
2. Why was the girls' mother reluctant to allow the elder sister to go to school?

3. At one point, the author acknowledges that being on their own allowed the girls to become more independent. What activities did the girls partake in that might be hard to imagine a Western child or teenager taking on?

4. In light of the parents' level of hardship and sacrifice, how can one account for the continued high level of migration within China?

"Rebirth"

1. Why did Hu Yan name her narrative "Rebirth"?

2. The writing demonstrates a good deal of introspection, but some gaps in the story are evident. Identify some of those gaps. Why might the author have left out certain elements?

3. What made the biggest impression on you as you read the two narratives, and why?

Break into teams of three or four and adapt the settings and circumstances of one of the accounts to India, the United States, Mexico, or South Africa by writing a narrative of similar length. After you have finished, discuss what you had to alter and why. What stayed the same, and why? Discuss whether it was easy or hard to adapt the story. How did the new set of narratives differ from each other?

ACTIVITY 4: Taking on the work of task forces

In this activity, you will take on the role of members of municipal task forces responsible for addressing some of the formidable challenges China faces, such as the disparities between rural and urban China, the growth of cities, and migrant issues including health care. Work in teams of four or five; each team will explore one issue. After reading the assigned documents (18.4–18.7), responding to the questions (Item 18.A on the CD-ROM), doing further research, and discussing the issue, each "task force" will prepare a public statement of approximately one page in length. Choose one person from your team to present your statement to the class.

ACTIVITY 5: The impact of Westernization on Chinese culture

Choose one of the three articles to read (18.8–18.10). After you have read and answered questions related to your article (Item 18.B on the CD-ROM), share information about the article with your classmates. Discuss:

1. Do Chinese traditions or holidays have a place in other cultures—in the United States, for example, or Canada? Explain.

2. Does the article about teahouses provide optimism that China will be able to retain unique aspects of its own culture in the face of rapid change? Explain.

3. How has China adopted the fast food business? What may be some of the consequences? How is this change related to culture?

CREATIVE EXTENSION:

Create a political cartoon or a comic strip portraying an aspect of cultural change in China.

ACTIVITY 6: **Discussing changing demographics**

Choose the topic that interests you most: "Sons' and Daughters' Responsibility to their Parents," "Marriage in the 21st Century," or "Women in Leadership." Read the articles from *Beijing Review* (18.11–18.13), answer the related questions (Item 18.C on the CD-ROM), and complete the writing assignment.

Finally, "gather in a teahouse" in groups that include representatives from the three topics. Describe the article you read. Keep in mind the demographic changes China is undergoing, along with the increased Westernization portrayed in Activity 4, Documents 18.8–18.10. Discuss how modernization appears to have affected Chinese citizens (children, young adults, the middle-aged, seniors). Identify what appear to be problems and suggest solutions.

ACTIVITY 7: **Role-playing "Oprah comes to China"**

In this culminating activity, you will role-play a television show: "Oprah comes to China." One student will role-play the famous talk show host, who will pose the question, "Is change coming too quickly to China?" Other students will take on roles as Chinese citizens listed below, while the remainder of the class will act as the audience. In role-playing and devising questions, call upon information in this chapter and any additional research you have done.
Among the guests should be a:
social worker, city planner, school teacher, migrant worker, child of a migrant worker, CEO of a Chinese auto manufacturer, architect, physician at a public hospital, nurse at a nursing home, university student, owner of a small business, or any individual about whom you have read in the articles.

EXTENDED RESEARCH:

Choose any one of the topics listed below. Working individually or in small groups, conduct research, using the most up-to-date information, and then present your findings to the class in a lecture, a visual display, or an electronic presentation using a program such as PowerPoint® or Photo Story 3®.

- Modernization has had an effect upon traditional Chinese architecture. In many cases, traditional buildings have been replaced by modern high-rise buildings.
  - Find out about the *hutong* in Beijing and traditional neighborhoods that are disappearing in many Chinese cities and the arguments for and against preserving them.
  - Discover the role of Western architects in China's cities. Explore the stories behind some of the most spectacular recent modern construction in major cities, such as the National Theatre, China Central Television offices, and Olympic Stadium in Beijing, and the Jin Mao Tower (Grand Hyatt) in Shanghai.
- Explore the issues facing elderly people in rural China.

- Find out about marriage practices in rural China. Which traditions continue and which have changed?

- Find out about government initiatives in the past three years that aim to change the divide between life in urban and rural areas.

- Report on Dayingjie, a village in Yunnan Province that has enjoyed significant success. What factors led to this success?

- How has the Chinese government addressed the needs of the "floating population" in the past three years?

- The Chinese and foreign press have reported on hundreds of protests in China in recent years. What are the main reasons for the protests? How is the government addressing the issues?

- Find out about the degree to which the press in China is free to report.

- Find recent articles in Western and Chinese publications (for example, the *New York Times*, *Washington Post*, *Los Angeles Times*, *Australian Financial Review*, *Sydney Morning Herald*, *Guardian*, *London Times*, *Daily Telegraph*, *China Daily*, *Beijing Review*, etc.) about China's growing economy and consumerism. In a written summary of your reading, compare the way British, American, or Australian and Chinese publications report on similar topics and explore what may account for some of the differences.

- The practice of religion in China has increased dramatically in recent years. Find out about the changes and explore reasons why.

■ A CLOSER LOOK

A Pedicab in Suzhou

- *Discuss: How does this photograph capture the changes in twenty-first-century China?*

(Photo by Elizabeth Lewis)

Suggested Resources

Books

Chen Guidi and Wu Chuntao. *Will the Boat Sink the Water? The Life of China's Peasants.* New York: PublicAffairs Co., 2006.
A one-sided portrayal of the plight of Chinese farmers. In particular, it focuses on their lack of legal recourse when trying to fight local corruption. In the process, it sheds some light on contemporary village life.

Gifford, Rob. *China Road: A Journey into the Future of a Rising Power.* New York: Random House, 2007.
An insightful, witty and beautifully written account of a National Public Radio correspondent's trip across China. A must-read for anyone interested in contemporary China.

Hessler, Peter. *Oracle Bones: A Journey Between China's Past and Present.* New York: HarperCollins, 2006
Eloquently written, with dabs of wonderful humor. Chapters 2, 4, 7, 11, 17, and 22 will be of strong interest to students wishing to learn about the lives of young Chinese adults in the new economy.

Websites

http://www.chinatoday.com A China-based and operated source of information with dozens of fun facts and additional links.

http://afe.easia.columbia.edu On the *Asia for Educators* website, go to "population" to find out more about contemporary demographic issues.

http://www.bjreview.com.cn The *Beijing Review* website provides up-to-date news and analysis on both national and international news. It is particularly helpful for anyone interested in the increasing role that China is playing in global affairs.

http://xiakou.uncc.edu/index.htm The Xiakou Village website hosted at the University of North Carolina–Charlotte is a work in progress. It explores the history, beliefs, folklife, and economy of a village in western Sichuan Province through long essays, images, video, and audio resources.

http://www.economist.com/markets/bigmac The *Economist*'s "Big Mac Index" provides reports on comparative purchasing power.

Films

China Blue (88 mins; 2005) *In Chinese (Cantonese and Mandarin) with subtitles and explanatory text. The powerful and disturbing documentary captures the lives of teen girls in a Chinese factory that produces denim jeans and notes the role that Western corporations and consumers play.*

China From the Inside (3-hour, 4-part series; 2007) *This PBS documentary looks at "Power and the People," "Women of the Country," "Shifting Nature," and "Freedom and Justice." More information at http://www.pbs.org/kqed/chinainside.*

China Revealed (102 mins; 2006) *The Discovery Atlas documentary explores where tradition meets modernity in China today. See http://dsc.discovery.com/convergence/atlas/china/about/about.html for more information.*

China Rises (3 hrs 20 mins.; 2006) *The Discovery documentary looks at the monumental changes unfolding in the People's Republic of China. Can be purchased from http://shopping.discovery.com/product-60261.html?rel_productId=63517.*

Primary Sources

DOCUMENT 19.1: "My Chinese High School" by Zhang Chengyan, 2006

DOCUMENT 19.2: "Schools and Students in China," a slide show, 2004–2007

DOCUMENT 19.3: Eye exercise diagram, translated and prepared by Livia Kohn and Kirk Goetchius (only on the CD-ROM)

DOCUMENT 19.4: "The Fight for Education" by Tang Yuankai, in *Beijing Review*, February 2, 2006

DOCUMENT 19.5: Essays by Dandelion School students, Beijing, 2007

DOCUMENT 19.6: American students' impressions of their stay at the Dandelion School, 2007

DOCUMENT 19.7: "Youth Under Pressure" by Zhang Xueying, in *China Today*, June 2006

DOCUMENT 19.8: "Growing Expenses" by Lu Rucai, in *China Today*, June 2006

Supplementary Materials

ITEM 19.A: Activity chart for Activity 4

CHAPTER 19

Growing Up in China

By Kongli Liu

Chapter Contents

Organizing Idea

Children growing up in urban China in the twenty-first century share much with children in developed countries worldwide. However, the experiences vary greatly between children in urban areas and those in the countryside.

Key Questions

What are the key features of China's education system?

What are the differences in education and the experience of growing up for students in urban as compared to rural areas of China?

What does the youth culture in China look like?

Essay

What does it mean to be growing up in China today? It means at a very young age being motivated or pressured to study hard in pursuit of a dream for a good life; it means being exposed to unprecedented opportunities and technologies that even the previous generation could not have imagined; it means growing up during the intersection of Chinese and Western cultures within the global village; it means being a witness and gradually a contributor to the enormous social, economic, and political transformations of one of the oldest civilizations on earth. As in any other country in the world, there is no single experience that captures "growing up in China." Unequal educational resources and opportunities make the experiences of rural and urban youth, in particular, very different.

An Overview of Public Education

The structure of China's education system is similar to that of many other countries. It includes five to six years of primary school, a three-year middle school, and three years of high school. Students can continue with their studies at a two- to three-year vocational school or a three- to four-year college or university, followed by graduate school if they wish. The 1986 Education Law in China mandates nine years of compulsory education, but it is not free. Students pay a nominal tuition fee, as well as for their textbooks, school uniform, and activities. All these combined cost a family about 500–1000 *yuan* a year.[1] This sum may mean little to an urban family, but can be an insurmountable burden for many rural families, whose children sometimes have to drop out for financial reasons alone. In 2001, the Chinese government began to gradually eliminate primary and middle school tuitions and fees in rural areas, with the goal of completing the reform by the end of 2007. This change will benefit 160 million students.[2] However, the primary reason for students in China not continuing education through high school or college is not financial, but the highly competitive examinations.

One Exam Changes Everything

Many children in China dream of attending college, a goal which may have been deeply rooted in their minds as early as primary school. This is especially true for children in rural China, because going to college and finding a job in a city probably is the only way to improve their lives and that of the next generation. One exam changes the fate of a Chinese teenager: the *Gao Kao* (高考, the National College Entrance Examination). More than 95 percent of colleges in China use an applicant's total score on the *Gao Kao* as the single criterion in the admission process. As a result, many students are not admitted to college because their scores fall below the admission score, sometimes by as little as half a point. In cities like Beijing or Shanghai, about 75 percent of students go to college, but in rural areas, this drops to only 10 to 20 percent.

An applicant can add up to twenty extra points to the total score if he or she falls into one of the following categories: someone who has won an award in an international or national academic competition; an individual with proven talent in the arts or sports; someone who has performed outstanding and recognized community service; or the son or daughter of a non-Han minority family, an overseas Chinese family, or a family of a veteran who died or was disabled while on active duty.

---

[1] About $60–$120 in U.S. dollars.

[2] China Education and Research Network, "China pledges elimination of rural compulsory education charges in two years," 1 Mar. 2006.

Exams: A Time-Honored System

Advancement through a series of exams dates back centuries in China's history. It formed the basis for China's civil service system created two thousand years ago. (See Chapter 2.) The present-day exam was established in 1950 at a time when China was very poor and educational resources were limited.[3] The country needed a relatively fair system to select the best-performing students to go on to higher levels of education. However, with the fast economic growth and social changes of the past two decades (see Chapters 16–18), both the Chinese government and the public have begun to realize that the education system has to be reconfigured and updated to meet the challenges and opportunities presented by globalization and the information age. As a result, there is ongoing national reform regarding academic standards and teaching approaches that encourage creativity and incorporate critical thinking and problem-solving skills into curricula. Also, school schedules have been restructured to allow students to engage in more extracurricular activities.

A Curriculum Designed for Success in the Global Economy

Schools in China emphasize academics above all else. Beginning in primary school, teachers are specialized in subjects, including Chinese, English, math, natural sciences, art and music, physical education, and moral education. Compared with systems in some other countries, where teachers do not specialize at the elementary level, this structure enables students to develop subject competence at a very young age. In particular, skills in English, math, and the sciences are stressed to ensure that students can compete in the global information age. Most children in urban China start learning English in kindergarten (in bilingual or immersion settings), and English is taught from primary school through college nationwide.[4] It is mandatory in all exams required for advancement, most exams for professional licenses or certificates, and exams to qualify for a college degree.

Extra Academics

Many students go to after-school classes provided by public schools, individual teachers, or private schools. The "catch-up" classes, called *buxiban* (补习班), and private tutoring are relatively expensive, even for some urban families, but most parents want their child to have as much extra help as possible in order to have a better chance of going to college. In rural areas, however, most students have conflicting priorities after school. On the one hand, parents want their children to have enough time to study hard and be better prepared for the *Gao Kao*. On the other hand, they need the children to help with farming and other chores so that the family can make a living and keep supporting their education financially. Therefore, many rural students simply do not have enough time to study. After-school classes and private tutoring are a luxury for them. In fact, after-school class providers usually do not serve rural areas, simply because most families cannot afford them.

Beyond the School Day

The life of urban students in China is comparable to that of children in developed countries. Common activities may include playing sports, watching movies and TV shows, studying

---

[3] The entire education system essentially shut down during the Cultural Revolution (see Chapter 14). Shortly after schools reopened, the college entrance exam was reinstated in 1977.

[4] An estimated 240 million students are learning English in China today.

music and the arts, visiting museums and parks, playing computer games, surfing online, reading books, socializing with friends, going to summer camps, and traveling with family in China or abroad. The activities of rural children cannot compare in terms of variety, exposure to technology, and recreational choices. However, they do have closer contact with nature, develop independence and survival skills, interact more with people, and gain real working experience.

Urban Youth Culture

The young generation in China today is experiencing and creating an urban youth culture that embodies two crucial themes in today's world: globalization and information technology. Young Chinese are very curious about the activities of young people in other parts of the world. They watch movies and listen to music from the United States, Hong Kong, South Korea, Japan, Europe and other parts of the world; they closely follow European soccer leagues, U.S. National Basketball Association games, Formula One car races, and tennis tournaments, which are all broadcast live in China. Many of them pay serious attention to international relations and world news as well.

China's urban youth embrace new ideas, express individuality, and pursue personal dreams. No better example can illustrate this than the sensational *Chaoji Nusheng* (*Super Girl Singers*, 超级女声), a singing contest show similar to *American Idol* launched by a local Hunan TV station in 2004 (see Suggested Resources for a sample). In 2005 alone, the show attracted more than 150,000 participants and 100 million votes via cell phone text message. The event even sparked a discussion of democracy and political reform in China—people joked that the winner was the first "democratically" elected public figure in Chinese history.

While youth culture in China today is influenced by Western pop culture, there has also been a revival of and renewed appreciation for traditional Chinese culture among young people and in the society as a whole. Students go to classes to learn traditional Chinese painting, music, or calligraphy, and many of them pursue dreams of a career in the traditional Chinese arts.

Meanwhile, globalization provides young people with opportunities to see the intersection between their own and other cultures. One of the most popular songs they listened to in 2006 was "Heroes of Earth" by Lee-Hom Wang, a Chinese-American who expertly mixed together hip-hop, rap, and elements from the traditional Beijing Opera (see Suggested Resources). Chinese youth are also witnessing the increasing popularity of their idols, such as NBA player Yao Ming and movie star Zhang Ziyi, among young people in other countries.

Information technology plays an increasingly important role in China's urban youth culture today. Many students chat online, write blogs, and play computer games. Many are using these technologies creatively to enhance their knowledge, finding e-mail pals in other countries and doing academic research online; many consider this just a way of life, creating their own online communities, sharing their art works online, or even starting social and business enterprises online.

Primary Sources

DOCUMENT 19.1: "My Chinese High School," by Zhang Chengyan, 2006

In my grade, there were nearly one thousand students divided into fourteen classes when I was in Grade 10. Every class has sixty to sixty-five students, and we stayed all day long in the same classroom with the same students. We had the same level of courses if we were in the same grade, and there is no AP or Honor courses. Because there were so many students have the same level of courses, schools arranged different schedules for different classes every day, and there are two to three teachers teaching the same subject for different classes.

In China, when we are in Grade 10, we have chance to choose area in which we are more interested, humanities or science. After we choose the area, we have fewer classes on the other area and by 12th grade none at all....

We do not need to run to different classroom for different classes, teachers come into our classroom for each class period. Every class has its own head teacher to not only teach one subject but in charge of daily affairs for the whole class, such as holds assembly for class every Monday, and contacts with parents when students have any problems. The head teacher arranges seats for students at the beginning of the year, so everybody has their own seat and it is unchangeable. It is the same for every class...

 The full text of **Document 19.1** is available on the CD-ROM.

DOCUMENT 19.2: Photograph of second-grade students in a school in Shanghai, 2006

(Photo by Sarah Dorer)

 The slide show "Schools and Students in China" is on the CD-ROM.

DOCUMENT 19.4: "The Fight for Education" by Tang Yuankai, in *Beijing Review*, February 2, 2006

As more rural laborers flock into cities in the search for employment–about 100 million[5] are moving between the countryside and cities, making up 10 percent of the country's total population–the education of their children has become a major concern. And it's an issue not only disturbing the parents, but also the government and society at large. According to conservative statistics from relevant departments, 7 million children in this group are at the school age of six to fourteen, and should be engaged in the nine-year compulsory education program.

Due to the current residential registration system, farmers are deprived of the same treatment as urban residents in education opportunities, social welfare and other areas. In recent years, however, changes have begun to take place....

SOURCE: Tang Yuankai, "The Fight for Education," *Beijing Review*, 2 February 2008.

 The full text of Document 19.4 is available on the CD-ROM.

DOCUMENT 19.5: Essays by Dandelion School students, Beijing, 2007

The Dandelion School is a middle school that serves children of migrant workers.

I'm from Yangou village, Tianshui, Gansu Province. Because my family was poor, my parents left for cities to make a living when I was very young. I was living with my grandparents, who never went to school. They couldn't control me. Nobody asked me about my school day when I was back home after school. Another excuse for my not studying hard was that I had to help with farming and raising cattle for my family. I failed exams and skipped classes sometimes. I was even thinking about dropping out of school and going with my classmates to a city to work. Finally, my grand-parents had no choice but to ask my mother for help. With help from relatives, I was brought to Beijing to go to school.

When I entered the gate of the Dandelion School, I saw a lot of kids with similar conditions like mine. I also realized that all of them are not Beijing natives, but from "five lakes and four seas"—all over the country. They just attend school here. At the beginning, I never listened to teachers and didn't concentrate in class. But with teachers' help, I began to realize the importance of study and that studying can actually be a joyful thing. Since then, I have decided to study hard and to not disappoint those people who have helped me....

SOURCE: Yan Zhiheng (student at Dandelion School, Beijing), unpublished essay, 2007. Trans. Kongli Liu.

 The full text of Document 19.5 is available on the CD-ROM.

---

[5] Current estimates are significantly higher.

DOCUMENT 19.6: **An American student's impressions of her stay at the Dandelion School, 2007**

During my stay at the Dandelion School, we were included in all of the students' games and activities, and everyone we met there was quick to introduce themselves and show us around. I had never had kinder hosts in any place that I stayed, and it made me feel really happy to be there. The teachers and the students alike were wonderfully open and caring, and everywhere we went we were greeted by big smiles and exclamations of "Hi! How are you?" The fact that we were from different backgrounds, and even that we spoke different languages didn't matter at all. On our very first day there I was walking around the school grounds. I had just met a girl named Lucy, and we were already friends. As we walked, she held out her right hand, looked at me, and asked, "Hand?" Smiling, I looked back at her, answered, "Yes," and clasped her hand in mine. As we walked together, swinging our hands, I smiled.

SOURCE: Lisa Randolph, Winchester, MA, unpublished essay, 2007.

 For the full text of Lisa's experiences as well as the experiences of other students , see Document 19.6 on the CD-ROM.

DOCUMENT 19.7: **"Youth Under Pressure" by Zhang Xueying, in** *China Today,* **June 2006**

Too much pressure and not enough sleep are common problems among China's primary and middle school students. One out of every three students suffers psychological problems, and 66.6 percent find it hard to fulfill their burden of study, according to a survey of 20,000 students in 500 classes at Beijing's primary and middle schools by the Psychology Institute of the Chinese Academy of Sciences. Educators say that although today is an era of freedom and opportunity for Chinese youth, it is also one of unprecedented pressure, particularly in cities....

SOURCE: Zhang Xueying, "Youth Under Pressure," *China Today,* June 2006.

 The full text of Document 19.7 is available on the CD-ROM.

DOCUMENT 19.8: **"Growing Expenses" by Lu Rucai, in** *China Today,* **June 2006**

The average urban, middleclass, young Chinese adult would not be seen dead in footwear other than that bearing the Nike, Reebok or Adidas label. Personal gadgetry of no less than digital camera, handset and MP3 is also mandatory for members of this trend-conscious social sector.

The need of young people to be instantly identifiable with their peer group by virtue of garb, hairstyle and accessories is nothing new. But exorbitant price tags on the image enhancers demanded by today's market economy generation set them apart from those of their antecedents....

Source: Lu Rucai, "Growing Expenses," *China Today,* June 2006.

 The full text of **Document 19.8** is available on the CD-ROM.

Activities

ACTIVITY 1: An overview of schools in China

Read the introductory essay up to "Beyond the School Day" and the description of Chinese schools by a teenager from Yunnan Province (19.1), and look at the slide show with photographs of schools (19.2 on the CD-ROM). In small groups, discuss what strikes you most about the schools and the education system. What surprised you? Where do the strengths lie? What appear to be weaknesses?

ACTIVITY 2: Exercising your eyes

Follow the instructions for exercising your eyes (19.3 on the CD-ROM). For the best effect, traditional Chinese music should be playing while you do this. The activity can take place at the beginning or during the middle of the class, since the exercises can also help a person renew his or her concentration. How did you feel during and after you did the exercises? Why do you think every Chinese student does these exercises daily?

ACTIVITY 3: Exploring education for children of migrant workers

Part 1:

Refer to Chapter 18 for more information about the migrant or "floating" population. Read the article about education for children of migrant workers (19.4) and the essays by some of the children themselves (19.5). Identify on a map the provinces from which the Dandelion School students come and their distance from Beijing. Consider as a class:

1. How is the government responding to the educational needs of the children of migrant workers?

2. What are the obstacles to implementation of existing policies?

3. How does a migrant student's experience in China compare with that of an immigrant student in a Western country? (Maybe classmates who are immigrants could share their experiences. Some literature on immigrant student experience would also be helpful.)

4. What struck you most about the student essays? What would you like to know more about? Compare each student's life to your own.

5. How do the essays contribute to your understanding of the lives of China's floating population?

Part 2:

Read about the experiences of American students who spent a week at the Dandelion School (19.6).

1. What is most striking about these accounts?

2. Why do you think the Chinese students were so warm and welcoming?

3. How did the American students react to this experience? Why?

4. What is the impact of this kind of student experience?

ACTIVITY 4: Comparing after-school activities

Fill in the top row of the Activity Chart (Item 19.A on the CD-ROM) with your typical activities. Next, fill in the second row, writing what you *guess* Chinese students do in their free time. Finish reading the introductory essay. Working in small groups, divide up Documents 19.7 and 19.8. Exchange what you learned from your reading with others in the group. Based on what you now know, fill in the bottom rows of the chart. Discuss:

1. If your initial guesses regarding Chinese students' activities were different from what you learned, what accounts for the differences?

2. What are the similarities and differences between students in urban and rural China? Why do these differences exist?

3. Compare your activities to those of many Chinese students. What can you conclude about Chinese education and culture based on this information?

ACTIVITY 5: Debate: Should the *Gao Kao* be abolished?

Form three groups: a pro-*Gao Kao* group, an anti-*Gao Kao* group, and the Ministry of Education. In your group, discuss what you've learned about the national exam. Compare it to exams with which you are familiar (e.g. the SAT, the ACT, or A-levels), and prepare your arguments. Debate the question. After the debate, the Ministry of Education group must summarize the advantages and disadvantages of the *Gao Kao* and come up with a plan for the future of the exam.

ACTIVITY 6: Rural education over time

Refer to Chapter 10, Document 10.3 (James Yen's efforts at rural education in the early 1920s) and Chapter 1, Document 1.2 (Fei Xiaotong's 1936 study *Peasant Life in China*). Compare the details of education in rural China described in those documents to the information you have learned in this chapter. What has changed over time? What challenges remain?

ACTIVITY 7: **Design a perfect school**

Working in small groups, design a "perfect" school by combining elements of your school and Chinese schools. Consider what the purpose will be of an education a student receives at your school and all the elements that will need to be in place to achieve that goal. Present your school plan to the rest of the class as if they were the members of the school board with the authority to approve your plan. "Board members" should take notes on all the proposals (in other words, all plans except their own).

NOTE: The activity can be broadened to include such elements as a design for the school campus, a promotional school brochure, or a school theme song.

■ Follow-up assignment: Choose the strongest school proposal and write an essay explaining why you feel it is the best one.

Suggested Resources

Books

Fong, Vanessa. *Only Hope: Coming of Age under China's One-Child Policy*. Stanford, CA: Stanford University Press, 2004.
This book by an anthropologist is the first in-depth study of the experiencees of the first generation of children born under China's One-Child Policy. What values, world views, goals and interests do these young adults now hold? What kinds of relationships do they have with their parents, families and peers? The book concludes that the One-Child Policy has largely succeeded in its goals, but with unintended consequences.

The Diary of Ma Yan. Edited and introduced by Pierre Haski, translated from Mandarin to French by He Yanping and from the French by Lisa Appignanesi. New York: HarperCollins, 2005.
Written by a young teenager from Zhangjiashu village in Ningxia Province. Ma Yan's diary covers two periods: September through December 2000 and July through December 2001. In simple, poignant language, the diary captures the vast divide between modern successful urban China, which most tourists see, and the abject poverty that exists in many rural areas. The book is a very quick read. A June 12, 2005 Washington Post review described the book as "one of those elemental, utterly artless works that simply stop you in your tracks." Additional information is available online at http://www.enfantsduningxia.org.

Websites

http://www.edu.cn/english_1369/index. shtml China Education and Research Network, a government-supported project supporting educational technology in China, includes statistics, reports, history, laws, and news about China's education system.

http://www.youtube.com/watch?v=qOh7vlJPUfM *Don't Cry for Me, Argentina* as sung by Liangying (Jane) Zhang, third-prize winner in the 2005 Super Girl Singers competition.

Film

Not One Less (106 mins; *1999*) *in Chinese (Mandarin) with subtitles. The film tells the true story of Wei Minzhi, a fourteen-year-old girl who is ordered to a remote impoverished village in Hebei Province to work as the substitute teacher for a month. Clueless when it comes to teaching, she is, however, extraordinarily determined to keep the class intact. Lead roles are played by the individuals themselves. Directed by Zhang Yimou.*

■ **A CLOSER LOOK**

(Photo by Liz Nelson)

Students answering a teacher's question, Dandelion Middle School for children of migrant workers, Beijing, May 2006

■ *Working in small groups, list all the objects in the photograph, all the individuals and details related to them, and the activities taking place. Compare what you see in this photograph to your own middle school experience.*

Primary Sources

DOCUMENT 20.1: Excerpt from "A Troubled River Mirrors China's Path to Modernity" by Jim Yardley in the *New York Times*, November 19, 2006

DOCUMENT 20.2: "Pollution from Chinese Coal Casts Shadow Around Globe" by Keith Bradsher and David Barboza in the *New York Times*, June 11, 2006 (not available on the CD-ROM)

DOCUMENT 20.3: "Riot Police, Villagers Clash in China," from The Associated Press in *The New York Times*, January 19, 2007 (not available on the CD-ROM)

DOCUMENT 20.4: "Internet Evolution" by Erica Schlaikjer in *Abroad View Magazine*, fall 2006

DOCUMENT 20.5: Excerpt from *Oracle Bones* by Peter Hessler, describing a nonviolent demonstration by Falun Gong followers in Tiananmen Square, Beijing

DOCUMENT 20.6: "What has the Qinghai–Tibet Railway Brought to China?" by Zhang Xueying in *China Today*, October 2006

DOCUMENT 20.7: Slide show with photographs of Tibet, 2005

DOCUMENT 20.8: "Profile: Rebiya Kadeer," BBC News report on a Uyghur activist, March 17, 2005

DOCUMENT 20.9: "China-Taiwan Trade Ties Increase," BBC News, January 17, 2007

DOCUMENT 20.10: Excerpt from "The Chinese Century" by Michael Elliott, *Time*, January 22, 2007

DOCUMENT 20.11: "China's Role in Africa" by Jian Junbo in *Beijing Review*, February 8, 2007

DOCUMENT 20.12: "Playing its Due Role" by Chen Xulong in *Beijing Review*, October 19, 2006

Supplementary Materials

ITEM 20.A: Questions for Activity 1, related to Document 20.1

ITEM 20.B: List of characters for Activity 1

ITEM 20.C: Questions for Activity 2, related to Document 20.2

ITEM 20.D: Additional activity examining the Three Gorges Dam

ITEM 20.E: Questions related to Activity 4, Documents 20.3–20.5

ITEM 20.F: Additional activity examining protests in China

CHAPTER 20

The Challenges Ahead

By Michael Abraham

Chapter Contents

Environmental Challenges
Social and Political Unrest
Tibet and Xinjiang
Superpower Status

Organizing Idea

As China's economy continues to grow and increasing numbers of people prosper, the Chinese government faces serious challenges at home and abroad.

Key Questions

What challenges have a large population and rapid economic growth placed on China? How does the Chinese government plan to meet these challenges?

What concerns arise from large-scale engineering projects that dramatically alter the environment, such as the Three Gorges Dam and North-South water diversion project?

How has the Internet affected the dissemination of information and the pace of political reform in China?

How does the Chinese government plan to further integrate the autonomous regions into the "new China"?

What is the Chinese government's position regarding reunification with Taiwan? How is it similar to or different from Taiwan's position and the position of the United States?

What are the short-term and long-term implications of China's many growing trade relationships?

Key Terms

Autonomous Region	multilateral	Security Council
developing nations	proliferation	sovereignty
diplomacy	reconciliation	sustainable development
dissident	rogue state	unilateral
geopolitical	sanctions	World Trade Organization (WTO)
human rights		

Essay

"The Chinese wouldn't put it this way themselves, but in their hearts I think they believe that the twenty-first century is China's century."

—Kenneth Lieberthal, senior director for Asia, National Security Council during the Clinton Administration, 1998–2000

China's prospects of becoming a world superpower have received considerable attention in the past two decades. Changes in China, since Deng Xiaoping (邓小平) launched economic reform, have been extraordinary. In 1978, 250 million Chinese people lived below the official poverty line; by 2004, the number had plummeted to 26 million.[1] But China's economic transformations have come at a price. As the twenty-first century unfolds, the Chinese Communist Party faces the challenge of governing a nation of almost 1.5 billion people, roughly equivalent to the population of the more than fifty countries of Europe and North and South America. China's government faces significant challenges both at home and abroad.

Environmental Challenges

Among the challenges is that of finding a sustainable level of economic development. Rapid industrialization and the efforts to raise the standard of living of 1.3 billion people have placed tremendous strains on the environment. The reliance on coal for 70 percent of the country's energy needs has caused appalling air pollution. Sixteen of the twenty cities with the world's worst air pollution are in China. Nearly half of river water cannot be used for agriculture

or industry. The government faces increasing pressure from a populace that is beginning to show the effects of poor health and from its Pacific neighbors who suffer some of the consequences. The challenge of providing clean energy is formidable, as a large portion of China's rural population has yet to experience the resource-intensive economic improvements.

One way in which Chinese leadership has tried to offset the heavy reliance on coal is through huge construction projects such as the Three Gorges Dam (三峡工程). Upon completion, its 26 turbine generators will generate electrical power equivalent to that of 40 coal-burning plants. But the dam has raised many concerns, including environmental ones. In addition, North China faces a critical water shortage in the near future. To address it, water will be diverted from the Yangzi River (长江) via three canals to northern regions.

In a country the size of China, natural disasters are an ever-present threat. The catastrophic earthquake of May 2008 and scores of aftershocks that followed caused enormous devastation in Sichuan Province and claimed tens of thousands of lives. But it also highlighted the central government's ability and willingness to respond immediately and effectively.

The Quest for Natural Resources

In the early years of Deng Xiaoping's economic reforms, China was able to supply its own energy needs. That is no longer the case. The country's unprecedented economic development has made the safeguarding and purchase of natural resources, especially energy, an increasingly important component of domestic and foreign policy. In part, the government's determination to keep the autonomous region of Xinjiang (新疆) stable is a result of that area's huge reserves of oil and natural gas.[2] Regional tensions include a dispute with Japan over

---

[1] C. Fred Bergsten et al., *China: The Balance Sheet. What the World Needs to Know Now about the Emerging Superpower* (New York: PublicAffairs / Center for Strategic and International Studies / Institute for International Economics, 2006) 18.

[2] Xinjiang is estimated to have 30 billion tons of oil (one third of China's total) and 13 trillion cubic meters of natural gas.

reserves of oil in the East China Sea. The Chinese leadership has made overtures to India (itself in need of energy) to avoid the two countries' outbidding each other for resources. In order to meet its growing needs for natural resources, the Chinese government has also turned to oil-rich regions such as the Middle East and Africa. Western nations have criticized Chinese officials for doing business with countries such as Sudan, Zimbabwe, and Iran, which are either involved in horrific human rights violations or are hostile to Western interests. China has also been criticized for selling weapons and sharing advanced weapons technologies with nations such as these. The Chinese, however, insist that they will not interfere with any other country's internal affairs, a stance supported by many developing nations.

Political Challenges at Home

On the home front, the Chinese Communist Party is keenly aware of income inequality. The growing divide is between skilled, educated urban residents and those less educated; it is between those living in a village far removed from a city and those in a village close to a city; it exists between coastal cities and inland ones. Various government initiatives seek to address the disparities. Chinese leaders are also examining ways to address the causes of thousands of spontaneous protests, primarily in rural China, over issues such as corruption and compensation for confiscated land.[3] In addition, the government, accustomed for fifty years to controlling the spread of information, is now in the midst of an increasingly connected age. For the more than 170 million Chinese who have access, the Internet allows contact with a source of largely unregulated information unknown to preceding generations. Despite government

efforts to crack down,[4] political blogs continue to serve as a way to discuss such topics as corruption, lack of governmental transparency, freedom of speech, and the limitations of one-party rule. Well-versed in their own history, which includes massive rebellions such as that of the Taiping (太平) from 1851 to 1864 (see Chapter 5, Item 5B) and the Boxer Uprising (义和团起义) in 1898 (see Chapter 7), Chinese leaders perceive well-organized groups such as Falun Gong (法轮功) as potential threats to the Party's stability and have no qualms about arresting and imprisoning members.

Xinjiang (新疆) and Tibet (西藏)

The Chinese government's control over culturally distinct minority areas is at once a domestic and an international concern. Despite being integral to what China now regards as its national borders, and despite efforts to increase the presence of Han Chinese in these regions, China's rule over minority areas—especially Tibet and Xinjiang—still appears harsh to parts of the world that are sympathetic to the Tibetan cause, and Muslim nations who sympathize with Xinjiang's large Muslim population. When protests erupt, such as in March 2008 during the period when the Olympic torch was being carried around the world, Chinese leaders insist these are domestic affairs and thus no one else's business.

China and the United States

The Chinese government has a complex relationship with the United States. The two have differed over issues such as trade imbalance, protections for intellectual property rights, valuation of the *yuan*, political reform, and

---

[3] China reported 87,000 "public order disturbances" in 2005, most of which involved 50 or fewer people. However, seventeen of these protests involved more than 10,000 people.

[4] The Ministry of Information Industry, Ministry of Public Security, and State Secrets Bureau together have some 30,000 individuals assigned to work as "Internet police." Bergsten 64.

human rights, but China's importance as a trade partner tends to prevent serious repercussions from the United States or other Western nations. Political scientist Harry G. Gelber has remarked, "[The U.S.] Congress and the public retain old and deep-seated illusions, such as the idea that American definitions of democracy or human rights are universally loved."[5] Experts at the Center for Strategic and International Studies concur, explaining that "some research suggests that at present, there is not widespread support within the general Chinese population for Western-style democracy, and that other 'preliminary steps' are more pressing: economic opportunity, clean government, and social stability."[6]

A tenuous strategic alliance between the United States and China has existed since the Bush administration's "War on Terror" began in 2001. The United States was eager to enlist the nominal support of a large secular nation, and China seized the opportunity to link its efforts to silence Muslim discontent in Xinjiang with the Bush administration's efforts against Islamic extremism. For the most part, however, the People's Republic of China chooses to be unaligned and independent. Using history as a guide (see Chapters 5 and 12), the Chinese government remains "deeply suspicious about long-term U.S. intentions toward China."[7] Chinese leaders look forward to a multipolar world to replace one in which the United States is the sole superpower.

China As a Superpower

Assuming that China's and the United States' current economic growth rates continue, China will become the world's largest economy, and by far the largest trading country, around 2035.[8] Since it became a member of the World Trade Organization (see Chapter 17), its booming economy has become tightly woven with those of the European Union, the United States, and Japan. Moreover, China has increasingly combined its economic leverage with its position as a permanent member of the United Nations Security Council to lend weight to global issues in which it has an interest. At the same time, the Chinese government has avoided open military engagements for decades, thus being able to focus on domestic issues: economic prosperity and modernization efforts.

---

[5] Gelber 440.
[6] Bergsten 71.

[7] Bergsten 13.
[8] Bergsten 9.

Primary Sources

DOCUMENT 20.1: Excerpt from "A Troubled River Mirrors China's Path to Modernity" by Jim Yardley in the *New York Times*, November 19, 2006

For centuries, the Yellow River symbolized the greatness and sorrows of China's ancient civilization, as emperors equated controlling the river and taming its catastrophic floods with controlling China. Now, the river is a very different symbol —of the dire state of China's limited resources at a time when the country's soaring economic growth needs more of everything.

"The Yellow River flows through all these densely populated parts of northern China," said Liu Shiyin, a scientist with the Chinese Academy of Sciences. "Without water in northern China, people can't survive. And the economic development that has been going on cannot continue."

China's dynamic economic engine, still roaring at record levels, is at a corrosive crossroads. Pollution is widespread, and a nationwide construction spree, tainted by corruption, is threatening to overheat the economy. China's leaders, worried about the unbridled growth, are trying to emphasize "sustainable development" even as questions remain about whether the party's rank and file can carry out priorities like curbing pollution and conserving energy.

The Yellow River, curving through regions only intermittently touched by the country's boom, offers a tour of the pressures and contradictions bearing down on China, and of the government's efforts to address them.

SOURCE: Jim Yardley, "A Troubled River Mirrors China's Path to Modernity," *New York Times* 19 Nov. 2006.

 The full text of **Document 20.1** is available on the CD-ROM.

DOCUMENT 20.2: "Pollution from Chinese Coal Casts Shadow Around Globe," by Keith Bradsher and David Barboza in *The New York Times*, June 11, 2006

The [Chinese] government has set one of the world's most ambitious targets for energy conservation: to cut the average amount of energy needed to produce each good or service by 20 percent over the next five years.... All new cars, minivans and sport utility vehicles sold in China starting July 1 will have to meet fuel-economy standards stricter than those in the United States. New construction codes encourage the use of double-glazed windows to reduce air-conditioning and heating costs and high-tech light bulbs that produce more light with fewer watts....

For the past three years, China has also been trying harder to develop other alternatives. State-owned power companies have been building enormous wind turbines up and down the coast. Chinese companies are also trying to develop geothermal energy, tapping the heat of underground rocks, and are researching solar power and ways to turn coal into diesel fuel. But all of these measures fall well short. Coal remains the obvious choice to continue supplying almost two-thirds of China's energy needs.

China must make some difficult choices. So far, the nation has been making decisions that it hopes will lessen the health-damaging impact on its own country while sustaining economic growth as cheaply as possible....

SOURCE: Keith Bradsher and David Barboza, "Pollution from Chinese Coal Casts Shadow Around Globe," *New York Times* 11 Jun. 2006.

The full text of the article is available online at www.nytimes.com with a free site subscription.

DOCUMENT 20.3: "Riot Police, Villagers Clash in China," from The Associated Press in *The New York Times*, January 19, 2007

Hundreds of riot police clashed with villagers protesting against an alleged land grab by officials in the southern Chinese province of Guangdong, a lawyer and Hong Kong newspapers reported Friday.

"Scores of villagers, even elderly ones, were taken away by police after being beaten," said Yang Zaixin, an activist lawyer who represents farmers in land disputes. The lawyer told The Associated Press that local officials in Chongyuan village illegally seized the farmers' land without approval from the provincial and central governments. Such allegations are common in booming Guangdong Province, one of China's biggest manufacturing centers. Officials are frequently accused of forcing farmers off land, which is later sold to developers who get rich building factories and other projects.

The *South China Morning Post* reported that hundreds of police armed with rifles, shields and electric batons broke up the sit-in protest Thursday in Chongyuan, part of the Nanhai district in Foshan city. After rounding up the large group of protesters, police released most of them late Thursday afternoon, Yang said. But five were still being detained, he added. Police withdrew after clearing away the protesters, but dozens of plain-clothes officials were watching the site, the *Post* quoted a protester, Chen Huiying, as saying.

The protest site, 66 acres of farmland, was first taken over by local government in 2005. Officials claimed the site was sold to a company that planned to build a warehouse complex, the *Post* reported. A spokesman for the local government, who only gave his surname, Chen, said he "did not know about the case" and declined to provide further information.

Hong Kong's *Ming Pao Daily News* quoted one villager as saying tensions have been simmering since 1992, when local officials began seizing large tracts of land. The villager, identified only by his surname, Tang, said officials never delivered on promises to compensate villagers with monthly deliveries of rice.

SOURCE: Associated Press, "Riot Police, Villagers Clash in China," *New York Times* 19 Jan. 2007.

DOCUMENT 20.4: "Internet Evolution," by Erica Schlaikjer in *AbroadView Magazine*, fall 2006

Chinese government censors have repeatedly blocked the free online encyclopedia [Wikipedia] in the Mainland over the past two years. The first block occurred in June 2004, during the 15th anniversary of the Tiananmen Square riots. It was lifted soon after two "Wikipedians," users named "Shizhao" and "Mountain," submitted a letter of appeal to their Internet service providers. The second block lasted only four days in September that year. The third block—arguably the most serious one—began on Oct. 19, 2005.

In all three instances, no explanation was given for limiting access to the website. People could only speculate—did someone post controversial articles about Falun Gong or Taiwanese independence?

The author of the first appeal, Shi Zhao, submitted another request to lift the most recent block last October, but to no avail. In his letter, he stated, "If we block Wikipedia, we lose the opportunity to speak with the world with a Chinese voice… we lose a channel through which we could access knowledge, a channel whose importance is rising constantly; blocking is no different from cutting away our own voice and tongue, or shutting our own eyes and ears; it is isolationism in the age of the Internet"…

SOURCE: Erica Schlaikjer, "Internet Evolution," *AbroadView Magazine*, fall 2006.

 The full text of Document 20.4 is available on the CD-ROM.

DOCUMENT 20.5: Excerpt from *Oracle Bones* by Peter Hessler, describing a nonviolent demonstration by Falun Gong followers in Tiananmen Square, Beijing

[A] small man directly in front of us drops into the lotus position. Shouts, commands, people running: a half-dozen plainclothes cops. By the time they force the man to his feet, a van is already speeding toward us from a far corner of [Tiananmen] Square. The protestor says nothing. He is about thirty-five years old, and he wears simple peasant clothes of blue cotton. His limbs go slack; they carry him into the van. Sheets have been tied over the windows so nobody can see inside…

[A few minutes later] a middle-aged woman tries to unfurl a banner in front of the flagpole. A plainclothes man tackles her hard. The next protestor is also a woman. She stands to the right of the flagpole and puts both arms over her head; two men run over and force her arms down….

Suddenly, there is a commotion at the flagpole. A dozen at once: men and women, shouting slogans, raising their arms. Another banner. The plainclothes men rush over; punches are thrown; people cry out. A man falls to the ground and gets kicked. Kicked again. Kicked again. One by one, the demonstrators are dragged away.

At the end, a child stands there alone. She is about seven years old, and probably she came with her mother or father, but all the adults have already been forced into the van. The girl wears a green sweater, with matching ribbons in her hair. She hangs her head as the cops march her to the vehicle.

SOURCE: Peter Hessler, *Oracle Bones: A Journey Between China's Past and Present* (New York: HarperCollins, 2006) 126–128.

DOCUMENT 20.6: "What has the Qinghai–Tibet Railway Brought to China?" by Zhang Xueying in *China Today*, October 2006

Tibet is considerably better off now than it was five years ago. Roads in Lhasa are wider and cleaner, ramshackle dwellings have been demolished and replaced with new Tibetan-style buildings and more people can afford private cars. Stores no longer resemble small workshops, and have signboards in Tibetan and Chinese and impressive facades. The post offices and public telephones most commonly seen five years ago are now vastly outnumbered by telecom companies and pharmacies, in front of which sit groups of Tibetan pilgrims. As one pharmacy assistant says, "Tibetan people pay great attention to their health, and in addition to Tibetan medicine also buy Western and traditional Chinese medicine."…

"As a Tibetan, I think the railway will bring a lot of changes that might influence the concepts of the Tibetan people," [a restaurant owner] says, thoughtfully. He cites an example. Ten years ago, Taiyang Island at the center of the Lhasa River was covered with trees, but no more. The island now has row upon row of two-storied buildings and has become the largest entertainment and gourmet center in Lhasa.

Tenzin, [a tour guide] aged 31, believes that such changes are inevitable, and that they cannot solely be attributed to the railway, which merely accelerates changes already underway. Tenzin asserts, "It is impossible to maintain the scenario of a century ago."

SOURCE: Zhang Xueying, "What has the Qinghai–Tibet Railway Brought to China?" *China Today*, Oct. 2006.

 The full text of **Document 20.6** is available on the CD-ROM.

DOCUMENT 20.7: Photographs of Tibet, 2005

Barley fields

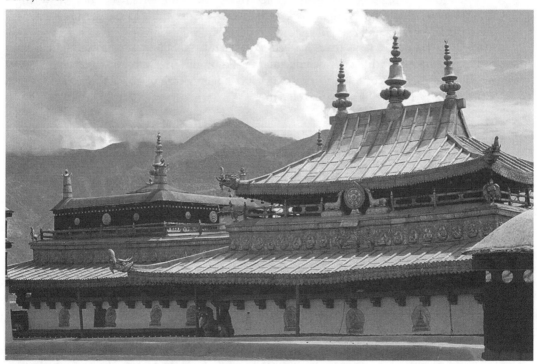

The Jokhang Temple in Lhasa is the most revered religious building in Tibet. Its origins date back to the seventh century, and over time it has undergone many renovations. The most recent was in 1980 after Red Guards desecrated the temple during the Cultural Revolution. *(Photos by Margaret Harvey)*

 The slide show is on the CD-ROM.

DOCUMENT 20.8: "Profile: Rebiya Kadeer," BBC News report on an Uyghur activist, March 17, 2005

Rebiya Kadeer was a successful businesswoman and philanthropist in China's restive Xinjiang until her arrest in 1999 for allegedly endangering national security. Her crime, the authorities said, was to send local newspaper reports about the activities of Xinjiang's ethnic Turkish-speaking [*sic*] Uighurs to her U.S.-based husband, even though these were freely available. It was a sharp reversal in fortunes for someone whose local achievements the Communist government had until then trumpeted. …

SOURCE: "Profile: Rebiya Kadeer," BBC News Online, 17 Mar. 2005.

 The full text of Document 20.8 is available on the CD-ROM.

DOCUMENT 20.9: "China-Taiwan Trade Ties Increase," BBC News, January 17, 2007

China's annual trade with Taiwan grew 18% to $107.8 billion (£54.8 billion) last year [2006], Chinese government figures show. China imported $87 billion worth of goods from Taiwan, up 16.6% on the year before, while Taiwanese firms invested $2.14 billion on the mainland.

Taiwanese firms have invested more than $100 billion in mainland China since the 1990s, with many manufacturers building factories there to take advantage of lower labour costs. China exported $20.7 billion worth of goods to Taiwan last year, a 25% increase on the year before.

Tourism boost

Despite restrictions on travel between the two countries, which requires most people to travel there via Hong Kong or another country, tourism has increased in recent years. According to a Chinese government spokesman, Taiwanese people made more than 4 million visits to China last year while more than 200,000 mainland Chinese visited Taiwan.

SOURCE: "China-Taiwan Trade Ties Increase," BBC News, 17 Jan. 2007.

DOCUMENT 20.10: Excerpt from "China Takes on the World" by Michael Elliott, *Time*, January 22, 2007

China's commitment to nonintervention means that it doesn't inquire closely into the internal arrangements of others. When all those African leaders met in Beijing [President] Hu promised to double aid to the continent by 2009, train 15,000 professionals and provide scholarships to 4,000 students, and help Africa's health-care and farming sectors. But as a 2005 report by the Council on Foreign Relations notes, "China's aid and investments are attractive to Africans precisely because they come with no conditionality related to governance, fiscal probity or other concerns of Western donors." In 2004, when an International Monetary Fund loan to Angola was held up because of suspected corruption, China ponied up $2 billion in credit. Beijing has sent weapons and money to Zimbabwe's President Robert Mugabe, whose government is accused of massive human-rights violations.

SOURCE: Michael Elliott, "China Takes on the World," *Time* 22 Jan. 2007.

 The full text of **Document 20.10** is available on the CD-ROM.

DOCUMENT 20.11: "China's Role in Africa" by Jian Junbo in *Beijing Review*, February 8, 2007

Is [China] a colonizing power or not when it engages Africa, especially as more and more Chinese [begin] to arrive on the continent at the beginning of the 21st century? Obviously, China hasn't occupied any African country. And as a country with a deep historical memory of being colonized by Western powers, China doesn't want to control Africa's economic and political systems. The Chinese Government neither appoints military consultants to African governments nor constructs military bases on the continent.

Moreover, China hasn't used deceitful means to steal and exploit African resources. Relations between China and African countries are grounded on reciprocal benefits, which is not just a slogan but a fact. Financial aid and other investments from China without political conditions are very helpful for African economies. For instance, in 2005, the rate of China's contribution to Africa's total economic growth was at least 5 percent. Simultaneously, China buys African resources at a fair price to fuel its rapid economic growth.

SOURCE: Jian Junbo, "China's Role in Africa," *Beijing Review* 8 Feb. 2007

 The full text of **Document 20.11** is available on the CD-ROM.

DOCUMENT 20.12: "Playing its Due Role" by Chen Xulong in *Beijing Review*, October 19, 2006

China has attached great importance to multilateral diplomacy and has strengthened its interaction with the international system. In response to some Western countries' promotion of Western ideology and values in the economic, social and human rights fields, China advocates building a multipolar world and establishing democratic international relations. China holds that all countries should respect the diversity of human civilization and social development models, and should attach importance to the role of the UN and safeguard its authority. ...

China is one of the five permanent members of the UN Security Council, which means that it should shoulder more responsibility than most of the other UN members in maintaining world peace. To achieve world peace and stability, China must pay attention to the coordination among major countries and push forward overall international cooperation. At the same time, as a representative of developing countries, China must consider and maintain the interests of developing countries in dealing with international problems, especially on the issues of development, environmental protection, human rights and humanitarian intervention....

SOURCE: Chen Xulong, "Playing its Due Role," *Beijing Review* 19 Oct. 2006.

 The full text of **Document 20.12** is available on the CD-ROM.

Activities

ACTIVITY 1: Role-play: The impact of rapid development

Read about the impact of development on China's Yellow River Valley (20.1) and answer the questions (Item 20.A). Next, role-play "In the Footsteps of Jim Yardley, Jake Hooker, and Lin Yang." You will retrace the authors' footsteps by setting up mock interviews with the individuals featured in this story. (See the list of characters in Item 20.B.)

- Take on the roles of Jim Yardley, Jake Hooker, and Lin Yang and the interviewees and prepare questions and responses ahead of time. (Check online for up-to-date information.) Conversations may be more extensive than how they originally appeared.

- The "authors" should conclude the oral story by responding to the question: "Has the Yellow River been damaged beyond repair?"

Extension activities:

1. Create your own storyboard or background scene for the interviews. Download images and create a slide show, or make a video of the story for viewing.

2. Read the following sources and recently published materials, then debate whether China's massive water diversion project is helping or exacerbating environmental problems. Keep in mind the origin of the articles and consider any possible biases.

- "South-to-North Water Diversion Project"
  http://www.water-technology.net/projects/south_north/

- "China's Water Diversion Project to Improve Environment"
  http://www.chinanews.cn/news/2005/2006-07-09/24878.html

- "400,000 To Make Way for Water Diversion Project"
  http://www.china.org.cn/english/index.htm

ACTIVITY 2: **Examining the global ramifications of China's reliance on coal**

Read about the problems that come from China's heavy reliance on coal (20.2) and work with a partner to answer the questions (Item 20.C). Check online sources for the most up-to-date information.

Next, stage a talk show that includes environmental and energy officials from Japan, Korea, the United States, Russia, India, and any other countries you feel should be included. Discuss the challenges related to China's dependence on coal. Also include individuals from the readings such as Wu and Cao, as well as those from other readings. In staging the talk show, an anchor person should pose questions such as:

1. What are the reasons behind China's heavy reliance on coal?
2. What are the difficulties involved in implementing pollution controls?
3. What is the potential for change?

ACTIVITY 3: **Class discussion: Solving the environmental problems**

Sketch a "balancing scale," with one side holding China's environmental problems and the other side holding potential remedies based on suggestions in the primary sources and your ideas. Discuss:

1. Has China waited too long to start addressing its environmental problems? Depict which side of the scale is heaviest by utilizing up and down arrows to indicate motion.
2. Is China's environmental damage unique among industrial nations? Are there any positive models that China may want to consider? Is the United States in a position to advise China on its environmental challenges?
3. Would China hold any advantages compared to other nations if it were to follow through on efforts to improve the quality of its environment?

NOTE: An additional activity pertaining to the Three Gorges Dam is on the CD-ROM (Item 20.D).

ACTIVITY 4: **Dissent: Writing an op-ed piece**

Divide documents 20.3–20.5 among class members. Read the accounts and answer related questions (Item 20.E). Reconvene as a class and report on your reading and discussions. Then consider:

1. What have you learned about China's political problems and the government's capacity for change?
2. Is China different from any other nation? How? Why?

Imagine that you are a journalist for *China Daily* and your editor has instructed you to write a short op-ed on the pace of political reform in China. He or she has given you no indication of what your stance should be. Keep in mind that you are writing for a paper subject to government censorship. Write the op-ed and share it with your classmates.

Extended activity: **Universal human rights**

Research the United Nations Universal Declaration of Human Rights (see Suggested Resources). Then compare and contrast the human rights records of the permanent members of the UN Security Council (the United States, Russia, the United Kingdom, China, and France).

ACTIVITY 5: China and its ethnic minorities

Part 1: Tibet and the Qinghai–Lhasa Railway

To better understand the issues surrounding Tibet, read the overview of Tibet's history (in Additional Resources on the CD-ROM). Then read Document 20.6 and complete the following:

1. Locate Golmud, Qinghai, and Lhasa, Tibet on a map that includes both political and physical features of China. Note the topography of the region.
2. Explain how life changed for Rintor, a Tibetan, once he took a job working on the Qinghai-Tibet railway.
3. Provide a direct quote or another piece of evidence that demonstrates the author's support for the railway.

Examine the photographs of Tibet (20.7 on the CD-ROM).

1. What do you find most striking about the images of Tibet?
2. Note six details that you find especially interesting in the photos of Tibetan people. Why did these details stand out to you?
3. Why do you think Tibet deeply stirs many people?

Prepare for a mini-debate around the question: "Is tourism having a positive or negative impact on Lhasa?" Compose an argument that includes two pieces of evidence, paraphrased or quoted directly from the reading, that support your position.

Part 2: Xinjiang

Read the overview of Xinjiang Autonomous Region and the Uyghur people and see the photographs of the region on the slide show (both in Resources on the CD-ROM). Then read the profile of Rebiya Kadeer (20.8) and find out more about her activities online.

1. What appear to be the key issues in Xinjiang?
2. Why does the Chinese government appear to be so intent on controlling the region?
3. What changes have taken place among the Uyghur since 2001?

Working in small teams,

1. Discuss whether these regions (Tibet and Xinjiang) deserve the title *autonomous*.
2. Identify China's goals in its policies toward Tibet and Xinjiang.
3. Check online for any recent developments.
4. Discuss how Han Chinese and these two ethnic minorities might work toward a mutually beneficial future.

NOTE: See Chapter 1 for more information on China's minority peoples.

ACTIVITY 6: Four-corner activity: China and Taiwan

Part 1:

Read the overview of Taiwan's history (in Additional Resources on the CD-ROM), information in Chapter 16 related to the relationships among Taiwan, China, and the United States, and Document 20.9 about the increased trade. Conduct research online to get a clear sense of the current situation.
Be prepared to address the following questions:

1. When and why did Taiwan become known as the Republic of China and begin to function as a separate entity from mainland China?
2. After Chiang Kai-shek and the Guomindang government moved to Taiwan in 1949 (see Chapter 12), why did the United States continue to recognize the Guomindang as the government of all of China rather than recognize the Communist government in Beijing?
3. Why did the People's Republic of China take the place of Taiwan in the United Nations in 1971?
4. Why did the United States shift its diplomatic recognition from Taiwan (the Republic of China) to the People's Republic of China in 1979? What does it mean to "recognize" a country?
5. What are the key provisions of the (U.S.) Taiwan Relations Act of 1979? (See Chapter 16, Document 16.5)
6. What have "trilateral" relations been like among the United States, China, and Taiwan since the late 1970s?

Part 2:

Consider each of the options listed below and write out possible reasons for supporting the course of action, as well as concerns regarding the option.
   Option 1 – China should set a timetable for reunification with Taiwan.
   Option 2 – Taiwan should declare itself independent.

Option 3 – The United States should take a more active role in bringing about a political solution.

Option 4 – Everyone should allow time and increased trade to resolve the issue.

Option 5 – Create your own option.

Choose what you consider to be the best option and draft a one-page statement that outlines your stance and rationale. Your statement should contain two or three specific pieces of evidence from the sources. Moreover, it should demonstrate a broad understanding of the situation.

Part 3:

Report to a corner of the room that has a sign designating your stance. (Undecided students will remain seated.) Once everyone has made an initial choice, begin the discussion. During the discussion, you can move to a different corner at any time. If you are not certain, you may remain seated. Students who are certain of their position need to persuade other students to join them. Once participants have aligned themselves, the facilitator may keep score as to which option wins the most converts or attracts the most undecided voters.

Comparative discussion question: In what ways is China's dilemma over Taiwan similar to and different from President Abraham Lincoln's considerations regarding the secessionist states in the South?

ACTIVITY 7: Trade and geopolitics

Define the following terms: "geopolitics," "nonintervention," "neocolonialism."
Read Documents 20.10 and 20.11 and consider:

1. How has Sino-African trade benefited each region?
2. What are the negative and positive consequences of Chinese officials not attaching political strings to their assistance and investment?
3. Why might trade with China be more appealing for developing nations than trade with Western nations?

Prepare a mini-debate among officials from China, the United Kingdom, France, India, and the United States over whether China's increased presence in Africa constitutes a form of neocolonialism. Finish with a class discussion on whether China's stance on trade, investment, and non-intervention is fitting for a major world power.

ACTIVITY 8: Is China a superpower?

Discuss what it means to be a superpower. Cite historical examples of nations and civilizations that fit your definition. What responsibilities and challenges come with being a superpower?
Read Document 20.12 and answer the questions:

1. The author describes four phases of China's involvement with the UN. Summarize China's involvement during the 1970s.

2. How does the author describe China's involvement from the early 1980s to the early 1990s?

3. How does the author characterize the period from the early 1990s to the turn of the twenty-first century? How does the author contrast China's approach to international relations with the approach of some Western nations?

4. How does the author portray China's role in the last of the four phases?

5. Among the different assertions the author makes, which do you find most plausible? Which appear somewhat dubious or less substantiated?

6. Why do you think the author uses the term "multilateral" so often?

Conduct small group discussions to identify the events or turning points that led to each new phase of China's involvement with the UN and the global community. Anticipate and discuss future turning points that could conceivably launch China into still another phase of UN and global involvement. What might that phase look like?

Conduct a class discussion on whether China fits the definition of a super-power. If you conclude that it does not, discuss what any nation must achieve to attain this status.

Note: If possible, before the discussion read the full article "China Takes On the World" by Michael Elliott (*Time* January 22, 2007, available online at www.time.com).

Suggested Resources

Books

Bergsten, Fred C., et al. Center for Strategic and International Studies/Institute for International Economics. *China: The Balance Sheet: What the World Needs to Know Now About the Emerging Superpower*. New York: Public Affairs, 2006.
A thoughtful, balanced look at China's extraordinary economic growth and its many implications. The book is short and very readable.

Chetham, Deirdre. *Before the Deluge: The Vanishing World of the Yangtze's Three Gorges*. New York: Palgrave Macmillan, 2002.
An excellent exploration of the impact of the rising water level upriver from the Three Gorges Dam.

Elliott, Michael. "The Chinese Century," *Time*. January 22, 2007.
The author leaves little doubt that superpower status is what China aspires to and describes the hurdles China must overcome.

Gifford, Rob. *China Road: A Journey into the Future of a Rising Power*. New York: Random House, 2007.
An insightful, witty, and beautifully written account of the National Public Radio correspondent's trip across China. A must-read for anyone interested in contemporary China.

Gladney, Dru. *Ethnic Identity in China: The Making of a Muslim Minority*. Fort Worth, TX: Harcourt Brace College Publishers, 1998. 11–23.
One of the best sources for understanding not just the Hui but also the whole issue of nationalities and minorities in China.

Harrer, Heinrich. *Seven Years in Tibet*. New York: E.F. Dutton and Company, 1953.
Highly relevant to an understanding of the Tibet issue. A true story about two Austrian mountaineers who traveled to India during World War II to summit peaks. Instead, they wound up in the service of the Dalai Lama. Harrer's account, originally published in 1953, generated significant outside interest in Tibet.

Hersey, John. *A Single Pebble*. New York: Vintage Books, 1956.
In this novel, a young American engineer voyages up the Yangzi with plans to tame the great river.

Li Li, "Eco Warrior Faces Up," *Beijing Review*. January 17, 2007. *About river pollution.*

Mayhew, Brad, ed. *Tibet*. Melbourne: Lonely Planet Publications, 1999.
This travel guide contains an excellent section on understanding Tibetan Buddhism, and includes illustrations of important Boddhisatvas, Tibetan gods and goddesses, Dalai Lamas, and manifestations of the Buddha in the Mahayana tradition.

Perlez, Jane. "China Competes With West in Aid to its Neighbors," *The New York Times*, September 18, 2006.

Rudelson, Justin Jon. *Oases Identities: Uyghur Nationalism Along China's Silk Road*. New York: Columbia University Press, 1997.
A very interesting analysis of Uyghur identity and the differences among Uyghurs from different oases.

Shakya, Tsering. *The Dragon in the Land of Snows: A History of Tibet Since 1947*. New York: Columbia University Press, 1999. 200–211.

Traub, James. "The World According to China," *The New York Times*. September 3, 2006. *This article offers a "behind the scenes" view of how China approaches international diplomacy, particularly in light of the history of European colonialism and China's own experience at the hands of colonizers.*

Websites

https://www.cia.gov/library/publications/the-world-factbook/index.html The CIA *World Factbook* provides excellent statistics on China today.

http://english.people.com.cn/constitution/constitution.html China's constitution, as amended in 1982.

http://www.un.org/Overview/rights.html The United Nations Universal Declaration of Human Rights.

http://www.chsource.org/Profiles.htm China Source, a California-based organization, provides introductory materials vital to the study of China. Their website includes an excellent set of ethnic profiles that are particularly useful for researching the less often depicted nationality groups.

http://www.tibet.com/index.html The official website of the Government of Tibet in Exile (the Dalai Lama and his supporters).

http://news.bbc.co.uk/2/shared/spl/hi/asia_pac/04/taiwan_flashpoint/html/introduction.stm This "Flashpoint Taiwan" website from the BBC News gives an in-depth understanding of the China-Taiwan conflict over time.

Slideshow

http://www.nytimes.com/slideshow/2006/11/17/ world/20061119_YELLOW_SLIDESHOW_1. html Online photographs of the Yellow River from 2006. Can also be accessed by searching for "Yellow River" under "Multimedia" on www.nytimes.com.

Films

Kundun (1997, 135 mins.) Directed by Martin Scorsese. *This film provides a unique opportunity for students to gain insight into some of the intricacies of Tibetan Buddhism.* Included *are excellent portrayals of the selection process involved for choosing a Dalai Lama, a portrayal of Bön shamanism, and a Tibetan sky burial. Overall, the film is rich in religious symbolism. Note: For use in the classroom, we suggest showing the movie from scene 12 to the end. This would take about 40 minutes. As a bonus, students can watch the earlier scene 4, when the young Dalai Lama is chosen.*

The Saltmen of Tibet (1998, 109 mins.) *A revealing, though slow-moving, visual portrayal of the ancient Tibetan practice of collecting salt, as well as a window into nomadic Tibetan life.*

The Story of the Weeping Camel (2005, 90 mins.) *This touching docudrama follows a Mongolian family in the southern Gobi desert during the camel birthing season. When a mother camel rejects her new colt, the family has to find a way to rectify the situation. The film provides a very rare look at steppe life and Mongolian identity. Note: Teachers may choose to describe the scenario above and show the second half of the film after the camel gives birth, as the delivery scene may be hard for some students to watch.*

Tibet: Cry of the Snow Lion (2003, 100 mins.) Tom Piozet, New Yorker Video. *Ten years in the making, this feature-length documentary was filmed during nine remarkable journeys through Tibet, India, and Nepal. Taking viewers to the long-forbidden "rooftop of the world" with an unprecedented richness of imagery, the film powerfully chronicles the dark secrets of Tibet's recent past through interviews, personal stories and archival images. Martin Sheen narrates; Susan Sarandon and Ed Harris provide voice-overs.*

"A Troubled River Mirrors China's Path to Modernity" (Part I and II) in "From the Lakes to the Sea" (November 17, 2006). *Excellent* New York Times *online video accompanies the Yardley article. Can be accessed by searching for "Yellow River" under "Multimedia" on www. nytimes.com.*

http://video.on.nytimes.com/index.jsp?auto_ band=x&rf=sv&fr_story=2922ba8a7952bca6a8 11ffae6e279e1289732bbe

■ **A CLOSER LOOK**

(Photo by Michael Abraham)

Street in Xi'an, Shaanxi Province, 2004, includes many green taxis. On the right is the city wall built during the Ming dynasty, 1368–1644.

■ *Access the photo in color on the CD-ROM. Examine all the details in the photograph, and then discuss how this image captures some of the challenges facing Chinese cities.*

Credits

We gratefully acknowledge the permission granted to reproduce the copyrighted material in this book:

1.2, 10.13 From Fei Xiaotong, *Peasant Life in China: A Field Study of Country Life in the Yangzi Valley*. New York: Oxford University Press, 1946. Used by permission of Cengage Learning Services Limited. **1.4, 8.6, 10.10, 10.12, 11.3** Courtesy of the Li family. **2.1, 2.2, 2.4** From *China in the Sixteenth Century* by Matthew Ricci, translated by Louis J. Gallagher S. J., copyright 1942, 1953 and renewed 1970 by Louis J. Gallagher, S. J. Used by permission of Random House, Inc. **2.3** Susan Naquin. *Peking: Temples and City Life, 1400–1900*. Berkeley: University of California Press, 2000. Used by permission of the University of California Press. **2.6** Kojiro, Yoshikawa: Five Hundred Years of Chinese Poetry, 1150–1640. © 1989 Princeton University Press Reprinted by permission of Princeton University Press. **2.9, 3.5, 10.9** Reprinted and edited with permission of The Free Press, a division of Simon & Schuster Adult Publishing Group, from *Chinese Civilization and Society: A Sourcebook*, edited by Patricia Buckley Ebrey. Copyright © 1981 by The Free Press. All rights reserved. **2.10** From Kang-I Sun and Haun Saussy, *Women Writers of Traditional China: An Anthology of Poetry and Criticism*. Copyright © 1999 by the Board of Trustees of the Leland Stanford Jr. University. **2.11, 6.1, 6.3** Used by Permission of Columbia University Press. **3.1, 7.2, 7.6, 10.11, 16.2** Excerpts from *The Search for Modern China: A Documentary Collection* by Pei Kai Cheng, Michael Lestz and Jonathan Spence. Copyright © 1999 by W.W. Norton & Company, Inc. Used by permission of W.W. Norton & Company, Inc. **3.2** From *Russia and China: Their Diplomatic Relations to 1728* by Mark Mancall. Harvard University Press, 1971. **3.6, 3.7, 3.8** Beijing: Foreign Languages Press **3.9** Freer Gallery of Art, Smithsonian Institution, Washington, D.C., Purchase—Anonymous donor and Museum funds, F2000.4 **Items 3.A, 3.B** Minneapolis Institute of Art. **4.6, 4.7, 4.9** Massachusetts Historical Society **4.8a & b** Courtesy of Lovers of Blue & White **5.1, 5.2** Courtesy of the Peabody Essex Museum, Salem, MA **5.7** Used by permission of the University of Washington Press. **6.4** From *The Autobiography of a Man a Who Brought the Gospel to China* by J. Hudson Taylor. 17th edition Minneapolis, MN: Bethany House Publishers, 1986. Used by permission of Baker Publishing Group. **6.7** Used by permission of Howard Spendelow. **6.9** Used by permission of the author. **7.9, 7.10** Reprinted with permission of Scribner, an imprint of Simon & Schuster Adult Publishing Group, from *Modern China: From Mandarin to Commissar* by Dun J. Li. Copyright © 1978 by Dun J. Li. All rights reserved. **8.1** From *Lu Xun: Diary of a Madman and Other Stories* translated by William A. Lyell. Copyright © 1990 University of Hawaii Press. Used by permission of the University of Hawaii Press. **8.2** From Lao She from *Teahouse* translated by John Howard-Gibbon. Chinese University Press, Hong Kong. **Items 8.A, 9.B, 9.C, 11.A** Maps courtesy of the Department of History, United States Military Academy. **9.1, 10.14** Used by permission of the University of Hawaii Press. **9.3, 9.5, 9.6, 9.7** Beijing: Foreign Languages Press. **9.10** "The Rebellion in Xi'an," a report in *The Manchester Guardian Weekly*, July 16, 1937. Used by permission of Guardian News & Media Ltd. **9.13** Peabody Museum of Archaeology and Ethnology, Harvard University/Lattimore Foundation. Used by permission of David Lattimore. **10.1, 10.3, 10.4** Reprinted by permission of

369

Glossary

abdication: stepping down from the throne

accommodation: the act of negotiating and compromising in relations with foreign countries

agrarian: related to farming

astronomy: the scientific study of the universe through physics and observation

autonomous region: an administrative area of China with its own local government and special legislative rights, often home to an officially recognized minority group

"barbarian:" the translation of a term formerly used by Han Chinese to describe anyone non-Chinese, especially someone who did not speak Chinese; a foreigner

Beijing: present-day capital of China, formerly known as Peking

big character posters: posters covered with writing that were hung in public places to communicate political messages

biological warfare: germ warfare that causes physical harm through the spread of harmful or deadly microorganisms, toxins, etc.

bourgeoisie: the middle class; according to Marxist doctrine the capitalists who exploit the working class

Boxer Uprising: an uprising in 1900 led by the Boxers United in Righteousness, a secret society that formed in China in 1898 and gained appeal with the landless, disbanded, and disempowered. During the uprising, foreigners and Chinese Christians were killed in Chinese cities.

cadre: a civil servant or bureaucrat in Communist China; someone who works for the government or Communist Party

Canton: former, English name for Guangzhou

capitalism: an economic system based on the private ownership of the means of production of goods, characterized by a free, competitive market and driven by profit

cartography: the making of maps

censorate: the part of the Chinese bureaucracy that made sure government officials did their jobs during the Qing dynasty

Chinese Communist Party (CCP): the political party that has governed China since 1949; the CCP was formally organized at its first Congress in 1921.

chinoiserie: a style of art and interior design that reflects Chinese style and influence but was developed overseas

civil service examination system: a system of exams in China that was used to choose appointees to government positions. Chinese civil service exams began around the sixth century and were based on different classical Chinese texts at different times; however, the exams always included the Confucian classics.

class struggle: The Marxist concept of struggle for political and economic power between the ruling class (bourgeoisie) and working class (proletariat)

coalition: an alliance of organizations, political entities, or nations in which each individual maintains its identity

collaborator: an individual, a group, an organization, or a country that works with another individual, group, organization, movement, or country. During wartime, the term has very negative connotations since it implies cooperating with the enemy.

collective: a group of farms managed as a unit, 1951–1958; farmers pooled their land and worked cooperatively. The product was shared primarily based on the amount of labor one had contributed.

commune: a mutually shared community in which property, possessions, and responsibilities are shared; in the "people's communes" organized in 1958 in China, all the land belonged to the government.

communism: a system of government in which no individual owns property and wealth is shared in a classless society by the members of the community

concubine: a woman who is the lover of a married man, but who is not his wife. She had the status of a subordinate "wife" prior to the founding of the People's Republic of China.

Confucian hierarchy: a rigid social hierarchy that endured for centuries in China. It placed scholar-officials at the top of society, followed by peasants, artisans, and at the bottom, merchants.

Confucianism: a philosophy of ethics and morality based on the teachings of Confucius, designed to cultivate civilized individuals and to establish an ordered, harmonious society

Confucius: (ca. 551 B.C.E. – ca. 478 B.C.E.) Chinese philosopher, whose philosophical teachings on ethics and morality became the foundation of the Chinese way of life

connoisseur: a person with expert knowledge and informed taste, especially in the fine arts

conservative: adhering to tradition and cautious about change

"coolie": an unskilled laborer in China (or India) often doing heavy work for very low wages

counter-revolutionary: opposing revolution; during the early decades of the PRC, the term was used against individuals who opposed or questioned Party policies

courtesan: royal female attendant who practiced and had talents in the arts, such as music, dancing, and poetry

decentralized: (regarding power or rule) spread out among many regions or individuals

Democracy Wall: a wall near Tiananmen Square where posters with criticisms of society and the government were hung in the 1980s

Democratic League: a liberal party that existed along with the Guomindang and the Chinese Communist Party (CCP) in China; established in 1939, it is one of eight legally recognized parties in the PRC today.

demographics: the distribution, density, vital statistics, etc. of a population

developing nations: countries in which the average income is much lower than in industrial countries; the economy is mostly agricultural and relies on a few export crops; farming is conducted by traditional, labor-intensive methods.

diaspora: the dispersion of a people sharing a common origin (in this case Chinese)

dictatorship: absolute power or authority by one individual, usually gained and/or maintained by force rather than election

diplomacy: the practice of and skill at managing communication, negotiation, and relationships between nations

dissent: to differ in belief or opinion, to disagree

dissident: an individual who disagrees with an established political or religious system or organization

dynasty: a succession of rulers who are members of the same family

edict: a proclamation

eunuch: a man who has been castrated; in imperial China, eunuchs worked as choral singers, actors, and servants, and were the only men permitted in the emperor's living quarters or in the vicinity of the emperor's courtesans; some rose to powerful positions.

extremist: an individual who holds extreme or radical political beliefs

"factory": the living and business quarters of foreigners trading in Guangzhou (Canton) up to the late 1840s

feudal Japan: period of Japanese history dominated by regional families and the military rule of warlords from the twelfth to the nineteenth centuries. During this period, the emperor remained but was kept in a figurehead position.

feudal system: a social, economic, and political system in which the people working the land do not own it and are often exploited by landowners

floating population: low-paid migrant workers and poor rural laborers who move to urban areas to fill manufacturing and construction jobs

foot binding: a tradition that lasted some 1,000 years in China in which young girls' feet would be wrapped in tight bandages to dramatically alter the shape and limit the size of the foot. Bound feet were considered highly desirable in a young woman; the feet would be so mutilated that a woman could not walk normally.

Foreign Direct Investment (FDI): the investment of one nation's funds into another country

Gang of Four: Jiang Qing (Mao Zedong's wife) and three others considered responsible for the worst excesses of the Great Proletarian Cultural Revolution

Generalissimo: the supreme commander of a combined military force of the air force, navy, and army; Chiang Kai-shek took on the title

gentry: the class of society who own land; upper class

geopolitical approach: a worldview approach to looking at politics or a political issue

Gross Domestic Product (GDP): a country's production of goods and services during the course of a given period

Guangzhou: the port city in southeastern China formerly known in the West as Canton

Guomindang: also known as the Nationalist Party; the party organized by Sun Yat-sen in 1912 and later led by Chiang Kai-shek; formerly spelled Kuomintang (KMT)

Han Chinese: the dominant ethnic group in China who make up more than 90 percent of the population; the name Han stems from the Han dynasty (206 BCE-220 CE), considered to be one of the high points in Chinese civilization.

hegemony: leadership; dominance

homage: anything given or done to show respect or reverence

human rights: the basic rights and freedoms to which each human being is entitled

ideology: an organized system of beliefs, values, and ideas that form a political philosophy or program

immigrant: an individual who has migrated to a country from another country

imperial power: power of one country over other countries or colonies

imperialism: the practice of extending rule or authority over other countries or colonies

incursion: a brief, hostile invasion of another country

indenture: a contract that commits an individual to serve a master for a specific time period

industrialized society: one in which machine-manufactured goods have replaced hand tools; one with large-scale industrial production

inflation: an increase in the supply of currency (money) leading to higher prices and to the money being worth less

"iron rice bowl": life-time job security in the PRC up until Deng Xiaoping's economic reforms

Jesuits: a Roman Catholic religious order of men known for their scholarship and commitment to education

jia: [in Fei Xiaotong's context] a family unit; individuals related by blood or marriage

kowtow: to kneel and touch the forehead to the ground to show respect to a superior in traditional Chinese culture

Kuomintang: former spelling of Guomindang or Nationalists; the party organized by Sun Yat-sen in 1912 and later led by Chiang Kai-shek

li: a traditional Chinese unit of distance; about one-third of a mile or 500 meters

literati: intellectuals or the educated class; those involved with literature or the arts

Little Red Book: printed by the millions during the Cultural Revolution, the small book contained quotations from Mao Zedong. Red Guards and proper revolutionaries carried it with them all the time, studying and memorizing the words of Chairman Mao.

loess: a fine-grained, yellowish-brown, extremely fertile soil deposited by the wind and sometimes by floods

magistrate: a scholar-official in imperial China responsible for provincial affairs, including administering the civil service exams, tax collection, public safety, and administering justice; sometimes used as a synonym for a scholar-official

Manchu: the name a people gave themselves from what are now China's northeastern provinces; they invaded China in the early seventeenth century and established the Qing dynasty (1644–1912).

Manchuria: region of northeastern China; now Liaoning, Heilongjiang, and Jilin provinces

Mandate of Heaven: For millennia, Chinese tradition dictated that a leader/emperor had to have legitimate authority from the gods in order to rule the country. Huge natural disasters or civil disorder were seen as signs that a ruler had lost this mandate.

manifesto: a public declaration of motives and intentions by a person or group with some public importance

mausoleum: a large tomb or burial monument

maxim: general rule, principle or truth

Meiji Restoration: a tremendous transformation in Japan in the late nineteenth century; as a result of this movement, Japan built a powerful militarized and industrialized nation.

memorial: a written appeal to a government official

migrant worker: a worker from another region (in the context of this book)

Ming dynasty: ruled China from 1368–1644; the era is known for its remarkable arts and culture and a vibrant commercial and urban life that contributed to great prosperity for some. In the late 16th century, however, rural populations were suffering as a result of government mismanagement and natural disasters.

mission schools: schools funded by foreign Christians and usually operated by foreign missionaries

modernization: the process of technological, industrial, and intellectual progress or advancement in a country

Mongols: nomadic people of (Inner and Outer) Mongolia; at various points in history, enemies of the Chinese empire

monsoon: a seasonal wind of the Indian Ocean and South Asia, blowing from the southwest from April to October, and from the northeast during the rest of the year

multilateral: many-sided; involving more than two countries

multinational company: one that conducts business in two or more countries

nationalism: loyalty and belief in one's country; (can be) excessive narrow patriotism

Nationalist: (in China) a member of the Guomindang, the Chinese Nationalist Party, the party organized by Sun Yat-sen in 1912 and later led by Chiang Kai-shek; formerly the Kuomintang (KMT)

occupation: the control of a country or area by enemy or outside forces

Peking: former English name of Beijing, present-day capital of China

"Ping Pong diplomacy": In 1971, at the 31st World Table Tennis Championships in Japan, Chinese players invited the American team to visit and play in China, which they did (with support from both governments). The Ping Pong players were the first American group allowed into China since 1949. The U.S. subsequently announced plans to end the trade embargo with China. Then the Chinese team reciprocated by visiting the U.S. These were early steps in the resumption of Sino–U.S. relations.

Politburo: one of the highest levels within the Chinese Communist Party made up of between 5 and 9 members, it effectively sets national policy and controls all administrative, legal, and executive appointments.

proletarian: relating to the working class in Communist terminology

proliferation: rapid spread or multiplication; (in this context) the spread of arms or weapons, such as nuclear or chemical weapons

propaganda: the use of words, symbols, music, art or any communication specifically to influence people's thinking and behavior; to promote a policy, doctrine, or cause

purge: to remove or overthrow opponents, rulers, or people considered undesirable

Qing: the Qing dynasty (1644–1911), also known as the Ch'ing or the Manchu dynasty, was the last dynasty in China.

queue: long, braided ponytail worn by the Manchus of central Manchuria, and imposed upon the Han Chinese during the Qing dynasty as a sign of submission

radical: an individual who favors making sweeping or extreme economic, political, or social changes

reactionary: an opponent to liberal or progressive social and political changes or reforms

reconciliation: the ending of a conflict or renewing of a friendly relationship between disputing people, groups, or nations

Red Guards: students who participated in the Cultural Revolution and took up Mao Zedong's call to destroy the Four Olds—old customs, old habits, old culture, and old thinking. Many were involved in extensive violence and destruction.

reeducation camp: "reeducation through labor," according to the Chinese Ministry of Public Security, is a system of reform through compulsory education for those who have committed minor offenses not considered legally criminal. The system was put in place in 1957 and it is not unusual for it to be used for political dissidents; conditions are harsh.

reform: social and political changes or improvement enacted by law

reparation: compensation for a wrongdoing given to one group or country by another

Republic of China (ROC): the name for China between 1912 and 1949; also the name of the government Chiang Kai-shek formed on Taiwan after his defeat by the Communists on mainland China in 1949

rickshaw: a small two-wheeled carriage with a seat, pulled by a person

rogue state: a subjective term used to describe a nation that does not adhere to international law or flouts international norms

rural: agrarian or farming areas; having to do with the countryside

sanctions: penalties imposed by one or several nations against another to try to force that nation to comply with international law

"save face": to politically or socially keep one's reputation intact

scholar-official: individuals who had passed China's civil service examinations and held government positions; educated in the Confucian classics, they were often amateur artists, and connoisseurs or patrons of the arts.

Security Council: the organ of the United Nations comprising five permanent members (China, the United States, Russia, the United Kingdom, and France) with veto power, and ten temporary members, charged with maintaining international peace and security

sent-down youth (*zhiqing*): approximately 12 million teenagers sent to the countryside between 1968 and 1975 (during the Cultural Revolution) to live, work, and be reeducated by the peasants

***simin*:** the four classes of people in traditional Chinese society: scholar-officials, peasants, artisans, and merchants

socialism: a political system that promotes government intervention to ensure a shared distribution of jobs and resources in a society and is usually characterized by some public ownership of industries

socialist: an individual who believes in socialism or belongs to a socialist party

sovereignty: authority or rule; independence from others

soviet (as in Jiangxi Soviet, for example): an area under Communist control; the Jiangxi Soviet began in 1928 as a hideout for Mao Zedong and a small enclave escaping the Guomindang.

Special Economic Zones (SEZ): geographical zones within China established for foreign investment; foreign enterprises receive tax breaks and other incentives

state-run economy: an economic system planned and run by a central government

struggle meetings or sessions: meetings during which individuals suspected of harboring "rightist" views that weren't in line with communist ideology were forced to confess and "struggle" to rid themselves of their bourgeois ways; these meetings were sometimes violent, especially during the early years of the Cultural Revolution.

sustainable development: economic progress that can be maintained over time without damaging the environment

***tael*:** approximately one ounce of silver, formerly used as Chinese currency

tariff: a duty or tax on imported or exported trade

treaty: a formal negotiated agreement between countries

Treaty of Versailles: the 1919 peace treaty that officially ended World War I

tributary relationship: a relationship between two states in which one acknowledged the other to be superior and paid tribute by sending representatives bearing gifts

unilateral: decided or acted upon by only one party or nation

vernacular: commonly spoken, everyday language

"victim literature": writings of individuals who experienced or witnessed terrible abuse during the Cultural Revolution; these books were for a while encouraged under Deng Xiaoping as a way for some to express their anguish. Some scholars note that these works, as a whole, give a one-dimensional emotional view of that period.

warlords: military rulers who had control over regions of China during the Early Republican period

World Trade Organization (WTO): the organization that oversees the rules of trade between nations worldwide

yuan: basic monetary unit of the People's Republic of China, also known as the renminbi (RMB)

Index

Page numbers appearing in **bold** indicate *A Closer Look* topic.